HARVARD HISTORICAL STUDIES, 122

Published under the auspices
of the Department of History
from the income of the
Paul Revere Frothingham Bequest
Robert Louis Stroock Fund
Henry Warren Torrey Fund

THE
FORMATION
of the
PARISIAN BOURGEOISIE

1690–1830

DAVID GARRIOCH

HARVARD UNIVERSITY PRESS
Cambridge, Massachusetts
London, England
1996

Library of Congress Cataloging-in-Publication Data
Garrioch, David.
The formation of the Parisian bourgeoisie, 1690–1830 / David Garrioch.
p. cm. — (Harvard historical studies ; v. 122)
Includes bibliographical references and index.
ISBN 0-674-30937-5 (alk. paper)
1. Middle class—France—Paris—History. I. Title. II. Series.
HT690.F8G365 1996
305.5'5'0944361—dc20   96-21146

FOR JAN

ACKNOWLEDGMENTS

Most of my intellectual debts are acknowledged in the endnotes. The one to E. P. Thompson is not, but his influence will be apparent. I have also been strongly influenced by the work of Natalie Zemon Davis, and Jonathan Spence's wonderful essay *The Question of Hu* inspired the presentation of Chapter 1, though I do not use his technique in the same way. Richard Cobb inspired a belief that history must be walked. Olwen Hufton prompted me to look more closely at parish life, and Denis Richet's stimulating seminars in 1981 showed me what could be done with parish records. I owe an enormous debt to Colin Lucas, whose methodology has greatly influenced me, and whose constant encouragement and assistance have been crucial. My own family have taught me more about the importance of kinship than any amount of historical research.

Some of the material in Chapters 4 and 7 was previously published in "The Revolution in Local Politics in Paris," *Renaissance and Modern Studies* (1989), and I am grateful to the editors for permission to reproduce it.

I would like to thank the helpful staff I encountered in a variety of Paris archives, and the parish priest of Saint Médard for allowing me to consult the parish archives. I owe much to the staff of the Monash University Library, particularly those in Inter-Library Loans. I would also like to record my gratitude to my colleagues in the Monash University Department of History, whose intellectual curiosity, cheerful determination to preserve a spirit of collegiality, and conscientious approach to teaching and research have helped to make the department an agreeable and stimulating place to work. Equally important in creating that atmosphere have been the efficiency and good humor of the administrative

Acknowledgments

staff of the department. My thanks, too, to the technical staff in the Monash Geography Department: Barry Carr, Rhonda Joyce, and Shannon Mattinson for photographic work, and Gary Swinton and Phil Scamp for the maps. Julia McLaren of CPEDERF rendered assistance in finding and copying some key documents. I also thank Elizabeth Suttell and Donna Bouvier of Harvard University Press for guiding me through the publication process, and Michael Brandon for extraordinarily careful copyediting that eliminated numerous errors and infelicities of style.

I have had indispensable financial assistance from the Australian Research Council, and from the Dean and the Faculty of Arts at Monash University. I began this project while a Junior Research Fellow at Saint Anne's College, Oxford. Special thanks to Alison Patrick, Colin Lucas, Bill Kent, Margaret Anderson, Patrice Higonnet, and to the anonymous reader of Harvard University Press, who have generously read and commented on part or all of the manuscript and who have saved me from many errors and misinterpretations.

CONTENTS

ILLUSTRATIONS

TABLES

THE
FORMATION
of the
PARISIAN BOURGEOISIE

1690–1830

INTRODUCTION

There was no Parisian bourgeoisie in the eighteenth century. There were merchants and lawyers, teachers, manufacturers, rentiers, *bourgeois de Paris*. But they did not form a united or a citywide class, did not possess the cross-city ties and identity that would make them truly Parisian. The political and social institutions of the city served to fragment rather than to unite the middle classes. This book is an attempt to trace, through the study of politics and of power at the local level, the way that politics, demography, ideology (including religious and gender ideology), and economic change conspired to create, by 1830, a Parisian bourgeoisie—a citywide political and social class with common interests and a strong sense of its own identity.

It was the Revolution that assembled the administrative and political structures and the social and political ideology upon which nineteenth-century bourgeois identity reposed. But it assembled them from components that were, in the main, already developing by the end of the Old Regime. By then, the commercial integration of the city was proceeding rapidly under the impetus of developing national and international capitalism and the accompanying domestic consumerism. A centralizing monarchy had constructed an administrative apparatus that was actively unifying and standardizing the urban environment. These changes, combined with new demographic and social behavior among the commercial middle classes, precipitated a turnover of population among the local elites from the middle of the century on. Simultaneously, the political debates of the period penetrated deep into the local consciousness of Parisians, creating cross-city alliances and perceptions of common interests. These were all preconditions for the formation of a Parisian bourgeoisie.

It was during the eighteenth century, too, that the ideological foundations of bourgeois identity were laid down. The ideology of domesticity, with its clearly prescribed gender roles, served to distinguish the middle classes both from the nobility and from the common people. So too, growing out of the improving material conditions of middle-class life, did a belief that property, virtue, and talent, rather than birth, should be the basis for privilege and advancement. Humanitarianism and a nascent utilitarianism—as well as a confidence in freedom of trade, curiously allied with reliance on state encouragement and assistance—also spread among the Paris middle classes in the final decades of the Old Regime. The revolutionary ideologues and their immediate successors took these strands and wove them into a new political system within which a Parisian bourgeoisie could develop and flourish. It was under the Empire and above all the Restoration, though, that this bourgeoisie formed the citywide identity that was needed to mobilize it politically and transform it into a class.

I did not set out to write about the middle classes. I wished to study changes in Paris society during the eighteenth century and to examine the effects of the Revolution. I chose to focus on a single quarter, because I felt that these questions required the study of individual families, businesses, and communities. But gradually I realized that the middle classes were the key to the enterprise, and that the documents I was studying provided privileged access to their world. At the same time, I became aware of how little we knew about the Paris middle classes. Apart from a few older works of the "daily life" variety,[1] few historians have chosen to examine this social group until very recently. Yet it has been, and remains, central to debates about the evolution of eighteenth-century French society and the origins of the French Revolution. Whatever precise definition of the "middle class" is adopted, there is no dispute about this group's considerable economic and demographic significance. Marcel Reinhard estimated, on the basis of rents, that in 1790 the moyenne bourgeoisie of liberal professions and business accounted for some

25,000 Parisian households, while the petite bourgeoisie represented an additional 22,000.[2]

Their numbers were matched by their influence in public life. From the 1720s to the 1760s, the Paris middle classes had played a major role in the religious disputes surrounding the papal bull *Unigenitus* and Jansenism. Later in the century they formed a major part of the "public" whose opinion became increasingly important in the minds and policies of France's rulers. In July 1789 it was they who led the municipal revolution in Paris and who dominated the districts. Subsequently they provided much of the leadership of the sections, even in the Year II.

In economic terms, too, the Paris middle classes were enormously significant, both as producers and as consumers. The industries they controlled helped to make France the center of fashion and of cultural production in the second half of the eighteenth century. And these same middle classes provided the principal market for a wide range of consumer products.

Following the Revolution, both the economic and the political weight of the Paris middle classes continued to grow. Napoleon's regime depended on the support of the "notables," most of whom, especially in Paris, were drawn from the financial and commercial elite and even from more modest merchant, scientific, and administrative circles. The Restoration, with its wider electorate and more powerful legislature (not to mention its bureaucracy), was even more dependent on the support of the middle classes. Its failure to retain that support—once again, particularly in Paris—was a crucial factor in its demise in 1830.

In the early nineteenth century, the first histories of the Revolution, by Thiers, Guizot, and Mignet, portrayed the upheaval mainly as a product of the growing power and influence of the middle classes. This theme was subsequently taken up by Marx and, with more or less subtlety, by a great many later historians, Marxist and non-Marxist alike. It is, paradoxically, the originally almost universal acceptance of the Revolution as "bourgeois" in this sense that largely accounts for the neglect of the eighteenth-century middle classes. The central historical problem of the Revolution appeared to be explaining the popular movement, rather than the role of the bourgeoisie.[3]

But misinterpretation of eighteenth-century sources and imprecision in the definition of "bourgeois" and of "middle class" have also blurred our picture of these social groups. Most definitions use some combination of wealth, status, and occupation, but this can be misleading. In the eighteenth century "bourgeois" still had a precise juridical meaning. It designated a person who had citizen rights within a particular city, and thus applied to most master artisans. It was nevertheless, in common usage, an ambiguous term, employed more restrictively in notarial documents, while used by artisans to mean simply their employer.[4] Very often it was synonymous with small business: "Le bourgeois est marchand; mais il n'est pas négociant" (The bourgeois is a businessman, but he is not in big business), wrote Louis-Sébastien Mercier at the beginning of the 1780s.[5]

By the mid–nineteenth century, the term tended to be applied to the liberal professions, to wealthy manufacturers and merchants, and to people of independent means. In much of the writing about the origins of the French Revolution, the use of a nineteenth-century definition of the term to describe Old Regime society has caused confusion. "Middle class" is a less problematic term in this respect, but it too is used in a variety of ways. For historians of the working class, master artisans and shopkeepers are often included in the "middle classes," whereas for students of the professions or of the financial elites such people have a very dubious claim to this status. In French, *classes moyennes* often refers to what English writers would call the "lower middle classes," but it may also be used to describe the professional and commercial middle classes.[6]

The problem is in part that eighteenth-century sources often do not reveal much about the wealth or status of an individual indicated as a shopkeeper, merchant, or artisan. A man or woman thus described may be a small retailer eking out a slim livelihood in rented premises but in some cases turns out to be a fat and wealthy property owner. The problem is particularly acute when dealing with the period 1792–1794, when titles and even the designations *maître* and *marchand* were generally dropped. This has further obscured the role of the commercial middle classes during the Year II, abetted by the myth, which originates with revolutionary rhetoric itself, that a sansculotte was a humble laborer or artisan. This combination of factors has prevented us from recognizing that the pioneering work of Richard Cobb and of Albert Soboul on the artisans and sans-culottes of Paris in fact dealt extensively with the middle classes. Many of the figures they wrote about were master craftsmen, small employers, and sometimes quite well-to-do merchants, former lawyers, schoolteachers, and members of the Old Regime bureaucracy.[7] Yet neither of them was interested in the middle classes, and Soboul in particular wished to see the sansculottes as autonomous, "a social group which, in many respects, was opposed to the bourgeoisie."[8]

Yet even the first challenges to the mainstream Marxist or Republican interpretation of the Revolution conspired to conceal the role of the commercial middle classes. Wishing to downplay the idea that the French Revolution resulted from the "rise of the [capitalist] bourgeoisie," Alfred Cobban stressed the role of officeholders, while others, building on a long historiographical tradition, emphasized the importance of intellectuals, lawyers, and journalists.[9] In some cases, the categories used for analyzing early modern society have—sometimes inadvertently—concealed the importance of the middle classes. Broad and diverse categories such as the middle class or the bourgeoisie fitted very uncomfortably into Roland Mousnier's "society of orders."[10] François Furet and Adeline Daumard popularized the use of "socio-professional" categories, dividing people by trade sector and by status: officeholders, liberal professions, masters and merchants, *petits métiers,* wage earners.[11] The "bourgeoisie" thus disappeared as a category, and in practice tended to be interpreted as synonymous with "liberal professions," while the commercial middle classes were divided among a number of categories, some of which—such as *maître-marchand*—could include people who had little but their labor, while "wage earners" embraced both lifelong wage earners and sons of rich craftsmen. The desire to quantify often led, in much subsequent work, to neglect of the definitional problems that these categories raised. Attempts to reconstruct the "social structure" of eighteenth-century France often produced a static hierarchy and took no account of geographical diversity or change over time.

By the 1970s many anti-Marxist historians dismissed the whole concept of a "bourgeoisie," preferring to describe eighteenth-century France as a society divided between "elites" and "people," between elite and popular culture.[12] Yet ironically, in rejecting the notion of a "bourgeois revolution," the so-called revisionists, following the lead of Alfred Cobban, made the role and nature of the eighteenth-century French bourgeoisie—and indeed of the middle classes throughout Europe—a matter of debate. Were the bourgeoisie revolutionary? Did they benefit from the Revolution? Were they "rising" in the course of the eighteenth century? Was French capitalism "bourgeois"?

The French bourgeoisie have thus at last become the subject of empirical studies, strongly influenced by the techniques of social, cultural, and economic history.[13] Exciting recent research has begun to reveal the silhouette of the Paris middle classes in the eighteenth century. Daniel Roche's pioneering work on material culture has begun to explore the commercial revolution of the eighteenth century, in which the middle classes played such a central part. Aspects of this subject have also been studied by Annik Pardailhé-Galabrun. With relation to the book trade some of the same themes have been covered by Robert Darnton. Roche's edition of Jacques-Louis Ménétra's memoirs is invaluable on the world of Paris master craftsmen in the second half of the eighteenth century. Michael Sonenscher's work recognizes the central role that master artisans and merchants played in structuring the work practices and the mental world of eighteenth-century artisans, and hence of revolutionary politics. Steven Kaplan has expanded enormously our knowledge of the role of masters and merchants in economic life in Paris. Less directly, Robert Isherwood's study of entertainments, my own work on local communities, and Arlette Farge's books on neighborhood and family have revealed aspects of the cultural and domestic world of the Paris middle classes. Christophe-Philippe Oberkampf and his partners are the subject of studies by Serge Chassagne.[14]

Some historians of the Revolution, too, have taken an interest in the social, economic, and political role of the middle classes, notably Richard Andrews, Haim Burstin, and Raymonde Monnier. The postrevolutionary financial elite has been studied in detail by Louis Bergeron.[15] Without the guidance offered by all these writers, as well as by a handful of older works, this book would not have taken the form it has.

My questions were also formed by the literature being published for the bicentenary of the Revolution. I became increasingly dissatisfied with the way that, in rejecting Marxist interpretations of the Revolution, some historians neglected and even attempted to throw out social history. The suggestion that the whole series of events could be explained by political ideology seemed to me to run counter not only to my study of the sources but also to the testimony of modern politics. This book arises partly, therefore, from a desire to explore ways in which political and social history interact, a subject I deliberately omitted almost entirely—I now think wrongly—from my earlier work on neighborhood. It has led me to conclusions I did not expect, not least about the Revolution and the Directory.

The best political history has always, of course, been aware of the importance of family networks, of patronage and indirect influence, and of religious affiliation. It has often, though, tended to see such relationships as constant, rather than as evolving and endowed with a history of their own. Social history has corrected this misconception, exploring the meaning of particular social bonds at different times. But the linking of long-term demographic and social change with the "short term" of politics is often difficult, and it has resulted in the construction of some very crude models. Feminist history, I think, shows the way, for feminists are trained to perceive the political in the private and are awake to the way that family behavior and ideology are reproduced in wider political life. They have helped to broaden the definition of "politics"; and in this book I am using the term to embrace areas of struggle that have always been ignored by those who defined politics as an activity restricted to the elites in society.

Rather than adopting a socioeconomic definition of "bourgeoisie" or of "middle class"—any particular measure of wealth or any occupational classification that might serve to distinguish the bourgeois from the worker—I have taken political behavior as the defining characteristic of the middle classes. This is because, as Edward Thompson argued many years ago, class is defined not so much by wealth or occupation alone as by behavior.[16] But it is also because political office was central to the identity of the middle classes of eighteenth- and nineteenth-century France. For middle-class families, more than for any others, local office was a central facet of social identity and of social power. The urban middle classes frequently found themselves thrust together with the populace, confused under the general title of "Third Estate." Most had little direct economic power. The liberal professions had few employees, and even a rich master or mistress might have only half a dozen. In a society in which rank was reflected in titles and privilege, thousands of members of the trades corporations, some of them very rich and some desperately poor, clung proudly to the title *maître-marchand*. Others, including former domestic servants and not a few master craftsmen fallen on hard times, prized the rank of *bourgeois de Paris*. But above all else, what publicly distinguished middle-class families from the rest—until 1830, when voting rights usurped this function, and except for a short period at the height of the Revolution when many of the middle classes withdrew from politics—was the dignity and honor bestowed by office. "It is a question often discussed among the bourgeoisie," reports Louis-Sébastien Mercier, "whether one should pay one's respects to one's neighbor, or if one might perhaps be dispensed from this obligation by some personal distinction, such as that of churchwarden, of syndic in a trade corporation, or of *quartenier*."[17] Office bestowed not only rank, but also rights, privileges, and power.

I have attempted to identify all the men who held local office in one quarter of Paris: for the Old Regime, the churchwardens of the parishes and the administrators of the Bièvre River; for the Revolution, those who belonged to the various committees; for the postrevolutionary period, the members of the Welfare Committee, the officers of the National Guard, and the men who served on the parish vestry. But office holding was rarely an individual achievement. A man's success, and very occasionally a woman's, was generally made possible by family resources. In return, the honor and power that office bestowed brought benefits to other family members. It is therefore important to go beyond the officeholders themselves and to study their family relationships: both their immediate kin and the families into which they, their siblings, and their children married. My sample therefore begins with politically successful local notables but extends to include many who did not hold public office. This is not a study of a socioeconomic group. I examine a local elite defined by their access to power and by the local and family relationships and the ideologies that placed political and social power within their grasp.

Yet as the institutions of France changed, slowly under the Old Regime and rapidly during the Revolution and the Empire, so the nature and meaning of local office evolved as well. In order to study the developing Parisian bourgeoisie, therefore, it was also essential to examine the nature of power at the local level—the ways it was used and the means by which it was acquired—and to study the structures of inclusion and of exclusion. This book therefore looks not only at those who defined themselves as middle class through their exercise of office but also at the changing meanings of office holding, and at the way the overt rules and the hidden conventions of power structured the local elite.

In the early eighteenth century, as the first chapters of this book show, the family, political, and emotional ties of the Paris middle classes were local. Like the sixteenth-century merchants studied by Robert Descimon, they belonged to the quarter and particularly to the parish in which they and usually their ancestors had lived.[18] Nowhere is this better illustrated than in the struggles over Jansenism between 1730 and 1760. The name Jansenist was applied to those influenced by the Dutch theologian Cornelius Jansen (1585–1638), who, interpreting Augustine, stressed the inability of humanity to achieve salvation without divine grace. An austere faith, Jansenism attacked the idea that regular attendance at the sacraments was sufficient. It particularly targeted the Jesuits, whom it accused of promising easy salvation to all who observed the external forms of religion, without sufficient attention to the state of the soul and of the conscience.

In the second half of the seventeenth century, the Jansenists took their campaign of moral reform into the seminaries and parishes of the kingdom, propagating a conception of the church as a community of the Chosen in which bishops, lower clergy, and the laity all had a central role. In the late seventeenth century, persecuted by the secular and ecclesiastical authorities alike, the Jansenist theologians found widespread support among the lower clergy and the laity, particularly in the diocese of Paris. When, in 1713, Louis XIV persuaded Pope Clement XI to issue a bull—*Unigenitus*—that condemned the work of the Jansenist theologian Pasquier Quesnel, the French church was split, particularly when Louis then attempted to impose the bull as a law in France. This aroused Gallican fears about papal influence over a French church proud of its independence. By the 1720s, the conjunction of Jansenism, Gallicanism, and questions about the authority of bishops over the lower clergy had produced an explosive political situation in many parts of France.[19]

In some Paris parishes, dominated by particular lineages, the battle between Jansenists and their opponents took on the character of a struggle for control, and even a defense of local family interests. My opening chapter shows the way that the elite of one such parish defined itself through the political and religious struggles within the parish. I have adopted a narrative form, partly in an effort to bring to life the characters of my story, but more importantly to attempt to portray unfamiliar relationships in a way accessible to twentieth-century readers. The following two chapters examine who the members of the local elite were and how they maintained their position. Chapter 4 considers the nature of office and of local politics in Paris during the first half of the eighteenth century.

The second part of the book, Chapters 5 and 6, deals with the dramatic changes in local office-holding and in social relationships that became visible from about 1750 to the 1780s, although the roots of many changes went much further back. Gradually, as intermarriage and residential movement across the city increased, the demography and family organization of the commercial middle classes were transformed, and simultaneously, the composition of the local elite. In the second half of the eighteenth century it became far easier for new men and new families to enter local politics. A crucial factor in this process was the development of merchant capitalism, but it operated more through the social power created by wealth and consumption than through the direct economic power of employer over employees.

Not until after 1789, though, were all the barriers removed. Chapter 7 studies the way that the Revolution changed the character of office and of local political power from 1789 to 1794. It broke the remaining hold of dominant local families on the quarters they inhabited, transformed the political institutions and the administration of Paris, and introduced a new way of thinking about politics. In the process, it redefined the local elite.

In response to the dramatic events of the early 1790s, the Directory constructed a system of power and subordination, now explicitly gendered, which was to last until the middle of the nineteenth century. At the same time, the political and military upheavals of the revolutionary decade set people moving in extraordinary numbers, and in Paris churned and mixed the middle classes. These changes created unprecedented residential and social mobility, accelerating a long-term process of integration but also changing the composition of the developing bourgeoisie, allowing new individuals and groups to join their ranks. Following the upheaval, the role of the Napoleonic state was very largely to consolidate the institutional and social changes that had taken place, while the contribution of the Restoration was to provide a framework and a challenge that brought the new bourgeoisie together, helping them to define themselves as a political and social class. This process of upheaval and consolidation is the subject of Part IV—Chapters 8 through 10—and the conclusion looks at the evolution of the Parisian bourgeoisie with a long-term perspective, relating it to the physical and social development of the city from the sixteenth to the nineteenth century.

The area I have chosen for close study is the Faubourg Saint Marcel, and in particular the parish of Saint Médard. This might seem, at first, a strange place to go in search of the Parisian bourgeoisie. It was on the fringes of eighteenth-century Paris and was renowned for its poverty. "If one makes the journey into that country it is through curiosity; nothing obliges you to go there," wrote Mercier in 1782.[20] Rousseau's hostile judgment on the area is well known and is echoed by other travelers.[21] Many of the streets were unpaved, and most of the houses along the narrow, winding rue Mouffetard were unprepossessing. The stench of drying hides was everywhere, a by-product of the local tanning industry,

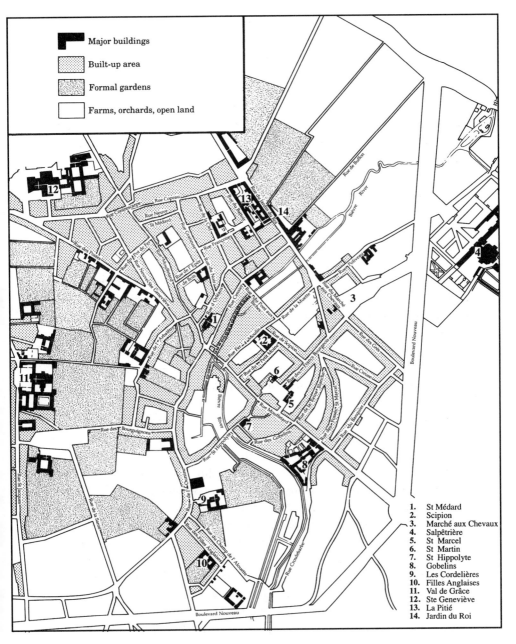

The Faubourg Saint Marcel in the late eighteenth century, showing land use and principal buildings (from the map by Jaillot, 1773).

and the Bièvre River was often languid and stinking. The starch makers produced a smell to rival that of the tanners, and the butcheries and breweries of the area contributed to the thick atmosphere of the quarter. It was neither a healthy nor a desirable place to live.

Nevertheless, the same industries that created these nuisances also produced considerable wealth. In contrast to the desperate poverty of many local people was the prosperity of the owners of the tanneries, breweries, butchers' shops and starch works, of the merchants who ran the substantial blanket-making businesses and the small silk industry based in the quarter, and of the dyers who were closely linked with both. Most lived in their places of work, but their homes were fashionably appointed. At the heart of the quarter lay the Gobelins manufactory, founded in 1607. It produced furnishings for the royal household and formed a hub of state-guaranteed prosperity. There were pockets of valuable stone houses where the richer people lived: at the top of the hill on the rue des Fossés Saint Marcel, within the close of the Abbey of Saint Marcel, along the rue des Gobelins next to the manufactory, and on the southeastern slope of the Montagne Sainte Geneviève in the rue Neuve Sainte Geneviève and the rue des Postes. There were some highly desirable properties on the rue Mouffetard itself, and in the rue de l'Oursine near the convent of the Franciscan sisters (the Cordelières), while some of the small streets on the flanks of the rue Mouffetard contained houses with large gardens and pleasant views.[22]

It is true that certain social and occupational groups were almost totally absent from the quarter. There were only one or two minor nobles, few lawyers or officeholders, and no financiers or bankers. Some of the most prestigious trades—drapers (who sold woolen cloth) and goldsmiths, for example—were virtually unrepresented, but there were some well-to-do mercers (sellers of furnishings, certain kinds of cloth, jewelry, and other items), apothecaries, and grocers *(épiciers)*. Wealthy families represented a smaller proportion of the population than in most parts of the city. This facilitated my quest. The local elite were exclusively middle class and did not play second fiddle to families of magistrates and rentiers on the fringes of the nobility. They are therefore more readily visible in the property records and the notarial archives, and their activities are far better documented than in areas dominated by more prominent social groups. The relatively small number of wealthy families made their reconstitution simpler. In many other parts of the city there was undoubtedly more competition for local office and less of an oligarchy than at Saint Médard. Yet this very feature made my study possible, for the domination of the quarter by a small group of lineages in the early eighteenth century was what enabled the parish vestry of Saint Médard to resist the ecclesiastical and secular authorities, giving us the sources necessary to penetrate the local political and social world of Paris during that period. But neither family behavior nor the nature of local politics was markedly different in the other parishes of the Faubourg Saint Marcel or, as far as I can ascertain, in other parts of the city.[23]

It is true that not all Paris parishes were as Jansenist as Saint Médard; but perhaps half of them were. Many of the laity in the four adjoining parishes—Saint Etienne du Mont, Saint Hippolyte, Saint Martin du Cloître, and Saint Jacques du Haut Pas—were strongly Jansenist, and so too were those of many city center parishes, including some like Saint Nicolas des Champs and Saint Séverin, which embraced wealthier areas and a wider social range. All the available evidence suggests that the social groups represented in this study, throughout the French capital, were solidly Jansenist in their sympathies.[24]

The marginal location of the quarter also distinguishes it. For some time I toyed with the hypothesis that the evolution I was observing was peculiar to the urban fringe, part of the integration of the faubourgs into the urban core. But there is too much evidence of similar patterns of behavior and ways of thinking from elsewhere in the city. I think it likely that the disappearance of local lineages among the commercial middle classes of the central districts, where the quarters were more cramped and the influence of the state more direct, occurred a little earlier than in the faubourgs. But the end date is probably about right: after all, the creation of a citywide bourgeoisie in the early nineteenth century was not complete until the outlying quarters were included.

One problem of sources is worth mentioning. I found almost nothing written by the people whose lives I was trying to trace. There are no letters or diaries (nor have I been able to locate portraits), and the difficulty is particularly acute when trying to find out about the women, on whom the other sources provide very little. Adeline Daumard points to this problem in her study of the early-nineteenth-century bourgeoisie, and the situation for the eighteenth century is no better. It is of course a common difficulty. At times I have been able to refer to evidence from other parts of Paris, but many gaps remain.

Introduction

As a twentieth-century city dweller who appreciates the relative ano-
nymity and the consequent freedom of a large Western city, I would not
have enjoyed life in early modern Paris and I would have found the
family life I describe here stifling. I can only hope that this has not too
greatly hindered my attempt to reconstruct the social world and attitudes
of an eighteenth-century city.

PART

I

THE JANSENIST YEARS

CHAPTER

THE WORK OF SATAN

What need have we of curé or priests in our parish?
—Moreau, master founder, 1730

1 December 1730

Father Jacques Coiffrel adjusts his vestments as he prepares to enter the church. The great wooden doors are open and he can see, white against the chill gloom inside, the faces of the people standing at the rear of the church, those too poor or too late to hire chairs for the long ceremony. The high windows—whose justly famed colored glass depicts scenes from the life of the Virgin and of Saint Médard, patron of the church—filter the winter light in tones of red and blue, dimly illuminating the great tapestries suspended along the nave. Coiffrel touches the open doors in a sign of possession, then steps forward to dip his fingers in the holy water. Slowly he makes his way to the front of the church, a figure at once of authority and of humility, aware of his responsibility for the flock whose shepherd he has become. On either side the people turn and jostle to catch what for many is their first glimpse of the new curé. Before the main altar he kneels and prays, then advances to kiss the cloth that covers it. Under the eye of the assembled clergy of the parish, of the representatives of the great Abbey of Sainte Geneviève, of which he is himself a canon, and of the most prominent parishioners, in their private pews at the front of the church, he touches first the gilded tabernacle, then the baptismal font, and moving up the aisle, lays his hand on the finely carved woodwork of the pulpit. Crossing to the side chapel, he does the same at the confessional. These symbolic gestures of possession completed, Coiffrel takes his place among the clergy at the front of the church while his letters of appointment are read out in a loud, clear voice.

The preliminaries complete, he celebrates his first high mass in his new parish—using the liturgy of Rome, not the more familiar one of Sainte Geneviève (the story goes that the parish adopted the Roman service in protest against its incorporation into the diocese of Paris). The office over, the great bells chime to proclaim the inauguration of the new curé. Yet the solemnity of the occasion, the great crowd in the church, and Coiffrel's awareness of the awesome task that confronts him cannot prevent him from being acutely and angrily conscious that the great pew in the front, opposite the fourth pillar of the nave, had been completely empty.

26 December 1730

There are perhaps forty men seated in the room. From the nearby church the chant and responses of the high mass can be distinctly heard. Different speakers address the assembly, exhorting, now angry, now triumphant. The mood in the parish, at least among the principal families, is determined. A petition has been circulated from door to door protesting against the imposition of this priest whom no one wants. The vestry—the assembly of past and present churchwardens—are holding firm: they unanimously boycotted his inauguration and refused to witness the official documents. Today's meeting is further evidence of their determination. Although the curé has, from time immemorial, participated in meetings of the vestry, Coiffrel has not been invited. To make doubly sure of his absence, the meeting is being held during the main parish mass. Already, at an earlier meeting, they passed a formal motion protesting the removal of M. Pommart, their much loved curé now in exile by order of the archbishop and the King's Council—though they know that this act of defiance is likely to bring down upon them the wrath of both ecclesiastical and royal authorities. When the vestry of the neighboring church of Saint Etienne du Mont passed a similar motion, a special order of the King's Council declared it null and void, and the churchwardens were obliged to witness the formal barring out of the offending paragraph from their register of deliberations. Nevertheless, the men of Saint Médard do not fear, for they know that they have God

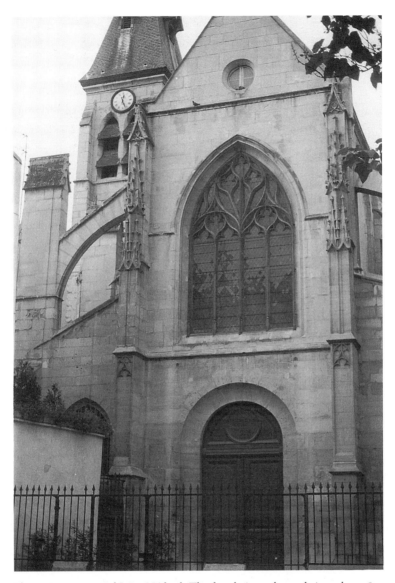

The main entrance of Saint Médard. The facade is unchanged since the 1780s.

and truth on their side. Nothing—not even the combined power of church and king—will make them renounce their faith or surrender to the imposter.

21 January 1731

Coiffrel is furious but helpless. The attitude of the churchwardens toward him is intolerable. They are avoiding all contact with him, even refusing to sign after him in the parish register to witness important baptisms. They vent their pique by referring to him as *"desservant,"* as if he were simply filling in for the real curé. They do not attend services at which he officiates. And now they have held yet another meeting without informing him—no ordinary meeting, either, for it was the annual election of new churchwardens, of the two men who for the next year will be running the temporal affairs of the parish. Even worse than their insults and insolences, for Coiffrel, is the fact that these men are leading astray the faithful of the parish, poor and simple folk, easily deceived. They openly encourage the population to seek the intercession of François de Pâris, as if he were a saint recognized by the church. True, the former archbishop, Monsignor de Noailles, had begun canonization proceedings because of the so-called miracles on Pâris' tomb in the tiny enclosed cemetery at the rear of Saint Médard. But the new archbishop, Monsignor Vintimille, suspended these inquiries. For it is well known that Pâris had strongly Jansenist sympathies, and like many of the Paris clergy, signed the appeals against the bull *Unigenitus,* the papal condemnation of Jansenism obtained by Louis XIV in 1713. The Jansenist press has made much of these so-called miracle cures ever since Pâris' death.

He was a holy man, certainly, though many found him overly given to fasting and self-flagellation, having modeled himself on Saint Francis of Assisi, whose name he bore. He was much loved by the poor of the parish for his charity and good works, but in Coiffrel's eyes his protests of personal unworthiness to partake of the Eucharist demeaned the priesthood and smacked of Jansenism. It was Pommart's failing that he encouraged Pâris, perhaps knowing how such action would increase his own popularity in the parish. But Monsignor Vintimille himself made it clear to Coiffrel that this illegal cult was not to be tolerated, and Coiffrel has no intention of letting it continue. If necessary, he will have the cemetery closed, though for that he will need an order from the King's Council.

Yet the greatest obstacle to reclaiming the parish is Collet Desroches, the sacristan. It is he who is animating the clergy against their new curé and goading the churchwardens to resist. To humiliate Coiffrel when he is to celebrate the mass, Desroches locks the sacristy so the vessels and altar ornaments have to be borrowed from a nearby convent. He is also known to distribute Jansenist books, and it is said that the underground Jansenist newspaper, the *Nouvelles ecclésiastiques,* is read openly at his table. He collects the testimony of those who claim to have witnessed miracles on the tomb and encourages people to seek the intercession of Pâris in their prayers, even in the church. Truly, a wolf in lamb's clothing, and a danger to the immortal souls of the faithful. Yet it is the church-wardens who appoint the sacristan, and in their present mood of rebellion they will certainly not dismiss him. Only the king can overrule them, and Cardinal Fleury, the first minister, is reluctant to take such drastic action. So Coiffrel is left to cope as best he can. He must win over his flock by words and example.

30 December 1731

The better part of a year has elapsed, but at Saint Médard the battle rages with increased intensity. The churchwardens have not ceased harassing Coiffrel, and they are refusing to attend the offertory, though they do occupy their places at the high mass. Their actions won them a personal rebuke from the lieutenant general of police, who summoned the four churchwardens currently in office to his residence where he ordered them to make an apology to the curé. In obedience to this command they went to visit Coiffrel, but once there informed him that they would never recognize him as their parish priest. In April the vestry began legal proceedings in the Grand Conseil, going so far as to claim that Pommart's dismissal was "arbitrary and despotic"—an action that led the archbishop of Paris to ask Cardinal Fleury to suppress the "defiance, indiscipline, and disorder" in the parish. After much deliberation, the Grand Conseil rejected the churchwardens' appeal and ordered them to show Coiffrel "the proper respect and deference owing to someone of his rank." The priest made much of this victory, preaching a fiery sermon and posting copies of the court decision all around the church, but as soon as his back was turned the people tore them down.

In July Coiffrel had an equally significant victory, when he obtained a lettre de cachet exiling Collet Desroches, the sacristan. He subsequently rid himself, in the same way, of two other Jansenist priests. Beyond the boundaries of Saint Médard, similar things have been happening. Priests have been exiled from Saint Etienne du Mont and other parishes. These have all been victories for the archbishop and for Coiffrel.

Yet in other respects, events have taken a turn against them. The cult of Pâris has grown astronomically since August, when people coming to his tomb seeking cures began undergoing the most extraordinary convulsions, leaping and contorting their bodies in a frightening fashion. There are those who say that this cannot be the work of God, but of Satan. Nevertheless, many cures have been reported, and pilgrims have begun arriving from all over Paris and from the provinces. The narrow rue Mouffetard has been jammed with carriages. Divine or satanic, the convulsions have been miraculous for the church coffers. A great many people have paid for masses to be said at Saint Médard, the collection boxes have overflowed, and the sales of candles have been prodigious. Portraits of M. de Pâris have been in heavy demand at the door and in the cemetery, and the hawkers claim that the churchwardens have given them permission to enter. Coiffrel can do little about all this, though he has obtained an order to close the cemetery when there are no services in the church. But the execution of this order is in the hands of the churchwardens, and Moinery, one of their leaders, often opens the cemetery gates at five in the morning and does not close them until eight or nine at night. The vestry are doing all they can to encourage the cult of M. de Pâris.

17 May 1732

Father Coiffrel writes a routine letter to Lieutenant General of Police Hérault. All the Paris curés have regular contact with the police chief, who sends royal decrees to read from the pulpit and often consults them on matters concerning their parish. Such is the present case, for Coiffrel is writing to acknowledge receipt of two petitions that Hérault has sent on for his advice. One is from two Irish priests who have complained of assault by a local wineshop keeper: the priest will have to make inquiries. It is the other petition that interests Coiffrel, though. It is on a personal matter, from a grocer in the rue Mouffetard named Nicolas Maurice. Seeking the priest's support, Maurice has already begun attending mass regularly. What is significant about this is that Maurice is one of the former churchwardens, who until now have remained united. But at

Easter Maurice joined the procession wearing his churchwarden's robes, even though the others all refused to attend. This is the first sign of dissent among them, and Coiffrel is inwardly exultant.

He seizes the opportunity to inform Hérault of affairs in the parish. The churchwardens have got wind of Maurice's approach to him—nothing can be kept secret in a parish like this—and they have declared that his inclusion on the list of former churchwardens was an error. More important, Coiffrel is still having trouble with the sacristan, the second since Desroches was exiled. This one, too, must be dismissed, for like the others he is harassing the priests whom Coiffrel has appointed, and he is favoring the cult of Pâris.

Over the last four months, Coiffrel has at last received the backing from the secular authorities that should have been forthcoming upon his arrival at Saint Médard more than a year earlier. On 27 January Cardinal Fleury at last had the king sign a decree closing the cemetery where Pâris is interred, and two days later, at four in the morning, hundreds of soldiers invaded the quarter. The entrance to the cemetery was bricked up so that no one could gain access, but the police were careful not to touch the tomb itself. The reaction of the people was remarkably subdued, and the churchwardens, who had been warned the day before, seemed overwhelmed by this show of force. Coiffrel had hoped initially that this might be the blow that was needed, and in his sermon the following Sunday had emphasized the virtue of obedience, but the churchwardens did not attend. The following day brought another victory, when the curé was able to enforce the archbishop's order preventing priests from outside the parish from saying mass there. Coiffrel had tried to do this himself six months before, but his order had been totally disregarded. This measure was necessary to prevent Jansenist priests from saying masses.

On the same day, however, it became apparent that the churchwardens' silence indicated sullen disobedience rather than reflection, for they appointed a new sacristan, who has made what should be a place of prayer into a marketplace and a den of thieves. He sells little packets containing linen and fragments of wood from the bed of Pâris. Within the church the Jansenists and followers of Pâris have taken to gathering at the chapel closest to the tomb, where they deposit their prayers on small squares of paper and light candles in such numbers that the chapel resembles a beacon. They fall to their knees and pray to Pâris, even when a service is in progress at the main altar, and they turn their back on the Host.

On 1 May, the anniversary of Pâris' death and therefore a day of great significance to the Jansenists, Coiffrel had buckets of water thrown over the stones to prevent the crowds from flinging themselves to their knees during the service. Foremost among them were many magistrates of the Parlement who, however great their devotion to Pâris, would not kneel on the muddy floor to say their prayers.

The Jansenists have become bolder, thanks to the support they have received from the Parlement. The brother of Pâris, himself a magistrate, took the archbishop to court over statements made about his holy brother. Fortunately for the archbishop the King's Council has removed the affair from the Parlement, and the king has forbidden the courts to accept any further cases concerning Saint Médard or the Pâris business, a considerable relief to Coiffrel. Other events in Paris have not made his task easier, though. The archbishop's order condemning the Jansenist paper, the *Nouvelles ecclésiastiques,* was proclaimed on 4 May, but twenty-one of the Paris curés refused to read it in their churches. At Saint Jacques du Haut Pas, only a few minutes' walk from Saint Médard, rumor has it that two thousand people left the church when the curé began to read it out. The same thing reportedly happened at Saint Landry, where only six parishioners remained in the church. Thus Coiffrel is not the only one facing opposition within his parish. He is convinced that the churchwardens are only the instrument of the Jansenists. But the actions of the Parlement and the agitation in other parishes make the task of winning them back much more difficult, for the churchwardens feel that they have powerful supporters, and this fosters in them a spirit of independence and revolt.

Coiffrel is still embroiled in a court case against them. Seizing on some technicality, they again appealed to the Grand Conseil, challenging his appointment. He had to suffer an excruciating session during which his opponents' lawyer contrasted him most unfavorably with his predecessor, Pommart, and also revealed that one of the priests he had appointed in the preceding year had some time previously been condemned by the Parlement. It was made all the more humiliating by the huge crowd that packed the courtroom. This case is still proceeding. Then, in April, the churchwardens again took him to the Grand Conseil over his appointment of a doorman for the church, an absolute necessity given the large numbers of people coming to pray and the disorder that frequently resulted. This, they claimed, infringed their privilege of making all appointments of church servants. This time the court decided in their favor.

Signatures of churchwardens of Saint Médard opposed to Jacques Coiffrel, 1732. The bottom two signatures are those of the notaries who witnessed the document.

Cardinal Fleury supported Coiffrel and obtained an order from the king appointing the doorman, but no sooner did this seem settled than the churchwardens were back in court claiming that the doorman had helped collect the offering, and that this was not permitted. Decidedly, they are determined to block Coiffrel at every turn. It looks increasingly as if his only chance of peace is to have them replaced—but it will not be easy to convince Cardinal Fleury of that necessity.

15 April 1733

To Monsignor Vintimille,
Archbishop of Paris

Declaration of Jacques Coiffrel, curé of Saint Médard

A spinster of Saint Médard, who appears to be paralytic and who therefore cannot go to the church, requested the paschal communion to be brought to her home. The curé agreed to take it himself, on condition that she show him a certificate of confession, and after having been to interview her first. The following day he therefore went to her, and on entering the room perceived a table ready for the Holy Eucharist, with several portraits on it, among them that of Monsieur de Pâris. At the sight of this portrait the curé observed either to the invalid or to members of her family who were there that it was not seemly thus to display on a kind of altar the image of a person who had not been recognized as a saint. After encountering much resistance, he finally managed to have it removed.

Notwithstanding the practice of the curé never to discuss politics in such circumstances, and particularly with women, he was nevertheless forced to state his opinion on the subject of the bull Unigenitus *because the family brought the conversation around to it. This gave rise to much dispute, which resulted only in everyone talking a great deal yet without persuading anyone. The matter was concluded only with the invalid and her entourage, who spoke on her behalf, declaring that the bull* Unigenitus *could only become the law of the French Church when a General Council of the church had thus decided, and even then, should there be a single bishop opposing it then it would still be permissible to take a position for or against; and whatever Monsignor the Archbishop might say, the voice of God spoke clearly through the miracles of Monsieur Pâris, which they regarded as genuine miracles, and they would never cease to believe with absolute certainty that he is a saint whose intercession may be invoked.*

The curé withdrew, having agreed that the matter would be put before Monsignor the Archbishop, and that it would be for him to decide.

The sick woman's name is Jeanne Tavignot, and her confessor is Father Tirmond of the Doctrine Chrétienne fathers.

(signed) Jacques Coiffrel, 15 April 1733.

3 April 1735

More than four years after his arrival at Saint Médard, it looks very much as though Coiffrel has won. He finally persuaded Cardinal Fleury that the churchwardens would never accept him voluntarily. It took a series of orders from the King's Council to win him access to his own sacristy: first the right to appoint the sacristan was withdrawn from the vestry and given to Coiffrel; then he was exempted from the need to offer a guarantor for his sacristan (the sacred vessels being of very great value)— he had been unable to find a guarantor anywhere in the parish. There then followed a lengthy dispute over who was to guard the sacristy at night, and yet a third royal order was needed to make the churchwardens finally hand over the keys.

At the same time, the interminable court battle over Coiffrel's appointment was finally decided in his favor. Thus defeated, the churchwardens in charge promptly resigned, and the vestry refused to replace them, feigning to take legal action to force them to continue. This left the church with no one to pay the bills, so the church and parish buildings are looking shabby and beginning to fall into disrepair. Worse still, for nearly the whole year the curé was left with next to no money for the poor, and almost no income himself. Even at Easter, only the personal intervention of the lieutenant general of police assured the provision of paschal candles. Without the 1,200 livres lent by Cardinal Fleury, Coiffrel would have been unable to pay his clergy.

Only after all this did Fleury agree that the vestry would have to be removed, and not until then was Coiffrel able to find anyone to replace them. At last, he managed to persuade Monsieur Dupin, a nobleman and undoubtedly the highest-ranking man in the parish, to accept the position of churchwarden of honor. Another four respectable parishioners agreed to take on the real work—no doubt the thought of walking in procession behind Dupin flattered their pride. But alas, no sooner had Coiffrel announced his plan to the cardinal and to the lieutenant general of police than Dupin withdrew. He had, he said, an important court case before the Paris Parlement, who would certainly be hostile if they learned that he was actively supporting the curé of Saint Médard.

For some time Coiffrel was in despair. He toyed with the idea of convening a meeting of the vestry with his twenty or so most implacable enemies excluded by order of the King's Council. But he knew that this was risky. Finally, in August last year, after many visits and much flattery, he found another solution. He was able to convince one of the former churchwardens, Antoine LeBis, to take over the parish finances. Admittedly, LeBis can read and write only with difficulty. But Coiffrel reassured him that it would in fact be the curé who handled the finances, and that he, LeBis, need only sign the receipts.

There are signs, too, that some parishioners are tiring of the dispute. On the Feast of the Purification, in February last year, there were murmurs in the church over the absence of candles on the churchwardens' pew. Then on 25 April the first indications emerged of divisions within the vestry, when a number of its members came to Sunday mass and occupied the pew. Six of them joined the procession, two even wearing their churchwardens' robes. There were not so many at Corpus Christi— only three—but that procession is much more public and they may have been afraid. Nevertheless, the opposition is gradually weakening. Since Coiffrel's arrival several leading members of the vestry have died, and this may have helped to undermine the churchwardens' resolve.

So Coiffrel can now, for the first time in years, enjoy some peace. Not that his worries are over, by any means. For a start, he is bankrupt, thanks to the repeated court cases that the vestry have brought against him: he has debts of nearly 2,000 livres. This leaves him nothing to give the poor, who at Saint Médard are very numerous; and a curé who cannot succor the least favored of his flock can expect little esteem in his parish.

Coiffrel has other concerns, too. The Pâris cult is still enormously popular in the parish. Many people come regularly to pray before the side chapel near the cemetery, and the church is littered with notes dedicated to Pâris. The parish schoolmaster is imparting Jansenist principles to the children, teaching them prayers to Pâris, and turning them against their curé. The priest has warned, from the pulpit, that those sending their children to this school will receive no alms from the parish, but the numbers have still grown. The schoolmaster is not a member of the clergy, so the curé is powerless against him.

Another concern is the Jansenist convents in the quarter. The Sisters of Sainte Agathe, for instance, used to run the parish school, but had it taken away when Coiffrel discovered that they were telling the children not to recognize him as curé and not to accept any of the parish clergy as confessors. But since then the number of private pupils at the convent has grown enormously. Behind all of this is the Jansenist party, with its powerful supporters in the Parlement. For a time, Coiffrel's refusal of the Easter communion to the invalid woman, Jeanne Tavignot, seemed to be getting him into very serious trouble: she appealed to the Parlement, which upheld her case, and only the cardinal's action in having the Parlement's decision reversed in the King's Council saved Coiffrel from condemnation, perhaps even exile. His position is secure only as long as he enjoys the support of Cardinal Fleury, the archbishop, and Lieutenant General Hérault, and all of them have powerful enemies at court.

Furthermore, the character of LeBis is uncertain. He is apprehensive lest the vestry begin legal proceedings against him, and ultimately his accounts will have to be checked—something normally done by the former churchwardens. Coiffrel may have to seek, yet again, the assistance of the crown.

18 March 1736

"All our hopes of peace have evaporated," writes Coiffrel in despair. For over a year he has been courting the churchwardens, at Cardinal Fleury's insistence. They have received him well and have consented to negotiate, but it has become clear that they have no real intention of yielding on any point. He is managing to run the parish from day to day without hindrance, thanks to the lettres de cachet that have reduced the vestry to angry impotence, but every time a major decision is required—repairs to the church, the acceptance of a bequest, the appointment of church employees—he must seek a special royal order. He finally, last year, replaced the troublesome parish schoolmaster, resorting to yet another order from the King's Council. But these are things no parish priest should have to do, and a burden borne by none of Coiffrel's colleagues. He greatly envies the cooperative spirit that some of them enjoy within their parishes. The financial management of a church is a task properly fulfilled by laymen, leaving the priest free for his pastoral duties. Not only does Coiffrel find it a distraction, but without their assistance parish income is reduced and he cannot meet the demands of the poor. He knows too that as long as this irregular situation continues he will never find true acceptance in the parish. Although for the moment the vestry can do him no harm, behind his back they have been threatening to take LeBis to court if there is any shortfall in his accounts. The poor man is quite intimidated and has declared that he will resign immediately after Easter unless his accounts can be checked by some outside body. The priest has been trying to persuade a number of the former churchwardens to resume at least some of their functions, for the good of the parish, and at one stage it had seemed that they were on the point of yielding. But now he can see that they have merely been leading him on, for today they have gone back to their original demands and claim that they never agreed to any concession. They would prefer, they now say, to remain forever in their present position rather than to accept any compromise. Perhaps they know of LeBis's threat to resign. If he does, Coiffrel's enemies will again have the ascendancy, and he will be right back where he began.

5 September 1740

Coiffrel is dead. The abbot of Sainte Geneviève has been busy, in the days since the priest fell seriously ill, compiling a list of suitable replacements. It is a delicate matter, for the church authorities cannot risk appointing a man who might reverse Coiffrel's good work at Saint Médard. The Pâris cult remains a serious headache for the supporters of the bull *Unigenitus*. Despite the best efforts of the police, the convulsionaries are still active and still claiming miraculous cures. Yet this is also an opportunity to seek reconciliation in the parish. It is ten years since Father Pommart was removed, and in that time some of the most hostile former churchwardens have died. Many in the parish are tired of the bitter dispute. The right man might be able to restore the vestry to their proper functions and heal the divisions.

But there is little time for reflection. For the churchwardens have a candidate for the position, Father Ramet, stepson of Guillaume Arnoult, one of their number. If he were appointed he would be a tool of the vestry, and thus of the Jansenist party. While it is technically the Abbey of Sainte Geneviève that makes the appointment, with the agreement of the archbishop, a long delay would give the churchwardens time to appeal to Rome. They are quite capable of so doing, and already Arnoult has been busily canvassing support. The abbot has written to warn the lieutenant general of police not to back Ramet, and has asked him to convey this message to Cardinal Fleury.

23 December 1740

Monsignor Vintimille,
Archbishop of Paris.

Rue de Bourgogne

Monsignor,
The deplorable state of the parish of Saint Médard leads a humble parishioner to take the liberty of addressing Your Eminence, to whose attention she has no claim other than her religion, of which you are the zealous defender.
The new curé *of Saint Médard is but a wolf in sheep's clothing, determined to seduce the flock that our much regretted late pastor tried so hard to bring back to the fold. He speaks ill of Monsieur Coiffrel, and repeats that the Archbishop had told him at table that he personally regarded Pâris as a saint, and that one day the church would recognize him. He is changing and overthrowing everything in the parish. He has reestablished a council of women, every one infected with Jansenism, to take over the distribution of alms, for he does not want to assume this responsibility. A priest, he says, should confine himself to saying his prayers. Among these women whom he has chosen, whose assemblies are held in his quarters, behind locked doors, are several whose husbands have been arrested and sent to the Bastille; they were among those poor fools who went with the convulsionaries to Port Royal and were arrested there planting a cross. One might even say that, to the shame of the Church, it is not a man who governs but fourteen women, all without education.*
I remain, etc.

(signed) Madame Tirman.

4 May 1741

The parish has once more been thrown into uncertainty. Less than a year after the new curé, Duquesnoy, was appointed, he has followed Coiffrel into the realm of the blessed. He had too little time to stanch the wounds that so weakened the parish, though he did achieve a partial reconciliation with the former churchwardens. Yet this set others against him, those whom Coiffrel had won over with so much effort. A flood of petitions to the archbishop and to the lieutenant general of police accused Duquesnoy of closing his eyes to the presence of the Jansenists, even of eating their bread. He had handed over the distribution of alms to Jansenist sympathizers and had approached the lieutenant general to obtain the withdrawal of the lettres de cachet against the vestry. He wished, so it seemed, to leave each parishioner to his or her own beliefs, and this displeased many who saw in the Jansenists a mortal threat to the church. On the other hand, it gave much succor to the former churchwardens and their party, who once again held the ascendancy in the parish, even though they were not restored to their official functions.

Once more, it seems, the Lord has intervened. A new priest must again be found.

13 July 1741

A meeting of the vestry has taken place, the first full one in years. Father Gerbault, the new curé chosen by the Abbey of Sainte Geneviève, has succeeded where his predecessors could not, in persuading the former churchwardens not only to attend but to recognize Antoine LeBis as the man officially in charge of parish finances. Not that this will avail LeBis: never prosperous, he is now virtually "on the parish" himself, no doubt in part as a result of his neglecting his business during the many years he has been in office. Unfortunately, the parish finances are in no better state. There are many outstanding debts, and it is high time that the vestry took charge once more.

Inevitably, there are people who are not pleased with the actions of the new curé. He has fallen out with Coiffrel's supporters, embattled ever since the loss of their patron. They claim that he is too sympathetic to the Jansenists and hostile to those appointed by his predecessors. He has abruptly removed Coiffrel's parish clerk and ardent supporter, Grandval, appointing instead one of his own relatives. He has fallen out most seriously with Coiffrel's two nephews, who hold the most senior clerical positions in the parish—those of first and second *vicaire*. Quick-tempered and strongly anti-Jansenist, they were even more vigorous than Coiffrel himself in their attacks on the Pâris cult. As a result, they have become the most hated men in the parish: three-quarters and half again of the parishioners, in Gerbault's expression, are so strongly against them that their continued presence in the quarter is an insurmountable barrier to reconciliation. They, in turn, have been showering Cardinal Fleury and the lieutenant general of police with accusations against him.

24 March 1742

For the third time in as many years the parishioners of Saint Médard have crowded into their small church to witness the inauguration of a new curé. First there was Father Duquesnoy, who died after less than a year. Then Father Gerbault, against whom there were so many accusations that the cardinal removed him a few months after his inauguration. Was it simply that he made enemies among those who had the ear of the lieutenant general of police and the cardinal, or was there substance to the reports that he did not pay his priests properly or pass on funds he had received for the poor, that he did not always honor his engagements, and that he listened too readily to supporters of the Jansenists?

Whatever the truth of the matter, his departure has opened the way to a new beginning. The new curé, Father Hardy de Levaré, has made an excellent impression. Perhaps seeking readmission to their places after so many years in the wilderness, eight of the churchwardens attended his inauguration and signed the register, and several others sent apologies. The very next day, the favorable impression was reinforced by the arrival of a new sacristan, Father Huguet, born in the parish and belonging to one of the principal and longest established local families. All his relatives live locally. His father was a churchwarden, but not strongly opposed to Coiffrel, and as a deacon the son always supported his curé. The Jansenists are not happy, and the vestry are displeased to again be deprived of the choice of sacristan, but others are very pleased to have someone they know, rather than an outsider. Many of the local people, it is said, have begun to turn away from the cult of Pâris, and there is every reason to hope that calm will return to Saint Médard.

31 July 1742

Alas, all hopes of peace have proved illusory. At first all seemed to be going well. The new curé was well received when he made clear his intention to reestablish the vestry. Although he insisted that he would not allow the Pâris cult in his church, his conciliatory tone reassured many of them, and they were flattered by his personal visits. In the Corpus Christi procession, at the end of May, the churchwardens agreed to carry the dais for the first time in twelve years.

The new man has much energy and has already found out more about his parish than any of his predecessors. He somehow discovered, for example, that despite their formal exclusion from parish government, for more than ten years the churchwardens had been secretly electing a *commissaire des pauvres* to distribute alms in the parish. Each year, without the knowledge of the curé or even of LeBis, they had obtained permission from the *procureur général* of the Parlement, who must have imagined that their request was legal. They then gathered at the house of the most senior former churchwarden and, needless to say, chose only men of their own persuasion. They had therefore been able to use the funds from the central poor relief agency, the Grand Bureau des Pauvres, to maintain their authority in the parish, while Coiffrel believed them to be totally disarmed.

Whether because of their annoyance at thus being discovered, or because of Hardy de Levaré's extraordinary efficiency in tracking down and denouncing Jansenist priests and schoolteachers, or because they felt that it was not the priest's place to convene a meeting, the churchwardens resolved not to attend when Hardy summoned them. Only LeBis, Maurice, and three others were present. The curé, far from being disturbed by this, within a week obtained a lettre de cachet excluding the others from future meetings and naming eighteen men to form a "Commission" to replace the vestry.

The churchwardens are furious. It now seems clear that this was a premeditated move and that the curé had already picked out a number of local merchants whom he would be able to dominate in assemblies.

1 May 1749

Never, since the cemetery was closed, have there been so many people at Saint Médard to mark the anniversary of the death of Pâris. The church is locked, as it is every year on this day and on 4 October, feast day of Saint Francis. The curé and his clergy have gone in procession to Sainte Geneviève, so they will not see the crowds who go down on their knees in the street to offer their prayers to Pâris.

The cult of Pâris has proved resistant to all the efforts of Hardy de Levaré to stamp it out. For seven years he has denounced convulsionaries and Jansenists. He has acted against the Sisters of Sainte Agathe and has accused the clergy of Saint Victor of accepting the confessions of renegades from Saint Médard. He has campaigned against Jansenist pamphlets and books and tried to exclude them from his parish.

For seven years, too, he has continued the struggle against the former churchwardens. Although the Commission has worked well, because of the dismissal of the old vestry many of the former churchwardens had never had their accounts checked. While some had undoubtedly put in money from their own pockets, others owed money to the church, and several have had to be pursued through the courts. Jacques Etienne LeSourd, for example, was finally judged to have collected some 2,000 livres more than he paid out, which with interest came to more than 3,000. Pursued relentlessly by Hardy de Levaré, he eventually repaid 2,400 livres. Bouillerot de Saint Ange died before his accounts could be checked, a circumstance that embroiled the curé in long and complicated proceedings with the heirs.

These have also been years of struggle on behalf of the poor. With 15,000 to 18,000 communicants, the amount of pastoral work at Saint Médard is very considerable, particularly as some 12,000 of those parishioners are so poor that even in good times they cannot survive without some assistance from the parish. And lacking the neighboring convents, the numerous clergy, and the Sisters of Charity with which many parishes are endowed, at Saint Médard the greatest weight of work falls upon the curé. The people come to their pastor, too, with their petty disputes, and even the better-off citizens often require his help. For example, he was able to obtain a reduction in the tax assessment for old Pierrusse, one of the members of the Commission. The Widow Ozanne, too, was shabbily treated by her husband's corporation after his death; Hardy wrote to the lieutenant general on her behalf.

Nor should anyone forget the priest's efforts to protect his flock from the temptations that abound in a large city. He has campaigned against those who work on holy days. He has exposed men and women who live in sin and prostitution, numerous in a quarter somewhat removed from the center, where the rents are low and there are large numbers of soldiers. The danger is illustrated by the fall of one of Hardy's own clergy, who was discovered visiting prostitutes. The curé is trying to raise funds to fit out a house next to the church where the priests of the parish can live as a community and be safe from such hazards.

Despite all these efforts, Hardy's relations with the Commission have deteriorated. When all those eligible to serve had done their term as churchwardens, they demanded a return to the old system. Hardy was strongly opposed to this, fearing that it would return too much power to the vestry. Last December the Commission sought to provoke him by inviting to the election of the *commissaire des pauvres* several of the

Rue d'Orléans, from the rue Mouffetard. In the eighteenth century a passage at the bend of the street on the right led to the side door of Saint Médard. The house that Hardy de Levaré eventually bought for his priests was one of those on the right.

former churchwardens. Then they changed the lock on the door of the room where the church ornaments are kept, to deny the curé access. The outlook is not promising.

29 December 1751

A debate has been going on at the highest level. On one side are the curé of Saint Médard and the archbishop of Paris, now Christophe de Beaumont. On the other is the new lieutenant general of police, Nicolas Berryer. The question is what to do about the troublesome churchwardens of Saint Médard.

After several years of tranquillity, thanks to the smooth operation of the eighteen-member Commission appointed by the King's Council, all the eligible men have taken their turn at running the parish. Hardy de Levaré and the archbishop have asked that a new Commission be appointed, and with the assistance of the old one the priest has put forward eighteen names. It has subsequently emerged, however, that many of those named have not been consulted, and several have threatened to contest any such arbitrary nomination. This would be to repeat the events of the previous two years, when the men chosen appealed against their election. At the beginning of the present year, the other members turned to the Parlement to force them: it was suggested by some that this was only a device to destroy the Commission. The King's Council removed the affair from the Parlement, which would almost certainly have supported the renegades. The government is reluctant to see the same thing happen again, for each time the Parlement has a new excuse to remonstrate, and this further inflames public opinion. Berryer's advice, therefore, is to return to free elections. The archbishop and the curé counter that this will set the members of the Commission—who were named by the King's Council—against those who are subsequently elected. Another option is to allow free elections, but to keep the Commission to make all important decisions. A decision must soon be made, for the new churchwardens would normally take up their duties early next year.

17 December 1752

The Jansenists have won another victory. The formidable curé of Saint Médard has gone into exile. The churchwardens, restored to their place of authority after years in the wilderness, are exultant, and a large crowd

of the common people of the quarter, shouting and jeering, gathered to
see Hardy de Levaré and his two *vicaires* on their way. They have not
forgiven him for his announcement at Easter that he would not allow
anyone to receive Holy Communion without a certificate signed by one
of his own priests, or by the Jesuits or the Capuchins. The parish at once
revolted, taking a protest signed by 1,500 bourgeois to the Parlement.
That came to nothing, but they see his present predicament as fitting
retribution.

The source of this new development is the archbishop's draconian
ruling that the last sacraments will not be administered to the dying
unless they have a certificate of confession signed by an approved priest.
In his relentless pursuit of Jansenists, the curé of Saint Médard has
carried out this instruction to the letter. A few days ago he was called to
the Sisters of Sainte Agathe to administer the last sacraments to one Sister
Perpétue, and knowing the Jansenist sympathies of the convent, he ques-
tioned her on her submission to the bull *Unigenitus*. On her refusal to
accept the bull, he and his *vicaires* denied her the sacraments.

It was not the first time this had happened in the locality, of course:
in 1749 the curé of Saint Etienne du Mont had refused the sacraments
to Charles Coffin, the principal of the College of Beauvais, and a year
later had done the same when Coffin's nephew died. Then in March this
year, the same curé again refused the sacraments to one of his parishioners. That time the Parlement ordered his arrest and, in April, ruled it
illegal to refuse the sacraments on the grounds that the dying person did
not have a certificate of confession or did not accept *Unigenitus*. So
Hardy well knew what the consequences were likely to be, and Sister
Perpétue may well have been testing him. She immediately appealed to
the Parlement, sparking yet another tussle between the Parlement and
the archbishop, who claimed that his clergy were not answerable to the
civil courts. Upon that, the Parlement issued an order for Hardy's arrest.
The King's Council can no doubt be relied upon to reverse the ruling,
but for the moment the Jansenists are rejoicing at the exile of one of their
most relentless enemies.

7 February 1755

Seventeen men are seated on leather-covered chairs around the table in
the vestry room at Saint Médard. They have assembled to hear Jean

Pichard and Louis Barre report on their visit to the *procureur général* of the Parlement, the man responsible for the parish churches of Paris. They had informed him of the death in February last year of Father Pommart, the former curé of Saint Médard, in exile in Troyes. They had also expressed their desire to honor Pommart's memory with a service, and recounted their efforts to persuade the clergy to allow it. Hardy, now back from exile, had given their request very short shrift.

The *procureur général* had listened patiently as they described the visit that their wives had made to the archbishop, Christophe de Beaumont. De Beaumont had retorted that if they were so keen to hold a service for their deceased priest, they should do the same for the other two who had died before him. Would this solution not be acceptable to them? the *procureur général* had asked. This was for the full vestry to decide.

When at last the meeting concludes, the churchwardens have resolved to ask the Parlement to order the curé to permit four services, one each for Coiffrel, Duquesnoy, Pommart, and Gerbault.

4 October 1759

The rain has been sweeping across Paris in gray sheets, splashing the cobblestones clean and washing the debris into the central gutters. On the Montagne Sainte Geneviève, the flood gushes down the rue Mouffetard toward the storm pipe that will carry it down beside the narrow bridge and into the swollen Bièvre River. It washes past the Gothic facade of Saint Médard, where a small congregation is celebrating the feast day of Saint Francis of Assisi.

The morning had begun as usual, with the ringing of the Angelus bell to call the working people to the first mass, before the start of the day's labor. By seven the gray light has grown, but all the candles of the faithful are needed to illuminate the somber church. At eight Hardy's secretary, also a cleric, officiates, and to the delight of the congregation the curé himself celebrates the solemn mass of the Blessed Sacrament at nine. The morning, thus sanctified, wears on, for it is a working day. There is another mass at ten, two services (one a funeral in a side chapel) at eleven. It being the first Thursday of the month, the curé leads the procession, after saying vespers as the light fades again, and then conducts benediction. Decorum reigns in the church, and in the parish all is quiet.

It is not quite a normal day, all the same. There have been fewer

services than usual, certainly for the feast day of a major saint. One of
the priests has gone away to the country and another two are unaccount-
ably absent. Nor have the preceding few days been peaceful. The curé
was summoned to an interview with the *procureur général* of the Parlement, who reminded him of his promise, a month earlier, that he would
say mass on the fourth. The archbishop, under heavy political pressure,
consented to allow him to say three masses. Then, only a few days ago,
the churchwardens met and decided to seek a court order obliging him
to say ten requiem masses, and a crisis was only averted by the intervention of the lieutenant general of police and the *procureur général.*

This is not the first year that services have resumed on 4 October, or
that the curé has officiated, despite his extreme hostility to the memory
of François de Pâris. Last year, also under pressure from the authorities,
he consented to say mass, though only after the churchwardens brought
a locksmith to open the sacristy, which he had had locked in the hope
of preventing any services that day. This was already an amazing concession from a man who, less than a month earlier, had stormed at the
churchwardens that he would never consent to a service on 4 October.
For one day in the year people could go to mass somewhere else, he had
fumed, and he would not succor a cult that the church condemned. They
were putting their eternal salvation in grave danger, he had warned them,
and as for himself, he intended to conserve his immortal soul in peace.
They had retorted that if he did not consent to say mass, they would
bring in priests from outside, even if it caused a scandal throughout
the diocese. It took all the efforts of the *procureur général* and his
brother the *avocat général,* of the lieutenant general of police, and
even the involvement of Cardinal de Bernis and of the First President
of the Parlement, Le Fèvre d'Ormesson, to avoid a full-scale confron-
tation.

Perhaps Hardy de Levaré's exile, from 1752 to 1754, and again from
1755 to 1756, has made him more flexible. Certainly, the churchwardens'
victories, first in having the church opened on 4 October, subsequently
in obtaining a service for Pommart and the other curés, have inclined
them to make concessions. They owe these things, of course, primarily
to the changed political circumstances in France—most notably to the
king's abandonment of the pro-*Unigenitus* party. It is true that their
differences with the curé have not been resolved, and never will be. Nor
will Hardy ever be popular with the majority of the parish. But for most

of the local people, the main concern is to have churchwardens to ensure that repairs are done and candles supplied; to have clergy to say mass and provide the sacraments; to have a curé who will look after the poor and help his flock in their need. After thirty years of bitter conflict, Saint Médard has become a normal parish once more.

CHAPTER 2

THE ELECT

*The election of churchwardens is not done by the bishop,
nor by the lord of the place, but by the inhabitants;
and in parishes where they are too numerous, it is the
former churchwardens who elect the new ones.*

—Encyclopédie, *article "Marguillier"*

In 1731 or 1732 an anonymous informant reported on the threatening situation at Saint Médard: "Popular fanaticism has made progress and will spread far if we are not careful." Anyone who did not support the churchwardens' cause, the writer explained, went in fear. "Someone of my acquaintance who has a house there where he lives, and who does not wish to be named because fear makes him regard these churchwardens as very formidable men, this person has spent two nights under arms with all his household until three in the morning . . . These villains have someone mount guard every night in the bell tower of Saint Médard and from time to time they fire gunshots as a signal."[1]

It is, to modern eyes, all rather melodramatic, as it clearly was to this anonymous correspondent, who portrayed the leading churchwardens as strutting opera buffa characters playing out semicomic roles on a very small stage. For all their self-importance, they lacked the dignity of seasoned political players. They could intimidate the naive, but they were really very small fry who should be dealt with swiftly.

A glance at the occupations of the Saint Médard churchwardens seems to confirm this analysis (see Table 2.1). Nearly all belonged to that diverse but undistinguished category of master craftsmen and merchants who made up the greater part of the Paris middle class. There were no

Table 2.1 Occupations of the churchwardens of Saint Médard, 1730–1732, and 1752–1760

Occupation	Number
Leather trades—master tanners and leather dressers[a]	35
Bakers	7
Brewers	5
Hosiers (*bonnetiers*)[b]	5
Grocers	3
Wineshop keepers	2
Candle makers	2
Ribbon makers	2
Hatters	2
Mercer	1
Butcher	1
Masons and roofers	2
Master potter	1
Starch maker	1
Blanket maker	1
Seller of cooked meat (*charcutier*)	1
Seller of prepared food (*traiteur*)	1
Apothecary	1
Market gardener	1
Minor officeholders[c]	2
Unknown	2
Total	78

Note: The years 1733–1751 are excluded because the men administering the parish during this time were appointed by lettre de cachet.

a. Leather dressers were those who cured skins without using tannin and who also made finer leathers.

b. Merchants who manufactured and sold stockings.

c. No other occupation given.

nobles, no lawyers or doctors, no holders of important offices. Even among the guildsmen, these were not the most illustrious. The most prestigious of the Paris corporations, the Six Corps—the drapers, mercers, goldsmiths, hosiers, furriers, and grocers—were poorly represented, and most of the churchwardens were in lesser occupations, nearly half in the insalubrious leather trades. Some were simple artisans, particularly the bakers, a clear rung lower on the ladder of occupational prestige in eighteenth-century Paris.

One might indeed have expected Hérault, the lieutenant general of police, or Cardinal Fleury, the first minister, to have dealt summarily with such puny opposition. A few lettres de cachet, a spell in the Bastille, and the episode would be over. The situation was, however, not so simple. Even in an absolute monarchy some legal niceties had to be observed, and even the most humble churchwardens had, by virtue of their office, a legal existence and civic rights. Furthermore, on the national scene the political balance was precarious. The authorities could not afford to take precipitous action, even against the rebellious churchwardens of a poor parish in an unimportant corner of Paris.

Nor, as it turned out, were the churchwardens as puny or as easily intimidated as their anonymous denouncer believed. Their resistance was long, stubborn, and resourceful. They proved surprisingly skillful in manipulating the complex legal system and in seizing the political initiative. It was partly their Jansenist-leaning faith that made them genuine opponents of the papal bull *Unigenitus* and of the monarchy's attempt to impose it on the nation. But the churchwardens were driven to public opposition by a conviction that as leading citizens they had a responsibility to speak out on behalf of the local population. They resented the interference of priest and government in the running of a parish that was their burden and their domain. In each of these respects the churchwardens of Saint Médard were, for all their humble status, little different from the local elite of most quarters of Paris in the first half of the eighteenth century.

The authorities at first attributed their "spirit of independence and revolt" to "the Jansenist party of which in this matter the churchwardens are but the instruments."[2] Manipulated, however, the churchwardens were not. That they were Jansenists in the spirit of Port Royal is unlikely: their theology probably did not run so deep. But they belonged to that sector of Parisian society in which "popular Jansenism" was firmly entrenched, manifested in opposition to *Unigenitus* and to the Jesuits, in a belief in the sanctity of the deacon Pâris, and in the conviction that the laity should play a key role within the universal church.

None of them, it is true, was ever refused the sacraments or imprisoned for Jansenism, though one was accused of hosting Jansenist meetings.[3] But there is ample evidence of impeccable Jansenist connections. The first refusal of sacraments in the parish, in 1733, was to the first cousin of churchwarden Jean Pichard.[4] A number of the churchwardens were close relatives of the anti-*Unigenitus* curé of Corbeil, Jacques Bouillerot.[5] Another of the Bouillerot family, a woman whose first name is not given, was sufficiently well known to be listed, together with the curé of Corbeil and one of the Pichard family, in a *"nécrologe des appelants"* that includes most of the prominent Jansenists of eighteenth-century France.[6] Sometime in the early 1730s, the son-in-law of one of the churchwardens of Saint Médard had given up his trade to spread Jansenist propaganda in the provinces. And among the churchwardens themselves, Nicolas Bouillerot owned at least one Jansenist catechism.[7]

In their running of the parish, too, the churchwardens of Saint Médard succored the cause of the Jansenist "party." The sacristan Collet Desroches, who according to police reports distributed Jansenist books, was their appointee.[8] The churchwardens also refused to dismiss the schoolmaster who, Coiffrel reported after purging the local clergy, "teaches openly that there is no confessor of sound doctrine at Saint Médard and that people should go elsewhere."[9] The first beadle, whom the vestry defended, kept a list of the miracles of Pâris and in the end resigned, "preferring to leave his position rather than to stop praying to Monsieur Pâris."[10] The churchwardens, not forgetting his services, later reappointed him as verger.[11]

In their administration, the vestry of Saint Médard displayed the care that Marie-José Michel has identified as characteristic of Jansenist parishes in Paris. They kept detailed accounts, issued receipts, maximized revenue from investments, and carefully maintained the church buildings.[12] Concern for the parish poor is likewise testimony to Jansenist principles: in 1704 the vestry funded a second bed at the Paris hospital for the terminally ill, for the exclusive use of Saint Médard; the parish poor schools were in place quite early (1662); and donations permitted the vestry to provide dowries for a number of poor women each year. The aunt and uncle of four of the churchwardens of Saint Médard, not content with looking after the poor of their own parish, donated a house to provide a school for the neighboring parish of Saint Hippolyte in 1706 and six years later gave 4,000 livres for a charity school in the third parish of the Faubourg Saint Marcel, Saint Martin du Cloître.[13]

Certain churchwardens displayed strong individual support for the cult of Pâris and tacitly encouraged the sale of relics. Antoine Moinery, an ancestor of the merchant involved in the so-called grocery riots of 1792, was assiduous in welcoming Jansenist visitors and in covertly allowing access to Pâris' tomb.[14] Another churchwarden dismissed a woman who had been employed to seek alms for the poor and replaced her with one who was more devoted to Pâris. It is true that the cult of Pâris was good for the church coffers, but there were signs of a more personal attachment to the holy man's memory. The wife of one churchwarden was noted by the police for her devoted observance of Pâris' feast day, even as late as 1757. Another member of the vestry, when the priest rebuked devotees of the deacon from the pulpit, replied indignantly from the pews that the preacher was "unfit for the care of souls."[15]

It was in part religious conviction, therefore, that gave the churchwardens the courage to tack against the ultramontane gales. The anti-*Unigenitus* cause depended on a deeply held conviction that personal salvation was not dependent on the blessing of priest or archbishop. Whatever moral pressure the curé brought, the churchwardens countered that he was, perhaps unknowingly, doing the work of Satan.

That they did not simply retreat into a sullen and private hostility, however, is due to the support they received both within and outside the parish. The previous curé, Pommart, had apparently been very popular; at any rate, he became so in retrospect. There was certainly considerable hostility to his abrupt dismissal. Police reports cite many instances of insults directed against Coiffrel.[16] Among the more educated parishioners there was little sympathy for the new incumbent, for he was unable to find anyone to replace the rebellious churchwardens or even to stand surety for the sacristan he appointed in 1732. The parish clergy also appear to have supported Pommart—he had presumably appointed most of them, and three-fifths of them had appealed against *Unigenitus*. The church servants, dependent on the churchwardens, were hardly likely to welcome the new curé, and even the regular clergy—notably the Sisters of Sainte Agathe and the priests of Sainte Geneviève—were largely pro-Jansenist.[17]

It is clear that the churchwardens were strongly seconded by their womenfolk. The wives of six of them visited the archbishop of Paris three times to request a service for their former curé. When Antoine LeBis singled out his principal enemies in 1741, he included the widows of former churchwardens Prevost and Dorigny. A year later, when the recalcitrant churchwardens were excluded, one of them angrily laid the blame on Joseph Bouillerot *and his wife*. Hardy de Levaré himself observed that the churchwardens' wives "share with their husbands the responsibility and the expense of their administration."[18] The support of the Jansenist women was indispensable to the campaign.

The opinions of the general population of the area are less accessible, but the overwhelming enthusiasm for Pâris is clear, and Coiffrel quickly made himself unpopular by attempting to efface his cult. The closure of the cemetery on 29 January 1732 was extremely provocative, not only because it forbade access to the tomb of Pâris but also because it put behind bars the sepulchres of a good many people's ancestors. Attempts to remove candles and ex-votos from the chapel nearest Pâris' tomb provoked near riots, with the populace "swearing and crying out against Messieurs the curé and *vicaire*." When Hardy arrived in 1742, he found it still strongly Jansenist.[19]

No less vital was the encouragement the churchwardens received from outside the parish. People flocked to the church once the news of Pâris' miracles spread, and the convulsions on his tomb attracted more pilgrims. Many believers paid for masses at Saint Médard, in hope of intercession by Pâris. Others enrolled their children in the local charity school. Many of the Paris curés and other clergy were frequent visitors, and in 1732 several of the curés refused to recognize Coiffrel's appointment.[20] Magistrates of the Paris Parlement honored the church with their presence, with Jérôme-Nicolas de Pâris, brother of the deacon, and Louis-Basile Carré de Montgeron the most regular. Henri-François Daguesseau, a member of the King's Council, came frequently in 1738. Later the prince de Ligne became a regular visitor, and in 1742 he drove the daughter of an upholsterer, a relative of the Bouillerot family, to the church in his carriage.[21]

Support from the neighboring parishes was also important. The dismissal of the curé of Saint Etienne du Mont at the same time as Pommart, in 1730, provoked a similar reaction in that parish, providing the churchwardens of Saint Médard with useful allies, many of them with legal training. In 1730 both vestries adopted similar tactics, and in 1734 the incoming churchwarden of Saint Etienne was acting as legal adviser to his counterparts at Saint Médard.[22] Meanwhile, opposition to a new, anti-Jansenist curé rocked the adjoining parish of Saint Hippolyte, and the Jansenists at nearby Saint Jacques du Haut Pas successfully prevented their new curé from ever gaining full authority in his parish. Later, when the churchwardens of Saint Médard seemed to have lost the battle, they could still find support not far away at Saint Victor, where the clergy were willing to hear confession by Jansenists and even convulsionaries.[23]

There was a sense, fostered by the Jansenist press, of citywide struggle against the forces of Jesuitism and the archbishop. Indispensable to the whole campaign, of course, was the support of a significant minority in the Parlement. Like Jansenist sympathizers throughout the city, the churchwardens of Saint Médard appealed repeatedly to the Parlement, and even though the King's Council regularly overturned its rulings, the churchwardens knew that powerful figures on the national scene supported their cause. The Parlement could, coincidentally, be of immediate assistance, as when François Nicolas Dupin, the only man of standing whom Coiffrel had been able to persuade to take the place of the churchwardens, withdrew his support, fearing the consequences for a lawsuit he had before the Parlement.[24]

The wider political situation afforded protection to the churchwardens of Saint Médard, making the archbishop and the agents of the government think twice before taking action that might provoke retaliation from the Parlement. And in the long run it was the victory of the Parlement that made possible that of the churchwardens. Once the crown had abandoned the pro-*Unigenitus* forces, priests like Hardy de Levaré who refused the sacraments to their parishioners soon found themselves on the run. At no stage was the local struggle independent of the wider political contest.

It was not, of course, simply an issue of faith at the local level and of politics at the national one. On the one hand, the Jansenism (or the anti-Jesuit feelings) of some *parlementaires* was perfectly genuine.[25] On the other, the conflict within individual parishes was political as well as doctrinal. It was a struggle for control, usually between curé and vestry. Embedded in the question of what kind of sermons were preached, of how the cult of Pâris was to be handled, and of what was to be taught at the parish school was the issue of who should decide. In the Jansenist parishes there was a powerful sense that the church was not the property of the archbishop or even of the curé, who was merely the incumbent. The church belonged to the local people, and the churchwardens were its custodians. It was not, therefore, as individuals that the members of the vestry of Saint Médard opposed the curé, but as notables acting on behalf of all the parishioners.

This attitude is comprehensible if one examines the role of churchwardens in eighteenth-century Paris. By law a strict division was maintained between the temporal and the spiritual administration of the parishes. The choice of clergy and the order and content of services were entirely the prerogative of the parish priest. Temporal administration, however, was in the hands of the churchwardens in office *(marguilliers)* and the former churchwardens *(anciens)*. Their job was to ensure the financial stability of the church—a formidable task in large parishes, whose annual financial turnover might be very substantial.[26] At Saint Médard it ran between 15,000 and 20,000 livres every year. In 1730 the value of the assets involved was well in excess of 130,000 livres, a very substantial amount for artisans and merchants to be overseeing if one considers that even the richest merchants in mid-eighteenth-century Paris rarely gave their daughters dowries of more than 30,000 livres.[27]

From this income, all the expenses of the church had to be met: the cost of candles, bread, and wine; upkeep of the cemetery, buildings, and ornaments. There were also the salaries and uniforms of beadles and doormen, grave diggers, musicians, bell ringers, and choirboys. The clergy were paid a fee for each memorial mass—nearly 4,000 at Saint Médard in 1781 and a larger number earlier in the century. In poor areas even the parish priest was heavily reliant on such funds. The curé of Saint Médard received about half of his 3,000 livres a year from the vestry, and at Saint Martin du Cloître, where there were no investments to boost the curé's revenue, they provided almost his entire income.[28] Of this he had to spend some 400 livres per annum to pay each of the two or three salaried priests (the others were paid only a fee for each mass they said).[29] When the churchwardens of Saint Médard refused to hand over the funds, the curé was reduced to real hardship. Control over the purse strings was a powerful weapon in their hands.

The former churchwardens *(anciens)* also played an important role. Their consent was required for any major expenditure. They also checked the annual accounts, selected the parish employees, and decided on legal action. The assembly of former churchwardens elected the new churchwardens each year.[30]

The position of churchwarden was onerous. Much time was spent chasing overdue payments and pursuing legal proceedings, and time was a scarce commodity for merchants struggling to keep a business afloat in the treacherous commercial world of eighteenth-century Paris. Not only that, but churchwardens often advanced substantial sums from their own pockets. At Saint Hippolyte in 1756, a total of 1,200 livres (in an annual turnover of 5,000) was owing to various former churchwardens, and it was not unheard of for a single individual to advance that much in the two years of his service.[31] Those elected were also expected to make a gift to the church—usually 200 livres at Saint Médard—and to distribute silver tokens *(jetons)* to the former churchwardens.[32] Not surprisingly, some men were not overjoyed at the honor bestowed on them, and occasionally it took the threat of legal action to persuade an unwilling appointee.[33]

Yet a great honor it was. The serving churchwardens sat in a prominent place near the main altar. Unlike the rest of the congregation, they received the Eucharist at their seats, and they accompanied the host in processions, wearing special robes. Everyone knew who they were and made way for them. The church employees were expected to display the "respect due to Messieurs the curé and churchwardens."[34] The *anciens,* too—the former churchwardens—sat near the front of the church, had a nicely furnished chamber, and enjoyed permanent access to the sacristy. On special occasions they might be the only parishioners with candles, or the recipients of the longest ones; and in a society in which every tiny mark of respect was highly prized, with long legal battles over the order of processions, such prerogatives bestowed a dignity that is hard for a twentieth-century observer to appreciate.[35] Lists of the churchwardens, in order of seniority, were often printed. The pride that men took in the office is reflected in the practice of mentioning it among their titles: "Deveaux, marchand chapelier, ancien juré et grand garde de sa communauté, officier juré porteur de charbon, ancien commissaire des pauvres et ancien marguillier de la paroisse Saint Médard."[36] Even in death the former churchwardens were honored—the vestry funded special services for the repose of their souls, and some parishes extended this to their wives.[37]

Perquisites of a more material nature were also available, such as the silver tokens that were distributed to the *anciens.* It was common for church contracts to be awarded to former churchwardens. And like any position of power in Old Regime France, the office of churchwarden gave opportunities both for personal advancement and for patronage. The parish churches provided considerable custom for local merchants and craftsmen. A young protégé of one of the churchwardens might hope for a post as choirboy, a position that would provide him with a free primary education and perhaps a free apprenticeship at the end of it. An older man might obtain employment as beadle or doorman. The church vestries generally accorded pensions to their employees, and often to widows and dependents as well.

A good word (or a bad one) from a churchwarden would influence the parish priest, who was often faced with a request for charity or for information about a parishioner whom he did not know personally.[38] The churchwardens knew more of the local people than the curé: most of them had grown up in the quarter, whereas he usually had not, and they belonged to the commercial and neighborhood life of the quarter. Their parish functions familiarized them with many of the local poor, with members of the confraternities, with tradesmen, and with the families of chapel and pew holders. They signed the baptismal and burial registers, assuming an authenticating role that was partly one of authority, partly one of patron. Churchwardens frequently signed certificates needed for a job or to satisfy someone letting a room that the applicant was suitable. The *commissaire des pauvres,* of course, had direct access to alms and might include or exclude people from the list of "deserving poor." Further occasions for the exercise of patronage were the concessions of private pews; the nomination of a sick parishioner to a bed in the hospital, paid for by the parish; the annual choice of poor young women whose dowry would be provided. A small number of people were permitted to invest their money in the parish in return for a pension. Even the clergy of the parish needed to have the churchwardens on their side, for both income and promotion: in 1758 one priest at Saint Médard wrote to one of the churchwardens to beseech his support in the forthcoming election of a sacristan.[39]

The wives and relatives of the churchwardens, too, had their local networks and carried much weight in the quarter. Some parishes—especially Jansenist ones, it would seem—entrusted the bulk of the poor-relief funds to a female treasurer who was automatically a member of the important *assemblée de charité*. This body was a major source of poor relief for "the indigent sick, infants fed on milk and on flour, and others who by convention and propriety can only be seen to by [women]."[40] Sometimes twinned with a male assembly, it provided women of the local elite with the opportunity to develop female patronage systems, for the surviving evidence suggests that only women applied to it. At Saint Jacques du Haut Pas the assembly was composed of wellborn women who visited the poor and distributed alms. A similar setup existed in the equally Jansenist parish of Saint Séverin, where a dossier of requests for assistance survives for the years 1734–1736. Most of the poor women asked for thread or for money to buy sewing materials, and most were elderly or widows with small children. Sara Robequin, a recent convert to Catholicism, was denied any assistance in 1734 because she had neglected her son's education. This example illustrates the moral rule that the *assemblée de charité* sometimes attempted to exercise. Its leading figures might also have authority over suppliers to the parish poor, such as the milkmaid rebuked by one of the *dames de charité* of Saint Médard, wife of a former churchwarden, when the supply of milk to the poor children was interrupted in 1742.[41]

Furthermore, the *assemblée de charité* was clearly an important center of sociability for the elite women of the parish. The *dames de charité* of Saint Séverin, at their meeting of 27 October 1757, exchanged information on the latest actions of the archbishop against certain of his clergy. They were apparently very well informed, for their conversation was reported to the *procureur général* of the Parlement, whom one might have expected to have such news from other sources.[42] Such women were politically aware and sometimes extremely influential, with ready access to the highest officials in the city. On at least one occasion the *trésorière des pauvres*—the woman in charge of poor relief—at Saint Germain l'Auxerrois wrote to the lieutenant general of police on behalf of a poor parishioner. The attacks on the prominent women whom the short-lived parish priest Antoine-Nicolas Duquesnoy admitted to positions of influence at Saint Médard suggest the power that these women could exert locally, and Hardy de Levaré later confirmed their influence when he complained that his load was increased by his inability to entrust the poor to their care.[43]

The power bestowed by the office of churchwarden inevitably produced rivalries. Individual churchwardens sometimes exceeded their authority, and there were endless opportunities for disputes within the vestry. In 1752 a churchwarden of Saint Martin du Cloître complained that two colleagues had placed their names before his in the printed list of churchwardens, and that "they attempt to place themselves in front of him both in processions and during the offertory, although he is more senior than they."[44] Such conflicts reflect the keen sense of importance that the position conferred, but also a concern to defend a domain. This impulse is most obvious in the conflicts between the vestries and other local interests, such as the administrators of the parish confraternities. The confraternity of the Saint Sacrement at Saint Hippolyte demanded in 1755 that its administrators occupy the place of honor at Corpus Christi. The Parlement ruled that the churchwardens should have this privilege.[45]

Generally the confraternities remained subordinate. Much more serious opponents were the powerful curés. Given the difficulty, in practice, of distinguishing between temporal and spiritual administration, conflict between vestry and priest was almost inevitable: over the choice of visiting preachers, over who controlled the choir of the church or the poor funds, over the choice of sacristan.[46] Sometimes the curé triumphed, for he was a personage of no mean importance. He was in direct contact with the archbishop, and with the lieutenant general of police and the Parlement, who relied on him to inform his congregation of new laws and to help keep order in the city. But just as often, it was the church-wardens who won these struggles.[47] Without their cooperation, the parish priest's life became fairly miserable. In 1734 the curé of Saint Jacques de la Boucherie bemoaned the reelection as churchwarden of a local lawyer whom he detested. "He accepted his reelection with a most solemn speech, in which he sorely mistreated me," wrote the priest. "My parish is going to fall into the greatest disorder, and there is no curé more to be pitied than I."[48]

At stake in these battles was control of the parish. When the church-wardens locked the priest out of the sacristy, or put locks on the poor boxes so the curé could not open them (as happened at Saint Germain l'Auxerrois), these were symbolic as well as physical acts of exclusion.[49] Jansenism was only one of many issues that provoked such conflicts—even if it was the most hotly contested, because it involved questions of conscience and was a national as well as a local battle in which the stakes were high. The struggle at Saint Médard was merely the most long-lived example of the power struggles that racked many Paris churches. The members of the vestries saw the parish as theirs and resented any attempt by the clergy—or anyone else—to dictate to them. The curé, of course, was equally determined. Coiffrel sought assistance from the authorities, as he said, "in order that he might become master of his church."[50]

It was therefore their responsibilities as churchwardens, as rightful rulers of the parish, that gave Coiffrel's opponents, already hostile to him on doctrinal grounds, both the means and the political will to resist. Yet the authority they wielded was not solely due to their office. They were chosen as churchwardens precisely because they were already notable citizens. The statutes of some parishes, such as Saint Jean en Grève, actually specified that "there will always be a first churchwarden from among the most respected persons in the parish, and notably from the principal officers of the sovereign courts; and one from among the practicing lawyers." Some parishes, too, had honorary churchwardens, people of the highest rank who occupied the first place in processions but "whose position and quality does not normally allow of their being named churchwarden in charge of the accounts." The prince de Rohan occupied this place at Saint Jean en Grève for sixteen years.[51]

Men of humbler status were chosen to do the actual work of administration, preferably merchants with a sound knowledge of bookkeeping. But—the statutes were generally clear on this point—no person exercising an *"art mécanique"* could be chosen.[52] Even in the poorest areas, where there were few wealthy men, the churchwardens were men with property in the parish and, at the very least, the rank of master in one of the trades corporations. Their property holding was a guarantee that church funds could be entrusted to them. Of course, the time, the expense, and the degree of education required effectively ruled out most of the population anyway. Even at Saint Médard, therefore, the churchwardens were men of property. It is instructive to compare the fragmentary information available on their material fortunes with the broader scale of wealth in the city. Three examples give a good idea of the range of fortunes within the vestry.

Perhaps the wealthiest was the tanner Etienne Bouillerot. In 1704 he and his wife provided their eldest daughter with a dowry of 7,500 livres. The other children received more, and by 1722, when the fourth daughter married, they were able to find 30,000 livres. In all, they provided 118,000 livres in dowries. On top of this, when Bouillerot died the balance of his property and investments was worth an additional 101,345 livres.[53] This placed him on a par with all but the wealthiest merchants in Paris. His estate was as large as those of any of the merchants in Annik Pardailhé-Galabrun's sample of eighteenth-century inventories. The dowries of all but the eldest daughter would have placed the Bouillerot children among the richest 9 percent of newly wed masters and merchants had they married in 1749, the year studied by Adeline Daumard and François Furet, and the fourth daughter, with her 30,000 livres, would have scraped into the top 1.3 percent. It is true that she and her spouse could not compete with the wealthier officeholders, yet her dowry was comparable with those of the richest 30 percent of nonnoble officeholders.[54]

The wealthiest of the Saint Médard churchwardens can be included, in strictly economic terms, among the Paris elite. For merchants they were rich, and in the impoverished Faubourg Saint Marcel they were the equivalent of millionaires. But possibly more representative of the majority of the churchwardens was the brewer Guillaume Arnoult. When

Rue de l'Arbalètre, corner of the rue Mouffétard. The café on the left was already a wineshop in 1688 and was owned by successive churchwardens of Saint Médard until the 1780s. The shop on the right was part of a large brewery that also belonged to churchwardens of Saint Médard throughout the eighteenth century.

he married in 1700, he gave his wife a modest income of 300 livres a year (which represented an investment of about 6,000 livres). She brought a minor office, that of *contrôleur des bois,* and possibly some brewer's tools. Their business must have flourished, for they were able to give both their children, and the wife's four offspring from her first marriage, a very good start. One of Arnoult's stepsons received an academic education and went on to become a canon of Sainte Geneviève. One of the stepdaughters received the considerable dowry of 15,000 livres. Arnoult's own son was apprenticed to their son-in-law, with 600 livres a year for maintenance—a very generous sum indeed.[55] Comparing the daughter's dowry with Daumard and Furet's figures for those marrying in 1749 indicates that she was close to the top 9 percent of the masters and merchants category.[56]

Perhaps the poorest of the Saint Médard churchwardens was the baker Antoine LeBis, who left an estate of just over 3,000 livres. This is not a fair measure, since his business suffered from his role in the vestry's dispute with the curé, but he was never rich. Alongside the workers and laborers of the Faubourg, though, he was a man of substance. He and his wife owned real estate—admittedly only a small house, in a back street, purchased for 1,500 livres in 1717. But Pardailhé-Galabrun has found that only 14 percent of her sample of Paris inventories in the seventeenth and eighteenth centuries included real estate, so even LeBis was a member of an elite.[57]

Most of the vestry members probably fell between these extremes.[58] They were very comfortable by Paris standards and in local terms were wealthy. Just as important, they were well known in the area and strongly committed to the parish. Most were born there and all owned real estate locally. Even the wealthiest owned very little property outside the parish, except for tanning mills (see map on page 124). They took no interest in rural estates, and when real estate in other parts of the city was inherited from distant relatives, it was usually sold quickly. Even the tanners, who accumulated several choice properties along the Bièvre River, did not venture upstream into the neighboring parish of Saint Hippolyte; they waited until the land was available locally.

Besides indicating their commitment to the parish, the property held by the churchwardens reflects their economic dominance of the area. The men who provided the principal opposition to Coiffrel between them owned most of the prime commercial property along the river. Many of

Tanneries on the Bièvre River (late nineteenth century), probably between the rue Mouffetard and the rue du Pont aux Biches. (Bibliothèque Nationale)

the remaining houses and tanneries along the Bièvre belonged to individuals who were subsequently elected churchwardens.

Dominant in landholding, as in parish affairs, these same men were often leaders in their trades. At least thirteen of the Saint Médard vestry of 1732 occupied the position of *juré,* or administrator, at one time or another: seven tanners, five leather dressers, and a hatter. Like the place of churchwarden, the position of *juré* in a Paris corporation was accorded primarily to the most prominent members of the trade.[59] The precise role of the *jurés* varied considerably, but it usually included fixing the capitation tax to be paid by each master or mistress, regularly inspecting workshops, and running the financial and legal affairs of the corporation. A man or woman who had served as *juré,* furthermore, retained (before the reorganization of the trades in 1776) a strong voice in the corporation through the policy-making assemblies to which, in most trades, all the past officials were summoned, along with a limited number of other masters or mistresses.[60] The office of *juré* provided valuable experience in financial management and leadership. It gave firsthand contact with powerful figures in Paris and familiarized its incumbent with the court system. On a more personal level, the office of *juré* bestowed a sense of individual worth and importance. These were all qualities and skills that the churchwardens of Saint Médard displayed keenly in their struggle with their curés.

Further evidence of the prominence of the men who were elected churchwardens of Saint Médard comes from their weight among the administrators of the Bièvre River. The Bièvre was the principal reason for the existence of the Faubourg Saint Marcel. By the middle of the eighteenth century it provided water for 42 tanners, 25 leather dressers, 4 dyers, 6 market gardeners, and 13 launderers. It also drove 23 flour mills. While taking much of the waste from the tanneries, the abattoirs, and the 20 starch makers of the quarter, it also provided water for ponds and fountains.[61]

Such extensive use of a small river—the Bièvre was only eight to ten feet wide and fairly shallow—created serious difficulties. The leather curers and dyers polluted the stream badly, whereas the launderers naturally required clean water. The millers demanded a constant and fairly rapid flow, whereas the market- and pleasure-gardens siphoned off water and often returned little to the river. Waste disposal exacerbated the problem. In 1671, therefore, the Grand Maître des Eaux et Forêts estab-

Rue du Pont aux Biches. The Bièvre ran under the street in two arms, on either side of the tall building halfway down the street. The three-story house on the right and the tannery behind it belonged to Nicolas Genneau, then to Jean Dorigny, both close relatives of the Bouillerot family.

lished regulations for the maintenance of the stream. The bottom and banks were to be cleaned annually.[62] An ordinance of 1678 provided for the election of syndics to enforce the rules, and by 1686 meetings of the principal users seem to have become fairly regular. In 1712 the convention was well established that there should be three syndics: a tanner, a leather dresser, and a dyer. By the 1730s a full-time river guard was employed to patrol the banks.[63]

During their two-year term, the syndics received daily reports from the river guard and took appropriate action. It might be necessary to rebuild a retaining wall, or more frequently to report someone to the Eaux et Forêts tribunal for dumping gravel into the stream. But the main task of the year was the summertime cleaning of the riverbed, at a cost of nearly a thousand livres. With the wages of the river guard and other expenses, in the years 1749–1750 the syndics spent nearly 3,000 livres.[64] In theory they were to be reimbursed later from a tax levied on all the river users, and they were responsible for keeping the tax rolls up-to-date. But there were so many disputes over who should pay the assessment that, in the words of an ordinance of 1756, "the said syndics prefer to write off the sums they have advanced, and fail to keep the tax rolls up-to-date."[65] There was indeed little incentive to do so, for they were often not reimbursed for years. In 1745 the syndics of the period 1734–1738 were finally paid the 6,438 livres they were still owed. Those who had served in the years 1738–1740 had to wait until 1750; and in 1757 the accounts for the span 1746–1748 were still not settled.[66]

The job of syndic was therefore financially onerous. Guillaume Edeline protested, following his election in 1754, that "he had only been established [in his own business] since last Easter, and that his means were insufficient to enable him to occupy the position, as he was totally unable to advance sums of money, his trade being very small, and he had much difficulty keeping it afloat."[67] The task was also very time consuming, yet without the honors bestowed on a churchwarden. So it is somewhat surprising to find men ready to accept the job. Yet in the twenty-seven years from 1732 to 1758, the period for which records of elections survive, thirty-one different individuals served. It is true that the syndics had a measure of power. The river users were required to allow them access to the banks at all times, so the job provided opportunities for the self-important. But on the whole, the men elected were those who, by virtue of their standing in the quarter, already possessed authority. The need to advance quite large sums of money, the amount of time required, and the fact that many syndics preferred to remain out-of-pocket rather than get involved in undignified and unpleasant battles with recalcitrant taxpayers—all these suggest that the syndics were men of substance. Edeline's objection to his election confirms this: it was those with well-established businesses of some size, he implies, who should be elected.

This was generally what happened. The de Jullienne family, founders and directors of the Gobelins manufactory and wealthy patrons of Watteau and a number of less noted painters, furnished five syndics between 1730 and 1760.[68] The dyer Antoine Guillaume Moinery, who served as syndic twice, was able to pay the huge sum of 44,000 livres for a large property in the rue des Gobelins in 1740.[69] Other syndics of the Bièvre were less wealthy, but all owned property in the area.

The syndics were, therefore, members of a local elite. In fact, they were members of a local oligarchy. They were elected by only a fraction of the people eligible to vote, and primarily by those who had themselves already served or were subsequently to act as syndics. In 1750 there were 76 dyers, tanners, and leather dressers on the tax roll, yet only 13 men voted. During the whole period from 1732 to 1756, the average attendance at elections was 18, and a mere 12 individuals were present at half or more of the elections, 10 of whom at some stage served as syndics.[70]

It is clear that the Bièvre administration was run by a small group of well-to-do merchants who elected one another and who did not doubt their fitness to speak not only for the 70 or 80 taxpayers and the 146 property holders within their jurisdiction (in 1757), but also for the many gardeners, millers, and laundresses, and indeed for the Faubourg as a whole. In the words of one of their number, the 10 or 20 men who elected the syndics every two years constituted "the assembly of the inhabitants of the Faubourg Saint Marcel, and of the riverside inhabitants both of the said Faubourg and of the country."[71] It is no surprise to find that of the 31 syndics elected in the years 1732–1758, at least 20 had served as churchwardens in one of the three parishes in the area. Of the 85 participants in the elections, at least 38 had been or later became churchwardens. The mantle of local office fell, as though naturally, onto the shoulders of a small number of prominent men.

That the churchwardens of Saint Médard were able to fight on for so long against their curé, in defiance of the police, the archbishop of Paris, and even the most powerful man in France after the king, Cardinal Fleury, was thus a result not only of their faith and of the support they enjoyed both within and outside the parish but—most important—of their key role within the quarter. They were "notables": men distinguished by wealth, by prominence in their trade, by churchgoing respectability, and by involvement in public affairs. They comprised a local elite with a shared sense of their role as the natural spokesmen and rulers of their parish.

CHAPTER 3

THE RULING FAMILIES

*Almost all the foundation masses were created by the
grandfathers of the churchwardens living today.*

—Mémoire *for churchwardens of Saint Médard, c. 1734*

A n errand boy dispatched in 1732 down the sinuous rue Mouffetard who, picking his path among the clutter of street stalls,
asked one of the stall keepers for "Monsieur Bouillerot" would
have been laughed at. "Do you mean Nicolas or Médard, Guillaume or
Jacques, Jean or Joseph?" The Bouillerot family were everywhere in the
parish of Saint Médard. Most were descendants of tanners who had
moved from Troyes in the mid–seventeenth century, when the city
authorities there imposed heavier and heavier taxes on the tanners.[1]

There were other prominent local families. The Genneau line provided
four churchwardens in twenty-five years, and many other families were
represented more than once. In all, fifteen family names account for
nearly half of the hundred churchwardens who served at Saint Médard
between 1690 and 1760. But even this does not adequately indicate the
monopoly held by a small number of lineages. An investigation of marriage connections reveals a web of relationships that does much to explain the solidarity displayed by the churchwardens. It demonstrates,
furthermore, the continued existence of a family form—local lineage—
that is well documented in medieval and Renaissance Europe but is
generally assumed to have disappeared, certainly from large European
cities, by the early eighteenth century.[2]

In 1732, when the struggle was at its height, the vestry of Saint Médard included no fewer than ten of the Bouillerot name.[3] They belonged to two family groups. The first centered on Nicolas Bouillerot and included two of his brothers (a third, also a churchwarden, had died in 1730), his son, and six first cousins. The other group gathered around Etienne Bouillerot, who sat in the churchwardens' pew with two of his brothers and his son. The second group's precise relationship to the first is not clear, but they were certainly related both by descent and by marriage.

Other vestry members were related to the Bouillerot family by marriage: Antoine Moinery, one of the ringleaders of the action against Coiffrel, was married to Clémence Bouillerot, and Henry Devaux's sister wed Jacques Médard Bouillerot. Thomas Besnard, a member of another well-known Faubourg Saint Marcel family, married Louise Michelin, granddaughter of another Bouillerot. Her uncle Nicolas Michelin had also been a churchwarden of Saint Médard, and her brother Jean had married the well-dowered daughter of Etienne Bouillerot. Thomas Besnard and Louise Michelin's daughter married the son of one of the Genneau brothers. Marriage ties also linked Jacques Delogny with fellow churchwarden Pierre Bouillerot and with Pierre Chevalier, father of a churchwarden of the same name, for they had married three sisters!

Overall, of the fifty-five churchwardens active in 1732, at least twenty formed what one might call a kinship cluster around the Bouillerot lineage. Most, furthermore, were linked not merely to one of the other churchwardens, but to the majority of the others in the cluster. Nearly all worked in the leather trades and lived close together along the Bièvre. Kinship, neighborhood, and occupation coincided to create an extraordinarily dense web of relations within the vestry.

This was the largest such cluster, but it was not the only one. Considerable intermarrying also went on among the bakers of the parish, although they were of necessity more dispersed. Even so, brothers-in-law and fellow churchwardens Jean Damane and Pierre Barre lived almost opposite each other in the rue Mouffetard. Antoine LeBis was probably Damane's nephew by marriage. LeBis was also linked through his daughter with another baker, Anne Hure, who became a churchwarden in 1745.[4]

The baker kin cluster is like a submerged mountain chain, only occasionally visible on the surface. Whereas the Bouillerot clan was sufficiently conspicuous to enable it to dominate the vestry, the baker families, less wealthy and less powerful, were represented at any one time by only a few individuals. There were, for instance, no members of the Moncouteau family among the churchwardens for nearly forty years. Nevertheless, the clan was indirectly represented by Pierre Barre, whose son was married to Marie Jeanne Moncouteau, and by Pierre Bonjean, whose wife was a Moncouteau. Her nephew, the baker Pierre Brot, was elected in 1757.[5]

These were the two main kin clusters, but other individual churchwardens were also related. The leather dressers Charles Gambart and Jean-Baptiste Laudigeois were linked through a common ancestor. Pierre de Noireterre, a wineshop keeper, was almost certainly related by marriage to the brewers François Duhamel and Guillaume Arnoult.[6]

It is of course not enough to demonstrate the existence of kin ties. For most of the Paris population during the second half of the eighteenth century, regular contact and kinship obligations did not normally extend beyond uncles and aunts, nephews and nieces, and first cousins. In higher-ranking social groups, on the other hand, such as among the *fermiers généraux,* more distant kinship ties were honored by those in a position to extend patronage.[7] As in other respects, however, nothing is known about the behavior of the "middling sort." The struggle at Saint Médard provides the perfect testing ground for exploring the family loyalties and political behavior of such people, and it is clear that "les Bouillerot" were perceived to constitute a clique within the parish. "The Bouillerots are the ones who are rousing all the parish," reported an official of Sainte Geneviève in 1730. A police report of 1733 included among the rebels all of the Bouillerots and others of their "party." About ten years later, Antoine LeBis complained of "the maneuvers of most of the former churchwardens, of their wives, relatives, and others . . .," and included at least ten members of the Bouillerot "cluster." There were several others, he added, who at their instigation behaved in the same way.[8]

Equally significant is the fact that none of them seems to have deserted during the thirty-years war at Saint Médard. Neither those whom Coiffrel managed to win over nor Hardy's "Commission" included any of the Bouillerot relatives. This is hardly surprising when one looks at other aspects of family behavior. Wills, for example, testify to the existence of kinship obligations beyond the requirements of the legal inheritance system. When Edme Bouillerot, a priest at Saint Médard, died in 1714, he not only left money to several Michelin cousins and to their children but also made provision for the apprenticeship of two other children, "either those in Paris, among my closest relatives, such as the grandchildren of cousin Edme Michelin, or those in Troyes." If there were no poor relatives, "either on the side of the Bouillerots or on that of the Michelins," the money was to go to the charity school at Saint Médard.[9] Cousins, even the children of cousins, are very much part of the family circle, no matter how geographically distant. The same concern is displayed for the education of girls and of boys. Furthermore, there is an equal commitment to both branches of the family; no distinction is made between the male and the female lines. This attitude, encouraged by the equal inheritance provisions of Paris customary law, is reflected in other wills. After the deaths of Etienne Bouillerot and his wife Madeleine Langlois, their portraits were passed on to Marie Louise Bouillerot, "as the eldest of the family."[10] This was not a purely patrilineal system.

Other evidence reveals the extent of family contacts and obligations. When Jean Tronchet married in the 1740s, those signing the marriage contract included a Tronchet uncle and two aunts, a Bouillerot uncle and aunt, three first cousins, his second cousin Marie Michelin, and his first cousin once removed.[11] Even though he resided in the Faubourg Saint Germain and most of them lived in the Faubourg Saint Marcel, the family stayed in touch. Whether this was by choice or by obligation is not clear, but fondness for relatives is often expressed in wills, through the voluntary bequeathing of money and of mementos to members of the extended family. Joseph Bouillerot lived with his cousin for some years before his death in 1747, and in gratitude he left her money, furniture, and his portrait.[12]

The choice of godparents and of guardians for minors is a further indicator of kinship obligations. Those most commonly selected, in the former case, were aunts, uncles, and grandparents. It was usual to select the godfather and godmother from opposite sides of the family, thus bonding the newly baptized infant to both, and at the same time creating an additional tie between the allied families. Two people who together held a child in the sacrament of baptism thereby formed a special relationship that was itself similar to kinship.[13] For guardians the responsibility was greater and immediate; hence the choice of kin for this task. Jacques Bouillerot's guardian was his cousin. Louise Bouillerot was chosen to look after two of her grandchildren, while her husband acted in the same capacity for her nephew.[14] The high mortality that made the appointment of guardians so common also required that the extended family remain in touch and close-knit, in the interests of all.

The no doubt well founded conviction that kin were more reliable is reflected in the close economic cooperation demonstrated by the Bouillerots and families like them.[15] It was essential in trades such as tanning. Although the actual tools were not so expensive—one finds estimates of equipment valued between 300 and 1,200 livres—a long-term investment in merchandise was unavoidable. Heavy hides took up to three years to prepare and lighter ones two years. First the skins had to be thoroughly soaked and cleaned in the river. They then spent a year packed in pits filled with lime, a procedure that allowed the hair to be removed, followed by up to two years in tannin, derived primarily from oak bark, to make them waterproof. By the 1740s, barley was often used in place of lime—a process that might save several months.[16] But leather still took a long time to produce, and a significant investment remained in the ground for many months. When Jacques Bouillerot de Longchamp went bankrupt in 1742, he had some 3,200 full hides in pits, another 800 drying, and another 2,200 calf-skins and cow-hides in various stages of preparation—with a total sale value of over 100,000 livres. This represented 75 percent of his total assets (and 85 percent of his commercial investment). The proportion was almost exactly the same for François Huguet when he went bankrupt in 1753, although his volume of business was very much smaller.[17]

Tanning thus required a major investment, with no return for two or three years. In the interim, workers, rent, and taxes had to be paid. It was usually family resources that enabled the Faubourg Saint Marcel tanners to meet these demands. It was family money, in the form of the combined dowries of husband and wife, that got them started. They had in many cases already cut costs by serving the five-year apprenticeship in the family; and as sons of masters, they paid less to be received into the corporation: 200 livres instead of 600. At this stage, too, the reputation of well-known parents was invaluable in persuading creditors to wait. Once established, cooperation with relatives continued. After the death of Joseph Bouillerot's wife in 1742, among the many creditors were his uncle, from whom the couple had borrowed 2,000 livres, his brother Roland, a Pierre Bouillerot (possibly their son), and his first cousin's mother, to whom some 4,000 livres was owed. Another two of the Bouillerot men were purportedly sharing the lime pits with Joseph—though there was no independent evidence to support this claim, and it may have been a way of protecting assets from the creditors.[18] Economic cooperation with family members was widespread and indispensable.

It was also common practice for parents, as they got older, to divide a considerable part of their property among their children. Nicolas Bouillerot gave his son half of a tanning mill at Essonne, as well as the very same house and tannery that his mother had given him, in precisely the same way, a generation earlier.[19] Technically, money was not given but lent, at legal rates of interest but on the obvious understanding that it would never have to be repaid. The same Nicolas Bouillerot and his wife lent a further 24,000 livres to their four surviving children shortly before he retired.[20] Catherine Prévost, wife of Joseph Bouillerot, had done the same in her closing years, transferring four houses to her sons and lending money to the other children.[21] This arrangement had the double advantage of ensuring the livelihood of the older family member, who did not relinquish total control of the assets, while furnishing the younger ones with much-needed capital.

Those with spare cash frequently lent to other relatives. Nicolas Bouillerot also lent 3,000 livres to his brother-in-law and 4,000 to the son of one of his cousins.[22] At a time when investments in state instrumentalities were still not widespread, loans to family members offered the best security and at the same time enabled relatives to avoid the usurious interest charged by professional moneylenders. The range of kin to whom these loans were extended is, of course, another indication of the span of family networks.[23]

It was not solely the tanning families who behaved in these ways. The brewer Guillaume Arnoult took one of his sons to be his apprentice, saving the usual fees. The second son was apprenticed to Arnoult's stepson, a grocer, who waived the fee. Both sons had already worked in the brewery. In the case of Louis Antoine Deheuqueville, his parents put up the 1,000 livres he needed to join the booksellers' corporation, and on his marriage they provided 2,000 livres' worth of books. His future in-laws, also booksellers, did the same. Since he had a brother and an uncle who were bookbinders and book gilders, another uncle who was a papermaker, and a first cousin married to an engraver, and since his intended had a brother, an uncle, two brothers-in-law, and a first cousin all of whom were booksellers, one imagines that he had little difficulty making his way in the trade.[24]

The prominent families of the Faubourg Saint Marcel thus behaved in a way similar to merchant families elsewhere.[25] They preferred to deal with relatives and they provided assistance for kin well beyond the immediate, conjugal family, in the female as well as the male line. Children grew up surrounded by relatives, learning the obligations that kinship imposed and what they could expect in return. They developed a powerful sense of family honor that made the interests of the lineage, on occasion, more important than those of the individual. This explains why so many Parisians had children, wives, and occasionally husbands locked up for bad behavior.[26]

Here, too, the Bouillerots were no exception. At eight o'clock in the morning on 5 April 1729, Hubert Bouillerot was whisked away to prison at the request of his father-in-law Nicolas Riou (another churchwarden of Saint Médard). The neighbors confirmed that Bouillerot lived with a woman who was not his wife. He frequently beat his three daughters, did not provide properly for them, and had given them no education, so that they "swore like true soldiers, were without religion, and did no work whatever." This was confirmed by two members of the Bouillerot family.[27]

Nor was Hubert Bouillerot the only bad apple. Four years earlier, Nicolas Dorigny, a distant relative of the Bouillerot clan, was imprisoned following complaints about his drunkenness and his allergy to hard work. His mother and his grandmother petitioned to have him locked away, a request supported by his uncle and aunt, two cousins, and a more distant relative.[28] The honor of the family was as much a matter for women as for men, and for a wide kin network: a black sheep might dishonor the whole flock, not only parents and siblings.

A further characteristic of this sense of family was that it extended even beyond the grave. It is reflected, for example, in the recurrence of Christian names over the generations. The first Bouillerots of whom there is evidence in the Faubourg Saint Marcel were called Pierre, François, and Jacques. Over the next hundred years—if for the sake of simplicity one looks solely at first names (though middle names came largely from the same pool)—there were at least 10 Pierre Bouillerots, 7 François, and 8 Jacques. Other prenames picked repeatedly by the family were Joseph (10), Nicolas (10), Etienne (6), and Jean or Jean-Baptiste (6). For women the favorites, excluding the ubiquitous and frequently disregarded Marie, were Madeleine (11), Louise (9), Elisabeth (8), and Jeanne (4). At first sight, these might seem to be simply the most common French Christian names, and comparison with the nearby Beauvaisis region does reveal that 40 percent of male children were baptized Pierre, François, or Jean.[29] But there, another 10 percent were called Louis, a name borne by only one Bouillerot boy in the whole century. Next came Antoine, totally absent from the Bouillerot repertoire. Charles was chosen for 4 to 5 percent of Beauvaisis boys, but never by the Bouillerots, while Jacques and Joseph, very popular among the tanners, came low on the Beauvaisis list. Few of the Bouillerot girls were baptized Marguerite or Marie-Anne, markedly the most common names in the Beauvaisis, whereas Louise, Elisabeth, and Jeanne were relatively low preferences there.

This is not simply a regional difference, for other lineages in the Faubourg Saint Marcel made different choices. The Michelin family, with whom the Bouillerots intermarried frequently, like them favored Jean, Louise, and Nicolas, but displayed a liking for Guillaume, which the Bouillerots largely eschewed. The Genneau clan liked Jean and Nicolas, but also went for Louis, and occasionally André and Charles. Some names appear only in one branch of the Bouillerot family, following a marriage that introduced them. One of the ten children of Joseph Bouillerot and Catherine Prévost, for example, was given her mother's name, and it reappeared twice among the grandchildren, but nowhere else on the entire family tree.

This strong continuity of first names suggests a respect for family traditions and a linking, in name and spirit, of generations. The church-wardens of Saint Médard in the 1730s had a strong sense of their forebears having created much of what they valued in the parish: "Almost all the foundation masses were created by the grandfathers of the churchwardens living today," they claimed.[30] Those same ancestors were buried beneath the floor of the church. Lest the living forget, the walls and floor were inscribed with reminders, like the marble plaque requested by Jean Michelin, "to be affixed next to the Saint Fiacre chapel where my ancestors are interred." Although he had long left the parish, Jean Michelin had not forgotten, and the marble was to record his bequest to the poor of the parish so that generations still there would not forget either.[31] Such attachment to the locality was common, according to Pierre Chaunu. Across the city, between 1650 and 1700 fully half of all testators in his sample requested burial in their parish, though this figure fell to 29 percent in the years 1700–1750.[32]

The same sense of family was inscribed on the urban landscape, on the houses themselves. Particularly on the recently constructed fringes of the quarter, it was often those same grandparents who had erected the first residential buildings. This was recalled, for those who knew, in some of the shop signs (enseignes). A house in the rue Censier owned by Joseph Bouillerot and his wife Catherine Prévost was called "Sainte Catherine." Another house in the same street, owned by Louis Genneau, was known as "l'Image Saint Louis." "L'Image Saint François" was almost certainly that in which François Bouillerot lived. And whereas the Sainte Catherine house, which remained in the hands of the Bouillerot family until 1789, retained its name, l'Image Saint Louis lasted only until purchased by Eustache Lecoq in 1759, after which it became "Le Coq." Other names came and went in the same way: a house in the rue Triperet, for instance, "le petit Saint Jean," became "l'Image Saint Nicolas" after its purchase in 1749 by Nicolas Lepy.[33] Naming houses was a way of imprinting one's identity on the landscape, and descendants of patriarchal and matriarchal figures generally respected their choices.

The significance of family property to the local bourgeois lineages, particularly in the seventeenth and early eighteenth centuries, is further reflected in the practice of *retrait lignager*. Under Paris customary law, when a property was sold to someone outside the family, any blood relative could repossess it by reimbursing the purchaser. When in 1719 Jacques Bouillerot and his wife Madelaine Brissart sold a house to one of their creditors, Jacques' brother Etienne obtained a court order allowing him to purchase it back. In June 1769, the creditors of Marie Jeanne Delogny, widow of a master butcher, seized and sold a house she owned in the rue Mouffetard that she had inherited from her mother. Seven of her maternal aunt's grandchildren (her first cousins once removed), who owned the house next door, clubbed together to retrieve the property.[34] This example again demonstrates the sense of lineage in the maternal as well as the paternal line.

Resort to *retrait lignager* was not common, perhaps because people normally sought a buyer from within the family in the first place, but it further illustrates the continuing bond between family and place. For the descendants of prominent local families, traces of their ancestry were all around. Even the inflexible curé Hardy de Levaré was aware of the importance of the sense of family and hesitated to offend it. When in 1758 he was pressed to consent to requiem services for deceased church-wardens and their wives, he felt he could hardly refuse "without making myself odious to the families."[35] This was in spite of the fact that those concerned included some of his most determined enemies, Jansenist sympathizers, and that agreeing to the services meant conceding a minor victory to his opponents.

If the dominant families of the area were acutely conscious of their ancestry, so too were parents and grandparents very much aware of the inheritance they were leaving. Concern for patrimony is reflected in the frequent use of entailment *(substitution)*. This was a caveat placed upon a person's estate that prevented an heir from disposing of property inherited. In 1732 Pierre Bouillerot, knowing that the business affairs of two of his sons were in disorder, wrote into his will an entailment that prevented them from realizing any of their inheritance: it must all be passed on to their children, although they would derive income from it.[36]

When Louis Gabriel Bouillerot added a similar provision to his will that substituted for his daughter Elizabeth her future children in legitimate marriage, he stressed that he was not acting through any ill feeling toward her, but because "she does not have enough talent to administer [the property]."[37] Often an entailment was designed to prevent the son-in-law from getting his hands on his wife's inheritance and thus depriving the grandchildren of their rightful portions.[38] It might also serve to protect the patrimony from creditors. "That part which should go to Marie Anne Lochet, wife of Antoine Delamarre, *marchand épicier* in Paris, will go by substitution to her children," specified Marie Moderat, whose husband had been a blanket maker and a churchwarden of Saint Médard. "She shall have the use of it, but it shall not be subject to seizure for debts."[39]

In each case, the purpose of the entailment was to ensure—from beyond the grave—that family property would be passed on. One extraordinary (and probably unenforceable) will stipulated that "wishing and desiring that the goods in my estate should remain in my family, I entail [them] until the third generation, so that they [the more immediate descendants] cannot sell nor in any manner alienate the goods that they will inherit from my estate."[40] Blood ties joined people across time as well as space.

Matriarchs and patriarchs deliberately used their control of property to ensure the continued prosperity of their line. Marriage contracts might serve the same end. A common procedure, and one specifically permitted by Paris customary law, was to stipulate, in bestowing a dowry, that no division of paternal property could be requested until after the death of both parents. If it were, then all the children would be required to return immediately everything they had received, and to pay interest if they had been given more than their share. This was designed "to maintain the peace and the union which have always existed in the family." It also ensured the future of the surviving partner and, equally important, retained property in the hands of the older generation, who could manipulate it in the interests of the entire lineage.[41] The elders were the ones with the widest view and responsibilities. The most bitter family disputes occurred over the wills of patriarchs and matriarchs no longer there to prevent strife.

In every domain, the prominent families of the Saint Médard parish operated as units, politically, economically, and socially. In this they resembled most Paris families. What they shared with the local and citywide elites, however, was a more extensive kin network than the large working-class population. This, and the economic and political power that such families possessed, enabled them to maintain their dominant position.

Inheritance strategies and economic cooperation were not the only techniques that enabled them to do this. Another mechanism was demographic. A striking thing about the Bouillerot family was their sheer number. One of their earliest representatives in the Faubourg Saint Marcel, Jacques, had 6 children who survived to adulthood. Two of the daughters married tanners in Troyes; 3 of the others had 4, 5, and 10 surviving children, respectively. Among these grandchildren, the families of 8 are identifiable. One had 2 children, 3 had 3, and the others had 5, 6, 7, and 10, all of whom survived to adulthood. The numbers are similar in other branches of the Bouillerot family. Overall, the 8 households of the Bouillerot lineage who were raising families in the second half of the seventeenth century had on average 5.8 surviving children each, and the 20 households in the next generation had 4 surviving children each.

Having large numbers of children had distinct advantages for those who could afford them. As most stayed in the quarter and went into tanning, these families came to dominate the industry. The parents bought up the best real estate along the Bièvre and installed their children there. Their numbers and wealth guaranteed them political dominance, both in the administration of the Bièvre and in the parish. There, of course, the system of election by the *anciens* favored any family that had already contributed many churchwardens, provided they stuck together. Some wealthy and notable families at Saint Médard never experienced the honor of being elected, conceivably because of the virtual monopoly held by the tanners.

Of course, the danger of large families in an equal-inheritance system is that the patrimony will be broken up into portions too small to allow future generations to maintain their position. Such fragmentation, though, is more of a problem in landed than in merchant families in thriving industries, where wealth may increase at a rate commensurate with numbers. Fragmentation was also offset by economic and political cooperation, as well as by two other strategies: endogamy and strategic marriage alliances with outsiders. Endogamy had the effect of retaining the patrimony in family hands. Peter Hall has explained how this worked among eighteenth-century Massachusetts merchants. One form was marriage between cousins. If a couple had four children and each of these in turn had two children, the second generation normally would each inherit one-eighth of their grandparents' estate. If first cousins married each other, however, two of the shares would be combined and the fragmentation of the patrimony would be slowed. The other form of kin marriage described by Hall is sibling exchange. If two sets of parents each had four children, the estates of the two sets of parents would be divided into eight. If two of the children from one family married two of those from the other family, the number of divisions would be six.[42]

Although neither of these forms of marriage was used systematically by the Faubourg Saint Marcel families, endogamous alliances did occur with some frequency. Marriage between second cousins was the most common; it may be that the church would not have permitted a closer alliance.[43] But sibling exchanges also took place. The most remarkable was in the Léchaudel family (a Gobelins dynasty): one son and one daughter married a brother and sister of the Chevalier family, while a second son and daughter wed a brother and sister from the Caron lineage.[44] The cumulative effect of such alliances was both to create a web of relationships binding the prominent families of the quarter and to maintain their combined patrimony within the parish.

Endogamy, however, was frowned on by the church, and was in any case not sustainable within a poor parish where the number of young people of suitable rank was quite small. Nor did it allow healthy infusions of new blood and money. The second type of marriage strategy, therefore, which enabled the Bouillerot family and others like them to maintain their economic and social position, was marriage alliances with suitable families in other parishes. This was, of course, facilitated by large numbers of sons and daughters.

Circumstantial evidence suggests that it was families, rather than the marriage partners themselves, who made the decision. For many of the local children, particularly the girls, the range of contacts with eligible partners was limited. On day-to-day errands young people would meet shopkeepers and neighbors, but many of them were already relatives—a factor that limited their marriage potential. The local church provided opportunities for contact with a wider pool of eligible young people, from all over the parish. This may have been where Clémence Bouillerot first met her future husband Antoine Moinery. Other weddings, however, were almost certainly entirely the work of parents or relatives. Just how François and Joseph Bouillerot met the daughters of Pierre Camet—the deputy mayor of Saint Denis, north of Paris—is anyone's guess, but their niece Catherine certainly encountered Jacques Camet through the existing link between the two families. Family contacts would also explain Louis Genneau's meeting his wife Charlotte LeBé, for his grandfather had married into the LeBé family, who were prominent in Troyes.[45]

In many instances, the source of the original contact is not obvious, but an arrangement between the young people themselves seems most unlikely. It is difficult to see how Marie Nicole Bouillerot could have met Jean François Delahaye, a jeweler on the Ile de la Cité, or how her distant relative Anne Bouillerot could have encountered the tailor Guillaume LeBorgne, also an inhabitant of the Ile de la Cité.[46] The most likely explanation is that the families chose these partners in accordance with their notions of suitability, leaving nothing to the vagaries of love or chance meetings. This does not, of course, mean that they had ambitious dynastic interests in mind. Like the Depont family of La Rochelle, they seem consistently to have sought partners of good bourgeois stock, in a social and cultural position similar to their own.[47]

Above all, marriages were designed to ensure the well-being both of the individuals concerned and of the lineage. They did not produce immediate social or economic advancement; in fact, large numbers of children precluded rapid capital accumulation. But such marriages did guarantee the local dominance of the kin network. Marriages outside the parish brought injections of outside money, and may have helped to cushion the lineage against the ups and downs of commercial life.[48] Equally important were the invaluable contacts they created. Two of the Bouillerot girls, for example, married *commissaires au Châtelet,* men with extensive functions and contacts.[49] Among the Michelin in-laws were two notaries, officeholders with considerable influence.[50] Immediate practical use was made of two of the Bouillerot sons-in-law—one of them a lawyer, the other a *procureur*—who advised the churchwardens of Saint Médard during the conflict with the curé.[51]

Useful outside contacts such as these were generally acquired in exchange for a daughter: it was invariably she who left the quarter to follow her husband.[52] Although Paris wives kept their own names after marriage, bourgeois women did become part of their husband's lineage. It was, in the end, with their husbands that they were buried, beside the decaying remains of ancestors not their own. Given the importance of lineage, this was possibly a real sacrifice.

Sons, on the other hand, if they remained in the tanning trade, normally brought their wives into the quarter. Of the original Jacques Bouillerot's 11 Bouillerot grandsons, all born after 1660, only 1 left the quarter: the only young man who did not become a tanner. Of the great-grandsons, 19 were born in the Saint Médard parish, roughly a decade either side of the turn of the century, of whom 12 became tanners and stayed. In the next generation, mostly born between 1710 and 1730, 17 male descendants of Jacques Bouillerot (not all of them bearing his surname) were born in the quarter and only 3 of them left. The same pattern held for most other branches of the Bouillerot, Michelin, and Genneau families. This had not only social but also political significance. It was overwhelmingly males who held political office. The retention in the parish of sons who would become notables and perhaps churchwardens in their turn helped families such as the Bouillerots to maintain their position.

A few of the sons took another course, although they, too, bolstered the position of the family within the parish. Displaying academic ability or a religious vocation, they became priests. A Louis Bouillerot in the late seventeenth century, and Edme Bouillerot and Jean Michelin in the early eighteenth, returned to serve at Saint Médard.[53] In the next generation were Roland Thomas Bouillerot, curé of Saint Gervais; Jacques Bouillerot, curé at Corbeil; and, later still, a nephew of the latter, Jacques Mignot. It was as if, having brought into the world enough sons to carry on the lineage, the family was prepared to make an offering, in each generation, to the church. Other prominent local families did the same, though less frequently, in proportion to their numbers and their importance. The Lebegue family provided Saint Médard with one priest. So too did the Huguet, Crevecoeur, and Auffray lines.[54] According to the *Nouvelles ecclésiastiques,* in 1731 most of the priests at Saint Médard were born and raised in the parish.[55]

A return to Saint Médard did not constitute upward social mobility for most of these men, for they became *habitués,* the humble priests who, unless they had independent means, could expect only a mean and precarious living. Promotion in the church was dependent on contacts, and the bourgeois families of the Faubourg Saint Marcel did not have adequate connections outside their own parish—at least not in the early part of the eighteenth century. It made sense, therefore, to come back to a parish dominated by kinfolk who could ensure, as churchwardens, that a reasonable number of lucrative masses went to relatives who had taken the cloth. Preferment was also more likely to be forthcoming in the home parish. When Jean Huguet became a candidate for the position of sacristan in 1741, it was reported that "several decent people *(honnêtes gens)* of the parish would be most content if this priest who was born there were to have this place rather than outsiders *(des étrangers)*. Besides," it was pointed out almost as an afterthought, "he is respectable and pious."[56] A few years later when a new sacristan was required, the abbé Auffray, son of one of the former churchwardens and nephew of another, won sufficient support in the vestry to be appointed, with both his relatives throwing their weight behind him.[57]

Joining the clergy was not a mark of upward mobility, but it did not involve any loss of status, either. A good local name gave the priest a head start among the parishioners, at the same time encouraging respect for the lineage that could thus offer sons to the church. Furthermore, having representatives among the clergy—particularly the sacristan, of course—could be very useful in local political struggles.

Daughters, however, rarely went into the church: only one descendant of the main Saint Médard families seems to have joined a religious order. It is hard to say why her example was so unusual. No serious loss of family property was involved, for although a nun took a small dowry with her it was customary for clergy to renounce any inheritance.[58] But in eighteenth-century Paris it was quite possible for women with a reasonable inheritance to remain single without becoming nuns, and quite a number of women in the Bouillerot and related families did so. It may be, too, that parents and daughters did not want to lose one another; for in entering enclosed orders the young women would be cut off in a way that sons were not when they became secular priests.

The ruling Saint Médard families thus maintained their position in a variety of ways. As in merchant lineages elsewhere, patriarchs and matriarchs had family goals. They strived to preserve their line and to maintain its social position, used their property to control their children, and created ties of interdependence over generations. It was presumably parents who decided on career paths for their children; and if they also had the major say in the choice of marriage partners, then several generations of Bouillerot, Michelin, Genneau, and Dorigny offspring were effectively tied to the parish by parental decisions. The local elite's political and economic role, too, bound them to the quarter. It is hardly surprising, then, that the ruling families should feel that the parish belonged to them. The church and the surrounding area were full of reminders of their lives and work. Their generosity was commemorated in plaques recording their bequests. Their names were read out week in and week out, in thousands of memorial masses.

How typical was this of Paris as a whole? It certainly corresponds closely to the pattern described by Orest Ranum in the seventeenth century.[59] For the early eighteenth century close study of other parishes is needed, but at Saint Hippolyte and Saint Martin the picture was broadly similar: a small number of interrelated families were overrepresented in the vestry, although no single family or kin cluster controlled either parish as the Bouillerots and their kin did Saint Médard. Records on 68 of the 101 churchwardens who served at Saint Hippolyte in the period 1670–1750 show 51 (75 percent) to have almost certainly been related to at least one of the other churchwardens, while a further 6 probably were. Forty (59 percent) were almost certainly related to *two* or more members of the vestry. Here too, kin clusters can be identified within the vestry. The Caron dynasty of cloth shearers provided Saint Hippolyte with 5 churchwardens between about 1670 and 1780, and was linked with the Léchaudel family, 2 of whom also served on the Saint Hippolyte vestry in the early years of the eighteenth century.[60]

The key families at Saint Hippolyte, like those of Saint Médard, had an occupational focus (see Table 3.1). There were four main groups. The brewers were one. Then there were those engaged in the preparation and dyeing of cloth: 20 of the 87 men whose occupations are recorded. A third trade was the ribbon makers (7 churchwardens). But the largest occupational group was composed of the diverse craftsmen who worked at the Gobelins factory: painters, tapestry weavers, furniture makers, a jeweler and a locksmith, a dyer and a warden (concierge). At least 41 churchwardens of Saint Hippolyte from 1670 to 1750 worked at the manufactory, which was renowned for its dynasties of highly skilled and well-paid craftsmen. The principal ones all intermarried: the Kerchove, Leclerc, Cozette, Chastelain, Montmerqué, Martin, Lefebvre, and Léchaudel families.[61] Like the families in the leather trades at Saint Médard, the Gobelins clans at Saint Hippolyte were in a position, if they joined forces, to dominate their parish completely. Did they unite to vote their kinsmen onto the vestry, or to elect a sacristan of their choice? The surviving records do not tell us.

Table 3.1 Occupations of the churchwardens of Saint Hippolyte, 1670–1750

Occupation	Number
Dyers	13
Painters	8
Tapestry weavers	8
Furniture makers	8
Ribbon makers	7
Cloth shearers (finishers of woolen cloth)	7
Brewers	6
Candle makers	3
Grocers	3
Market gardeners	3
Quarrymen	2
Farriers	2
Concierge of Gobelins	1
Saddler	1
Locksmith	1
Toolmaker	1
Saltpeter maker	1
Vinegar maker	1
Starch maker	1
Mason	1
Jeweler	1
Rope maker	1
Fruiterer (seller of produce)	1
Wineshop keeper	1
Hatter	1
Pastry cook	1
Engraver	1
Architect	1
Officeholder	1
Unknown	14
Total	101

The picture in the adjoining parish of Saint Martin du Cloître was broadly similar. Of the 137 churchwardens who served in the period 1699–1750, the family connections of 86 are traceable. Of these, 51 (59 percent) were related to at least one of the others, and a further 21 probably were (a combined total of 84 percent). Between 33 percent and 40 percent had family ties with at least two of the other churchwardens who served during this time. Here too, kin clusters can be observed.[62]

The starch makers—the Goulet, Moulinet, Levé, Véron, and Porthault families—congregated in the rue Poliveau, where their children learned the trade, met, and married. The Chevalier, Clabaux, Guenebault, Osmont, and Beschepoix claɴs of leather dressers, who lived along the rue Mouffetard near the Bièvre, were similarly linked by multiple marriage alliances. Here again, the kinship ties within the vestry were dense—to the extent that some individuals were related to each other on both sides of their family!

At Saint Martin, as at Saint Hippolyte, no single clan dominated the vestry. Rather, the pattern was similar to that of the baker families at Saint Médard, who only from time to time contributed a churchwarden. There were many eligible families, none of whom commanded a majority. For example, the enormously prolific de Beaune lineage, all farmers, were allied with the Poiret, Gelmont, and Leclerc families, who were each represented in the vestry of Saint Martin. Although only one de Beaune is recorded as a churchwarden between 1699 and 1760, this does not reflect the clan's real influence.

Despite the absence of a single, dominant clan, both Saint Martin and Saint Hippolyte were governed by a small number of lineages, most of them geographically concentrated, often within a single trade. Further evidence comes from the considerable overlap between the vestries and the Bièvre administration: seven of the dyers who served as administrators of the river were churchwardens of Saint Hippolyte, and nine of the leather dressers were both river administrators and churchwardens at Saint Martin.

What of the rest of Paris? It is impossible to analyze every parish, but the lists of churchwardens available for Saint Gervais and Saint Laurent indicate that there too a number of prominent families were overrepresented in the vestry. Certainly, neither parish had more than four or five churchwardens with the same surname over the hundred years between 1650 and 1750, compared with the eleven members of the Bouillerot family who served at Saint Médard during a somewhat shorter period. Nevertheless, many surnames recur. In each case, 15 percent of the churchwardens shared ten surnames, only slightly fewer than at Saint Martin. This of course takes no account of marriage alliances, which certainly existed. At Saint Gervais a churchwarden of 1664, Louis Boucherat, married two of his daughters to men who were subsequently elected to the vestry. His third daughter married the grandson of a former churchwarden. In the following generation at least one of the boys born of these alliances was elected, and he married into another family that later provided a churchwarden. A second kin group, distantly linked with the first, centered on the Le Peletier family.[63] There may have been others. Many of the Saint Gervais vestry were from the top ranks of Paris society, but otherwise the situation was rather like that at Saint Martin, where many prominent local families contributed only a small number of churchwardens each yet were indirectly represented by several more.

What seems to set Saint Médard and Saint Hippolyte apart, therefore, is not the existence of extensive kinship ties among the principal families but rather the small number of these families. This reflects the socioeconomic character of the quarter: the huge difference in wealth between the few well-to-do families and the very poor population that surrounded them. The tanners of Saint Médard, the artists of the Gobelins, and the dyers of Saint Hippolyte were wealthy even by the standards of merchant families in central Paris, but they faced far less competition for places in the vestry.

Even if the dominance of these families was unusual, local lineages—clans based on geographical proximity and often on occupation, who acted together to further their political and economic interests—were widespread among the commercial middle classes of Paris in the late seventeenth and early eighteenth centuries. It is very noticeable that each parish had surnames that recur frequently within the vestry but are uncommon elsewhere, even in the adjoining parishes. This reflects the concentration of lineages within particular areas of the city.

Other evidence points to such geographically concentrated lineages. Clustered along the rue de la Mortellerie, near the ports of central Paris, were allied families of grain merchants. Clans of butchers could be found around Saint Jacques de la Boucherie (indeed, until the seventeenth century the whole trade was in the hands of only four families). The Porcherons quarter, on the northern fringe of Paris, was dominated by the Sandrié family, whose fidelity to the building trades, collaboration in business, and local networks are strongly reminiscent of the Bouillerot family. Closer to the center of the city, in the Saint Benoît parish, lived the Cochin family, who for most of the eighteenth century remained on the rue Saint Jacques, marrying into other local families.[64] The Notre Dame de Bonne Nouvelle parish, especially the rue de Cléry, was home to intermarrying dynasties of cabinetmakers.

High levels of professional endogamy also characterized the furniture trades of the Faubourg Saint Antoine, the drapers of the rue Saint

Honoré, and the *fripiers* (sellers of secondhand clothes) in the parish of
Saint Eustache. Such patterns were equally widespread among the booksellers, printers, bookbinders, and papermakers concentrated in the Saint
Séverin and Saint André des Arts parishes. At Saint Nicolas des Champs
in the 1750s, three of the clergy belonged to a prominent local family
largely composed of gold beaters and ribbon makers. Around the central
market, too, according to one study, three-fifths of the children of master
butchers, bakers, and *fruitiers-orangers* (sellers of fruit, butter, eggs and
cheese)—all trades with high rates of endogamy—lived in the same parish
as their parents.[65]

This occupational endogamy and dynastic continuity set the commercial bourgeoisie apart from more modest families whose sons and daughters were far more likely to enter a different occupation.[66] Local lineages
were a form of family organization largely confined to the better-off
sections of Paris society, and the solidarity of lineage formed the basis
for the economic and political ascendancy of the commercial middle
classes in many parts of Paris in the first half of the eighteenth century.

CHAPTER 4

POWER AND LOCAL POLITICS

The textbook portrait of Old Regime France contains few political actors. There are the peers and princes, ministers, and powerful noble families. There are courtiers—nobles and a few commoners—jostling for the favor of the king. The queen and a series of royal mistresses, although possessing no official powers, exert a strong influence both directly on the king and indirectly through their patronage of favorites. Outside Versailles, the parlements and the other "sovereign" courts are recognized political players, as are the archbishops and bishops, the periodical Assemblies of the Clergy, and, occasionally, lower courts such as the Châtelet in Paris. City councils from time to time enter the field. Then, in the second half of the eighteenth century, something called "public opinion" appears, exerting an influence on politics even if those responsible for creating and holding it—the writers and their middle-class audience—are not full participants.[1]

Yet if one adopts Keith Baker's definition of politics as "the activity through which individuals and groups in any society articulate, negotiate, implement, and enforce the competing claims they make one upon another,"[2] then what can be more "political" than the maneuverings of the churchwardens of Saint Médard? They were, in the same way as the provincial parlements and estates or the municipalities of French towns and cities, struggling to defend their community, their jurisdiction, and their privileges against the impositions of the royal government.[3]

And they were not alone in doing so. Other vestries resisted attacks on their beliefs and their control of parish affairs, albeit generally with less success. Nor were such struggles confined to religious bodies. The trades corporations of eighteenth-century France struggled to defend themselves against the fiscal intrusions of the crown, the reform efforts of particular ministers, and the infringements of other corporations. Masters resorted to petitions and litigation, lobbying of powerful government figures, bribing, and electioneering. Even journeymen, as Michael Sonenscher has demonstrated, had a keen sense of how to operate the patronage networks and the complex court structures of the Old Regime.[4] The restricted textbook view of Old Regime politics will no longer do.

The great difficulty today in understanding how Old Regime politics worked is that it did not take place in institutions of the type widely familiar to us. There were no professional politicians (except perhaps at the royal court), no elections or representative assemblies of the modern type. Instead, politics was conducted in the courts, within privileged corporate institutions, and within the administration itself; no public opposition to the government could be tolerated without undermining the whole basis of the regime, so issues of public policy were debated within a corporate, patriarchal structure consciously modeled on the contemporary ideal of the family. Local politics was conducted within town councils, parishes, and trades corporations, and in local courts and administrative bodies, each one of which formed, within the wider family of the kingdom, a smaller family.[5]

The local political scene in eighteenth-century France may be unfamiliar today—particularly in Paris, where so many sources have disappeared—but despite the increasing authority of the monarchy in the preceding two hundred years, local politics remained extremely lively. For many eighteenth-century French people, it seemed more significant than distant struggles at Versailles. Even for Parisians, in normal times national politics remained distant. The central government was not easy to influence, whereas local struggles were immediate and open to a much wider range of people. At the same time, local affairs frequently assumed wider significance when some parish matter served as a flash point for a national conflict because it raised issues and principles of a more general nature. The convulsions at Saint Médard are one example; and parish affairs came to national prominence repeatedly during the refusals-of-sacraments controversies from the 1730s to the 1750s. The Calas Affair, which involved a Protestant wrongly condemned for the murder of his son, is another example of a local religious dispute with national ramifications.[6]

There was thus constant interaction between local and national politics in Old Regime France. Many of the minor actors who briefly appeared on the national stage were in fact political players of considerable local experience. They may have belonged to provincial troupes, but they were familiar with the conventions and techniques of political performance. This is partly why examining local politics is instructive—particularly where it had national implications. It is a way of exploring the political understandings of the increasingly vocal mass of people whom the eighteenth century termed "the public." It was not solely, perhaps not even primarily, through reading and observation that these people gained political know-how, but through active apprenticeship, served in innumerable local organizations and institutions.[7]

The long dispute at Saint Médard opens a curtain onto a local political stage rarely glimpsed. Because struggles within parishes and corporations were (often literally) of parochial interest, they are usually poorly recorded; seldom is much known about the individuals concerned. In this case, however, because of the importance of Jansenism to the authorities, quite detailed records were kept on the struggle between the vestry and the curé over a fair span of years. Even though the individuals concerned left very few writings that can be identified as theirs, a good deal about them can be discovered from the surviving sources. At times it is even possible to pick out more minor figures—an indication of the dimensions of local political participation. One can even sense the reactions of a wider "public" that influenced the way the parish leaders behaved.

This chapter explores the methods used by both sides in the dispute at Saint Médard, the sources of legitimacy that each side claimed, the bases of power within the parish, and the interaction between local and national politics. But it also seeks to identify the unstated bases of local politics. A lot of historical work in the last few years—feminist writing, in particular—has emphasized that the political realm extends much further than traditional definitions acknowledge, and that those definitions are themselves an ideological tool: one designed to deny a voice to people formally excluded from power, and to remove from the "political" agenda issues of importance to women and other oppressed groups.

Even political battles within elites, whose outcome does not greatly affect the overall distribution of power within society, draw upon understandings about that wider distribution of power. At Saint Médard the actions of churchwardens and curé alike reposed on shared assumptions about who the legitimate political actors were; about the proper roles of men and women; about the bases of status.

When Jacques Coiffrel, the new, anti-Jansenist curé of Saint Médard, arrived in 1730, the first action of the churchwardens was simply to refuse to recognize him. They boycotted his inauguration. They called him *"desservant"* (priest in charge) or "Monsieur Coiffrel" rather than "Monsieur le Curé," forms of verbal rejection to which both he and the onlookers were extremely sensitive. "They treat me badly in their public actions," he complained in 1733.[8] They held meetings without notifying him, although it was customary for the parish priest to attend. They refused to participate in processions and services, for doing so would have amounted to recognition of his status. These were forms of exclusion, both real and symbolic. He was denied access to the mechanisms of power, for if he did not attend meetings of the vestry he could not have a full say in the government of the parish. At the same time, they were denying him the right to the symbolic power that a curé gained from leading a magnificent procession through the streets of the parish. The black-robed figures of fifty churchwardens parading directly behind their pastor, or kneeling to receive the host from his hands at the front of the church, were symbols of authority that the unfortunate Coiffrel was to be deprived of throughout his ten years at Saint Médard.

Refusal of recognition was but the first blow in a propaganda war waged within the parish and beyond its limits. The churchwardens had *mémoires* printed to argue publicly their claim that Coiffrel's appointment was illegitimate—a common maneuver in any local struggle or court case.[9] Both sides trumpeted their victories, the curé posting all over the church copies of the order of the King's Council upholding his position. (It was promptly torn down by enraged parishioners, according to the Jansenist newspaper *Nouvelles ecclésiastiques*.) Nearly thirty years later, the churchwardens would ostentatiously issue printed invitations when they were at last permitted to hold a service for the Jansenist curé whose dismissal had sparked the whole struggle.[10]

At every point they made maximum use of rumor. Word that the churchwardens were likely to win their case against Coiffrel in the Grand Conseil "only too easily finds credence among the *petit peuple*," moaned the priest.[11] Of course, boycotting the inauguration and excluding the curé from meetings of the vestry were in part propaganda. So too were petitions. One of the churchwardens' first actions, in 1730, had been to organize a petition against the removal of the former curé; another, in 1752, was signed by 1,500 parishioners to protest when Hardy de Levaré, Coiffrel's successor, announced that everyone taking Communion would require an approved *billet de confession*.[12] Even after legal action by the churchwardens became clearly pointless, because the King's Council systematically overruled the Parlement, they persisted: such proceedings kept the issue alive in the public mind and aroused sympathy among many people scandalized by the irregularity of the government's actions.

The churchwardens also resorted liberally to the sort of bluster and bravado that are already familiar from disputes within the neighborhood communities of Paris.[13] Their leader Moinery was reported to have promised that "even if it cost him his beard he would expel [Coiffrel] from his post or else from this world."[14] The same anonymous informant's claim that the churchwardens mounted guard in the bell tower of Saint Médard and fired off a gun from time to time "as a signal" is laughable until the reader notes that at least one family was so frightened they stayed up all night expecting to be attacked. Another anonymous note records that the curé "is not safe even in his own house."[15] The very fact that the police archives contain such reports demonstrates the success of the churchwardens' informal campaign of bluff.

Yet it was no more than bluster. Even LeBis, the baker Coiffrel brought in to handle the parish finances after the dismissal of the churchwardens, and the person most vulnerable to their wrath, suffered no more than insults. In fact, his greatest concern was that they would find something amiss in his accounts and prosecute him.[16] Nor were several vestry members afraid to break ranks as the dispute dragged on. The first deserted to the curé in April 1732, despite public expressions of disapproval; then another five defected in April 1734.[17] The only incident in which there appears to have been any serious likelihood of violence took place during a funeral in September 1733, when a crowd seemed to be turning nasty. An element of premeditation is apparent in the crowd's action, with some evidence of organization, and although there was nothing to link the churchwardens with the event, they were rumored to be behind it and were, it seems, happy to allow this suspicion to stand.[18] Nevertheless, while they were prepared to use threats of violence and to engage in a certain amount of rabble-rousing, actual violence was not part of the game. Even in their most desperate straits, the churchwardens were not prepared to countenance physical force.

They did use most other weapons at their disposal, though, beginning with legal action. First came the challenge to the legality of Coiffrel's appointment, followed by a court action over the election of new churchwardens—a case that attracted considerable attention. "All of Paris is going to hear the lawyers plead in this case," reported the diarist Mathieu Marais.[19] Coiffrel retaliated by initiating proceedings to oblige the churchwardens to pay his clergy. A little later he engaged a doorman, whose main job was to prevent the curé from being insulted in his own church. The churchwardens immediately claimed that Coiffrel had no authority to engage church employees. They won that case, but the decision was reversed by the King's Council. Almost immediately the vestry began a new court proceeding, arguing that the doorman had been improperly employed to accompany the woman who took around the offertory box. This too was dismissed by the King's Council.[20]

In August 1732 the churchwardens again began legal moves with a formal complaint that Coiffrel and his sacristan had caused a "scandal" in the church by removing candles placed in one of the chapels.[21] In October, despite agreeing to allow the curé access to the sacristy, they formally appealed against his occupation of it. When ordered by a magistrate to hand over the keys to the church, the churchwarden in charge, Joseph Bouillerot, refused because he had registered an injunction.[22] And so it continued until the vestry was finally suspended.

In 1750 the legal moves resumed, this time initiated by the two churchwardens elected by the "Commission" that curé Hardy de Levaré had put in place to run the parish. This was followed by other legal action designed, so the priest claimed, to destroy his system of parish management.[23] Such maneuvers indicate a mastery of the complex legal machinery of the Old Regime. At the same time, they reflect a keen political opportunism, for given the national political situation in the early 1730s, any appeal to the Parlement against an anti-Jansenist priest would receive a sympathetic hearing.

The churchwardens were also well aware of the importance of informal power networks and did not neglect them. They courted important visitors to the parish, particularly members of the Parlement. Later they approached the *procureur général* of the Parlement directly and went to see the powerful *secrétaire d'état* in charge of the king's household, Saint Florentin. The wives of six of the churchwardens visited the archbishop of Paris on three separate occasions. They wrote to officials in the Châtelet court.[24] There is little evidence of political naivety here.

In conjunction with legal action and gestures designed to win over the local and wider public, the churchwardens made full use of their control of parish finance and administration. For two whole years they refused to pay Coiffrel or his clergy, leaving him with few priests to say mass and almost bankrupting him personally. They withheld money for the poor of the parish, whom they knew were beating on his door. They engaged him in costly litigation, using parish funds for their own expenses.[25] Their ultimate sanction was abdication of their functions, a ploy designed to paralyze parish administration.

The curés however, had one weapon that the members of the vestry did not: their privileged access to authorities outside the parish. This they were able to use in two ways. First, they had recourse to the arbitrary authority of crown and church, through Cardinal Fleury, through the lieutenant general of police, and through the archbishop. Without numerous lettres de cachet, and the intervention of the King's Council, the curés would have got nowhere. Naked force was used to close the cemetery of Saint Médard and François de Pâris' house. The archbishop's ban on regular clergy officiating at Saint Médard, and ultimately his threats of excommunication, were measures that the churchwardens did not dare defy openly.

Second, the curés used their access to outside authority to build local patronage networks. They were frequently called upon to support parishioners in dealings with the police and other institutions. In 1734 Coiffrel supported a petition to the police by Edme Huguet, who was not then a churchwarden but was later to become one. He did, however, have a close relative already in the vestry, François Huguet, and it is perhaps telling that François Huguet abstained from any action against the priest. He was sufficiently uncertain in his loyalties for the churchwardens to exclude him from the position of *commissaire des pauvres*.[26]

Hardy de Levaré, too, was later able to use his credit with the police to good effect. For two years in a row he wrote to the lieutenant general on behalf of Pierrusse, whom the King's Council had named as a member of the Commission that replaced the vestry throughout the 1740s. On at least the first occasion the curé was able to obtain for Pierrusse a reduction in his capitation tax.[27] In 1743 Jacques Dosseur, a candle maker in the rue Mouffetard and also a member of the Commission, had a problem with his neighbors; Hardy de Levaré tried to get them to leave the quarter. Dosseur was again mentioned in January 1744, when the priest hoped that the lieutenant general might be able to get some confiscated goods restored to him. The same man's wife approached Hardy in May 1744, seeking support to get their son into the priesthood.[28]

But the local position of the curé owed even more to his symbolic and spiritual functions. The sacred vessels, the churchwardens of Saint Médard insisted in 1758, could only be handled by an ordained priest.[29] The altars were the priests' territory, particularly the high altar. The baroque screens that divided the church marked the limit of lay access, and indeed the whole choir, according to the statutes of many parishes, belonged to the curé. The pulpit, of course, was a crucial source of authority—a symbol of the Counter-Reformation (the pulpits in most Paris parish churches dated from the seventeenth century)—and it was denied not only to the laity but even to most of the clergy. Its use was confined to the most important services, and it was from the pulpit that the curé exhorted and chastised—for the anti-Jansenist clergy made a specialty of sermons on obedience and submission to authority. It was from the pulpit, too, that royal decrees were read out.[30] The association of the curé with these sacred objects and locations lent him substantial social power.

The churchwardens benefited to a more limited degree from the aura created by participation in ceremony. The liturgical calendar was full of colorful rituals, foremost among them the Corpus Christi processions, major productions with tapestries and flowers adorning the buildings along the route. All the local authorities had their place on such occasions, and exclusion from the ceremony, or the demotion represented by marching farther back, represented a serious loss of status. It was the authority that flowed from presiding over such elaborate and well-attended displays that the churchwardens of Saint Médard sought to deny to Coiffrel. Yet the same ceremonial events were the source of some of their own status. Sitting in the churchwardens' pew, or in one of those reserved for the governors of the confraternities, conferred prestige that mere heads of families, even wealthy ones, did not possess. After the grocer Nicholas Maurice broke ranks and marched in the Easter procession of 1732, the vestry declared that his inclusion as a former churchwarden was an error: he had no real authority.[31] The robes of office; the right to march behind the clergy or to carry the dais with its sacred

The pulpit of Saint Médard, donated by three retiring churchwardens in 1718.

burden in the Corpus Christi processions; undisputed access to the church, chapels, and sacristy—these were symbols that bespoke real authority.

In the end, there seems little doubt that the churchwardens won the public-relations battle. But Coiffrel and Hardy de Levaré put a lot of effort into winning local hearts. Both courted the churchwardens themselves, with limited success. Some in the parish were more responsive, however, and enjoyed sufficient local prestige to replace the members of the vestry if they chose. It is worth looking closely at who these people were, for their presence indicates the existence of alternative sources of local political power. When Coiffrel at length decided that he would have to dispense with the vestry, he turned to other prominent parishioners. Some were sympathetic, but they declined to take over the role of the churchwardens. Eventually, however, the priest persuaded François Nicolas Dupin, "without doubt the most distinguished of our parishioners," to help him.[32]

Dupin was a nobleman and former governor of the town of Coulommiers. He owned one of the most valuable properties in the area, the Hôtel d'Harcourt in the rue neuve Sainte Geneviève, which he had bought from the prince de Guise in 1729.[33] He clearly was above local politics, and while he was too distinguished to be asked to do the actual parish administration, he was the perfect person to head the vestry as honorary churchwarden. Coiffrel therefore sought and found four men willing to join Dupin on the churchwardens' bench: Cousin, a local manufacturer of gold and silver ribbons; Huet, a mercer; the butcher Cretté; and a hatter named Delestre.[34] Very little is known about these men. Delestre owned a modest house in the rue Mouffetard, and Cretté probably belonged to the family of that name that was well established in the Saint Hippolyte parish.[35] What seems certain is that none of the four had any connection with the dominant clique among the churchwardens of Saint Médard. Like Dupin, they were outsiders. They must have had sufficient means to be credible as churchwardens, yet it is equally clear that the curé's proposal to replace the vestry depended on the prestige of Dupin, for when he withdrew the scheme collapsed. Dupin's authority, furthermore, was derived from outside the parish, for he had no historical connection with it, no family ties, and in fact no interest in the area except his ownership of a valuable property. He fell into the same category as the magistrates and other high-ranking people whose carriages forced the street traders aside as they made their way to the tomb of Pâris.

Hardy de Levaré was more fortunate. Not suffering the same initial hostility, and arriving in a parish weary of ten years of conflict, he was perhaps also more politically astute, for he managed to exploit long-standing divisions within the local elite. Unable to win over the church-wardens, he, like Coiffrel, turned to people outside their circle, but with more success. He found "eighteen of his own supporters," as his opponents called them, to make up the Commission. When all of these men had served, another twelve were added.[36]

Some of these individuals were fairly obscure, but the records reveal the occupations of twenty of them, and what is striking is the total absence of tanners, who dominated the vestry. Four bakers and three brewers provided the core of this alternative local elite, the others mostly coming from a range of shop-based trades. This is reflected in their geographical distribution: eleven lived in the rue Mouffetard and six in the rue de l'Oursine, while the rues Censier and Fer à Moulin, where the tanners congregated, are unrepresented.

The Commission members had a few links with the former church-wardens, but in nearly every case had them with those who had either supported or not opposed Coiffrel. Anne Hure, for instance, came from a baking lineage and was distantly related to the baker Pierre Petiton, one of the half dozen churchwardens who had marched in the Easter procession behind Coiffrel in 1734 and who had been excluded by the other members of the vestry.[37] Another member of the Commission was Antoine Merillon, a relative of Etienne Merillon, one of the half dozen former churchwardens to attend the first meeting convoked by Hardy de Levaré in 1742. Merillon was also related to the Cretté family, one of whom had been prepared to assist Coiffrel in 1733. Jean-Pierre Moncouteau, another baker on the Commission, was brother-in-law to Pierre Bonjean, one of Coiffrel's few supporters.[38] The disqualification of the former churchwardens had opened the door to the baker families, who had long been a minority within the old vestry.

Most members of the Commission, however, had no previous connection with the vestry of Saint Médard. Several were related to families in the neighboring parishes of Saint Martin and Saint Hippolyte. Only three had any definite connection with the Bouillerot clan, but all three were elected under protest, and all were to oppose Hardy de Levaré in the

1750s, once free elections to the vestry were restored. Their inclusion may have represented an attempt by the priest to confer legitimacy on his Commission by including docile members of the dominant local lineages.

Several other members of the Commission almost certainly had arrived at Saint Médard after the dispute began. Four of them purchased property in the parish in the late 1730s or early 1740s and may therefore have been complete outsiders. Alternatively, of course, they may have been men of rising prosperity who saw in the vacancy created by the dispute their opportunity to obtain positions of local prominence. In either case, Hardy's supporters were men who might never have become churchwardens had the old vestry remained in place. Most lacked the necessary family and patronage connections. They were also less wealthy than those customarily elected, as Hardy de Levaré himself admitted when he warned of the inadvisability of leaving parish funds "in the hands of people who have no other assets than their work."[39] Some may have been younger men who had not yet reached the peak of their careers and fortune. One had recently been elected an official of his trade corporation, and two others were only later to assume this position.[40] These men were possibly potential future churchwardens who received accelerated promotion because of the dispute.

Among the remaining members of the Commission, of whom next to nothing is known, there is an intriguing hint of another source of local authority. Together with Cretté, the butcher selected to serve as churchwarden under Dupin, at least two had been administrators of the foremost confraternity at Saint Médard, that of the Saint Sacrement.[41] The confraternities of the Paris parish churches are little known, but deserve closer study.[42] At Saint Médard there were at least five at the beginning of the eighteenth century, each with its own pew reserved for the present and former administrators, who like the churchwardens wore robes and bands. Each had services said on the feast day of its patron, as well as for any of its members who died. The administrators had a place of honor in processions, particularly on their feast day, and like the churchwardens were elected by their predecessors. Many confraternities also had a charitable function, assisting the "honest poor" or providing dowries for poor girls.[43]

Becoming administrator of a parish confraternity was a mark of local prestige and like service in the vestry was recorded among a man's titles. Jean-Baptiste Bignot, a butcher in the parish of Saint Etienne du Mont,

was described in invitations to his funeral as "former *juré* of his corporation, former administrator of the confraternity of the Saint Sacrement
in his parish."[44] The office offered a highly visible ceremonial role, a sign
as well as a source of local notability.

In each parish there was a pecking order among the various confraternities, with the Saint Sacrement almost always first.[45] In some parishes,
such as Saint Laurent, the churchwardens were chosen (until 1748) from
among the former administrators of the two leading confraternities, both
of which recruited their leaders from the local elite.[46] More commonly,
the membership of the confraternities and of the vestry did not overlap.
There was often little social difference between them, and this gave rise
to innumerable disputes over precedence and independence. In 1755 the
administrators of the Saint Sacrement at Saint Hippolyte sought the right
to march directly after the host in the Corpus Christi processions, ahead
of the vestry. The men in charge of the same confraternity at Saint Jean
en Grève complained that the vestry tried to run their elections and to
take funds rightfully theirs.[47]

At Saint Médard one of these quarrels was quite fresh. In 1731 the
vestry had threatened to abolish any confraternity that did not produce
papers proving that it had been legally established. Neither the Saint
Sacrement nor the Sainte Vierge could produce such documents, and both
made formal declarations to this effect before a notary.[48] Soon after, they
were able to retaliate against the churchwardens, who were boycotting
official ceremonies, by taking their place in the Corpus Christi processions and carrying the dais bearing the host.[49] Among those who had
signed the statement for the Saint Sacrement, and who presumably
marched in procession, were Jacques Cretté, Louis Dechard, and Jacques
Dosseur, all of whom were to support Coiffrel or Hardy de Levaré. It is
quite possible that other allies of Hardy de Levaré during these years
were drawn from the Saint Sacrement confraternity.

Administration of a parish confraternity thus provided an alternative
source of authority that could serve as a power base for participation in
local politics. Many of the disputes between confraternities, or between
confraternities and the churchwardens of the Paris churches, were indis-
tinguishable from the power struggles within the vestries and between
curés and their churchwardens. Confraternities in some parishes threw
in with the Jansenist cause in the 1730s. The administrators of the Saint
Sacrement at Saint Benoît, for example, sought permission to say a
requiem service for a Jansenist priest who had belonged to the confrater-

nity, thus provoking a dispute within the chapter of Saint Benoît. The lieutenant general of police in the end intervened personally to rebuke two of the administrators of the confraternity.[50] When Hardy de Levaré was exiled in 1761, the *procureur général* of the Parlement received four petitions on his behalf from notables of the parish, including one signed by several churchwardens who had supported him in the 1740s, and another from the administrators of the confraternity of the Saint Sacrement.[51] Their office, like that of churchwarden, gave them authority to act and to speak on behalf of the parish.

Office had still further significance. It provided the indispensable basis for legal action and for dealings with higher authorities. The churchwardens' challenge to Coiffrel's appointment could not have been undertaken by individuals—at least not with any hope of success. It was the official status of the vestry, as a local corporation with legally recognized privileges, that formed the basis for many of its actions. Petitions to the *procureur général* of the Parlement were taken seriously because they emanated from a legally constituted authority, not from a crowd of unruly tanners. This was why in 1736, Coiffrel sought a lettre de cachet that would "reduce them to the status of simple parishioners, incapable of hindering us."[52] The authorities took the churchwardens seriously despite their humble occupations, because they were officeholders and therefore men of substance, honor, and authority. This was fundamental to Old Regime political culture: to treat them otherwise would have been to undermine the whole basis of subordination upon which the regime reposed.

For this reason, the corridors of influence in eighteenth-century France were far more accessible than has been recognized. Corporate office was open to a large number of people, including many whom neither the theorists and authorities of the time nor historians since would normally consider political actors. There were roughly fifty parishes in Paris in the early eighteenth century, each of which had at least twenty or thirty vestry members.[53] Most parishes also harbored up to a dozen confraternities, and many more were to be found in the churches of religious orders: a total of probably well over three hundred confraternities in the city as a whole.[54] Every one bestowed the privileges of office on as many as twenty administrators and former administrators, most of them masters in different Paris trades corporations.[55] Nor, in the list of offices, should one forget these corporations themselves—126 of them in 1691.

Each had two or more *jurés* in office each year, and many accorded some responsibility and privileges to large numbers of former officials. The decision-making *bureau* could be up to fifty or sixty strong.[56]

Most of the several thousand individuals who thus gained access to office, and to the honor, status, and rights that it bestowed, were masters and merchants. Often they were among the richest in their respective trades, but there were some openings for humbler people. There existed, for example, at least forty-seven confraternities of journeymen in Paris in the course of the eighteenth century, in thirty-six different trades, a good many of them legally established.[57]

Even more unexpected, given the dominant patriarchal ideology, is that a small number of women, too, won rights by virtue of holding office. There were five exclusively female corporations listed in the edict of 1691: the linen makers *(lingères)*, seamstresses, midwives, flower sellers, and hemp makers *(linières)*. The midwives were under the surveillance of the (male) surgeons, but the others had their *jurées* and their *anciennes*. Those of the seamstresses were eighty in number in 1762. In addition, the grain sellers admitted women as mistresses, two of whom served each year as *jurées*.[58]

Certain confraternities, too, were restricted to women and had female office bearers. There was one at the Quinze Vingts hospital, and the parish of Saint Jacques du Haut Pas had two: in 1766 the "Dames Marguillière, Gouvernante et ancienne[s]" included the widow of a sad-dler and the wife of a *marchand fripier* (seller of secondhand clothes).[59]

Parish administration, too, particularly in Jansenist areas, offered places to women, some of whom became quite powerful local figures. A Mademoiselle de Thienne at Saint Jacques du Haut Pas was *trésorière des pauvres* through the 1770s and 1780s. Not only did she handle much of the poor-relief money, but her office entitled her to sit on the board of the parish hospice, later the Hôpital Cochin.[60] It was common in Paris for prominent local women to administer a proportion of the parish poor funds. They decided on the distribution of poor relief and collected the offerings of the congregation at the principal parish services. At Saint Médard the woman in charge, the *trésorière* herself, was normally god-mother to the first child born in the parish on Christmas Day.[61] Such ceremonies, like visits to the poor and *quêtes*—collecting money, both in the church and from house to house—were more than charitable gestures. Undertaken principally by the wives and daughters of local notables, they were also local reaffirmations of authority and of deference.[62] This ceremonial role, like that of the churchwardens, was both a privilege of office and a very real source of power.

Yet at the same time, what also emerges from the tumult at Saint Médard is the importance of local public opinion. The intense concern of both sides with legitimacy; the churchwardens' petitions and the curé's struggle for recognition; the public-relations exercises, the boycotts, the rumors and bluster—all of these demonstrate that financial control or outside support were rusty weapons if support within the parish was lacking. A stream of lettres de cachet could reduce the vestry to legal impotence, but they could not win Coiffrel the respect of his parish. Even in an absolutist state, power flowed in both directions.

For legitimacy depended not solely on royal decree but, even more fundamentally, on public acceptance. The only players who could mount the political stage, the only people who could exercise power, were those recognized by the public to be legitimate political actors. Those who occupied offices and who were thereby given access to the mechanisms of political action, whether they were appointed or elected, had to possess what mainstream opinion in French society recognized to be appropriate qualifications. They had, in short, to be "notables."

This usually meant, to begin with, that they were male and married. There were immediate practical reasons for being married, particularly for the merchants and master artisans who were numerous in the humbler parishes. Without a wife to run their affairs and govern the family while they went about parish business, their commerce might collapse or the church funds be put at risk.[63] But there were also fundamental symbolic reasons why officeholders should be married. The household was, along with the workshop, one of the basic models of power relationships in Old Regime society.[64] Metaphors of familial relationships were used to describe the kingdom itself. The king was the father of his people, and this imagery helped to link office with married status as well as with masculinity. At the same time, because the family was perceived to have a semicorporate status, its head possessed a certain public identity that bestowed civic rights. Hence the hesitation of a Paris police inspector who in 1769 wrote to his superior that he needed a special warrant to arrest the leaders of the journeymen painters and decorators who were then taking industrial action: they could not simply be thrown into prison on the inspector's own authority, because they "are domiciled

. . . they have wives and children . . . they even have a certain standing" *("un certain état").*[65] Being married, and hence "established," mature and stable, was therefore a component of notability; I have not found any unmarried churchwardens at Saint Médard or elsewhere. Ironically, this semicorporate character of the family allowed female heads of households, particularly widows, to exercise a public role of sorts, by engaging in commercial and legal enterprises and acting on behalf of sons and daughters.

The "notable" also had to be adult (which usually meant over twenty-five) and Catholic, though it was possible to enter an office under the usual age, and in certain cases, such as those of John Law or, later, of Jacques Necker, to be a Protestant. This was an issue that did not normally arise in Paris local politics. More important, at that level, was appropriate rank, measured very largely by occupation. The statutes of several Paris vestries specifically excluded artisans *(les gens mécaniques).* Merchants were quite acceptable, even desirable for the sake of good account keeping. But while master artisans were undesirable, from time to time they had to be admitted because there were no other suitable candidates. In such cases, their selection took into account other criteria, which normally, in the case of nobles, officeholders, and professional men, could be taken for granted: education, appropriate wealth, and respectability *(honnêteté).* Without these, a man could not hope to be considered for office.

But my study of the Saint Médard churchwardens indicates the importance of other factors too. Local commitment was important, measured by property ownership but also by participation in the economic and religious life of the parish. A man who ran a substantial business was well known in the locality; and if he employed a number of journeymen or servants, he possessed further authority, the habit of command.

Above all, family connections were crucial. Even more than wealth or rank, these were a guarantee of probity. Belonging to a prominent local family, particularly one that had furnished churchwardens before, was a sign of commitment to the quarter and a surety of local acceptance: parish affairs should not be entrusted to outsiders *("étrangers"),* but to local *enfants de famille.* The selection of administrators of the Bièvre betrays precisely the same criteria, within the appropriate trades. These also underlie, in a less local context, the selection of *jurés* in the trades corporations. The qualities of masculinity, rank and wealth, occupation, reputation, and family fashioned the "notable." They were the prerequisites for office and hence for entry into active political participation in the first half of the eighteenth century.

But these criteria were not of equal value and were not necessarily all present in every case. Paris had a hierarchy of eligibility, of notability.[66] Obviously, selection to the highest municipal office, that of échevin, required a higher level of notability than election as a churchwarden. There were variations, too, according to the social composition of individual parishes. Local hierarchies were reflected in the order of parish processions. To be eligible for election to the vestry required higher rank, greater wealth, and better family connections than selection as administrator of a confraternity. The governors of the Saint Sacrement required a higher degree of notability than those of the Sainte Vierge.

In some cases the various criteria of notability did not overlap perfectly. Thus, for instance, a man might not be as wealthy as most churchwardens, but if his family qualifications were impeccable he might still win office—particularly, of course, if his kinsmen were well represented in the vestry. A woman of good family, while not satisfying the usual gender requirement, might exercise more power within a parish than males of lesser pedigree. The Dame—subsequently Widow—Delaribardière who was trésorière des pauvres at Saint Médard was not the wife of a churchwarden, but she did belong to the same family as one of the pro-Jansenist churchwardens (she was possibly his sister). Her office was not due to her husband's position but almost certainly to her family connections.

At all levels of Old Regime society, therefore, the bases of power were the same. Political power depended first and foremost upon office, which bestowed legal recognition and gave access, formal and informal, to courts and higher-ranking authorities. It is important to remember just how many men, and a surprising number of women, held offices of various kinds and had access to the privileges, responsibilities, and power that such positions conferred. This was what gave corporate institutions in eighteenth-century Paris their vitality.

It has often been said that the trades corporations were backward-looking, insular, moribund; that confraternities were declining anachronisms in an age of Enlightenment. The parish vestries are generally forgotten altogether. Yet the picture of such institutions conveyed by the court records and other sources is quite different. They were in reality active bodies upon which much of the political energy of the capital (and other places) was focused. This was why they survived. Corporations were the means by which a wide range of people who had no direct influence over government struggled to defend themselves through the legal and patronage systems of France. They provided a mechanism for *bourgeois,* merchants, and even artisans to win some say, however limited, in the administration of their locality, their parish, their trade. Such people were therefore able—to a degree that neither the powerful in eighteenth-century France nor most historians have recognized—to manipulate higher authorities and to bring middle-class concerns to official notice.[67] The people thus empowered might have been players only on the local level, but the rules of the Old Regime political system—the "political culture," as it has been termed—were essentially the same whether the stakes were large or small, local or national.

Office, in turn, depended on notability. But notability, it must be stressed, was not an *individual* attribute in the early eighteenth century. Rank, wealth, and reputation could only very rarely be acquired by a man on his own, and still less by a woman. Rather, they were possessed by families. Even in bourgeois and petit bourgeois lineages, rank depended on the position of one's family, and not just one's father. Even when substantial wealth was derived directly from the art and industry of the individual household (for it must be remembered that nearly all businesses in eighteenth-century cities were household ones), its indirect basis was still the patronage, credit, support, and initial impetus that derived from membership in a prominent family. Bourgeois families, even in an area of equal inheritance like Paris, developed strategies for maintaining their economic and social position across the generations.

The role of extended family ties at this level of society has wide implications. It points to the significance of demographic patterns for the consolidation of power at the local level. The assistance afforded by wide kinship networks made it difficult for newly arrived immigrants, in the first half of the eighteenth century, to achieve any degree of power unless they had well-established kin in the area or trade. Churchwardens—and, as far as the sources are available, officials of the trades corporations and women in the parish charity companies—usually belonged to families with deep local or at least Parisian roots. Moreover, the correlation of power and office with extensive family ties suggests that a kind of natural selection took place: those families with both high fertility and the economic resources to raise, establish, and marry off large numbers of children were the ones that prospered and accumulated local political office. Any lineage with few offspring was much less likely to succeed at this level of society.

But power is never static. Its forms and language change greatly over time. The structures within which power was exercised in the parishes and quarters of Paris in the late seventeenth century and early eighteenth century were far from permanent. Evidence suggests that the vestries and confraternities that played such an important role in local political life during this period owed some of their liveliness to Jansenism. Marie-José Michel has suggested that it was the Jansenist clergy who opened up parish offices to the laity, according the churchwardens new honors and greatly increasing the rewards of this office.[68] This may be true, but it may also be that pressure from the Jansenist laity was a major contributing factor. Undoubtedly, as at Saint Médard, the conflict over *Unigenitus* brought a large section of the population into local politics.

Whatever the reason, the vestries certainly seem since the mid–seventeenth century to have replaced earlier sources of authority. In the sixteenth century, officer rank in the militia and ownership of the municipal offices of *quartenier, dixainier,* and *cinquantenier* had been the principal mechanisms for the exercise of local political power. But the militia had disappeared, and by the early eighteenth century the monarchy's takeover of the municipality had drastically reduced the standing of these local offices.[69] The parishes offered an alternative, though possibly less effective, power base.

Yet the parishes too, for all their longevity, were neither eternal nor unchanging. In the second half of the eighteenth century, even before the cataclysm of the Revolution, the structures of power at the local level were to change further.

II

THE CHANGING OF THE GUARD

CHAPTER 5

THE DECLINE OF LINEAGE

*In a well-to-do family, it would be odious to have
more than one heir.*

—*Butini,* Traité de luxe, *1774*

A former parishioner returning to Saint Médard in 1760 after an absence of two decades would have found the church unchanged. The Gothic facade remained, as did the sixteenth-century altars and the seventeenth-century glass that conspired with the low vault to make the church very somber. The pews at the front were the same as twenty years before and the marble plaques on the walls recorded the same names. Tapers still burned in rows before the chapels, though perhaps a little less brightly in front of the chapel of the Virgin, the one closest to the tomb of the deacon Pâris, where those seeking his intercession still came to pray.

If it were a Sunday or feast day, the observant former parishioner would have recognized many faces, most of them more lined, the young men and women now in middle age, the children grown. The visitor might, however, have noted with surprise an absence that could not be accounted for by the passing of the generations: the Bouillerot family, who had so dominated the parish less than a generation earlier, had all but disappeared. The pews they had squeezed into at the front of the church were now occupied by other families. Among the former churchwardens, where for fifty years up to a dozen male representatives of the Bouillerot name had claimed a place, only one individual of that lineage would, on the right day, have been present to reassure the visitor that a mere twenty years had passed.

Had some disaster—an epidemic, perhaps—swept them all away? Or had they all, for some reason, left the quarter in the preceding two decades? Or again, had only daughters survived to adulthood, young women scattered among the pews of other local families, their children heirs of the Bouillerots in all but name?

The answer to the riddle could have been provided by any of the locals. It also lies in the property records and those of the notaries. No sudden disaster had struck the family. They had not suddenly died out, though the older generation had disappeared. Some of their descendants were still to be found in the parish, but they were few in number, and some bore other names. Most had left the quarter for good. Having dominated the parish and the tanning trade for the best part of a century, the family had moved on, adopting other occupations and other parishes, leaving only a few of its less affluent offshoots on the banks of the Bièvre.

The declining local influence of the Bouillerot lineage can be traced in their diminished representation in the vestry of Saint Médard. At a well-attended meeting in December 1758, only one Bouillerot was present: Nicolas, who had served as churchwarden in 1754. In stark contrast to the balance of forces within the vestry twenty years before, he had only three relatives sitting with him. Two were his second cousins, the third hardly a relative at all: the brother-in-law of his first cousin once removed! They were hardly close kin, and in the event—the election of a new sacristan which caused a serious rift within the vestry—they did not vote together. The two second cousins voted for one candidate, Bouillerot and his more distant kinsman for another.[1]

Shortly after, in 1760, another Bouillerot became a churchwarden, the last of the name to sit in the churchwardens' pew. At some stage in the 1770s one more distant kinsman was elected: Jean Charles Dorigny, descended from the Bouillerot family through both his father and his mother. But the addition of these two men did not appreciably strengthen the clan's influence in the vestry, for Nicolas Bouillerot died in 1766 and his second cousin Jean Dorigny in 1764. Their deaths left only four members of the vestry with any Bouillerot blood, but with little trace of kin solidarity between them.[2] After more than a century, the succession lay vacant.

Despite its apparent suddenness, the departure of the Bouillerot family from the parish of Saint Médard—and indeed from the whole Faubourg

Saint Marcel—was in fact accomplished over several generations. Mobility occurred by branch rather than through individual departures scattered across the entire family tree. This was no doubt related to the means and expectations of the couples who made career and marriage decisions on behalf of their children, but it was also consistent with the corporate nature of lineage ties. The first to leave, in the late seventeenth century, were all five sons of tanners Pierre Bouillerot and Marie Copoix, and the one son of Pierre's brother François. The latter moved to Versailles. One of Pierre's sons became *maître d'hôtel* of the duchess of Orléans; another studied at the university, then moved on elsewhere; a third was employed by the Paris municipality; and the fourth became a cavalry officer and subsequently *receveur des tailles* (a collector of taxes) in Bernay in Normandy. The fifth son's occupation is unknown, but in 1733 he was living in the right-bank parish of Sainte Croix de la Bretonnerie. Four of the five bought country estates and took titles—Sieur de Vinente, Sieur de Marail, Sieur de Blonville, and Sieur de Marsenne.[3]

This branch of the family thus behaved in the way that eighteenth-century bourgeois are often described in the history books as behaving: they made some money, invested in land, and abandoned trade. But Jacques and Edme Bouillerot and their immediate descendants did not do this, even though they were equally wealthy. Instead they remained in their traditional trade and stayed to people and dominate the faubourg. Jacques had three sons, all tanners. His three daughters married tanners, two in Troyes and one in Paris. Of Edme's five sons, four became tanners, while the fifth was a priest at Saint Médard. His one daughter apparently did not marry.[4]

Only in the third generation does this pattern change, and then only among the women. Jacques and Edme between them had eighteen Bouillerot grandsons, sixteen whose careers are known. One was a priest at Saint Médard and fourteen became tanners in the same parish, though one later moved to another quarter of Paris. Only one broke with the family tradition. He purchased the office of *greffier* (secretary) of the *connétablie,* the tribunal that judged cases concerning soldiers and the military, and moved to the rue de la Harpe. But the careers of the thirteen Bouillerot granddaughters of Jacques and Edme, between about 1700 and 1730, were quite different. Only three stayed in the quarter, one remaining single and two marrying local tanners. Those who left made advantageous matches, either with minor officeholders—*procureurs,* a *commissaire au Châtelet,* a *contrôleur des rentes de l'Hôtel de Ville,* the president of the *grenier à sel* at Nogent-sur-Seine—or with men in the most prestigious Paris trades: a jeweler, a grocer, and a mercer. Most moved to the central districts of the city.[5]

In fact the difference in the behavior of the men and women of this generation was not as different as it at first appears. The grandsons were tied to the quarter by their trade, but like their sisters most married outsiders. Only two married within the parish: they wed distant cousins. Two more married into prominent families in adjoining parishes. Nicolas Bouillerot married a little farther afield, choosing the daughter of Jacques Mignot and Marie Arnault, prominent citizens in the rue Saint Jacques. Two more grandsons wed daughters of Pierre Camet, deputy mayor of Saint Denis, while Jean Bouillerot's father-in-law, Jean Testard, lived near Saint Merri and was a former judge in the commercial court *(juge consul).*[6]

All of these were advantageous alliances, although they should not automatically be taken as evidence of a conscious strategy of upward social mobility. Had that been the goal, the Bouillerot parents would no doubt have sought more prestigious careers for their sons. They might also have sought some advancement for themselves, purchasing land or offices. But instead they remained in their own trade (and in the quarter, insalubrious as it was). The mix of local marriage partners and outside ones served to maintain the local position of the lineage and to retain the patrimony in male hands within the quarter while exchanging daughters for infusions of new wealth. Of course, this was already a departure from the marriage behavior of the preceding generation, who overwhelmingly chose other tanning families, either in Troyes or in the Faubourg Saint Marcel. The new strategy was probably in part a reflection of the growing prosperity of the lineage. Financial success meant that they could no longer find suitable matches locally: there were few families in the Faubourg Saint Marcel who could offer the 30,000 livres in dowry that Geneviève Bouillerot took with her, or even the 20,000 livres that her sister Marie Madeleine received.[7] The local marriage pool had become too small for fish as large as the Bouillerots.

The consequence of the wider alliances that they were now contracting, of course, was to integrate them into a citywide network of merchant and office-holding bourgeois. This gave them contacts that not only assisted in local political battles but that provided the means for further departures from the quarter in subsequent generations. It is likely, for example, that Marie Bouillerot's son Jean Michelin obtained his position as *greffier au Parlement* with the assistance of his two uncles by marriage, both of whom were in legal professions. His sister was also to marry a legal-office holder.[8]

This was the beginning of the end. In Edme Bouillerot's line the next generation was the last in the Faubourg Saint Marcel: his great-grand-children, who were making career decisions in the 1740s and 1750s. Partly because of departures in the previous generation, they were already fewer in number—four male and six female children—and although the destiny of two is unknown, it seems that only one of the ten remained in the quarter: one of the older ones, Marie Anne Bouillerot, who married the tanner Louis Dorigny in 1739. Another of the girls followed the example of most of her aunts, marrying a mercer and moving to the city center. The other three remained unmarried, but unlike earlier Bouillerot spinsters two of them moved away, perhaps to be near relatives elsewhere in the city.[9] All four sons disappeared from the parish of Saint Médard and from the faubourg. One entered the church and in 1761 became curé of the important central parish of Saint Gervais. A second young man purchased the office of *contrôleur des domaines du Roi* in Normandy and moved there, while a third also bought an office, that of *greffier des bâtiments,* and joined his sisters in central Paris. With these departures the male line of Edme Bouillerot's family disappeared from the Faubourg Saint Marcel and never returned.[10]

Jacques Bouillerot's descendants tarried longer, perhaps because they were less affluent. Jacques' great-grandchildren in the male line included at least seventeen boys and seventeen girls, half of whom stayed in the quarter. Eight of the males joined the local tanning fraternity, but Joseph Bouillerot and Jeanne Camet broke with family tradition by apprenticing one son to a mercer and another to a grocer, perhaps benefiting from the alliances that Joseph's sisters and female cousins had made with these prestigious occupations. Their third son went even farther afield: in 1734 he was in Germany, having before that lived near Saint Germain des Prés.[11]

The other three male children of the same generation also left the quarter. One moved to central Paris, one to Rouen, the third to Versailles as one of the sixteen *huissiers de la chambre du Roi*—one of the most important positions in the king's household.[12] Of the girls, six married locally but only three chose tanners. Two of the four who left the quarter did so by marrying wineshop keepers in the neighboring parish of Saint Etienne du Mont, one by wedding a grocer in the city center, and the last by marrying an official in the duc de Maine's household at Sceaux.[13]

These departures caused the Bouillerot numbers in the faubourg to dwindle sharply. The following generation in the male line—Jacques Bouillerot's great-great-grandchildren—contained only five sons and four daughters born in the area. Two of the girls married into Gobelins families, and a third married outside the quarter, although exactly where is not known.[14] Of the boys, one left to become a *procureur au Châtelet*. The other four stayed, but they no longer ruled the Bièvre. Only two of them worked as tanners, but one later moved into brewing. The last tanner in the once dominant dynasty declared himself bankrupt in 1788.[15]

So far I have concentrated on those in each generation who bore the Bouillerot name. But what of the female line? Obviously, its chances of local survival were precarious with more daughters than sons leaving in each generation. Nevertheless, sufficient numbers of Bouillerot girls married local men for the family to make a considerable contribution to the gene pool of the Faubourg Saint Marcel. Edme had five non-Bouillerot great-grandchildren born in the quarter. The one male departed to occupy the office of *greffier au Parlement*. Of the four women, one married a *procureur* and also left. The others appear to have stayed, but remained unmarried. As for Jacques' descendants in the female line, two of his four locally born non-Bouillerot granddaughters married local tanners and the other two married outside both the quarter and the trade.

In the following generation—those born in the 1720s and 1730s—there were six non-Bouillerot women and twelve non-Bouillerot men who were descended from Jacques and grew up in the Faubourg Saint Marcel. Four of the women married outside the quarter, a fifth married a local leather dresser, and the last remained single. Five of the men, bearing the Genneau and Dorigny names, became tanners. Another became a priest at Saint Médard, and one more—whose occupation is not known—also remained in the area. Two became dyers, working near the Gobelins, and the other three left altogether: one became a bookseller, one a silk merchant, the third a minor officeholder in the Châtelet courts.

In the two branches of the Bouillerot family that set down roots in the Faubourg Saint Marcel, therefore, the pattern was broadly the same in male and female lines alike, although the timing varied. After a long period when sons became tanners, daughters married local tanners, and all of them set up close to where their parents lived, the process of departure was begun when several of the sons and daughters married outsiders, although the sons remained in the family trade and in the quarter. Most of their children, male and female, would then leave the area. But departure required money, in the form of dowries for the girls and the purchase of offices or shops for the boys. This was why Jacques' descendants were slower to depart than those of Edme. The Genneau and Dorigny descendants did not prosper like the others, and they remained in the area well into the second half of the century.

The near disappearance not only of the Bouillerot name but of the entire lineage from the quarter they had once dominated thus resulted in large measure from success: not as individuals but as a family. It was parents who gave their sons the education necessary to enter the most prestigious trades in the city. Sons and daughters alike were given the cultural and educational grooming necessary for entry into the best bourgeois homes. It was families who provided the dowries and who negotiated suitable alliances. Inherited wealth and dowries were used to buy offices and *maîtrises* (masters' qualifications).[16] Movement took place by generation and by branch, rather than through individuals breaking away on their own. These were all quite traditional forms of behavior in the bourgeois lineages of Paris. Yet the new pattern of careers and marriages that the Bouillerot children were embarking on in the first half of the eighteenth century represented a marked departure from past family practices, a major shift in their relationship both with their trade and with the locality in which the older generation continued to dwell. The lineage was no longer identified with the parish. As children moved to other quarters, the dense network of ties within the faubourg and within the tanning trade gradually thinned.

These changes were not confined to the Bouillerot family. The Chevalier family, chosen by Adeline Daumard as typical of the local notables of Paris in the early nineteenth century, provides another example. They had been in the Faubourg Saint Marcel since at least 1700, when the leather dresser Noel Chevalier and his wife Anne Ferret purchased a house at the top of the rue de l'Oursine. Their only son, Pierre, married the daughter of another leather dresser, Jean Osmont. Osmont was an important figure in the area, married to a local woman with whom he owned three prime properties on the rue Mouffetard, and successively an official of his trade corporation and a churchwarden of Saint Martin. Two of his daughters married leather dressers, the third a tanner, all of them locals. Pierre II, eldest son of Pierre Chevalier and Marie Osmont, was therefore descended from prominent local people through both his parents, and it is not surprising to find him adopting his father's and both his grandfathers' occupation of leather dressing. Nor is it surprising that he should have been elected churchwarden of Saint Martin in his turn.[17]

One of his brothers also became a leather dresser, but the other was a grocer near Saint Jacques de la Boucherie. Their sister married a grocer and went to live in the rue Saint Honoré on the other side of the city. This was in about the 1740s. It was the beginning of a change, for while one of Pierre II's sons followed the family tradition and became a leather dresser in the rue Mouffetard (though according to Daumard was later a brewer), two of the others set up as mercers in other parts of the city. One of the daughters married a local mercer, and another a *négociant* (businessman) in the city center.[18] Like the Bouillerot family, and at about the same time, this lineage deserted its old habits and spread across the city.

It is quite likely that in the central quarters of the city the change was less marked. After all, the bourgeois marriage pool was larger there and children did not need to move quite so far. It may well be, too, that the decline of local lineage took place later. But there is evidence of a similar change taking place. The Cochin family, for example, mercers on the rue Saint Jacques, had arrived in Paris in the late seventeenth century and settled in the parish of Saint Benoît. For a century they intermarried with other mercers and with printers in the same quarter. It was not until the second half of the eighteenth century, after one of the family entered the church and became curé of Saint Jacques du Haut Pas, that the family began to spread. The brother of the curé moved to Saint Jacques du Haut Pas in 1787. His son, born in 1757, was the first to study at the university, despite the fact that the family could have afforded to give sons this education at any stage in the eighteenth century. He qualified in law in 1776 and then set up a private bank. His sister married a notary.[19]

The greater residential and occupational mobility that many bourgeois families seem to have adopted during the eighteenth century had important consequences for family relationships. The forms of day-to-day solidarity, cooperation, and mutual assistance that had enabled the clan to dominate the area and the trade were no longer either possible or necessary. Kin remained in touch, and continued to help one another, but parents no longer set up their sons or sons-in-law next door. The tanners could no longer put their sons—now in other trades—in touch with reliable butchers who might offer credit on hides because of the sound family reputation, or with the owner of a tanbark mill who delivered on time and who might also be prepared to wait for payment. A son who was establishing a mercer's business on the other side of Paris might be open to advice on investments, but for news of suitable shops available, or of likely bankruptcies among suppliers and customers, he would have to find other sources. Daughters too had to set up completely independent households, build up new support networks, find their own baby-sitters.

Beyond that, of course, the possibilities for parental control once children left the neighborhood were no longer the same. Those who moved away while still single were perhaps more likely to find their own marriage partners. A young couple's household was of necessity more independent once removed from the dense kinship ties of their natal parish. Parental expectations changed accordingly. The marriage contract between tanner Marin Derenusson and his second wife, Suzanne Labbé, signed in 1769, specified that the couple would be responsible for Derenusson's children from his first marriage, "and that each of them would be taught whatever trade they wished to follow."[20] There was no expectation that the sons would automatically become tanners, or even that their parents would choose a career for them.

Other signs of change, too, can be detected among the Bouillerots and their affines. The pool of first names, long characteristic of the lineage, now broadened, particularly for females. In the generation born in the middle years of the eighteenth century, one finds, for the first time, the names Adelaide, Victorine, Nicole, Henriette, Julie, Eulalie, Jean-Jacques, and even Marc Antoine. This broadening of the pool of names, a widespread phenomenon in France, took place earliest in urban areas.[21] It is evidence of an openness to outside influences that may not have been present previously—a reflection, perhaps, of the wider contacts of the family outside the quarter. But equally, it suggests a reduced attachment to the lineage, a diminished desire to stress family continuity by identifying the child with an aunt, uncle, or grandparent.[22] The choice of such names may also, as André Burguière has suggested, indicate a desire for social advancement that was absent in earlier generations: these were names that elevated the child above the mass of the Jeans, Maries, and Marguerites, placing the individual—and the family—instead in the more illustrious company of classically educated and upwardly mobile office-holders.[23]

What was happening here, it seems, was a dramatic change in the organization of merchant bourgeois families in Paris: the decline of local lineage, of an extended family group living in proximity and cooperating economically and politically. These structures were being replaced by networks of more independent, geographically dispersed households. There is certainly other evidence to support this hypothesis. Attachment to the parish was declining: requests in wills for burial in the parish of residence fell from roughly half in the seventeenth century to 29 percent of wills in the first half of the eighteenth, and to 6 percent in the second half of the century. Pierre Chaunu situates the turning point in the 1730s, thus at around the same time as the changes in the Faubourg Saint Marcel.[24]

An equally dramatic transformation was taking place even at the very moment of the Bouillerot ascendancy—a change that was to have far-reaching implications not only for this lineage but for the way bourgeois families operated in general, and for the whole system of local politics in Paris. Since the late seventeenth century, an appreciable decline had occurred in the numbers of Bouillerot children in successive generations. If one takes both the male and female lines together and excludes celibates, the eight members of the Bouillerot clan in the Faubourg Saint Marcel who were reproducing in the mid–seventeenth century had on average five or six children each. The generation they reared—the twenty-one men and women who began families between approximately 1680 and 1710—averaged about four children each. In the following generation, born between about 1705 and 1730, that average fell closer to three, and in the one after that it dropped below three. If, in order to increase the size of the sample, one includes allied families in the calculation—the siblings of those who married into the Bouillerot lineage where these are known—the averages are slightly lower in most cases, but the progression is the same (see Table 5.1).

It is the trend of declining fertility that is significant, of course, not the individual averages. The sample is too small for the figures to have any direct comparative value. Moreover, the available sources give no information on infant mortality, so that the real numbers of children born may have been significantly higher. But there is no reason to suspect that infant mortality increased during the eighteenth century; on the contrary, all the evidence is that it fell. And sufficient information is available in

Table 5.1 Mean number of recorded children in Bouillerot lineage and allied families, by generation

Approximate dates of birth	Mean number of children	
	Bouillerot only	Bouillerot and allied families
1650–1680	5.75	4.59 (17 households)
1680–1710	3.95	3.75 (32 households)
1710–1740	3.39	3.41 (39 households)
1740–1760	2.72	2.65 (20 households)

the notarial records to support the conclusion that the figures are not the result of premature death interrupting the childbearing of some couples in the later generations.

There appears to be no precise turning point at which the change occurred—no "demographic transition"—partly, of course (but only partly), because the concept of a "generation" is fuzzy, and becomes more so as the years pass. In some cases the youngest children of one generation were little older than their nieces and nephews. In one instance a marriage took place between second cousins of different generations but of about the same age! Moving the younger members of one generation into the next for statistical purposes makes no difference to the overall trend, however: by the mid–eighteenth century, the Bouillerot clan were having significantly fewer children than their great-grandparents or even their grandparents. Some form of family limitation was being practiced by the Bouillerot lineage from the late seventeenth century on.

Was there a correlation between declining family size and departure from the quarter? This does not seem to be the case, for those who stayed and those who left, where they can be traced, had similar numbers of children. It seems, furthermore, that the decline in birth rates was not peculiar to this lineage but shared by others of similar social standing. If one takes the churchwardens of Saint Médard as broadly representative of this social group, the pattern is similar (Table 5.2).[25]

This sample includes both the children and the families of origin of the churchwardens and their wives, where these are known. The dates of birth are not certain, but working from the evidence available, I have divided them into rough cohorts (assuming, again on the basis of the data available, that the churchwardens on average were forty-five years old when elected, got married in their late twenties, and usually took wives

Table 5.2 Mean number of recorded children in families of churchwardens
of Saint Médard (excluding Bouillerot family and affines)

Approximate dates of birth	Mean number of children
1640–1670	4.9 (16 households)
1670–1700	4.4 (21 households)
1700–1730	3.3 (29 households)
1730–1780	3.9 (14 households)

no more than five years their junior). These groupings are necessarily
very approximate, and the samples very small, but taken in conjunction
with the Bouillerot households they represent a very high proportion of
the notable households of the parish. In the mid–seventeenth century, the
tanning families appear to have had slightly larger numbers of recorded
children than the other churchwardens did, but in the mid–eighteenth
century they seem to have had comparatively fewer. Nevertheless, the
sample suggests an overall decline in fertility among the local merchant
elite.

This conclusion, although based on very imperfect data, is absolutely
consistent with recent findings for some other cities during the same
period. In Rouen, fertility declined conspicuously after about 1670, and
higher status groups—though merchants less noticeably—began limiting
births slightly ahead of other social groups. If this also happened in Paris,
as recent work by Jean-Pierre Bardet also suggests, it might account for
the difference between the Bouillerot lineage and the churchwardens as
a whole, since the later included families of lower status. The findings
match those for Geneva in the same period, and in Lyon, too, the
principal bourgeois families reduced their average number of children
steadily from nearly eight per couple in the generation of the mid–
seventeenth century to fewer than four in the second half of the eighteenth. In Chartres, many couples were limiting the size of their families
by the beginning of the eighteenth century.[26] Perhaps aware of this, the
clergy intensified their condemnations of "unnatural practices" between
1700 and 1750.[27]

It is tempting to speculate about why these well-to-do merchants and
craftsmen would wish to limit their families. They were wealthy enough
to raise large numbers of children without financial strain. The equal-
inheritance system did not dismay them: they had evolved family strategies that effectively balanced the negative effect that division of patri-

mony might entail. Indeed, large families were advantageous politically, for they were the key to the doors of local office and of patronage. It seems difficult to argue in this case, as some authors have of the French bourgeoisie in general, that family limitation was a deliberate strategy of social promotion.[28] Furthermore, the families of the Faubourg Saint Marcel were strongly religious: the argument that declining religious practice and family limitation went hand in hand is not applicable here.[29] Why did the members of successive generations of the Bouillerot clan, and of other Faubourg Saint Marcel families, produce smaller households than those in which they had themselves grown up?

It is easiest to think of reasons why many women might want to have fewer children. Childbirth and pregnancy were, in the words of the wife of a Toulouse magistrate expecting her third baby in the 1780s, a *"vilain métier,"* painful and involving a very real risk to health. A century earlier, Madame de Sévigné's letters to her daughter reflect a similar view. A great many women would no doubt have preferred to have fewer children.[30] Yet with the cooperation of their husbands, family limitation was not difficult: it was successfully achieved by millions of French peasants long before effective contraceptive devices were available, and there is clear evidence that a range of birth control techniques were known throughout the early modern period.[31]

If many women indeed had a strong motive for limiting the size of the family in the mid–seventeenth century but were unable to do so, perhaps the attitudes of husbands and the nature of the relationship between the married couple can explain why this was the case. Jean-Louis Flandrin suggests that elite men in the late eighteenth century may have displayed a new respect and concern for their wives, and therefore been more prepared to cooperate in limiting their families—a view for which Margaret Darrow has found persuasive evidence in Montauban. Angus McLaren sees this explanation as too simplistic, but he, too, is prepared to argue that French husbands "acceded" to their wives' demands.[32] Yet the changes in many cities began much earlier, in the second half of the seventeenth century, and in the Faubourg Saint Marcel among merchant tanners, not nobles or officeholders. It seems that the evolution in family attitudes conventionally associated with the eighteenth century took place over a much longer period, at least in certain social groups. Just as the Enlightenment owed many of its basic principles to seventeenth-century developments, so family attitudes among literate Parisians even of modest rank were undergoing a profound transformation during this whole period. Norbert Elias identified the later seventeenth century as central in the history of manners, and there is no reason to believe the changes were confined to the court of Louis XIV.[33]

The key, in the case of the Paris tanners, may well be Jansenism. The decline in fertility seems to begin at about the same time that Jansenism was taking root in Paris. The Faubourg Saint Marcel was close to Port Royal and was one of the areas most influenced by the new theology.[34] Jansenism encouraged in its adherents an independence of mind and a personal moral certitude discouraged by mainstream Catholicism. Given that church writers of the period roundly condemned the use of birth control, its adoption suggests a willingness to disregard mainstream church teaching that was characteristic of the Jansenists, with their emphasis on the community of saints and a greater role for the laity in the church.[35] Furthermore, this emphasis on the independence of the laity extended to women, whose considerable role even in aspects of parish administration was examined in Chapter 2.[36] Certainly, many of the Bouillerot women behaved in a most independent manner, and it would come as no surprise if it was they who determined the number of children they wished to have, though—and this is important—in accordance with the norms of their generation, a cultural factor that may help to account for the gradual nature of the change.

This is not to deny the possible importance of economic factors—in this case growing prosperity rather than hardship. Alfred Perrenoud sees family limitation as a response to a sudden increase in fertility produced by a marked improvement in the economic situation. Exactly what the economic position of the Paris middle classes was in the second half of the seventeenth century is not known, but the Bouillerot family certainly prospered. Did they adopt family limitation in response to increasing fertility and subsequently use it to reduce the number of children further, as the religious limitations on the practice weighed on them less? Family limitation may well have begun for one reason in the seventeenth century and continued for quite different reasons.

In order to understand what happened, much more needs to be discovered about the demography of Paris in the seventeenth century and about how children fitted into their world. Between the late seventeenth and the late eighteenth century, major changes occurred in the family relationships of bourgeois Parisians and in the material objects with which they chose to pad their lives. Both sorts of changes may have influenced family size. Although decisions about numbers and spacing of children are made by individual couples, they are strongly influenced by community and family expectations. In the eighteenth century the households formed by those children who married outside the quarter were of necessity more independent, less susceptible to the pressures that the older generation and extended family might apply. Particularly because in the early eighteenth century it was more often women who left the quarter, this probably weakened the traditions of mothering that were passed on in the female line from one generation to the next. At the same time, they received less assistance, a change in circumstances that, depending on the use made of servants, made child rearing potentially more onerous. Simultaneously, the social group to which the Bouillerot family belonged was becoming less susceptible to neighborhood opinion as the eighteenth century progressed.[37] This greater independence from family tradition and from the pressure of relatives and neighbors alike left successive generations more open to new models of family behavior. As lineage gave way to household, it was women, too, who were arguably more receptive to, and certainly more immediately affected by, the new ideology of domesticity.

It is equally likely that the evolving material expectations of bourgeois Parisians played a part. With the development of merchant capitalism and the accompanying consumerism, apartments were more and more richly furnished. Between the mid–seventeenth century and the late eighteenth, paintings and decorations, silverware, books and musical instruments, and new types of furniture all flooded into domestic interiors. Growing specialization of rooms indicates changing ideas of space and new notions about the way it should be used.[38] Where, in these newly organized spaces, did the children play? Did material objects in a sense displace them? If parents felt that children needed more space, better furnished, with more toys and trinkets, then they could not provide adequately for so many. Letters or diaries are needed to reveal the place of children in people's vision of their own future, especially among those in a position, economically, to realize their material aspirations.[39]

Whatever the explanation for the steady, slow decline in family size among the local elites, it is clear that a combination of powerful, long-term forces was changing the family organization of the middle-class merchants who since the mid–seventeenth century had dominated the Faubourg Saint Marcel. Smaller numbers of children and more dispersed family networks in turn wrought important changes in a local political system that had formerly favored large kinship groups. It became more difficult for a single lineage to dominate the parish, as the Bouillerot family had done at Saint Médard. There were fewer men of the right age and standing who could serve as churchwardens, and fewer daughters whose marriages into other local families could provide valuable support within the vestry, either on matters of policy or to elect a younger kinsman. In the second half of the eighteenth century, the division of the Saint Médard vestry into two large kin-based factions (with about another third independent of both) vanished.

This is not to say that family ties disappeared within the vestry: far from it. The rump of the Bouillerot faction—six of them—remained until the early 1760s. A trace of the baker faction survived with Louis Moncouteau and his nephew Pierre Brot, both distantly related to another churchwarden, Louis Jean-Baptiste Barre. Three members of the Pichard family are recorded, as are several father-and-son teams. In all, sufficient information survives on fifty churchwardens in the period 1752–1791 to reveal any close kin ties. Forty (80 percent) and perhaps forty-two were related to at least one other churchwarden who served during these years. This compares with 89 percent of the churchwardens from 1690 to 1732. But a more significant difference emerges if one looks at the later vestrymen who were related to *two* or more of their fellows: 34 percent for the years 1752–1791, but 69 percent for the earlier period. The dense tissue of mutually reinforcing solidarities that characterized the vestry in the early decades of the century had begun to thin.

The same thing seems to have happened at Saint Hippolyte and at Saint Martin du Cloître. In the first half of the century, as at Saint Médard, it was fairly common for men from the same family to be elected as churchwardens. Six names appear more than once among the churchwardens of Saint Hippolyte in the period from 1700 to 1750. From 1750 to 1791, however, there are only two, and no examples of brothers or of father and son being elected during those years. At Saint Martin, in the first half of the century nineteen surnames appear more than once, with three members of the same family sometimes being elected. Again, this practice disappears in the second half of the century, when only two names recur. Furthermore, in both parishes many entirely new names appear, while families continuously represented on the vestry since the late seventeenth century now vanish. Although the change was not as dramatic as at Saint Médard, a similar evolution is visible.

The most immediate effect of these shifts was the admission of a wider number of families to the ranks of the elite and the spreading of the political influence that had been concentrated, at Saint Médard, among the leather trades and, in second place, the bakers. Greater opportunities emerged for those without long-established local family networks. The second half of the eighteenth century saw an influx of such people, bourgeois from other parts of the city and members of the provincial middle classes. Rapid population growth, increased economic development, and the new commercial opportunities of the period brought to Paris large numbers of immigrants, from every social group, and there were perhaps more challenges from new arrivals than at the beginning of the century. At the same time, as the local kinship network became less important, the weight of other components of notability grew: personal reputation, size of business, and particularly wealth. It was not only the personnel who changed, but the system itself.

One may also postulate an evolution in the character of patriarchy, at least in the long term. In a society of lineages, power was patriarchal in the older sense of that word: it was vested in the head of the lineage. It could be exercised most effectively when the patriarch retained direct control over adult children. As long as they lived close by, and particularly if they had the same trade, the patriarchal system worked reasonably well. Once the children moved away, into other occupations and more distant circles, once they made their own marriage and career decisions, the authority of the older generations was more limited. It did not extend nearly as effectively beyond the household unit, and the equal-inheritance laws of the Paris region made the threat of disinheritance a very ineffectual tool. Within the simple family of the "companionate marriage"—the more close-knit domestic unit that many historians believe emerged in the eighteenth century—marital and paternal authority was less influenced by the couple's parents, or by any other kin. It was more concentrated within the household, leaving opportunities for either greater female independence or greater domination by the husband. This change may underlie the obvious concern about paternal and marital roles that is expressed in the novels and social literature of the later eighteenth century.

More isolated households also entailed important consequences for bourgeois family ideology. The autonomous conjugal family became the "normal" one. Both family limitation and the companionate marriage constitute part of the shift that Roland Mousnier described some years ago, from a society of lineages to a society of households.[40] The ideology of domesticity had greater relevance to couples who lived some distance from their other kin yet who retained ties of family, occupation, friendship, and patronage across the city and were therefore likely to remain outside the neighborhood community.[41] Doubly isolated, in this sense—deprived both of the sense of family that accompanied lineage structures and of the neighborhood identity facilitated by more plebeian trades and habits—they found an alternative social identity in the new ideals of behavior that I have termed the "quality" model. It set them apart both from the mass of "the people" and from the decadent and worldly aristocracy.

"Well-to-do artisans and rich merchants have left their station," commented the lawyer Edmond Jean François Barbier (himself an archetypal example of the old system, son of a churchwarden at Saint Séverin and a local notable who lived throughout his life in the same house as his parents before being buried in the family chapel). "They no longer consider themselves to belong among the people," he went on. "And, in truth, in such a great city one must distinguish between the people, who are innumerable, and the bourgeois."[42] Already in 1745, a perceptive observer such as Barbier was able to identify the emerging social identity of a Parisian—as opposed to a local—bourgeoisie.

C H A P T E R

THE NEW FAMILIES AND THE NEW POLITICS

*You have neither wealth nor birth, you have no chance
of success; devote yourself to commerce.*

—*Mathematics examiner in Paris to Charles-Joseph Panckoucke, c. 1757*

In the houses and neighborhoods of the French capital in the second half of the eighteenth century, an enormous silent change was taking place among the commercial middle classes. Family sizes had dropped dramatically, and the local bourgeois lineages that had competed for influence in the parish vestries and in local administration—families like the Bouillerots—were reaching out across the city. Changes of such magnitude necessarily had a major impact on a political system in which local lineage had until then played such a vital role. But the second half of the century was also the period when Enlightenment ideas became part of the currency of everyday educated life, and when the material lives of better-off Parisians were transformed by new products and by growing prosperity. The role of the church was challenged, and new political and family ideologies competed with inherited ways of thinking. The commercial dynamism of the Paris middle classes, their growing numbers, and their education and local dominance placed them at the center of these changes. They were agents of some of the new trends, but at the same time their own composition, world view, and political role were being transformed. The second half of the eighteenth century was a crucial period in the formation of the Parisian bourgeoisie.

The immediate impact of the dilution of middle-class lineages can be

Property owned by churchwardens of Saint Médard elected 1690–1732.

Property owned by churchwardens of Saint Médard elected 1752–1791.

gauged from the changing composition of the vestry of Saint Médard. The occupational and geographical distribution of the churchwardens altered, shifting away from the Bièvre. And new men appeared, individuals who despite their recent establishment and their lack of a local kinship network were nonetheless able to win office.

The change is obvious if one compares the property owned by the churchwardens of Saint Médard elected in the period 1752–1791 with that owned by their predecessors (see maps). In the first part of the century only one of the churchwardens owned a house outside the parish, and most of their properties were clustered along the Bièvre and the rue Mouffetard; after 1750 they were scattered more widely across the parish, and several of the churchwardens owned real estate beyond its boundaries.

The new geographical distribution reflects a shift away from the riverside occupations, particularly tanning and leather dressing (see Table 6.1). The other industry whose representation declined markedly was silk: both the ribbon makers and the hosiers *(bonnetiers)*, who dealt extensively in silk stockings, all but disappeared from the vestry. This probably reflects the concentration of the industry in fewer but larger enterprises, rather than its decay.[1] The places that the hosiers and the tanners had formerly occupied were now taken partly by retail traders and artisans, among whom bakers and grocers remained prominent and apothecaries made an appearance, but also partly by men engaged in other manufacturing industries. Brewers now constituted the second-largest occupational group. The extra starch makers and the introduction of saltpeter manufacturers, both long-established trades in the area, suggest the rising wealth and status of these occupations.

Equally interesting is the appearance of new industries: dye production and wallpaper. Dyeing had been an important trade in the Faubourg Saint Marcel since the days of the Gobelin family in the fifteenth century, but early in the eighteenth century the dyes themselves were imported. After the 1750s they began to be manufactured locally, in response to the boom in production of printed cloth. Oberkampf's large manufactory at Jouy, farther upstream along the Bièvre, produced between 20,000 and 30,000 pieces of printed cloth each year from 1771 to 1790, and more thereafter. This encouraged cloth-dyeing trades within the Faubourg Saint Marcel itself, enterprises like that of Jean-Baptiste Vérité, who purchased *bleu de Prusse* from Antoine Robert Dheur, one of the two dye manufacturers who appeared in the churchwardens' pew at Saint

Table 6.1 Occupations of the churchwardens of Saint Médard, 1690–1732 and 1752–1791

Occupation	Number	
	1690–1732	1752–1791
Leather trades	30	15
Hosiers (*bonnetiers*)	8	2
Bakers	6	6
Brewers	4	7
Grocers	4	5
Wineshop keepers	4	1
Ribbon makers	2	0
Sellers of cooked meat (*charcutiers*)	2	1
Pastry cooks/sellers of prepared food (*traiteurs*)	1	2
Potters/tile makers	2	4
Candle makers	2	1
Hatters	2	0
Minor-office holders[a]	2	0
Butcher	1	0
Mercer	1	0
Starch makers	1	3
Metal founders, nail makers	1	1
Blanket makers	1	1
Market gardeners	1	2
Masons and roofers	1	1
Apothecaries	0	3
Furniture maker	0	1
Dye maker	0	1
Saltpeter maker	0	2
Wallpaper manufacturers	0	2
Occupation unknown	4	5
Total	80	66

a. No other occupation given.

Médard in the final years of the Old Regime. *Bleu de Prusse* was a new product invented early in the eighteenth century, and there were three factories producing it in Paris at the end of the Old Regime.[2]

Wallpaper making was another new industry in the second half of the eighteenth century. By 1789 there were some fifty workshops in Paris producing different kinds of wallpaper, the most famous of which was Jean-Baptiste Réveillon's factory. In the Faubourg Saint Marcel, the Saint

Médard churchwarden Jean Nicolas Legrand employed more than 100 workers in the 1770s and 1780s.[3]

The new industries were often introduced by men without local ties. Robert Dheur had moved to Paris from the Auvergne, possibly in the 1740s, for his son Antoine Robert was born in the parish of Saint Eustache in 1750. He was well enough established at Saint Médard to be elected as churchwarden in 1779. His son followed him into dye making and into the vestry, and seems to have married locally, though not in the same parish.[4] Jean Nicolas Legrand, the wallpaper manufacturer, may have arrived in the area around 1770, for he claimed in 1791 to have been running his business (primarily exporting printed paper to Russia, Poland, Germany, Switzerland, and America) for twenty years. A second paper manufacturer in the rue d'Orléans, Philippe Antoine Legrand, perhaps Jean Nicolas's brother, was born in the parish of Saint Germain l'Auxerrois in the center of Paris. Jean Nicolas Legrand was economically an outsider, too, since upon his marriage in 1768 he was able to contribute only 200 livres to the marriage community and his wife's dowry was only 300 livres: tiny sums alongside the tens of thousands that the Bouillerot family were by then giving their children. His was a different world.[5]

The appearance of self-made men like Dheur and Jean Nicholas Legrand in new and expanding industries reflects the economic and the demographic changes that were taking place in the Faubourg Saint Marcel. It is unlikely that either man would have become a churchwarden at Saint Médard earlier in the century, when the leather and baking dynasties dominated the vestry. But the new men were not solely in the new industries. The cabinetmaker Etienne Perreve had come from Burgundy in 1743 and bought a house in the parish in 1774; he may have been at Saint Médard the whole time, working his way up. He was forty-seven when he was elected as churchwarden, and in 1791 was employing eleven journeymen—quite a substantial number for a cabinetmaker.[6] Another relative newcomer was the leather dresser Louis Lucien Duchemin, born near Beauvais and a resident of Paris since the 1740s. He bought a house in the rue Censier in the mid-1760s, and became a churchwarden around 1780.[7]

Even among the tanners there were new faces. The Auffray brothers, Jean and Antoine, both of whom became churchwardens of Saint Médard in the early 1750s, first appear in the records in 1734, when Antoine rented a small tannery in the rue Censier. Both the brothers are included in the 1738 Bièvre tax list. In 1741 Antoine married the daughter of Louis Lafillard, a member of a well-established local family and a former churchwarden. By 1757 the couple owned two houses in the rue Censier, where Jean also bought a house in about 1751.[8]

But the most successful of the new men among the tanners was Jean Antoine Derubigny de Berteval. Born in Picardy in 1732, he described himself on one occasion as a "former farmer," and probably came to Paris while in his late twenties. He appears on the Bièvre tax list of 1764 as the tenant of a tannery in the rue Censier, a property he bought about four years later. In 1772 he purchased the adjoining house, formerly owned by the Bouillerot family: an appropriate transfer, for Derubigny was in a sense heir to their leading political role in the quarter.[9] The following year he was elected to the vestry of Saint Médard, and subsequently purchased the office of *dixainier*. Like Antoine Auffray, he formed an alliance with an important local family, wedding the widow of one of the Huguet brothers. The Huguet family were a tanning dynasty of long standing but of recent prominence, and Derubigny's link with them no doubt helped to consolidate his position in the quarter. By the time of the Revolution, he owned four houses as well as the Manufacture Royale de Maroquin in the rue Saint Hippolyte.[10]

Even more than in the new industries, the success of these outsiders in the long-established trades of the faubourg depended on the old families making room for them—both physically and figuratively. The departure of the Bouillerot lineage meant that the best riverside properties were at last up for sale. It was here that Antoine Robert Dheur had his dye works and Derubigny his first two tanneries. Antoine Auffray's tannery had belonged to Louis Genneau, cousin to the Bouillerot churchwardens. At the same time, the decline of the old lineages also left room in the vestry for men who formerly would have been hard pressed to compete with "inside" candidates.

The success of Derubigny is all the more remarkable in that the second half of the eighteenth century witnessed a prolonged crisis in the tanning industry. The number of tanners in Paris, according to one source, fell from forty in 1759 to twenty in 1775, and the production of large hides dropped from 36,000 to 10,000 in the same period.[11] The number of tanneries along the Bièvre declined dramatically. The tanners themselves blamed this on the royal edict of 1759, which changed the way taxes were levied on leather and established a *régie* to administer the new system, a form of bureaucratic supervision that the tanners claimed was very costly.[12] But the decline was not solely attributable to the *régie*. The later eighteenth century witnessed increasing English competition and the progressive closure of export markets in Germany, Italy, and Spain as those countries' governments sought to protect their domestic industry.[13]

All the evidence suggests that this contraction of the industry facilitated its concentration in a smaller number of larger enterprises. In the Bouillerot days the establishments run by individual tanners were quite small. The Bièvre tax roll for 1738 includes the number of lime pits each one contained. Jacques Médard Bouillerot had just over 20 pits, located in four different houses. Guillaume Bouillerot had 20, and Joseph Bouillerot and Jean-Baptiste Michelin 19 each. The average number was 10, the smallest number 2. If these figures provide a reasonable guide to the amount of business being done by each individual, it appears that the wealthiest tanners, who did a far larger trade than the smallest, had about twice the average number of pits. Furthermore, a single large tannery provided sufficient room for all the hides a tanner had in lime at any one time.[14]

By the end of the century there were about fourteen tanners left in the area. The largest trade was probably being done by Derubigny de Berteval in his two tanneries in the rue Censier and his manufactory in the rue Saint Hippolyte. A large commerce was also run by Jean Edme Huguet, and another by the Widow Derenusson, whose husband had died in 1791 leaving a business worth 85,412 livres. The Huguet and Derenusson enterprises were at least as big as any owned by the Bouillerot dynasty, and Derubigny's was certainly larger—this after years of depression in the industry. During the Revolution, Derubigny lost his first place to the Salleron brothers, who by 1807 were employing 30 to 40 workers. The son of one of the brothers had a similar number on his payroll, somewhat more than the 20 to 30 taken on by Derubigny in 1791 and 1792 and considerably more than the average of nearly 16 workers per employer in a list of 1791.[15] The growth was to continue, too, for when the social hygienist Jean-Baptiste Parent-Duchâtelet described the industries found along the Bièvre in 1822, he listed, alongside a number of small tanneries, a "very large" one belonging to Monsieur Salleron, another "vast tannery" in the rue du Fer à Moulin, and the huge establishment belonging to one of the Salleron brothers: "it has over 100 pits in a vast covered workshop, not counting the ones, at least as numerous again, located in the open air."[16] There was nothing anywhere near this size in Paris before the Revolution.

Looking outside the Faubourg Saint Marcel to the city as a whole, one finds evidence of the same growth. In 1802 the Coulon brothers had over a million francs invested in leather, with half of it in the lime pits.[17] This far exceeded anything that the Bouillerot family possibly could have imagined. What appears to have happened in the last decades of the Old Regime, and on into the Revolution, is that the largest enterprises held on or grew, despite the apparent decline of the industry. A number of smaller businesses managed to survive, but many went under. The trade was concentrated in fewer hands.

The same can be said of the brewing industry, which also declined in the later eighteenth century. The brewers, like the tanners, complained of time-wasting inspections and regulations, and their number had apparently dropped from fifty or sixty (in the whole city) to a mere sixteen in 1791.[18] Yet those who remained were by local standards wealthy. In 1777 André Arnoult Aclocque, a churchwarden of Saint Martin, married the cousin of a Paris notary. To her dowry of 4,000 livres, he added 3,000: a respectable though not enormous sum. In 1780, however, he paid 50,000 livres for three houses in the rue Mouffetard, and on the eve of the Revolution bought a house in the country. Like Derubigny, Aclocque also invested in the largely honorific position of *dixainier*.[19]

These were hardly signs of declining fortunes. Nor were the achievements of Charles Delongchamp, the owner of at least six houses, who on the marriage of his son was able to transfer property and goods worth some 120,000 livres.[20] Antoine Joseph Santerre, also a son of the Faubourg Saint Marcel, though he worked in the Faubourg Saint Antoine, was worth 140,000 livres when he married for the second time, in 1778, at the age of twenty-six.[21] In the brewing industry too, circumstantial evidence suggests that the wealthier manufacturers did not suffer from the crisis, but benefited from the concentration of the trade in fewer hands.

Partly as a consequence of industrial concentration, a similar concentration took place in the ownership of real estate in the Faubourg Saint Marcel. As Table 6.2 indicates, between the 1720s and the 1770s there was a significant drop in the percentage of houses whose owner actually lived in them. By the 1770s houses in the faubourg were somewhat more likely to be owned by someone who lived outside the quarter—further evidence of the commercial integration of the city and the dilution of local ties. Above all, a significant rise took place in the proportion of houses owned by people living elsewhere in the quarter, many of whom

Table 6.2 Place of residence of owners of real estate in the Faubourg Saint
Marcel, 1720s and 1770s

	1720s		1770s	
Owner's place of residence	Number	Percentage of total	Number	Percentage of total
In owned property itself	80	40.8%	60	24.2%
Elsewhere in faubourg	33	16.8	63	25.4
Outside faubourg	83	42.3	125	50.4
Total	196	99.9[a]	248	100.0

Sources: S*1953 (1), déclarations au terrier de Saint Marcel, 1695–1743. S*1954 (2),
déclarations au terrier de Saint Marcel, 1762–1778. S*5693, papier terrier du Fief de
l'Oursine, 1717–1725. S*5683, terrier du Fief de l'Oursine, 1773–1777.
   a. Does not total 100.0% because of rounding.

owned several properties. This contrasts with the earlier pattern. Although the Bouillerot family collectively owned much real estate along
the Bièvre, individuals rarely owned more than one or two houses. Yet
by the 1770s several local notables possessed not only the house in which
they lived but adjoining properties as well. Sometimes this represented
an industrial investment, and the properties were combined into a single
large manufactory. At others, it was a purely financial strategy, and the
houses were let to tenants. In either case, real estate in the faubourg was
held by a smaller number of local people.

   The changing occupational composition of the vestry of Saint Médard
over the course of the century reflects the decline of the old bourgeois
lineages and the rise of new families and individuals. This change was
neither sudden nor complete. Some new men were never elected to the
vestry even though they were wealthier than some of the established men
who were: the brewer Jean-Baptiste Santerre, for example, brother of the
future revolutionary general. Many well-established families probably
continued to function as they had during the Jansenist years, and there
is ample evidence of continuing local and occupational endogamy. A
great many of the old family names of the Faubourg Saint Marcel—Fre-
min, de Beaune, and DeVitry, Dorigny and Moncouteau—were still there
at the end of the eighteenth century. Some of the newcomers were assisted
by marriage ties with the old clans: both Antoine Auffray and Derubigny

formed alliances with old tanning families, although not until they had become well established in the quarter. Nor did kinship become less important. Local office had become more accessible to outsiders and political influence was spread among a larger number of families.

The new openness was not confined to the parish vestries. The other institution through which the inhabitants of Paris could in some way govern themselves and have an influence on government policy was the trade corporation. Physiocratic critics of the corporations condemned them as closed oligarchies, and in trades as diverse as hatting, printing, tailoring, and wig making, there was a small core of large employers and a "periphery" of small masters. This remained true right up to the Revolution.

But before 1776, in the very large corporations of more than a thousand masters, only fifty or sixty belonged to the central *bureau* and made decisions (though these could be challenged in the courts). This control was legitimized by the statutes of many corporations. The seamstresses' regulations, for instance, stipulated that all the former officials were to be called to meetings, together with forty of the longest-established mistresses in the trade, twenty mistresses of less seniority, and twenty of the most recently admitted women. The shoemakers were to summon the former *jurés*, fifty to sixty strong, as well as twenty men of some years' standing and twenty more recent masters.[22] Even these rules were not always observed. A complaint in 1764 by a number of shoemakers accused officials in their corporation of arbitrarily reducing the number of ordinary members present. In 1775 "a private meeting of [the] principal manufacturers" among the card- and papermakers was similarly accused of effecting a change of trade policy to the detriment of the majority of small employers. It was common for a small group of *anciens* to dominate the corporation.[23] These officials, furthermore, were frequently linked by kinship or marriage. This was true of the tanners and brewers, and it almost certainly applied to the butchers. In the glaziers' corporation, both the uncles of Jacques-Louis Ménétra were *jurés*, and Michael Sonenscher has discovered that Ménétra's father was also a member of the central *bureau*. This was perfectly consistent with the spirit of the rules governing so many of the trades, which waived fees and other requirements of entry for sons of masters.[24]

Although surviving information on the trades is very scanty, it is likely that in the later part of the century these strongly endogamous occupational dynasties found their hold weakening in the same way as did the oligarchies within the vestries. Family size probably dropped, as in the Faubourg Saint Marcel, and with it the number of kin eligible to become *jurés* and hence *anciens;* this left more room for outsiders: not necessarily people from outside Paris or even from outside the trade, but men and women who did not belong to any of the dominant families. Certainly, recent work has demonstrated that, far from becoming more restrictive in their membership, some corporations were, if anything, increasingly open. Of the Paris locksmiths acquiring their *maîtrise* (master's ticket) in the years 1735–1776, only about a third were sons of masters in the same trade. The turnover of names within the ranks of the master masons also suggests relative openness to outsiders; and the age composition of the workforce of various trades provides further evidence that entry was certainly not restricted to sons and daughters of masters.[25]

It is difficult to see how the old oligarchies, supposing they remained intact in the 1770s, could have survived unscathed the changes made by the royal edict of August 1776. The number of trades corporations was reduced from about 120 to 44, mostly through amalgamation, though a small number were abolished and their ranks opened to all comers. These changes in themselves may have made control by the previous leaders difficult to maintain. But equally challenging to oligarchies within the trades were the innovations that the same edict made in the system of electing *jurés* and syndics. The old system had accorded greater representation to the *anciens,* the former officials of the corporations. As long as they remained united, they could defeat the representatives of the very much larger number of ordinary masters. Under the 1776 edict, however, two-tier elections were introduced. In certain respects these were less democratic than the old system, for only those who paid the highest taxes—the top 200 in small trades and the top 400 in large ones—were eligible to vote or to be elected. They gathered 100 at a time to elect deputies, who in turn chose the syndics. These same deputies—24 or 36 of them, depending on the size of the corporation—formed the policy-making body of each guild.[26]

This new structure had two obvious effects. One was to make it impossible for modest masters to be elected as officials of their corporations, something theoretically possible before, even if it rarely happened. The other was, because of the enlarged electoral base, to make it harder for the trade dynasties and reigning oligarchs to retain their dominance. The syndics were no longer to be selected by virtue of a single ballot within a small assembly that might be dominated by their kin. And they were no longer, once elected, life members of the ruling elite, automatically summoned to every meeting. The new system, of course, did not make it impossible for them to remain in place. But now they would have to persuade the 200 or 400 wealthiest masters or mistresses to elect them, not once and for all, but repeatedly.[27]

The new system was apparently based on proposals originally drawn up by Lieutenant General of Police Antoine Gabriel de Sartine, a man well placed to study the disadvantages of the old corporate structure.[28] In three important respects it constituted a radical departure from the habits of mind of the Old Regime. First, it made wealth the principal formal prerequisite for participation and for election. Second, by abolishing the assembly of *anciens* and making continued influence conditional on repeated election, it turned its back on the deeply ingrained respect for seniority and experience. An aging former *juré* who no longer paid much tax might now be totally excluded from the government of the trade.[29] And third, the new structure made it possible, as it had not been before, for an individual to be reelected. Formerly, a *juré* had served for a fixed time and then become an *ancien,* making way for someone else.

The new system was much better suited to energetic individuals who did not necessarily belong to the old family oligarchies. Provided that they could muster sufficient support in the trade—and no longer solely among the *anciens*—they could win office and stay there, free from the surveillance of the former oligarchs. It is not certain whether this happened. Perhaps habits of deference or the influence of the powerful led the masters and mistresses summoned to elections to vote for the same people who had governed the corporation before 1776. Yet the brewers' corporation, in the years following the reforms, elected as *jurés* men like Jean-Baptiste and Antoine Joseph Santerre, both born in the Faubourg Saint Marcel where their father had a brewery but where the family had no roots. Another *juré* in the brewers' guild, André Schveinfelt, was an even more recent arrival: he first appears in the same quarter in 1780.[30] Whether new men and women made their way into the decision-making elite of other corporations after 1776 is not clear. The most prestigious trades—the goldsmiths, drapers, and mercers, and others like them—probably remained difficult for outsiders to penetrate. But there was a new spirit abroad, a fresh approach.

Turgot and his supporters believed that they were removing barriers to commerce when they urged the abolition of the corporations. The restoration of these organizations following Turgot's fall is often seen as a defeat for the Physiocrats. But neither of these interpretations is entirely accurate. The Paris corporations do not seem to have hindered commercial development greatly, and were probably most onerous and bothersome for the unfortunate immigrant workers and small masters for whom inspections represented a significant loss of working time and confiscations a real disaster. The reestablishment of the corporations may well, at least in the long run, have completed what Turgot set out to do: destroy oligarchy within the Paris trades. The irony is that these oligarchies were probably already moribund.[31]

Yet the change in local and corporate politics was more far-reaching than this. It was not simply that the dilution of the old lineages left more room in the vestries, and probably in the government of the corporations as well. There was also a change in the definition of notability. No longer was a long-standing commitment to the quarter, exemplified by belonging to a well-established local lineage, so important in the vestries. Local implantation did retain some relevance: in the absence of family reputation, personal knowledge of a man and his family who had lived in the parish for many years, even if not born there, was important when the *anciens* gathered to elect a new churchwarden. Certainly, all those elected at Saint Médard seem to have been in the area for years and were owners of property there. Other considerations are harder to gauge. Regular church attendance may have been one, although it is likely that, the Jansenist years spent, any religious elements in local reputation became less significant.[32] Further indications of suitability for election as churchwarden were, naturally, other marks of notability already acquired: the office of *juré* in one of the trades corporations; or that of *dixainier* or *cinquantenier.*

But other factors now became more significant both in the vestries and in the corporations. In particular, wealth, the solidity of a thriving business, and personal energy and talent could give an individual the wide reputation that once had been assured by lineage. Recognition by the authorities was both a source of publicity and a guarantee of worth: possession of a *privilège* and the honor of adding "royal" or "du Roi" to the name of one's manufactory or title were, if not entirely new forms of recognition, certainly much more common. "Manufactures royales" proliferated in Paris toward the end of the Old Regime; more than two dozen existed in the late 1780s.[33] Elevation to the status of local notable might now have little to do with family or with commitment to the parish but could result instead from royal favor, which was in turn dependent on success in invention and a flair for self-promotion.

All this points to a major change of attitude. The Old Regime was now prepared to broaden—although often parsimoniously—the range of those on whom it conferred the honorific rewards that were so important in scaling the degrees of its social and political hierarchy. The change in official thinking was signaled by the introduction of such honors as the Necker gold medal, an award granted for innovations that enriched French industry. But at a more profound level, even in the more humble but perhaps more telling domain of local politics, Old Regime society was beginning to recognize talents that it had previously regarded with scorn. The newcomers, whether in recently introduced or long-established local industries, had been obliged to make their own way. With few or no relatives to pilot them through the storms of the Parisian commercial world, without surnames that automatically opened doors, they required skills of self-promotion and perhaps invention. They had to be entrepreneurs, not simply merchants.

Here Derubigny provides the perfect example. Acknowledged in J. E. Bertrand's *Descriptions des arts et métiers* as an experienced and particularly able tanner, he had apparently invented a method of waterproofing leather.[34] He had investigated, if one can believe his own not particularly modest claims, the tanning techniques used in England and in Liège, had brought in specialized workers, and had conducted experiments of his own. He claimed to have invented a way of "disinfecting hides infected with epizoic diseases to make them usable." He had—again by his own account—corresponded both with the Académie des Sciences and with Diderot about tanning techniques.[35] His credentials obviously impressed the royal authorities, for he was able to obtain a *privilège* for his manufactory in the rue Saint Hippolyte. This presumably gave him a monopoly on the use of his tanning techniques, but above all it freed him from corporate regulation and gave him the advertising advantage of government recognition. He may also have obtained tax privileges.[36]

From the mid-1770s, Derubigny campaigned tirelessly against the *régie* governing the tanning trade. He bombarded the authorities with letters and *mémoires,* and published several pamphlets, one of which landed him in the Bastille in 1777. Before this he had won the support of Turgot for his campaign and had managed to obtain a personal interview with the king. In 1787, still pursuing the abolition of the *régie,* he attended the Assemblée des Notables. In 1789 he produced his own cahier, returning to the same issue, among others. It was presumably about this time that he also published his *Observations économiques sur le commerce et l'agriculture.*[37]

Derubigny was in many respects typical of entrepreneurs of his generation. The eighteenth century, and particularly the last four decades of the Old Regime, was a period of extensive innovation and growing public interest in industry—best exemplified, of course, in the *Encyclopédie,* but also in the publications of the Académie des Sciences and in a flood of more minor works.[38] Much of this work was done outside— even despite—the official governing bodies of the trades: witness, in the glazing trade, Jacques-Louis Ménétra's technically illegal importation of Baccarat glass from Alsace, and the introduction to Paris of Bohemian glass by independent entrepreneurs and by master glaziers who had obtained their qualifications by royal caveat, not by satisfying guild regulations. The authorities tolerated the establishment of cotton manufactories, despite repeated government prohibitions on the industry. Prominent ribbon makers in Paris introduced the Dutch loom, despite bans on its use.[39] Lamoignon de Malesherbes—in charge of censorship— and de Sartine tolerated and even protected writers and publishers whose works were technically illegal. Derubigny was, like Ménétra, a member of a Paris guild, yet he owed his success in some measure to his having obtained exemption from the restrictions of corporate organization.[40]

If Derubigny owed his prosperity in part to royal favor, this was in turn thanks to his ability to persuade the authorities that he was a genuine innovator and worth supporting. In this sense, too, his career is paradigmatic. One finds other new men in the faubourg making the same attempt. Self-styled "entrepreneur" Pierre Barrois sought the renewal of royal letters patent in 1765, confidently asserting that the leather manufactory he ran was "unique." Of Barrois it is known only that he was churchwarden of Saint Hippolyte in 1759 and that he owned a property in the rue Saint Hippolyte, but like other local entrepreneurs he appears to have had no family or long-standing connections with the Faubourg Saint Marcel.[41]

Many similar examples can be given from other parts of the city. In the Faubourg Saint Antoine, Jean-Baptiste Réveillon was a self-made man whose success was in part due to a new division of labor in his manufactory but also in large measure to the fame he acquired in 1785 from winning the Necker gold medal. Réveillon claimed to have found the secret of English woven paper *(papier vélin)*, though one of the Didot brothers (probably François-Ambroise) and one of the Montgolfier brothers claimed that he was not the first. (The Didot brothers were no mean innovators themselves, and the Montgolfier brothers provide yet another example of successful and self-made late-eighteenth-century entrepreneurs).[42]

Réveillon's famous neighbor Antoine Joseph Santerre provides another example in a more traditional trade. A descendant of brewers through both his father and his mother, Santerre innovated in many small ways, finding a new use for processed hops and introducing new types of beer in imitation of English ones. He too fought a campaign against the heavy duties imposed on his trade.[43]

Also in a centuries-old Paris industry was the bookseller Charles-Joseph Panckoucke, who built a publishing empire on the success of the *Encyclopédie* and, later, the *Encyclopédie méthodique.* He had arrived in Paris in 1762 and, despite having "no friends, no credit" in Paris (so he later claimed), within a decade had risen to be the highest-taxed member of the prosperous booksellers' corporation. Panckoucke came from a family prominent in bookselling and printing in Lille, and married into a printing family based in Orléans. He seems to have had no help from relatives in Paris (though his mother's father had been a Paris bookseller) and owed his success partly to business acumen, partly to the protection of the police chief de Sartine.[44]

Yet another example is Christophe-Philippe Oberkampf, founder of one of the largest factories making printed-cotton cloth in Europe. He came to Paris in the early 1750s, and after 1769 built up his business with considerable skill both as a negotiator and as an advertiser. His too was a new industry, and the factory's location outside Paris at Jouy helped evade opposition from the Paris corporations.[45] Oberkampf was unusual in his skill and success, but many others in the same industry were just as much outsiders as he was. Of the first generation of cotton manufacturers in France, between 1760 and 1785, fewer than half were already employers in other industries, and a third were born outside France.[46] For new men such as these, success depended less on family connections than on individual initiative.

The same crumbling of the invisible barriers that had hitherto made access to local office in Paris difficult for outsiders facilitated the entry of a small number of bourgeois women into business. The decline of local lineages and the greater freedom of action it afforded individual households provided the potential for either increased paternal authority within the conjugal family or greater female autonomy. Of course it was quite common, in the seventeenth and throughout the eighteenth century, for widows to run successful businesses, and married women frequently kept the books of smaller family enterprises. But now the growth of businesses and the opportunities for entrepreneurs outside the trades corporations allowed a small number of women to fashion business careers that were difficult to match either in the early eighteenth or the early nineteenth centuries. Most often it was in an auxiliary capacity, at least officially.

The example of Marie-Catherine-Renée Darcel, wife of Oberkampf's business associate Sarasin de Maraise, is probably the one known best. She handled the accounts of the Jouy manufactory for twenty-two years, managing them so well that in its capital base it became the second-largest business in the entire country. But she was also, on many occasions, the public face of the company, representing it in transactions with clients and creditors, in dealings with the authorities, and in religious ceremonies. She illustrates perfectly the way that, in late-eighteenth-century Paris, a woman with the will and energy to do so could combine business and an attachment to domestic ideology. A firm believer in maternal breast-feeding and in the virtues of motherhood, she supervised the upbringing of her six surviving children. She skillfully manipulated her dual role as accountant and mistress of a bourgeois household, inviting clients and suppliers to dine, entertaining her husband's business associates, and employing female networks—such as her connection with Madame Necker. Daughter of a Rouen mercer, she was doubly an outsider: a woman and a provincial. Yet she was remarkably successful in business, thanks partly to the fact that the industry was a new one, outside corporate restrictions on women, and partly to the expansion and greater mobility within the Paris business world.[47]

Marie-Catherine Darcel was not alone. In the equally new porcelain industry, Louise Croizé was in sole charge of accounts and sales for the factory founded in 1781 by her husband, Antoine Guérhard, in partnership with Christophe Dihl. She was sufficiently influential to be consulted in 1786 over a decree concerning Paris manufacturing by the director of the *bâtiments du Roi,* d'Angivilliers.[48] Another successful businesswoman, this one single, was Madame Bertin, who made a fortune designing and creating fashion clothes for women, even supplying Marie Antoinette. She was from a humble family in Amiens and succeeded in the capital through a combination of talent and entrepreneurial skill.[49]

Most of the new men and women were keen adherents of Enlightenment and, particularly, Physiocratic ideology, elements of which had special appeal to them (the edicts of 1776 opened almost all occupations to women). Marie-Catherine Darcel combined Jansenist sympathies with a mild anticlericalism and a Rousseauist attitude toward the early education of her children. She was a friend of the popular doctors Samuel Tissot and Jacques-René Tenon, with their modern medical ideas.[50] Less cultured, yet able to cite Rousseau in one of his petitions, the tanner Derubigny was equally typical of a whole generation of entrepreneurs who emerged in France in the second half of the eighteenth century. Whereas Marie-Catherine Darcel confined her literary skills to personal letters, he was typical of males of his class and generation in his propensity for scribbling. He wrote not only in quest of *privilèges* and personal advancement, but also for the public good, about all manner of things. In his 1789 *cahier*, he not only dealt with tanning but also sought a reduction in the duty on wine entering Paris: this would help to keep workers on the job, because they would drink locally and be less tempted to abandon their work for a daylong excursion to the duty-free *guinguettes* (taverns) on the outskirts of the city. Among other recommendations, he opined that male religious orders could be rendered useful to the nation by being obliged to teach children Latin, religion, geography, arithmetic, the elements of the Paris legal system, and agriculture.[51]

A number of such *cahiers* were drawn up. Another from the Faubourg Saint Marcel was that of André Arnoult Aclocque, the brewer and churchwarden of Saint Martin. He sought freedom of the press; the suppression of venal offices; the abolition of barriers to trade within France, including taxes on raw materials; a unified system of weights and measures; and improved poor relief paid for from the revenues of the monasteries. Like Derubigny's document it is a stereotypical bourgeois *cahier*, overflowing with ideas for reform—utilitarian, humanitarian, and stressing the benefits of free trade.[52]

But such writings were not solely a result of the reformist fervor of 1789. *Mémoires* and projects were produced in large quantities throughout the second half of the eighteenth century. In 1766 one of the Auffray family, too, had produced his "Considérations sur le commerce de la tannerie," an attack on the *régie des cuirs* containing a thinly disguised request to be commissioned to prepare a report on the state of the industry.[53] What makes Auffray's document particularly interesting are its literary pretensions, which testify to his reading of Enlightenment literature. He begins with universalizing statements about the basic needs of man: life and clothing. It is the latter that distinguishes civilized man from the savage. In civilized countries, rich and poor alike require clothing, whether it be of wool, linen, or hemp, or of leather. Of these, leather is the most neglected . . . and so on to specific criticisms of the edict of 1759 and the current state of the trade. In the conclusion Auffray again betrays his literary aspirations.

> The commerce of tanning, in its present state, may be likened to a vast, arid, uncultivated field, yet one which is well situated, and which awaits only an expert hand that knows how to open its breast, to prepare it to receive the dew which alone can develop in it the juices that it holds, give it a new existence, and, so to speak, create it.

Despite the mixed metaphors, the prose suggests a man who has read and appreciated literature. Although the surviving records do not reveal what books the Auffray brothers possessed, they do include an admirable description of the five-hundred-volume library owned by Jean Auffray Jr., who was either the son or the nephew of the author of the "Considérations." It included Ovid, Horace, and Lucian, a range of religious works, an English dictionary, the *Révolutions du Portugal,* Montaigne, and a *Dictionnaire comique.* Jean Jr. also owned two thermometers, a barometer (still rare among Paris bourgeois in the 1770s), and a number of maps.[54] All of this points to a man with some general culture and certainly wide interests. This was a very different world from that of Nicolas Bouillerot, whose somewhat smaller library sixty years earlier had contained almost exclusively religious works. The change confirms the penetration of intellectual influences into the ranks of merchant tanners, even in the Faubourg Saint Marcel, where, if Louis-Sébastien Mercier can be believed, they were least to be expected.

Under the benevolent despotism of the Paris lieutenants general of police de Sartine and Jean Charles Lenoir, the government was deluged with *mémoires* like those of Auffray and Derubigny.[55] Invention was the spirit of the age. Some innovations were indisputably genuine, such as Pierre-Simon Malisset's economic milling, Solignac's machine for kneading bread, and Derubigny's waterproofing. Oberkampf perfected a new way of engraving copper cylinders used in textile printing, then a washing machine in 1795, and in 1808 a green dye, the secret of which had been sought for some years.[56] Many other "inventions," of course, turned out to be fraudulent, like the medical treatments that ranged from ointments to cure baldness to Mesmer's devices for putting "animal magnetism" to worthy use. Some innovations proved to be products less of mechanical genius than of talented advertising. Réveillon's commercial success, partly based on his ability to supply good wallpapers at low prices, owed even more to his extraordinary talent for publicity.[57]

Of course, there had been inventive entrepreneurs before: in the Faubourg Saint Marcel the name Gobelin springs to mind. And Jean Glucq, who came from Amsterdam in 1667 and who in the 1680s obtained the name "manufacture royale" for his establishment.[58] Men like these had succeeded outside the corporate system, with royal support. The difference was that in the second half of the eighteenth century many more such people appeared and some of them were gaining access to the honors and the institutions of political life in Paris.

Yet, ironically, even as new men and women were beginning to enter the grass-roots political institutions of the Old Regime, profound social and economic changes were reducing the role and influence of the parishes and of the trades corporations. After the total suppression of the Jesuits in 1764, the bitter controversies of the first half of the century, which had continued through the 1750s with the refusals of sacraments, now subsided. Gallican liberties apparently safe, the Parlements turned to issues that, if in other ways similar to those that had provoked constitutional crises during Louis XV's reign, had no religious implications. The storms within the parishes calmed as pastors and flocks were no longer divided by burning religious and political differences. Even at Saint Médard, Hardy de Levaré was able to return in 1771 to spend his last years at peace with his parishioners and with his conscience. The *procureur général* of the Paris Parlement, the man responsible for parish affairs in the capital, was able to close many of his files, no doubt with relief, and devote his time to what were now more pressing secular matters.

The change is reflected in the apparent unconcern with which some parishes saw the numbers of churchwardens reduced in the 1780s. This happened at Saint Médard, following the scandal caused by the bankruptcy and disappearance in 1780 of the churchwarden in charge, with some 500 livres owing to the parish. The Parlement ordered that henceforth, in order to prevent the second churchwarden from possibly being held legally liable for the actions of the first, only one new churchwarden would be elected each year. At Saint Laurent the same reduction had taken place in 1757, following a nine-year dispute between the vestry and the two leading confraternities. A different sort of attack was the complete abolition of five parishes on the Ile de la Cité.[59] These examples illustrate an official spirit of innovation that disregarded ancient loyalties; and the apparent lack of opposition reinforces the impression that the affluent Parisians whose views constituted "public opinion" no longer set great store by parish boundaries or clung to the vestries as an indispensable part of local life.

The confraternities declined even more markedly. This was partly because of an official campaign against certain devotional organizations that were seen as little more than dining clubs. In 1760 the Parlement ordered that all the confraternities in the churches of the diocese must provide proof of their legal status in the form of royal, papal, or episcopal approval and properly drawn-up statutes. Needless to say, a great many confraternities were unable to produce these documents. Not all were abolished as a result, but some did disappear immediately.[60]

But the confraternities were also under attack from other quarters. Very often it was the vestries that wanted to be rid of them: to liberate a chapel or, as in the case of the confraternity of the Sacré Coeur at Sainte Madelaine en la Cité, because it was "very onerous to the vestry because of the expenses it incurred."[61] Financial instability also killed a number of confraternities. Even the principal one at Saint Martin du Cloître, the Saint Sacrement, ran into trouble in 1751, as had the confraternity of Saint Nicolas and Saint Fiacre two years earlier. At Saint Laurent the confraternity of Sainte Anne disappeared in 1756 owing a considerable debt to the vestry.[62]

One of the reasons for financial difficulties was probably declining membership. Many confraternities established during the wave of religious enthusiasm of the seventeenth century found themselves high and dry once the tide receded. The one in the church at Les Porcherons found the takings in its collection box declining throughout the middle years of the century, despite a considerable increase in the population of the quarter.[63]

In addition, the honor of election as an administrator was frequently insufficient to balance the cost in time and money, especially in the humbler confraternities, which came well back in processions and might be limited to one day of glory per year, on the feast of their patron. Even this was not safe, as the reorganization of the religious calendar during the eighteenth century amply demonstrated: several saints' days were struck off—an unfortunate thing to happen to one's patron! Many confraternities therefore collapsed because administrators could not be found.[64] In 1743 the vestry of Saint Jacques de la Boucherie bemoaned "the impossibility of finding notables willing to accept the task of administering the confraternity [of Saint Charles Boromé]."[65] By 1786 the problem was so severe that the Parlement saw fit to issue an exemplary condemnation of men who had refused to accept their election as administrators of the prestigious confraternities of the Saint Sacrement at Saint Etienne du Mont, Saint Sulpice, and Saint Roch.[66]

For a mix of reasons, then, the confraternities declined to varying degrees in all the Paris parishes, as they did elsewhere. At Saint Médard the number fell only from four to three during the eighteenth century, but at Saint Laurent it went from at least twelve down to three that appear to have survived until the Revolution. At Saint Gervais ten existed at the beginning of the century, of which six seem to have lasted.[67]

It was not just as political institutions that the parishes were declining. I have already referred to the ever-diminishing percentage of affluent Parisians requesting to be buried in their parish. Reformers launched a long campaign against the health hazard of burials in crowded town centers, prompting a vigorous debate in which Paris churchwardens were frequently on the side of conservatism, yet in which an increasing weight of enlightened opinion supported change. Eventually a royal edict of 1776 forbade burial in the churches, and by the 1780s few opposed the complete transfer of inhumations (and the physical transfer of bones and bodies from the infamous Holy Innocents cemetery) to new sites right outside the city.[68]

In France as a whole in the second half of the eighteenth century, fewer requiem masses were being requested, fewer men were entering the priesthood, and fewer people were being recruited into religious orders. Evidence shows a relative decline in the numbers of religious books. Another reflection of the declining social role of the churches was the gradual disappearance of private pews, from the middle of the eighteenth century onward.[69] This is consistent with the movement of the notable families who until then had occupied them. The dispersal of the local bourgeois lineages meant that the parish was no longer a central component of their family identity.

Nevertheless, the decline of the parishes in local politics was not total. Disputes over precedence continued, both within the vestries and between them and the confraternities—an indication that the honor they conferred remained significant in local terms. Conflicts over control of the parish continued to set the clergy and the churchwardens at loggerheads. And there were still occasions when the vestries represented their quarter in dealings with external authorities. In 1780 the vestry of Sainte Marguerite, unable to prevent the transfer of the hospital for the blind (the Quinze Vingts) to its jurisdiction, nevertheless made two claims. One was on their own account, for the loss of revenue to the parish that would result from the opening of a new church in the hospital. But they also, on behalf of "the inhabitants of the Faubourg, whose taxes paid for the site and the buildings," made "every possible remonstrance and protest against the alienation of the site and of the buildings . . . in support of a demand for exemption from the tax for the billeting of soldiers which the said bourgeois, notables, and inhabitants have earned by the payments they have made."[70]

Here we see the vestry acting in defense of local interests, not just parish ones. In a case like this, there was no other body that could represent the local population. Later, in the crisis of July 1789, many citizens again turned to their parishes—though not to the vestries. At the district meeting at Saint Séverin on 13 July, only parishioners were admitted, while at Saint Germain le Vieil, Saint Pierre des Arcis, Sainte Croix-en-la-Cité, and other parishes the churches provided the venue for meetings that organized a citizen militia, even though they were not used for district meetings.[71] While they aroused less enthusiasm than fifty years before, the parishes thus remained at the heart of local political life, for a certain sector of the population at least, and were able to respond to new types of issues. The position of churchwarden remained an essential addition to the curriculum vitae of any man aspiring to local leadership.

The vestries, nevertheless, were not always the only arenas for local politics. In the Faubourg Saint Marcel, the Bièvre administration was another, but unlike the parishes it retained all its vigor. This is clear from the leadership it provided in the campaign against a proposal to divert part of the Bièvre's flow and pipe it to Paris to provide drinking water. From 1787 to 1789 the Bièvre syndics campaigned vigorously against the plan, taking their case first to the Forests and Waters administration, subsequently to the Parlement, and finally to the King's Council. Early in 1789 sixty-one river users put their names to a fifty-six page printed pamphlet setting out their case. They eventually won, though this may have been thanks to the Revolution.[72]

The internal organization of the Bièvre administration seems to have remained unchanged after about 1720, but its structure was always less exclusive than that of the vestries. Within the limits imposed by the obligation to choose the syndics from the tanning, leather-dressing, and dyeing trades, newcomers were readily admitted to the job. One finds the tanner Marin Derenusson and the dyer Etienne Cayrol, both relative newcomers to the quarter, becoming syndics in 1774, and Derubigny, too, seems to have done a stint as administrator.[73] An openness to new men, together with the importance of the river to industry, ensured that the Bièvre administration retained its vitality.

The trades corporations, on the other hand, like the parishes, became less able to influence the government and probably less significant in the lives of Parisians. The development of dynamic new industries not covered by the corporations reduced their role in the economic life of the capital. The growth of rural industries further weakened their hold.[74] But the government was also responsible. Jean Antoine Chaptal was later to state that on the eve of the Revolution it was not the corporations but the *inspecteurs des manufactures,* the government-appointed inspectors, who played the dominant role in industrial organization.[75] This is an exaggeration as far as Paris is concerned, yet in tanning the *régie des cuirs* and in brewing the Ferme Générale dominated the industry, making rules, inspecting, and controlling the manufacturing process. *Régies* were now the favored way of organizing new enterprises: the postal service, for example.

The government had also done much to undermine the corporations through the creation of *manufactures royales,* which were exempt from certain corporate rules. The granting of royal *privilèges* and of *brevets* (exemptions accorded by the crown) allowed many individuals to bypass the corporations. In the Faubourg Saint Marcel, the prosperous tanner Derenusson had never qualified as a master but was permitted to process hides because he had a *brevet.* When Réveillon was challenged by the engravers and other corporations that until then had had a monopoly on wallpaper, he got around their opposition partly thanks to the protection of the lieutenant general of police and partly by buying into their ranks.[76]

The government's motivation in such cases had less to do with encouraging industry than with raising money. Of course, this was one of the key reasons why the trades corporations had been established. They not only had played a central role in collecting taxes on behalf of the crown but also had been ruthlessly milked of their savings, as in the final years of Louis XIV's reign, when new offices were repeatedly created and sold back to corporations anxious to retain their autonomy. Now the monarchy found it could raise money by creating new structures, and the government was not concerned by the threat these posed to the privileges, autonomy, and political role of the trades corporations.

Thus, in the second half of the eighteenth century, a very complex conjunction of changes was affecting not only the composition of the limited number of political institutions in which bourgeois Parisians could participate but also the very role of such institutions in the power structure of the city. Merchant capitalism thrived and the consumer boom gathered pace, increasing the general prosperity of half the city's population and at the same time providing openings for bold spirits with a flair for business. A greater optimism was abroad, linked both with economic improvement and with the diffusion of Enlightenment thought. This in turn was accompanied by a more secular spirit, a shift from religious to secular issues in politics.

As new blood was flowing in, the dominant institutions of local political life were declining. There were fewer vestries, fewer confraternities, and fewer trades corporations—and hence, far fewer offices available at a time when, thanks to the commercial expansion of the eighteenth century, the number of well-to-do bourgeois families in the city was growing. And those offices that did exist in the parishes and in the trades were less influential, both locally and with the government. Although some of their functions were taken over by other bodies, none of these allowed the commercial middle classes the influence they had earlier been able to wield through local and trade-based corporate institutions.

Certainly, those families—and they were numerous—whose commercial success or profitable marriage alliances provided connections with the ranks of the venal-office holders and government officials might by that means possess limited behind-the-scenes influence. They, together with others who worked in the centralized tax farms and *régies,* might be able to exercise powers of patronage. But those unable to form such connections were potentially alienated from the new power structure. The mass of the commercial middle classes now had even less place in the honorific and political structure of Paris society than similar people had enjoyed at the height of absolute monarchy under Louis XIV. On the eve of the Revolution, there were probably fewer opportunities for formal political participation by the local notables than at any time in the preceding three hundred years.

Not that local notables or the commercial middle classes formed in any sense a uniform group. They were divided by considerable differences of wealth and status, and in some cases by occupational and provincial loyalties, while local ties remained significant for others. Yet they were in a sense united by their common exclusion. Whether members of corporations whose position was being eroded by government agencies, or outsiders who had struggled against entrenched privileges—and Derubigny and Aclocque fall into both categories—they were likely to identify with and respond sympathetically to criticism of "tyranny." The development of a public opinion critical of the government at the end of the Old Regime may therefore have been, at least in Paris, a reflection of disenfranchisement as much as of growing bourgeois power.

Derubigny, deluging the administration with petitions and paying to have his pamphlets printed and distributed, exemplifies the new public and the new relationship between government and local elite. The ideology of equality before the law and before government, the belief in rewards based on merit and talent, not on birth, appealed to outsiders in a wide range of ranks—not just bourgeois—who possessed considerable social and economic power but lacked accompanying political influence even at the local level. For them, "privilege" meant the government-protected *régies* like the Ferme Générale, or the *chambres syndicales*—the governing bodies of the publishing industry—which Panckoucke attacked in a pamphlet of 1790 as "petits corps aristocratiques, despotiques."[77] It meant the old dynasties and the old habits that were in decline but that might still make it difficult for new arrivals to gain access to positions of profit, honor, and power. The political crisis of the Old Regime, in which these issues were central, thus did have profound social and economic roots (if not those of classic Marxist analysis) as well as financial and political ones. Far-reaching change of some sort was inevitable. That it took the form of Revolution was largely a consequence of the particular circumstances of 1789.

The commercial middle classes had much to gain from political and social change. If the "tyranny" of government agencies were removed, then they would be free to develop their commercial and political potential. Yet those who had labored to win government support for their new techniques or products had no wish to see their own privileges disappear. In the political sphere, what was later to be called "representative government" would be very much to their advantage, but participatory democracy had few attractions. Revolution offered both opportunity and danger, therefore. In either case, the local elite could not remain indifferent: their public position required them to take a stand. They responded not as a group but individually, in a variety of ways. Some supported the Revolution initially but later turned against it, in some cases re-emerging after the tempest had passed. A small number remained in the storm's eye throughout, adroitly riding the swift tides of the revolutionary years. None, however, remained unaffected.

PART

REVOLUTION

THE REVOLUTION IN LOCAL POLITICS

*[The working men] will tell you frankly that they have
not the necessary knowledge for employment in the
administration of the common weal*
(la chose publique).

—*Manifesto of the Arsenal Section, 13 December 1792*

The French Revolution transformed totally the character of local politics in the French capital. It established new institutions and new rules by which elections, meetings, and local administration were to be guided. It also drastically extended the political sphere to include men and women who had previously had no place—not, at least, in any formal sense. The criteria for participation were spelled out in legislation, and they were radically different from those, largely unspoken but generally observed, that had reigned for most of the eighteenth century. And the Revolution introduced a new way of thinking about politics. In the process, it was to have a considerable influence on the composition and the ideology of the Parisian bourgeoisie.

One can distinguish three phases in local politics between 1789 and 1794, each of which brought different groups into public life. Each phase was based on slightly different principles. The first was the era of what might be termed "outsider notables," when office and power rested in the hands of men who, while members of the Old Regime bourgeoisie, had for the most part not been active in public life before. The second phase was that of the professional politicians, men whose position depended less on their wealth, occupation, or local ties than on their ability to persuade the electorate of their ability and their patriotism. The third phase was that of the government servants. As the Terror was constructed, elected local officials were increasingly subject to surveillance and control by external authorities, and in the end the local political process was totally subverted. The qualities required of officeholders had become administrative ability, loyalty, and obedience to central government.

The first two of these phases were products of ideology and of the new structures that resulted—of the shift in "political culture" that has been the subject of much recent historical research.[1] In local politics, two broad and very significant principles of Old Regime thinking were rejected by the Revolution from the outset: respect for precedent and a corporate approach to social and political organization. Before 1789, the more well established a practice, the stronger the argument for retaining it. Lawyers and writers on jurisprudence devoted acres of text to proving that the particular practice or rights they were defending could be traced back to a distant past—the further back, the better. Antiquity was a source of legitimacy and, as the Parlements were quick to realize in their long-running battle with the monarchy, perhaps the only one that could be used successfully to counter the claims of the crown.

The same principle dictated respect for seniority. The *anciens* were the guardians of tradition, as the curé of Saint Médard obviously believed when in 1755 he wrote, in the course of the dispute over the funeral service for the dismissed parish priest Pommart, that "if there had been an established practice of this sort, the six *anciens* would have known of it and would have required it to be followed."[2] His opponents, for their part, wheeled in the oldest member of the confraternity of Notre Dame de Charité to testify that both the vestry and the confraternity had held a service for Pommart's predecessor.[3] All sorts of honorific privileges were attached to being the doyen—the longest-serving member of any body. In the case of the vestries and of many similar institutions, it conferred a place well to the fore in processions and ceremonies. The doyen had the power to call and preside at meetings, and to speak first. In the trades corporations of eighteenth-century Paris, until 1775, the longest-established masters had greater representation in assemblies than more recent arrivals. The office of *juré*, like that of churchwarden, was in practice reserved for older people; positions in the vestries usually were held for those in their forties and fifties. Much the same was true of any corporate body in Old Regime France: in every area of public life, seniority—and the underlying principle of age and experience—bestowed privilege and power.

Equally fundamental to Old Regime political culture was a corporate mentality. Society was imagined as both organic and cellular. Everyone belonged, or should belong, to one or more collegiate bodies, be they professional, occupational, religious, or honorific. The parish vestries and the confraternities, the trades corporations, religious congregations, town councils, and the associations formed by those holding the same office (from the porters in the Paris grain market to the high-ranking *maîtres des requêtes*) are all examples of the sometimes overlapping and often conflicting corporate institutions that composed the body social and the body politic of the Old Regime. There was no sense of an undifferentiated mass of more or less equal individual citizens making up the nation. Rather, the kingdom was composed of a host of bodies, of corporations, and it was only as members of such institutions that individuals enjoyed civic, pecuniary, and honorific rights. Corporate status allowed journeymen artisans the right to plead in court, even against their employers—a privilege denied to domestic servants who had no corporate standing.[4] Even women, who in law had no right to hold office or to engage in legal proceedings, could do so if they belonged to a trade corporation or if they were acting on behalf of a religious community.[5] The whole notion of privilege, central to prerevolutionary political culture, depended on this image of society.

The Revolution rejected this organic image of society. The only cells remaining, in this sort of society, were family or household ones, for it was a first premise of most revolutionary lawmakers that women and those with a similar dependent status—like servants and, for some legislators, journeymen and other employees—could not be citizens. In the place of a kingdom composed of corporate institutions, broadly organized into a hierarchy and each with its own privileges, the revolutionary constitution-makers espoused a vision of a nation made up of property-owning male citizens each of whom possessed the same civic rights (men without property were not deemed to be citizens). These individuals, collectively, were considered to be the sole source of legitimacy and power: in other words, they possessed sovereignty. Antiquity and seniority no longer had any legitimizing value.[6]

The legislators further believed that French citizens, guided by reason, would inevitably reach agreement on all important issues, once freed from the institutions of the past. This, indeed, was one of the motives for destroying corporations, for any sort of special interest group was deemed a threat to the revolutionary consensus. The family, however, did not constitute this sort of threat because the interests of women and of children and other dependents were felt in most things to be identical with those of the household head.

The concept and practice of politics that resulted from this new image of society were necessarily very different from the old system. There could be no legal distinctions between citizens, or special privileges, and all should have an equal say in the government of the nation. The practical impossibility of the whole mass of citizens governing themselves directly made a system of representation necessary. If sovereignty was to be retained by individual citizens, however, public office had to be of fixed tenure and revocable. Hence, politics was no longer fought out within and between corporate institutions. Gone were the legally organized interest groups within which an individual seeking power, either through personal ambition or to achieve the implementation of some policy, had formerly been obliged to work. Gone, therefore, were the long court battles through which rival bodies had sought precedence. The new politics took two forms: parliamentary and electoral politics. It was fought out on the one hand between individuals and groups within representative institutions and between those institutions, and on the other hand between individuals seeking election by a relatively large number of citizens.

The implications of this for local politics were dramatic. The vestries, the confraternities, and the corporations, the institutions within and through which the struggle for power and the defense of local interests had been waged, were now replaced by a series of elected institutions: the district and later the sectional committees; the justices of the peace *(juges de paix)* and the *commissaires de police;* the officers of the National Guard; and, at a higher level, the succession of municipal and departmental assemblies. Election to office was no longer by a small and self-selected group of *anciens*. The numbers of voters were usually much larger—the potential numbers greater still, for participation rates were never high.[7] The political class, if those holding office can be so called, was no longer self-perpetuating. It was much more difficult, therefore, for one occupational group, one family, or one clique to dominate, at least in theory.

With the Revolution, furthermore, came important changes to the formal criteria that a candidate had to meet. Not in every respect, of course: the principle of independence dear to the Old Regime was retained, so that servants, minors, and women were not eligible to vote or to run for election. Nevertheless, for most males the way that independence was now assessed was different. Formerly the essential criterion had been that subtle and hard-to-define quality of being "established." This was now replaced with the easily quantifiable measure of the amount of tax paid. It is true that wealth had always been an important prerequisite for election to office, even in the Faubourg Saint Marcel. But now a particular sum was specified: initially a tax assessment to the value of three days' labor to become a voter, and ten in order to become an elector in the second stage of elections.

These new principles were a response to profound changes in French society over the preceding decades, and this is why they gained immediate acceptance in Paris. I have described the effects of these changes in the Faubourg Saint Marcel, notably the decline of the old lineages, with a concomitant loss of attachment to the parish and reduced respect for long-established practice. By 1789 the most dynamic section of the local elite was composed of men and women who had come to Paris in the middle decades of the century, sometimes with their parents and sometimes alone, often from humble origins.[8]

It was primarily men from this elite, energetic and determined, who stepped forward in the crisis of July 1789. A former *procureur,* Antoine-Joseph Thorillon, and the wealthy brewer André Arnoult Aclocque were the most active—Thorillon a recent arrival, Aclocque second generation. Of the first District Committee as a whole, over half almost certainly had no kin ties in the quarter and only a third of the members belonged to long-established local families. To anyone familiar with the locality under the Old Regime, two other things stand out about the members of this first District Committee. One is the absence of family ties between the members; there was possibly a marriage connection between two of them, but that is all I have been able to find. The other conspicuously new thing is the presence of occupations that were not found in the vestries before 1789: three schoolteachers, a writer, and a *feudiste* (an expert in seigneurial dues).[9] They included the two men who, of all the representatives of the Faubourg Saint Marcel, were to play the most prominent role in the Revolution: Bourdon de la Crosnière and Bernardin de Saint-Pierre, neither of whom was to remain in the area for long.

The committee of 1790 differed little from that of 1789. Twelve of its members had served the year before. Of the fourteen whose places of birth are known, five belonged to families who had been in the area since the beginning of the century, and another four—once again, among the most active—had arrived or were sons of men who had arrived in the quarter in the 1740s and 1750s. The other five had come in the 1780s. Eleven were linked by birth or marriage to other local families. This confirms Richard Andrews's observation of the central role that successful immigrants played in local revolutionary politics.[10]

The kin ties within the 1790 committee were more extensive than in 1789: two of Aclocque's relatives (his cousin and a kinsman of his wife) had been elected; and there were now two father-and-son teams. But such ties were insignificant compared with the web of relationships that had existed in the vestries of the quarter. And far fewer of the committee members were major property owners—only six of the twenty-five can be traced in the property records of Saint Marcel and Sainte Geneviève, though there may have been others who had recently bought houses there.

It is striking that few of the men elected in 1789 and 1790 had been churchwardens. Of the thirty lay members of the first committee, only Aclocque, Pierre Cozette (one of the three "entrepreneurs" who ran the tapestry workshops at the Gobelins), and five or six others had served one of the local parishes, while another six belonged to families that had provided a churchwarden at some time during the eighteenth century. In the committee of 1790, four or perhaps five had been churchwardens. Although the parish vestries remained in place and continued to elect new members until 1791, they were now of no political significance. Their subordination to the district was already made clear late in 1790 when the General Assembly at Saint Marcel decreed that it would no longer send representatives to elections of churchwardens but would require the election to be held in a meeting of the district.[11]

The only occasion, after 1789, when the vestry of Saint Médard raised its voice was in July 1792 when the Commune ordered the removal of the church bells. Its members signed and distributed a formal protest, an action later to put many of them into prison, suspected of counterrevolutionary sentiments. At the time, though, they were swept aside, their protest hardly noticed.[12] Already of decreasing significance in the years immediately preceding the Revolution, after 1789 the vestries ceased to have any mobilizing power at all. Furthermore, the fact that so few of their members made the leap from the old institutions to the new indicates that the Revolution swept away not only the old system of local politics but, at the same time, the vast majority of those who had occupied local public office under the Old Regime.

The Revolution had much to offer the newcomers who now entered local political life. If they were in poorly regarded occupations, with few prospects, or if they were newcomers with the barriers of privilege to climb, or even if they were successful but still faced the condescension of the Paris bourgeois toward parvenus, they had no reason to defend the Old Regime. If they were locked in battle with the corporations, or if their entrepreneurial efforts were hindered by government-bestowed privileges or monopolies, the disappearance of the old institutions and the victory of free-market principles operated in their favor. Some of them ardently advocated such reforms: Aclocque, scion of a brewing dynasty but one not established in the Faubourg Saint Marcel for very long, wrote a personal *cahier* in 1789 in which he urged the abolition of all internal customs barriers and duties and of "all the hindrances to trade."[13] Jean Antoine Derubigny, who for years had been fighting the authority set up by the royal edict of 1759 to regulate the leather trade, seized the opportunity to attack this edict in his personal submission to the Estates General. A similar if less vehement attack was included in the *cahier* of the Saint Marcel district, which Derubigny helped to compose.

To such men, the abolition of the Old Regime meant the removal of taxes, of inspections by government officials, of what they saw as corruption in public life—things they had found a hindrance in their own successful careers.[14] The Revolution promised new opportunities for men of talent and enterprise, not only in the economic field but also in government and administration. The barriers—however permeable—that the Old Regime had placed in the path of up-and-coming men, outsiders with wealth but often of modest origins, were to be swept away.

When they had the opportunity, therefore, in the municipal revolution of July 1789 when power was seized by the local notables, these were precisely the principles they put into practice. Spontaneously, long before the National Assembly got around to drafting its law on municipal government, they rejected the notion of the *anciens* selecting their successors. Instead, they opted for limited democracy, opening local office to all men of property. As the National Assembly was later to insist, independence was essential—no women, servants, employees, or men without means were elected to the district committees. Local residence was also a prerequisite, but those chosen had not necessarily been in the area for a long time and did not need to belong to established local families. The idea of limited terms of office was warmly embraced, the committee stating in September 1789 that "it is right for all citizens in turn to participate in the administration of the Commune."[15] Reelection was nevertheless permitted. Election was now to be based above all on property, on willingness to serve the nation, and upon personal qualities of leadership and capacity that had been demonstrated in the recent crisis: on principles dear to the bourgeois notables of Paris.

In practice, of course, the very success of the new men who swept all before them in mid-1789 was an indication that major changes were already under way. The political principles they put into practice, and which the National Assembly was soon to endorse, had begun to be applied, paradoxically, by the Old Regime itself. It was for the elections to the Estates General in early 1789 that the tax qualification and the age, nationality, and residence requirements were introduced. But the tax qualification and the two-tier electoral system had been in use in the trades corporations since 1776. Only those masters paying the highest tax could vote, and they did so in primary electoral assemblies that selected deputies who in turn chose the *jurés*.[16] This new system, like the later revolutionary changes, enlarged the electoral base and made it more difficult for trade dynasties and oligarchs to dominate the corporations. They could continue in office only by dint of constant reelection and no longer by virtue of a single ballot within a small assembly. By abolishing the assembly of *anciens,* the reformers of August 1776 (most prominent among them the former lieutenant general de Sartine—himself an immigrant, a successful outsider)[17] were already turning their backs on the Old Regime respect for seniority and experience.

The arrangements for the elections to the Estates General thus had a significant precedent in the post-1776 structure of the Paris trades. The changes made in both 1776 and 1788–1789 demonstrated that the old system of local politics was already moribund. They reflected changes of thinking at the top, but these were in part a reflection of very significant social changes within Parisian society.

The Revolution reinforced the new principles that had been introduced in 1789 and applied them consistently. Among the formal conditions for office included in the law of 1790 were affluence (in the form of a property qualification), independence, French citizenship, residence in the electoral district for at least a year, and adulthood, deemed to be twenty-five years of age. The law also explicitly outlawed close family relationships within local government institutions: fathers and sons, fathers-in-law and sons-in-law, uncles and nephews henceforth could not serve together.[18] The Old Regime had seen nothing wrong in close family ties within vestries and other bodies; on the contrary, a good family name was a guarantee of respectability. After 1790, however, the hold the Bouillerot clan had had on the vestry of Saint Médard would have been both illegal and, in Paris at least, impossible.

A further change that helped set a term to the old oligarchies, if any had survived until the Revolution, was the reorganization of local jurisdictions, a logical consequence of the belief in equality of rights across the nation. For it followed that if all citizens were to be equal, then electoral circumscriptions should be as nearly equivalent as possible, or at least that the ratio between the number of voters and the number of elected representatives should be as uniform as was feasible. Hence, the boundaries of the Paris sections were drawn carefully with an eye to enclosing a roughly equivalent population within each one. Even the sixty districts had been a step in this direction, for uneven as they were, they were far closer in size and population than the old parishes.

As a result, the basic units of local political life were redefined. Streets that had not belonged to the parish were included in the electoral district, while others that had been part of the parish were now excluded. The networks of local notables within each parish were thereby disrupted. The district of Saint Marcel included a large part of each of the three parishes of Saint Médard, Saint Martin, and Saint Hippolyte, all of which had had their own dynasties and ruling families. After 1790 the sectional boundaries in turn divided the district, combining most of Saint Martin and Saint Hippolyte *intra muros* with part of Saint Médard to form the Gobelins Section. But other parts of Saint Médard went into the Observatoire and Jardin des Plantes Sections, while part of Saint Hippolyte (and most of Saint Jacques du Haut Pas) also joined the Observatoire Section.

The new church organization, admittedly of short duration and little political significance, combined two of the former parishes into one and redrew the boundaries of all three. Former vestrymen and notables of Saint Hippolyte living on the north side of the rue de l'Oursine now found themselves in the Observatoire Section, while their erstwhile companions were in the Gobelins Section. The tanners of Saint Médard found themselves cheek by jowl with the dyers and starch makers of Saint Hippolyte and Saint Martin, while other churchwardens of Saint Médard

Approximate addresses of the members of the Saint Marcel District Committee, 1789–
1790. The map reflects the integration of the three elites of the Faubourg Saint Marcel:
the tanners along the Bièvre; the clergy and notables of Saint Martin, around the
cloister of Saint Marcel; and the elite of Saint Hippolyte, centered particularly around
the Gobelins manufactory.

joined the blanket makers of the rue Saint Victor and professors from the Jardin des Plantes. A formidable mixing of the local notables of Paris had begun.

These changes, which disrupted any parish oligarchies that had survived into 1790, had other unintended consequences, too. They risked depriving parish leaders of their notability, since a family known to everyone in one parish might be foreigners in the neighboring one. The male householder would therefore not enjoy the certainty of recognition and, perhaps, election. At best, he would now be competing for office with notables from other parishes. This had a leveling influence, forcing voters to assess a man on his words or on hearsay rather than on personal knowledge of his family and reputation. It thus provided an entry for outsiders: for men who thanks to their impressive rhetoric at assemblies could attract support; or quite simply for those whose "notable" qualities were evident but who were not sufficiently well established in a particular parish to win election as churchwardens.

It certainly favored men who for professional reasons were well known across the whole area of the new electoral division. The various legal officers—notaries, *procureurs*, and probably *avocats*—were often figures of wide reputation, with a clientele concentrated in several neighboring parishes.[19] Priests too were widely known figures, principally within the one parish, but those skilled in preaching were frequently invited to other churches on major feast days. The importance of such sermons in political life has been almost universally overlooked. The abbé Claude Fauchet, for example, who was to shine during the Revolution, had already quite a reputation as a preacher.[20] *Avocats,* like priests and, to a lesser extent, schoolteachers, were often practiced public speakers, and this was a considerable help in the new electoral conditions. The effects of such natural advantages were already visible in the elections of April 1789, when 42 percent of the men elected in Paris were lawyers and another 3 percent members of various academies.[21] They were clear, too, in the district committee of Saint Marcel, where priests and schoolteachers, the writer Bernardin de Saint-Pierre, and other talented outsiders played a key role.

Other unforeseen consequences of the new principles that now applied to public life—some of them less palatable to the men of 1789—were to follow. One was far greater access to office for younger men, who were often more ambitious and radical. The rejection of precedent and of seniority, and the opening of the way to talent rather than solely to those with the right connections, made this possible, although it did not happen immediately. The change is only just perceptible in the average ages of revolutionary officials: in the Saint Marcel district committees of 1789 and 1790, the averages were forty-eight and forty-six, a little higher than for the churchwardens. Among the committee members and electors of the Gobelins/Finistère Section from August 1792 to June 1793, the average age was forty-three, and in the Year II (1793–1794) it was forty-three for the Revolutionary Committee and forty for the Civil Committee. It might have fallen further had the war not brought compulsory military service for younger men.[22] The same general evolution is visible in the three sections of the Faubourg Saint Antoine, where the electors of 1790 had an average age of forty-six, but three-quarters of the Revolutionary Committee members were under forty-five and a third were under thirty-five.[23] The same thing happened in both citywide and national politics. Although opinions vary about the age distribution in the Legislative Assembly, the average age in the Convention was lower.[24]

The change is more marked, however, if one considers the range of ages of revolutionary officials. Whereas the prerevolutionary churchwardens were almost all in their forties or fifties when elected, after 1789 the proportion of younger men grew steadily. Of the 1789 committee of the Saint Marcel District, 17 percent of those whose ages are known were under forty. The figure crept to 30 percent in 1790, then to 40 percent of the electors and committee members of 1792–1793 and 38 percent of the committee members of the Year II. In this quarter very few men in their twenties were elected at any stage of the revolutionary experiment, but quite a number were in their early thirties. In the Faubourg Saint Antoine, however, four members of the revolutionary committees were in their early twenties. Again, in city and national politics the picture was similar: the percentage of Paris electors under thirty-five doubled between 1791 and 1792.[25] Age and experience were no longer held to be nearly so important in candidates for office.

It is true that in the revolutionary assemblies it was still the oldest men who presided while a ballot for officeholders was held. An attempt was also made to celebrate old age in a number of the revolutionary festivals. In this respect the Revolution was heir to the growing emphasis in eighteenth-century literature and theater on respect for old age, on the need for filial piety, and on the virtues of wisdom and dignity that the old were now seen to embody.[26] But the new emphasis on respect was shadowed by a view of the old as weak and to be pitied. Institutions—old people's homes—began to be created for them, replacing the religious institutions that had formerly provided some assistance to the infirm poor but in the process making them a category to be removed from everyday life, along with the insane. In every area of revolutionary practice, despite the rhetoric, age lost its aura.

As in political life, where there were no longer automatic advantages for seniority, in family legislation the Revolution brought the young greater freedom from parental control. The law of 17 Nivôse Year II (6 January 1794) that introduced equal inheritance was to deprive testators of most control over their estates. This had no effect in Paris, where equal inheritance already applied, but the earlier law of August 1792 did: it prohibited entailment, the disqualification of an immediate heir in favor of his or her successors, thereby weakening the influence that propertied parents had been able to exercise. The Convention also abolished paternal control over children who had attained majority, which was now reduced, like the voting age, to twenty-one.[27] Although the ideological justification for these measures was the destruction of paternal tyranny, the new laws amounted to a rejection of the idea of a patrimony that must be protected and passed on across generations: each generation was free to use its inheritance as it saw fit.

The abolition of venal office also assisted this trend. Under the Old Regime a great many of the offices that conferred influence in public affairs—in the administration or in the courts—were private property, and could therefore be inherited. In sensitive positions, the crown often chose the new incumbent and forced the heirs to sell, but most offices were not in this category. Thus a man was able to provide his children with a lucrative inheritance—very few offices lost value during the eighteenth century—and with a position that provided status and perhaps influence. In replacing venal office with elected office, the Revolution, as Margaret Darrow has remarked, obliged each generation to win public office (and the prestige accompanying it) anew. Here too the role of elders was undermined.[28]

It is tempting to see in these developments an indirect consequence of the demographic changes of the second half of the eighteenth century. With the increase in population and the decline in mortality from the 1740s onward, the rising generation was more numerous than its predecessors.[29] The tide of migration to Paris and the growing importance of many new individuals and families in the local economy and in local affairs was already a reflection of this pressure of population. The Revolution consolidated a turnover of generations that was already under way, flinging open doors that were previously only ajar.

But it was not only younger men who found access to public life easier during the Revolution. It was also those who did not have family connections to assist them. The image of the nation as a collection of individual citizens, replacing the notion of a kingdom composed of corporations, naturally placed the emphasis on individual responsibility. The outlawing of close family ties within municipalities was an indirect consequence of this approach, in practice further undermining a concept of notability and a system of local politics within which extended kin ties had been of vital importance. Not only were close family ties between members of a committee now illegal, but the larger numbers of voters made it impossible for a united group of *anciens* to ensure the election of younger relatives.

Other revolutionary changes apparently unconnected with political life further disenfranchised kin networks. The abolition of venal office, which meant that existing officeholders could no longer pass on their positions to their heirs, put individuals whose families had not previously played any political role on a more equal footing with the sons and nephews of those already in office. The new inheritance rules reduced the rights of nephews and cousins by allowing a couple without children to leave as much of their property to each other as they wished. The Revolution was consistent in espousing a narrow view of the family: the political and legal system no longer favored lineages but, rather, smaller family units and individual heads of households.[30]

In this new world, the elected citizen had to make his own way through the tempest of political life. And not only once: he had repeatedly to remake it. Tenure of office being limited, he had to face the voters frequently. That meant, in turn, that he had to perform his functions and to behave publicly in a manner that not only satisfied his superiors—the minister, the Commune, or the National Assembly—but also his fellow citizens. It was a delicate balancing act, and all the more so amid the rapid changes of the revolutionary years. The route to reelection, furthermore, lay through uncharted territory where parents and relatives could no longer provide guidance, and where safety was to be found in seeking the company of the largest possible number of like-minded fellow travelers: in "party," in the older sense of a loose coalition of the like-minded, rather than in the corporate and family networks of Old Regime political culture.

For despite the dangers, within the revolutionary system an ambitious and politically talented individual could go far. Within every Paris section, as at the national level, there were dramatic success stories. Few were as spectacular in either their rise or their fall as Danton, Varlet, Hébert, or Roux, but there were others who under the Old Regime had at best a modest future in public life yet during the Revolution were able to exert an influence that belied their origins. The career of Charles-Alexis Alexandre is one example from the Faubourg Saint Marcel. From not spectacularly successful stockbroker under the Old Regime, he rose through the National Guard to become a general. Or consider the barrel maker Antoine Gency, only thirty-two years old in the Year II, who was an elector for the deputies to the Convention in 1792 and subsequently a member of the Commune.[31] Such examples could be multiplied for every section in Paris. Neither of these individuals owed any part of his rise to his family connections, and neither had relatives in the section in which he rose to prominence (except in Gency's case, his father, who offered him little support). The Revolution offered unprecedented opportunities for the talented individual, without the need for family or other connections.

This said, family ties certainly did not become suddenly irrelevant in revolutionary politics. A young man who was known to few of his citizens but who came from a highly regarded local family might, as under the Old Regime, quickly win office. The revolutionary careers of Philippe Vavoque and his brother François were certainly not harmed by their belonging to a well-known Gobelins family, nor by their both being active in the section.[32] Other staunchly revolutionary families were also well represented in local office in the Faubourg Saint Marcel. Nicolas Levé was a member of the first district committee, an elector of 1793, and treasurer of the section in the same year; his brother-in-law Joseph Véron was a member of the Revolutionary Committee and a militant in the popular society. They joined forces in Floréal Year II (May 1794) to denounce Guillaume Boulland.[33]

It was quite possible that a united kin group with a reputation for patriotism could sway the sectional assembly to elect one of their number. Richard Andrews gives several examples of families in the Faubourg Saint Antoine that played a central role in local revolutionary politics. Of some importance, too, were kinship ties across the city that helped to link different sections. Antoine Joseph Santerre's brother-in-law was Joseph Etienne Panis, elector of the neighboring Arsenal Section and subsequently a Jacobin deputy in the Convention. Santerre's brother Jean-Baptiste also played a prominent role, for a time, in the Faubourg Saint Marcel. No direct evidence suggests that such connections helped the careers of any of these men—though it is hard to believe they did not. But men like Santerre belonged to intensely political families whose upbringing and social position predisposed them to take on the responsibilities of office.[34]

Family thus remained important in revolutionary politics. Yet it is striking, for anyone familiar with Old Regime politics, to observe just how many key figures constructed their own entirely new political base and made remarkable revolutionary careers. New talents were now both necessary and sufficient for political success. Oratorical skills had become an essential tool for the budding politician. Guillaume Boulland provides an outstanding example of the previously unknown orator who within a remarkably short time could assume a position of influence and leadership in the section.[35] Others made their way through sound committee work, through the National Guard, or through cultivating opinion makers in the sectional assemblies.

The National Guard was a major source of authority in local affairs, yet has been almost universally overlooked in histories of the Revolution in Paris. In the Gobelins/Finistère Section, as in a number of others, it directly contravened the regulations, becoming a neighborhood organization with each company drawn from adjoining streets.[36] Five members of the Revolutionary Committee of the Year II lived near one another in the rue de l'Oursine, and all served in the same company, as did a sixth member of the committee. Three key members of the Société Lazowski belonged to this company as well. They probably knew one another as neighbors, but even if they did not, fortnightly service on regular street patrols, drilling at intervals, and mobilization at moments of crisis brought them together.

Command of a company was a way for an individual to demonstrate his personal authority, and his men quickly got to know his qualities and his opinions. The position also provided considerable discretionary power. In dealing with the brawls that frequently shook Parisian taverns, captains in the guard regularly decided whether to send the contestants on their way, perhaps having imposed a settlement of their dispute, or to take them to the *commissaire de police,* who on the basis of the captain's report might even send them to trial. The fate of a person accused of some petty theft might similarly rest in his hands. Officers of

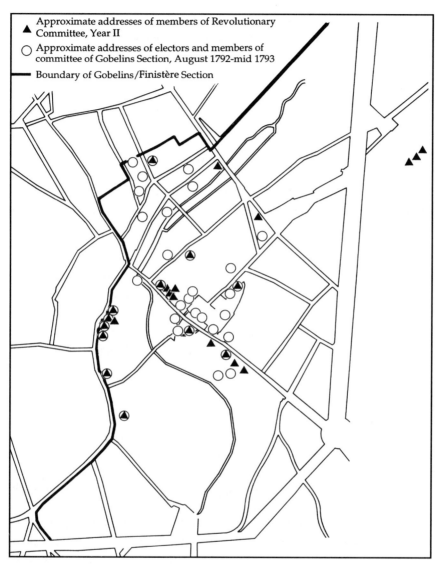

Approximate addresses of the electors and members of the Gobelins/Finistère Section Committee, 1792–1793, and of members of the Revolutionary Committee, Year II. The distribution of electors and committee members reflects the opening of the section committees, after August 1792, to a wide cross-section of the local bourgeois, spread across the whole area. The triangles at the far right represent officials of the Salpêtrière Hospital.

the National Guard were sometimes given particular administrative tasks, such as—in the Finistère Section—recording the names of those who had participated in the *journées* of 31 May and 1 and 2 June.[37] This gave them an additional aura of authority.

Officer rank in the National Guard therefore provided a key route to influence and to local political office. Aclocque provides the earliest example of this, for it was his effective organization of the bourgeois militia in mid-July 1789 that marked him as a local leader. Later, the careers of Charles-Alexis Alexandre and Claude Lazowski again demonstrate the importance of service in the National Guard. Alexandre does not seem to have played any role in sectional assemblies or committees, though he was an elector. He became captain of the artillery company in 1791 and battalion commander soon after. Although attacked for his role in the sugar riots of February 1792—protests over the sharp rise in the price of sugar—and again after 20 June 1792, he retained his post and led the battalion to the Tuileries on 10 August. This brought him promotion to legion commander, and appointment as minister of war followed, though it was immediately revoked. He was subsequently to serve as *commissaire des guerres* and to be a candidate for the Directory in 1797. By this stage he had long left the Saint Marcel quarter, but it was there, at the head of his company in the rue Mouffetard, that his political career had begun.[38]

Lazowski's rise was cut short by his sudden death in April 1793, but in 1792 he was lieutenant in the artillery company and soon after was elected captain, then battalion commander. Although he owed his local reputation partly to his oratory in the section and the popular society, and perhaps also to his close ties with the Jacobins, his original local base, following his arrival in the quarter sometime in late 1791 or early 1792, was the National Guard.[39]

The political importance of the National Guard was not confined to the early stages of the Revolution. In the Year III, five members of Jean-Baptiste Villain's company, based on the rue d'Orléans near Saint Médard, rubbed shoulders on the Civil Committee.[40] The sense of solidarity that united some companies is evident in their persistent loyalty toward their commanders. The first company of the Finistère troop signed two petitions in favor of Claude Foucault after he was arrested as a former "terrorist" in the Year III. Jean Vedrenne's company was similarly supportive of him. The remarkable thing is that although the evidence against both men was very strong, some of the signatures are those of men who were themselves moderates.[41]

Other kinds of personal loyalties also provided dynamic individuals with a power base, serving both to mobilize the small proportion of the electorate who attended any one election and to determine how they voted. A man who belonged to extended local networks could assemble the support necessary to be elected *commissaire de police* or justice of the peace. The backing of workers at the Gobelins manufactory was most probably crucial in the choice of the painter Augustin Louis Belle as a member of the District Committee, then as an elector in 1792, and subsequently in his election to the Civil and later the Revolutionary Committee. He was director of the manufactory in the Year II. Other Gobelins figures played similarly prominent roles: Cozette (who ran one of the tapestry workshops) and his son; the Vavoque brothers; later the tapestry makers Jean Louis Laronde and François Manguelschot. Educated and highly skilled, the Gobelins workers were bound by complex family and work ties, and the manufactory was one of the major centers of revolutionary ferment in the quarter.[42] One can safely assume that it was well represented in section meetings.

Similar networks, within other trades and streets, probably gave certain employers an advantage, though in the absence of attendance and voting lists from the sectional assemblies, this cannot be tested. The success of grocers in local revolutionary politics, while perhaps an echo of the status they had previously enjoyed, is more likely to reflect their very wide clientele. As sellers of candles and coffee, sugar, soap, spices, and occasionally spirits, they were well known within their neighborhoods. As retail merchants, who in an area like the Faubourg Saint Marcel often dealt in tiny quantities, they were likely to have some sympathy with the common people who made up the bulk of their clients. The revolutionary system, from 1789 right through to Thermidor, worked in favor of those with the ability to activate such networks and to mobilize support from key groups within the section. Together with the ideology of equality and hostility to privilege, it allowed in many people previously excluded from political life.

While thus widening access to local politics, though, these factors nevertheless ensured that those elected were not a microcosm of the society of the section. There were always important limitations on the choice of committee members and section officials. To begin with, the voters could choose only from among those who were prepared to accept office. In practice, a process of self-selection and self-elimination went on, determined not only by each man's ambition, civic spirit, or assessment of his own worth, but also by pressure from friends, supporters, or enemies. This eliminated a large number. Many could not afford the time required: lots of merchants, shopkeepers, artisans, and even professional men could not abandon their business, although wealthier men who had shop assistants or foremen might do so. A report written in 1799 on a doctor/surgeon in the Pantheon Division recalled that although "he showed himself an ardent patriot in popular and political meetings, . . . he has never accepted office because his practice would have suffered too much."[43] Of course, where a man's wife and family worked with him, they might be willing or constrained to replace him while he served the nation.

Employees and workers might be prepared to abandon the uncertainties of their trade for those of political life, particularly when local officials were paid (from September 1793 for the revolutionary committees and from late April 1794 for the civil committees). At least one member of the Revolutionary Committee of the Finistère Section was in this position: Jean-Baptiste Rognon, who was employed as a supervisor in the butchery at the Hôtel Scipion. He was actually able to improve his financial situation by having his brother stand in for him at Scipion at twenty-five sous per day, while he earned another seventy-five carrying out his patriotic duty.[44]

Other potential candidates, those with both time and strong civic instincts, were nevertheless excluded because they did not have sufficient education. The members of the sectional committees, particularly during the periods of crisis when they worked in shifts, twenty-four hours a day, drew up and signed thousands of documents. Their signatures nearly always indicate considerable familiarity with the quill.

Means, time, and education limited the choice offered to voters, throughout the Revolution. But it is not certain, even had the range of candidates been far wider, that the men elected would have been very different. For there undoubtedly existed an unconscious image of the suitable officeholder, a hidden agenda of unspoken criteria. Ineffable qualities of speech and dress, posture and gesture almost certainly played a role. Given an equal measure of patriotism and correct principles, it was the more eloquent candidate who would win votes, the man who possessed the rhetorical techniques of his age, the gestures and inflections

Signatures of members of the Revolutionary Committee of the Gobelins/Finistère Section: Deflandre, Hardon, Hagnon, Droulot, Dumont, Barre, Laronde, Baron, Pamelart, Langlois. The other signatures are those of members of the Revolutionary Committee of the Twelfth Arrondissement.

that impressed his hearers. It was the man who possessed authority and inspired respect.

To some extent simply possessing a powerful voice and imposing physique was important: this was in part the secret of Danton's success, and there were more minor figures—like the cabinetmaker Charles Balin in the Quinze-Vingts Section—whose booming voices were commented upon.[45] But "natural" authority was a subtle quality more likely to be acquired by the employer than by the employee; by the notable whose wealth, breeding, and everyday work accustomed him to speak first and to be listened to; by men whose training as priests, lawyers, or teachers had developed their public-speaking skills. In the National Guard the officers had to inspire respect, perhaps by their personal courage or physical stature, but more often—to judge from what is known of them—by the habit of command in the workplace. The well-to-do butcher Pierre Courtois, who became commander of the Saint Marcel battalion in 1793, undoubtedly employed a number of butcher's boys—a group notoriously violent and unruly—so he was probably a forceful man accustomed to making himself obeyed.[46]

Such factors conspired to create a revolutionary "political class" composed overwhelmingly of educated men who fell into two very general categories.[47] One included merchants and shopkeepers who were wealthy and well established enough to devote considerable time to public affairs. The other was made up of various professional men, many displaced by the Revolution (clergy, lawyers, bailiffs, teachers), and others who had never found a secure place under the Old Regime. Even at the height of the Jacobin ascendancy, very few elected officials in Paris really corresponded to the Père Duchesne's description of "the honest sansculotte who lives from day to day from the work of his hands."[48] The largely bourgeois composition of the revolutionary leadership and of the civil committees in particular, even at the most radical stage of the Revolution, has been frequently commented on, and the Finistère Section was no exception (see Tables 7.1 and 7.2).[49]

It was not only the qualities required for participation in local politics—the way power was acquired—that changed after 1789. The fashion in which power was exercised also altered. Under the Old Regime the churchwardens and the administrators of the Bièvre formed an oligarchy that made decisions on behalf of the local population. They enjoyed prestige as members of such bodies—particularly the churchwardens, whose preeminence was symbolized by their place in the church

Table 7.1 Prerevolutionary occupations of members of the Finistère Civil
Committee, 1792–1795

Occupation	Aug. 1792–June 1793	Year II (1793–1794)	Year III (1794–1795)
Professions			
Professor	0	0	1
Law	0	1	1
Government service (unspecified)	1	1	2
Painters	1	1	0
Masters and merchants			
Grocers	1	1	2+1[a]
Mercers	0	1	1
Goldsmith	0	0	1
Apothecary	1	0	0
Brewer	1[a]	1[a]	1
Dyer	1	1	1
Tanners	0	0	1+1[a]
Wood merchant	0	0	1
Starch makers	0	0	2
Furniture maker	0	0	2
Candle maker	0	0	1
Bakers	0	1	1
Wineshop keeper	1	0	1
Linen maker	0	1	1
Market gardeners	0	0	2
Artisans not masters			
Tapestry weaver	1	0	1
Jewelery mounter	1	0	0
Tailor	0	1	1
Harness maker	1	0	0
Other			
Clergy	0	1	0
Building contractors	2	0	1
Dancer	1	0	1
Rentiers	1	0	2
Soldiers	0	1	2
Unknown	7	2	12
Total	21	14	44

a. Known to be rich.

Table 7.2   Occupations of members of the Finistère Revolutionary
Committee, 1793–1794

Occupation	Number		
	April 1793	June 1793	Early 1794
Professions			
Government service (unspecified)	3	4	2
Painters	1	1	1
Inspector of manufactures	1	0	0
Masters and merchants			
Mercer	1	0	0
Brewer	0	1	0
Apothecary	0	1	0
Grocer	0	0	1
Tavern keeper	1	1	0
Market gardener	0	0	1
Linen maker	0	0	1
Artisans, unspecified status			
Tapestry weaver	1	1	1
Fruiterer (seller of produce)	0	0	1
Gauze maker	0	0	1
Furniture maker	0	0	1
Tailor	0	0	1
Other			
Building contractor	1	1	1
Propriétaire (investor in real estate)	0	0	1
Unknown	2	3	4
Total	11	13	17

and in processions. They wrote recommendations for people and defended the parish against outsiders. These activities reinforced their status
in the quarter. Only rarely, however, did such men give direct orders in
the exercise of their functions, except, of course, to the church or Bièvre
employees.

During the Revolution, the commanders in the National Guard and
the members of the civil and revolutionary committees had much more

immediate contact with the population whom they represented. A captain in the National Guard issued orders to his troops, but also to people who were infringing some regulation, and to those who queued at the city gates. The Revolutionary Committee was continually interviewing and interrogating citizens, and increasingly issuing commands. Through its power to issue or refuse certificates of patriotism, it exercised enormous authority. Even a member of the Civil Committee posted in the market-place might find himself issuing orders to the stall keepers or to the women queuing to buy.[50]

The presidents of the sectional assemblies, too, were often authoritarian: they probably had to be if meetings were to retain any sense of order. The *commissaires de police* had to issue instructions and rulings every day. The greater range of men who held local office, the diversity of their backgrounds, and the fact that many were unknown to people in the area meant that their authority had to be indicated by a cockade or a sash. It was a more direct and immediate power in that their ability to make people obey them depended not on their being known so much as on dress, on personality, and on presence. The personal qualities required for successfully exercising office were similar to those needed in obtaining it.

So far this chapter has been concerned with the ways in which the general principles and basic structures laid down in 1789 changed the forms of local notability and of local political life. Those principles remained largely unchanged until 1794. But the danger of comparing revolutionary and Old Regime political culture is that it obscures the very great changes that took place during the Revolution itself. The general picture of a revolutionary political class is profoundly misleading if no account is taken of its evolution. Three major factors brought about very significant changes in local political life between 1789 and 1794: the considerable extension of the electorate; the increasing radicalization of that electorate and of revolutionary politics in general; and the changing relationship between central authority and local administration.[51] These three factors profoundly modified the sources of power, the nature of notability, and hence the balance among the types of people elected to local political office.

The effective electorate of 1789 was tiny. In April, in the elections for the Estates General, only eighty-seven men were present at Saint Marcel.[52] No figures exist for the period after July, but in December the general assembly of the district met in the house of Bourdon de la Crosnière in the rue des Gobelins. The numbers therefore cannot have been large, and the private, bourgeois nature of the premises may have discouraged some from attending. Furthermore, the meetings were held during working hours. By March 1790 they had been moved to Saturday evening, and to the church of Saint Marcel, permitting many more voters to attend.[53]

Nevertheless, the first hard evidence of a major enlargement of the electorate comes from the municipal elections of October 1790, when the newly established sections drew up lists of those eligible to vote. In the Gobelins Section there were 1,154 active citizens, of whom between 121 and 176 turned up over the several days of the elections. Despite the very low rate of participation, this represents a doubling of the effective electorate since the previous year. Little further change occurred before June 1791, when between 93 and 183 citizens chose the electors who were to select the Paris deputies to the Legislative Assembly and the administrators of the Paris Department. At the end of 1791 a petition against the Department bore 109 names, and one of February 1792 seeking the release of those arrested after the sugar riots was signed by 149 persons.[54] Given the passion aroused by the latter affair, the first number is probably a more accurate indication of the numbers who were meeting regularly. This was fewer than in most of the sections during this period, but represented roughly the same proportion of active citizens as in other parts of the city.[55]

The second change took place after 10 August 1792, once universal male suffrage was introduced and the voting age was reduced to twenty-one. The number of potential voters in the Finistère Section increased to more than 3,700, roughly in the middle range of Paris sections. No attendance figures exist for the following period, but Soboul's statistics for other sections indicate that between 200 and 400 voters at elections was not unusual from mid-1792 to mid-1793, with the figure rising in late 1793 and early 1794.[56]

This extension of the active electorate was not enormous in absolute terms, but it had a major impact on local politics. The larger the numbers, the harder it was for a small group linked by ties of kinship, trade, or locality to impose its own candidate. The larger the assembly, too, the more important were the oratorical skills of the candidates, and the less significant their private qualities, their wealth, and their standing in the street where they lived. An influx of new voters who better represented the modest character of the bulk of the population, furthermore, allowed new concerns to be voiced. It became important to express popular concerns in vernacular language, rather than in the semiliterary vocabulary of the local elite. The move from an extended electorate of notables to one open to any male citizen thus changed both the form and the content of political debate, and opened participation in local office to men of more limited means.

These changes were accompanied by a radicalization of local politics. This is documented in innumerable histories of the Revolution that trace the growing importance of popular economic demands, the increasing emphasis on direct democracy, and the struggle over sovereignty between the sections and the Commune. As early as June 1791, the Gobelins Section had sought voting rights for all male residents over twenty-five. After March 1792, section by section, passive citizens were admitted.[57] The radicalization that accompanied this change is reflected, by mid-1792, in the declining numbers of moderates attending meetings. After 10 August, when the great enlargement of the electorate took place and the sections regained control of the National Guard, power returned decisively to the local level, freed from the restraining hand of the municipality. The creation of welfare and surveillance committees late in 1792 or early in 1793, in response to the deteriorating economic and military situation, gave the sections new powers and functions, and greater control over local affairs. The practice of sending deputations from radical sections to more moderate ones further encouraged radicalization. After 2 June 1793 the sections were firmly in the hands of the radicals and where necessary the committees were purged.[58]

The victory of a more popular version of democracy and of equality not only allowed the participation of larger numbers of citizens but also, in many sections, permitted the presence of women. Already in early 1792 one finds six women named as delegates of the Gobelins Section to the Legislative Assembly, even though those chosen were not present at the sectional assembly. All were married, two of them to local militants who, while never holding sectional office, played a major role in the popular society. Another was probably the wife of a lawyer who had been an elector in 1790. I have not been able to identify the other three or their families, except that one had been among the notable women who had presented the National Guard with their flag in 1789. This suggests that they may have owed their selection to their own position, perhaps within women's networks in the quarter, as well as to their known patriotic principles, and not primarily to the position or role of their husbands. The issue at hand—the imprisonment of a number of men and women after the February 1792 sugar riots—was a matter of considerable concern to the women of the quarter. Their inclusion in the delegation testifies to a new openness to the interests of local women.[59]

Soon after, in July 1792, a petition demanding the release of Boulland following his fiery call for a new insurrection after 20 June was signed by several women, an indication both that they were fully engaged with local politics and that they were able to participate in this way. Subsequently women attended section meetings regularly, and in March 1794 were accused of having so much power that they "destroyed all the work of the patriots" in the section, under the evil influence of Aclocque's brother. They participated fully in the popular society. The wife of Dumenil, claimed one militant in the Year II, had played an active role there on 20 June 1792. Marie Jacqueline Beschepoix admitted in Prairial Year III that she had been a member and had been sent on various missions for the society. Women also assisted the Paris revolutionary armies.[60] Although they never held office, the appearance of women changed the character of meetings, introducing new voices and concerns that were not always the primary ones of the male militants. It also helped change the composition of the local political elite, encouraging the election of men like Hébert and Roux—or in the Finistère Section, Boulland—who were prepared to demand the maximum and to stress the needs of consumers and families.[61]

The radicalization of revolutionary politics and the extension of participation also led, as Haim Burstin has pointed out, to increased stress on each man's politics, on his revolutionary fervor, and on the role he had played since the beginning of the Revolution. There was a Paris revolutionary catechism of a kind, in which the key questions concerned a man's actions on 20 June, on 10 August, on 31 May. It made relevant the sort of political skills with which we are now familiar: the ability of a candidate to present himself as faithful to the will of the people and to point to the failings of his opponents. "Party" allegiances became significant (although also dangerous).[62]

The new electoral politics thus produced a considerable change of personnel at the local level from 1792 on. It brought in men of lower social status and lesser means. The barrel maker Gency, born in Reims but possibly a resident of the faubourg for some years, appeared on the political scene early in 1792. Guillaume Carrel, who as a result of the Revolution had lost his position as a performer at the opera, was not the sort of man likely to be chosen to represent the Faubourg Saint Marcel in 1789 or 1790, but he was elected to the Civil Committee in 1793. These men and others like them were never excluded by the formal electoral rules. They were already active citizens in 1791. But the political conditions were not conducive to their election before 1792.[63]

The radicalization of the electorate probably helped to shift the balance in local political office toward former officeholders and away from the wealthy merchants who had dominated sectional politics hitherto.[64] On the whole, those with a substantial stake in the existing socioeconomic hierarchy were unlikely to welcome extreme democratization or measures that placed a substantial financial burden on the well off. Nor did they have a strong economic interest in office, unlike the displaced lawyers, clergy, former government employees, and such people, who often had no other jobs awaiting them. After September 1793, when committee members began to be paid for their time, those who would otherwise have been unemployed had a vested interest in office, a consideration that may have helped to radicalize their opinions at the same time that the shift to the left took place within the sectional assemblies.

Increasing persecution of the church also played a major role in driving some people out of public life. This took place less along socioeconomic lines, although affluence was a factor, since the old parish structure had accorded the places of honor to the wealthy. Whatever they thought of the constitutional church, such people—perhaps particularly the women, who the evidence suggests were more attached to religious practice and to whom the new regime offered no compensating prestige—were likely to react negatively to the removal of the bells, the banning of processions, and, finally, the closure of the churches. Very few former churchwardens had joined the committees of the years 1789–1791 in the Faubourg Saint Marcel. By the Year II there were none, except in the Welfare Committee, which continued the poor relief formerly undertaken by the parishes.

The third major factor that profoundly affected both the character and the personnel of local politics in Paris was the changing relationship between central authority and local administration. Ever since mid-1789 when the districts seized power, many political struggles were over who was sovereign—the local assemblies, the municipality, the Department, or, for that matter, the National Assembly. The municipal law of 1790 and the creation of the sections attempted to destroy the radical independence of the districts and removed their control of the National Guard.

The districts seized back the National Guard after 10 August 1792, at the same time winning the removal of the Department's control over Paris and the election of new justices of the peace, *commissaires de police,* and section committees, all of whom now came under the control of the sectional assemblies. The sections now met whenever they wished—usually daily—and by the end of the year most had set up their own "surveillance committees." In March and April of 1793, in an atmosphere of crisis, these were to be revived as "revolutionary committees" with very extensive, even unlimited powers. In December the sections formally regained control of public charity when the municipality abolished the parish charity committees, recognizing a transfer of authority that had in reality already taken place. Throughout this period the sections insisted that their elected representatives were revocable at any time and should always express the will of the section. Power had returned decisively to the local level.[65]

In an electoral sense, of course, it had always resided there. Since 1789 the districts, then the sections, had chosen their own office bearers and named the members of the committees. The sources of local power and local office ultimately lay in the district and sectional assemblies, even if at certain moments other sections or the municipality might try to intervene. As a consequence, local recognition and acceptance remained the crucial determinants of election, despite the changing size and composition of the electorate. But the importance of each individual's role and relationships within the section was never greater than in the months between August 1792 and September 1793, when the sections not only ran their own affairs but very largely those of the whole city.

By late 1793, this was changing. The sections began to lose control of their own committees. On 5 September 1793 the Convention placed the revolutionary committees in charge of the identification, arrest, and disarming of suspects, but decreed that first they would be purged by the municipality. The principle of election by the sections was thus partly undermined, as they were quick to perceive. Then, on 17 September 1793, the Law of Suspects required the revolutionary committees to report directly to the Committee of General Security. In practice, from late September onward, only candidates acceptable to the Committee of General Security joined the revolutionary committees. On 4 December (14 Frimaire Year II) the Committees of General Security and of Public Safety were given the power to purge and reorganize any public authority, even an elected one, and members of any such authority were forbidden to meet without permission. This was directed against the Commune, but increased central control over the local committees as well.

Finally, on 13 March 1794 (23 Ventôse Year II), the Committee of Public Safety was authorized to remove any public official and was specifically instructed to purge the revolutionary committees. Henceforth, new members were not elected by the sectional assemblies but proposed by the committees themselves or by the municipality and appointed by the Committee of Public Safety or the Committee of General Security. The same applied to the National Guard, whose officers were no longer elected after March 1794, but appointed by the Committee of Public Safety.

At the same time, external control of the committees' activities increased. Since 5 September 1793 their members had received payment to compensate for the time they put in—three livres and then, after 1 November, five livres. This was originally a democratizing gesture in intent and in effect, yet had the potential to turn the committees into servants of their paymasters. The same payments were extended to the civil committees from 25 April 1794.[66] By the end of May 1794, the committees of the Convention were in total command and now rarely encountered any opposition from the sections. Sovereignty had been surrendered to the center.

This meant that, over the nine months before Thermidor, the criteria for election were changed drastically. It was no longer so important to be well regarded locally, particularly for election to the revolutionary committees, which were now the most powerful ones in each section. A good revolutionary record was still vital, but the Committee of General Security did not use exactly the same criteria as voters in the sectional assembly. They required obedience, and a more legalistic turn of mind, which would ensure that the documents forwarded from the section were legible and in the required legal form.

Subservience to the committees of the Convention now came before service to the citizens of the section. As the Committee of General Security put it in mid-1794, "if the Section proceeded to this nomination [to a vacancy on the Revolutionary Committee], the goal of public utility might well be totally forgotten."[67] By then, good revolutionary committeemen were not necessarily good orators, nor necessarily committed to the goals of the popular movement. In fact, as the revolutionary government clamped down on that movement, fidelity to sectional and popular interests became a liability. In short, what the central government required in the sectional committees were government servants, not elected representatives of the people. Hence the appointment to the Finistère Revolutionary Committee of a man like Pierre Nicolas Droulot, who seems to have had no other occupation and was probably totally dependent on the Committee of General Security for employment and income: he had been a paid secretary to the Revolutionary Committee before becoming an elected member. Joseph Véron did have another position—he ran the laundry at the Salpêtrière Hospital. But that too was a position entirely dependent on the goodwill of the government, his employer. Jacques Langlois had been a gauze maker but never returned to this occupation: after the Revolution he undertook a profitable street-cleaning business—dependent, of course, on government contracts. His stint on the Revolutionary Committee was quite possibly his escape route out of the very uncertain textile trade, which had suffered during the Revolution, and into public service.[68] Such men were pliable tools for the Committee of General Security, just as some of them had previously been willing appointees of the sectional assembly.

Over the course of the Revolution, therefore, the structures and personnel of local political life—and at the same time, the nature and sources of power—evolved considerably. The first great change came in 1789, when "outsider notables" took over local affairs: men who, while members of the Old Regime bourgeoisie, were in some instances recent arrivals in the area, in other cases men who lacked the local connections necessary under the Old Regime; outsiders in both instances. It is possible, of course, that some had simply not chosen to become politically involved before but had been inspired by the excitement and opportunities afforded by the Revolution. They were elected by men who for the most part were like themselves: an expanded notability that certainly included many of the churchwardens, governors of confraternities, and other public figures of the Old Regime, but that took in newcomers to political life. The selection was done according to criteria that were in part new, in that they accorded a greater role to education and a lesser one to local implantation, but that produced electors and district committees scarcely distinguishable in socioeconomic terms from the former churchwardens. Their authority arose not only from office, but also from their personal position in the quarter as employers, property owners, or educators.

The second phase, that of the professional politicians, was a response to the operation of the new political structures. As the electorate grew, allowing greater pressure from below and the expression of new opinions, and as events both locally and at the center pushed the Revolution in a more radical direction, the men elected began to look less like Old Regime notables and more like modern politicians, able to win office on the basis of their opinions and policies as well as their ability to persuade the voters. They were not necessarily locals at all, and many, having no personal authority as notables, drew their legitimacy exclusively from their elected office. The crucial qualities, therefore, were verbal skills, a sense of timing, and an ability to construct a local power base. They had the support of other recognized patriots in the sectional assembly and on the committees, men who not only could speak for them if they were denounced or challenged but could also persuade and influence members of the section to support them.

In the final phase, that of the government servants, legitimacy came from outside the section and local officeholders owed allegiance to government rather than to their fellow citizens.

The causes of this evolution in the local political elite—from powerful, locally elected notables to faithful government servants—are entwined with the wider history of the Revolution. The early stages, from "outsider notables" to professional politicians, were enshrined in the logic of the revolutionary ideology and the structures that resulted. The move from a highly democratic and very open political system to one closely controlled by government was partly a product of external and internal war, insofar as these facilitated the creation of a Jacobin monopoly of power at the center. But it was also, at the local level, a perhaps inevitable consequence of weariness and disillusionment: The weariness of men who for months, in some cases years, had given freely of their time and energy with little or no payment. The weariness of men who had devoted all their waking hours—and many of what should have been sleeping hours—to service on committees and in the National Guard, buoyed in some cases by a thirst for power but in others primarily by a sense of civic duty.

It was the weariness of citizens who voted repeatedly—far more frequently than in a modern democracy—for assemblies, administrators, committees, mayors, judges, and officers in the National Guard; who devoted hours to sectional meetings and popular societies. And of wives whose husbands were rarely home and brought little money when they did return; who spent hours in bread queues, and who even if they had servants to do that work had to feed their families with lower quality food at higher cost; who could no longer find consolation in the church.[69]

It was the disillusionment of those who had believed in the dawn of a new age: the men of 1789 whose dream of peaceful and prosperous rule by the enlightened had turned sour; the humbler patriots whose weariness was unrelieved by evidence of genuine betterment, either moral or material. The disillusionment of women who were not treated as citizens, solely because of their sex, and who in the brave new world still battled to make ends meet.

In the longer term the consequences of all this, for the evolving Parisian bourgeoisie, were enormous. In the short term, the old bourgeois elite lost power to a new one, which was in turn driven out by a far more mixed and open political "class." By 1794 the power and status of public office were enjoyed by men who today would be called bureaucrats, a group of minor significance under the Old Regime, but whose star was now in the ascendant.

IV

PARIS OF THE NOTABLES, 1795–1830

CHAPTER

INTERREGNUM

We did not wish to return to the times when [the vestries]
behaved as if they were in command.

—*Archbishop of Paris, 1803*

Between 1789 and 1794 the notables who had dominated local political life before the Revolution were driven out. Few of the churchwardens continued to hold office under the new rules, which initially favored men and families whose star had already been rising in the 1770s and 1780s but who for the most part had not succeeded in achieving recognition in the form of local office. They were often, as Richard Andrews has pointed out, migrants or sons of migrants of long standing, and some remained prominent throughout the early 1790s.[1] Increasingly, however, the Revolution offered opportunities to other outsiders: to very recent immigrants and to people who had previously been excluded by their occupation or their poverty yet who possessed the personal abilities now required for office. These changes created, by mid-1794, a composite political elite in which the commercial middle classes remained prominent, together with displaced officeholders, lawyers, and teachers, but that also contained a sprinkling of people of humbler social origins.

To some degree, therefore, the Revolution divorced political power from economic power and from local notability, a trend reinforced in the Year II by the centralization of authority. The Revolution also, particularly through the struggles between the sections and the Commune, created citywide political alliances that similarly helped to reduce the significance of local notability. Both of these developments had longer-term consequences for the Parisian bourgeoisie that will be examined later, but their immediate effect was to exclude most of the prerevolutionary notables and the men of 1789–1790 from political office. The second half of the 1790s was to witness the reemergence of a local bourgeois elite, though not the prerevolutionary one, and a struggle between this new elite and a series of governments.

After 1794 the Convention, then the Directory, dismantled the framework within which local political life had gone on over the previous half decade. Over the next thirty-five years, and despite profound differences in official ideology, the directorial, consular, imperial, and royal governments attempted to destroy all political activity in Paris. Alarmed by the democratic possibilities of the Revolution, they endeavored to control every possible avenue of agitation and to limit access to power.

Politics and power struggles, however, go on even when open opposition and debate are not permitted. Just as the church vestries, the corporate structures, and the courts of the Old Regime had provided opportunities for political life, so too in the postrevolutionary era individuals and groups in Paris struggled to control their own affairs. There were essentially two domains in which people could operate politically: in various locally elected or even government-appointed bodies that oversaw the administration of the city, or within the government structure that now extended further into the local scene than ever before and offered ample opportunities for behind-the-scenes struggles of influence. The opportunities open, in each case, varied according to the strength and ruthlessness of the government.

Under the Thermidorean Convention and the Directory, the swings of national politics and the confrontations of Jacobins, moderates, and royalists opened up possibilities for action at the local level, just as during the Jansenist years the struggles between the archbishop, the Parlement, and the crown had allowed the humble churchwardens of Saint Médard to ride boldly into the lists. After two and a half or three years during which most of the local notables had withdrawn or been excluded from power, they now began to find ways of reasserting their authority.

The wavering religious policy of the Thermidoreans provided the earliest opportunities. As soon as the law permitting the reopening of religious establishments was passed, on 3 Ventôse Year III (21 February 1795), the sixty-one-year-old tanner Jean Antoine Derubigny de Berteval, churchwarden of 1775, pamphleteer, veteran of campaigns on behalf of the tanners of France under a succession of governments, and survivor of a revolutionary prison, announced his intention to rent the church of Saint Médard and reopen it for religious services. He may not have been acting alone: one historian states that several former churchwardens were responsible. It was nevertheless he who, without awaiting permission, obtained the keys from the former beadles, who of course knew him both as a prominent and pugnacious local notable and as an authoritative former churchwarden.

When challenged by the local Civil Committee, Derubigny threatened to denounce its members to the committees of the Convention. Fearing that he might in fact do so, the Civil Committee decided to get in first, warning its superiors that "if someone who, like the Citizen Rubigny, bears a heavy responsibility, is allowed to seize hold of everything he wants, then we will return to those unhappy times when the rich could act with total impunity."[2] The local *commissaire de police* also denounced Derubigny's action, but neither the Committee of General Security nor the Paris Department (to whom the matter was referred) took any action. The first mass went ahead on 5 April 1795, celebrated by the constitutional bishop Jean-Baptiste Royer, and on 1 May (anniversary of the death of the *diacre* Pâris) the service was very well attended. Corpus Christi also attracted large crowds—a sign that religious sentiment had gone underground but not been eliminated by the de-Christianization campaigns.[3]

In a number of other parishes, it was the clergy themselves who reopened the church. At Saint Leu and at Saint Marcel, individual priests hired the building and began saying mass.[4] But more often it seems to have been the laity who took the initiative. At Saint Merri ten men met on 30 Messidor Year III (18 July 1795) to receive the keys of the church, and the first service was held the following day. The use of the former church of the Saint Sacrement was requested early in 1796 by "citizens exercising the Catholic religion in the Popincourt, Temple, Homme Armé and Indivisibilité Sections." At Saint Eustache the church reopened on 3 Messidor Year III (21 June 1795), and an assembly met the next day to decide on practical and financial arrangements.[5]

As at Saint Médard, the support of a good part of the population was indispensable for successful reopening of the churches. Police reports emphasized the presence of women, perhaps trying in this way to play down the significance of the large numbers.[6] The *Journal des Munici-*

palités reported on 24 Ventôse III (14 March 1795) that "several churches were this morning so full that the overflow of the faithful formed long lines just as at the doors of the bakers and butchers."[7]

Although the paper reported that it was "the laboring class that is the most attached to religion," it was generally local notables who led the way. Even where the clergy got things moving again, they relied on the better-off citizens to donate furnishings and altar ornaments. In the former parish of Saint Gervais, the first mass was held on 8 March 1795 in a chapel rented by a local wine merchant and supplied with ornaments, books, and furniture by faithful parishioners. At Saint Marcel, local people supplied a painting, a missal, and a candelabra, though there was less support than in some other churches, perhaps because of the priest's political and religious convictions: he was both a nonjuror and strongly anti-Jansenist, an unpopular combination in the Faubourg Saint Marcel.[8]

At Saint Médard items donated or lent to the church between 1795 and 1802 included a large silver cross and candlesticks, a processional cross, a font, chasubles and copes, even chairs.[9] The donors included two former churchwardens: Derubigny, and the wealthy brewer Jean-Baptiste Hannen, who had played an active role throughout most of the Revolution. He had served on the Welfare Committee in 1791, on the Revolutionary Committee from April 1793 until the Jacobin purge of Brumaire Year II (late October 1793), and on the Civil Committee just before Thermidor. He was again a member of the Civil Committee in December 1794, and worked briefly on the Surveillance Committee of the Twelfth Arrondissement from January to March 1796.[10] Other donors to the reopened church included local notables who had not previously played any political role. There was Etienne Albinet, a blanket maker soon to become one of the largest employers in the faubourg, with eighty people working at his establishment in the rue d'Orléans and more than three hundred in other parts of Paris and in the countryside. He had arrived in the quarter in 1783.[11] The wealthy tanner Bricogne, son of a rich mercer, provided some church furniture, as did one "Bacquet"—probably Bacot, another blanket maker with a large local workforce. Neither of these men appears to have had any connection with the quarter either before or during the Revolution.[12]

The other donors mentioned are the Pelart sisters, who in 1789 had helped provide a flag for the local National Guard. They were daughters of a lawyer, and one of them had been arrested as an "aristocrat" in the

Year II.[13] It is likely that at least some of the men mentioned were among the "administrators" of the parish who are reported to have met on 7 Floréal Year V.[14] One could hardly ask for a better cross-section of the local bourgeoisie, those soon to become known as *"citoyens notables."* They included all political views except Jacobinism and overt royalism. Furthermore, in contrast to the local elite of the prerevolutionary period, none of the individuals involved in reopening Saint Médard was related to any of the others.

Elsewhere the pattern appears to have been similar. At Saint Laurent several of the twenty-four members of the new "directory" were former churchwardens. At Saint Etienne du Mont the president of the administrators, presumably one of the 138 signatories of the petition requesting the reopening of the church, was Charles Agier, a former member of the Constituent Assembly and post-Thermidorean president of the Revolutionary Tribunal. At Saint Merri, among those involved were at least four former churchwardens and the notary formerly employed by the vestry. With them were a jeweler, two upholsterers (one of them, Louis Augustin Grandin, probably related to the wealthy family of upholsterers of that name in the Faubourg Saint Antoine), and two gilders: all prestigious trades. The deputy of the Department who handed over the keys was a former mercer in the parish, and had also been a churchwarden. This group in turn called another meeting, attended by nineteen local citizens, who chose sixteen administrators for the church, one of whom was Bricogne, father of the tanner who helped to reestablish Saint Médard.

At Saint Eustache, too, where some sixty citizens attended at least one of the regular administrative meetings, the evidence indicates that those actively involved were local notables. The president of the assembly was a wealthy stockbroker, selected to represent the arrondissement in the elections of the Year III. Another man who regularly attended was an administrator of the municipality. Most of the others seem to have been prominent local merchants or manufacturers. At Saint Gervais they were lawyers and shopkeepers.[15] All the indications are that those who took charge of the reopened churches in 1795, and 1796 were representative of the most notable citizens in each area.

The system of administration adopted by the Paris parishes between 1795 when open religious observance was legalized, and 1803, when an imperial decree established common rules for all parishes, varied considerably. Where a hard-line nonjuror priest officiated, there was far less lay participation, although there are traces of local citizen organization at

Saint Roch in November or December 1795, when a petition asked the government to repair the church clock, and also at Saint Jacques du Haut Pas, where there were regular meetings of lay administrators.[16] At Saint Marcel, the curé Louis Bertier was doubly hostile to the involvement of the laity, being both a nonjuror and staunchly anti-Jansenist.

But where the restored cult was the revolutionary Constitutional Church, as in half of the churches officially reopened, a highly democratic system operated. At Saint Médard, in accordance with Henri-Baptiste Grégoire's attempted reorganization of the Constitutional Church that envisaged the election of priests, an assembly at Saint Médard on 26 July 1795 chose Augustin Baillet as the new curé and a number of "administrators" to look after the temporal administration. At Saint Laurent, a two-tier electoral system operated, with a "general assembly of the faithful of this church" meeting on 16 August 1795 to select a "directory," whose members in turn chose the curé. Their decision was then confirmed by another general assembly, on 11 October.

At Saint Merri, the former *curé* seems to have come back uncontested, but the eighteen administrators were to be elected annually by an open and well-publicized meeting of all parishioners. The president, secretary, and treasurer were to be chosen by the administrators themselves. Saint Eustache had six, and subsequently nine, administrators, among them the curé, all chosen by assemblies of the faithful—though the numbers attending were small. There the clergy, too, were elected, and women were permitted to vote. The assemblies of administrators at Saint Eustache not only were responsible for church maintenance and finances but also decided what religious services would be held, and when. Similar assemblies existed at Saint Etienne du Mont and at Saint Gervais.[17]

Although the various bodies elected to administer the churches had no legal status, they provided a new forum for local politics. The administrators acted both on behalf of the parish and in defense of their own rights. Incessant conflicts arose between the administrators and the curés at Saint Thomas d'Aquin, at Saint Paul, and at Saint Laurent. In 1801 a dispute at Saint Merri between the administrators and the clergy, who wanted more of a say in the running of the church, involved a number of other local residents, also including "fifteen to eighteen *dames* and *demoiselles*" who burst into a meeting, one of them announcing her intention to replace the existing administrators. It appears that one grievance of the intruders was a ruling by the administrators authorizing men formerly elected to that position to attend meetings, in the same way as in the old vestries. The ladies had a further complaint: another decision of the assembly excluded them from the area around the main altar during certain services.[18] The details of this dispute are not clear, nor is the outcome, but it suggests that local politics was thriving in the Saint Merri quarter. Nor was conflict with the clergy unusual. In 1802 Jean-Etienne-Marie Portalis, minister for religious affairs in all but name, wrote to the newly appointed archbishop of Paris.

> I have received, Citizen Archbishop, several complaints from citizens who, before your installation, administered the temporal affairs of the different Paris churches; most complain that the curés have not allowed them to participate in the administration of matters in which they have an investment and an interest; they point out that they have contracted debts for which they are answerable to the workers whom they have employed, and that they should maintain active supervision of things that result from these debts.[19]

The assemblies also defended themselves against increasing outside interference. After the coup of 18 Fructidor Year V (4 September 1797), they had to contend with the Théophilanthropes, the nationalist religious group that enjoyed official patronage between 1797 and 1799. At Saint Médard there is no evidence of local support for the Théophilanthropes, and the pressure for their implantation seems to have come from outside.[20] At Saint Laurent, following a dispute over the use of the church, the curé was exiled, and subsequently the church was closed to the Catholics, leading to a local campaign to have it reopened. A similar thing happened at Saint Thomas d'Aquin.[21] At Saint Etienne du Mont, only a few months earlier, a dispute set the local citizens against the ecclesiastical authorities. The constitutional priest having departed, the former abbot of Sainte Geneviève had tried to return to the prerevolutionary practice and impose his own candidate. He had the support of the émigré bishop, but the parishioners called a meeting and elected a priest themselves, refusing to return their church to the counterrevolutionary fold.[22]

The valiant efforts of the administrators to retain full local control of their churches were nevertheless doomed to failure. Napoleon's ascendancy was reflected in the increasingly authoritarian character of the regime and in a gradual clamping down on all independent administration and political activity, especially in Paris. In May 1801 the prefect of the Seine ruled that henceforth the administrators of the churches could no longer carry out any repairs or other work without the approval of the building inspector of the Department. This provoked a strong but fruitless protest from the assembly at Saint Merri.[23]

But it was the Concordat of 1801, promulgated in 1802, that heralded the end of the independent assemblies. On 7 May 1802 the archbishop, working closely with the government, announced the creation of thirty-nine parishes in Paris and set out their boundaries. He also named the twelve curés who would be in charge of these churches, one for each of the new arrondissements.[24] This put an end to the election of priests. Furthermore, the men chosen by the archbishop—like Bertier, the new parish priest at Saint Médard—were authoritarian figures determined to, as the prelate himself put it, "tighten . . . the bonds of subordination that our troubles have slackened." "We did not wish," the archbishop announced, "to return to the times when [the vestries] behaved as if they were in command."[25]

The 1803 decree on parish administration established vestries composed of seven members, one of whom was the *curé*. One new member was to be chosen each year from among those who paid the highest taxes or from among the public officials living in the arrondissement, and all elections were to be approved by the archbishop. The annual accounts were likewise to be presented to the archbishop. The curé was to play a leading role even in financial matters and was to be one of the three members entrusted with a key to the cash box. The new vestries, the decree insisted, "have no right to represent the parishioners, nor to write petitions in their name." Initially, to ensure that the right people were chosen, the curés were to draw up a list of candidates for their vestries, from which the archbishop and the prefect would choose the six members.[26]

These measures, for all their thoroughness, did not leave the new vestries entirely supine. In December 1803 the curé of Saint Leu wrote to the Minister that he had called a meeting of the men appointed, but that "they had got together in advance and replied unanimously that, without refusing the position, they could nevertheless not accept it as long as the government had not made a decision on the vote of the municipality concerning the budget for religious affairs. Here I am, therefore, without a vestry, and probably soon without a church; for our lease expires in two weeks. I have neither the right nor the means to renew it in my own name."[27] Nevertheless, the new vestries were a far cry from the fiercely independent bodies of the Old Regime, which had been legally independent of both the ecclesiastical and the secular authorities. They were very different, too, from the elected local assemblies of the post-Thermidor and Directory years, although both were composed of notables.

The postrevolutionary story of the parishes is one of initial independent action by local notables, followed by increasing government control and, finally, the virtual elimination of opportunities for local political activity. It is repeated in other areas of administration. The Faubourg Saint Marcel was unusual in its dependence on the Bièvre River, whose maintenance had been assured under the Old Regime by representatives of the local tanners, dyers, and leather dressers, who had levied taxes on river users and riverside properties so that the river could be cleaned annually. This system had collapsed during the Revolution. The last election of syndics was held in 1788, when Antoine Moinery (owner of the premises attacked by the "sugar riot" crowd in 1792), Antoine Poilleu, and Jean Edme Huguet were elected for two years. After 1790, when the Bièvre in principle was administered by the section, little was done until the Year IV (1795–1796), when the Department of the Seine paid for the river to be partially cleaned—though who was responsible for initiating this action is not clear.

Then, in October 1796, an unofficial meeting of local property owners decided to employ a river inspector and obtained permission from the municipality. The meeting also chose three syndics: Jean-Baptiste Vérité, a substantial dyer; Joseph Salleron, the tanner; and Huguet, the same man who had held this office in the years 1788–1790. All three were solid Directory notables. Vérité was a member of the Surveillance Committee of the arrondissement in the Year III. Salleron had served on the Welfare Committee of his section from 1793 until 1795, and on the Civil Committee in the Year III. Huguet had played no formal political role, though his nephew had been active until early 1793 and like Vérité had served on the post-Thermidorean Surveillance Committee. All were wealthy and were large employers.[28]

Their activities, however, did not go uncontested. At the beginning of 1797, the municipality received a letter from Derubigny opposing the appointment of the river inspector, Baltet. This man, he pointed out, had earlier been removed from the very same position for malpractice. The authorities responded by convoking a meeting of all the river users on 12 Thermidor Year V (30 July 1797). This assembly, attended by twenty-two citizens of the Faubourg Saint Marcel—among them, Vérité and

Salleron—condemned the earlier meeting on the twin grounds that it was not properly advertised and that the election of syndics was illegal under the laws dissolving the corporations. Instead, one man from within Paris—Derubigny—and one from the country were chosen to draw up the tax list and ensure that work on the river was done. The new river inspector was to be Jacques Rivaud, former *commissaire de police* of the Finistère Section, who had spent the Terror in prison and who had been a deputy for the arrondissement in the elections of the Year IV.[29]

The municipality soon had cause to regret the choice of Derubigny. Within two months it was being deluged with his complaints: against those who refused to pay for the maintenance of the river; against his predecessors, who refused to hand over the previous tax rolls; against Rivaud, who refused to accompany him on inspections. Rivaud responded that Derubigny was himself contravening the regulations by closing off access to the river bank and by illegally drawing off water into his tannery. Throughout the first half of 1798, hostility between Rivaud and Derubigny grew, with both men drawing in whatever local allies they could find, until the municipality finally stepped in to conduct its own inspection. It then convened a meeting, in mid-July 1798, to lay down rules for the maintenance of the river. Rivaud was retained, but Derubigny was replaced by Jean Edme Huguet. Not until the third ballot was this decision reached—a prolonged process that suggests deep divisions among the twenty-one men present. Derubigny did not attend and refused to accept the decision, for he continued to bombard the municipality with letters signed "*commissaire de la Bièvre* until Thermidor Year VII," and to complain about Huguet. Huguet, in return, reported that Derubigny's accounts were wrong and that he should not be repaid what he claimed to have advanced.[30]

At the beginning of August 1799, the municipality received a new petition, signed by 94 people (the tax list for that year bears 109 names). It recalled a law of 11 Frimaire Year VII specifying that all aqueducts, ditches, and bridges were to be maintained from the public purse. "You will understand equally," the petition continued, "that under article 355 of the Constitution, we no longer have any corporations or communities, privileges, *maîtrises* or *jurandes,* still less any syndics of owners or of those with an interest in the maintenance of rivers." It therefore followed, the petitioners argued, that the municipality should assume the cost of cleaning the Bièvre. The mover in this case appears to have been Huguet's nephew Claude Roland Huguet, who had already played a significant role in local politics from 1789 until 1793 and again since Thermidor. His was the first signature, and over the following months he was to lead a campaign of civil disobedience, persuading other river users not to pay the tax.[31]

It was almost certainly this dispute that produced, a few months later, a decree of the consuls removing responsibility for the Bièvre from locally elected officials and placing it in the hands of the prefect of police and the prefects of the departments through which the river flowed. As the minister of the interior explained in a letter to Derubigny, leaving such matters up to individual citizens gave rise to far too many disputes and abuses.[32] But it was perfectly consistent with the government's action on church administration: all independent and potentially troublesome local bodies should be eliminated or brought firmly under control.

The same process is observable in every other area of local administration. It had been, of course, the Jacobin government that brought the revolutionary committees to heel, then used them to control and purge the sections. The same government dissolved the popular societies and robbed the sections of their right to name representatives to the Commune and to elect the local revolutionary committee and the officers of the local National Guard.[33] But none of these powers was restored after Thermidor. On the contrary, the new government continued the suppression of democracy, in August 1794 reducing the general assemblies to one meeting every ten days, and two months later replacing the civil committees, which were originally elected by the sectional assemblies, with men chosen directly by the Convention's Legislation Committee. Three new members were to be appointed by the Legislation Committee every three months. In December the welfare committees were also placed under direct control of one of the Convention's committees. Well before this, back in August 1794, the revolutionary committees of the sections had been dissolved, and replaced by twelve new revolutionary committees—one for each of the arrondissements, which were now formed from the grouping of four sections. The new committees were made answerable directly to the Committee of General Security. Finally, in 1795, the Convention abolished elections for the *commissaires de police,* who henceforth were likewise to be appointed by the Committee of General Security.[34]

Ironically, this streamlining of control by the center had initially restored to the local notables a degree of power they had not possessed for some time. The abolition of the revolutionary committees, which during

the Terror had increasingly come to control sectional affairs, now renewed the influence of the other local authorities, particularly the civil
committees. Although the Legislation Committee appointed the members
of these bodies, it relied on the general assemblies of the sections to
provide a list of candidates. While asked for twice as many names as
there were places to fill, very often the sections provided only the same
number, "in a sense making the appointment," the Legislation Committee
complained in July 1795.[35] The Finistère Section did this repeatedly, and
to judge from complaints about long delays in appointments, the Legislation Committee was too overworked to eliminate the practice, although
it did occasionally reject a candidate. In effect, the section named its own
civil committee, with the central agency merely exercising a veto.[36]

Most of the men chosen by the sectional assemblies, now dominated
by the moderates who had returned after Thermidor, were local notables
with experience of office, accustomed to exercising authority, usually
moderate revolutionaries. Of thirty-one men who served on the Finistère
Civil Committee after Thermidor, nine had been either *dixainiers* or
churchwardens before 1789. At least six had held positions in 1789 or
1790, another four in 1792, and thirteen had been committee members
in 1793, before the Jacobin ascendancy. Three had served on the Jacobin
Revolutionary Committee, but had departed a respectable length of time
before Thermidor. In addition, there was a striking continuity from the
Welfare Committee of the Year II to the post-Thermidor Civil Committee: seventeen men served on both.

Most of the Civil Committee members were well established in the
quarter, though very few were drawn from the old parish dynasties. Their
previous administrative experience had brought them into contact with
much of the local population. Many were also major employers.[37] There
was Hannen, the wealthy brewer mentioned earlier, and François-Joseph
Gandolphe, who had taken over the wood business built up by his
millionaire uncle.[38] Not all were this rich, and indeed some had only the
small income from their committee work, but as a group they were
markedly more prosperous than the Civil Committee members of 1793
or the Year II.

They were also, on the whole, older: this was consistent with the
choice of well established local figures. The average age of the eighteen
men whose date of birth is known was forty-eight, not including the
seventy-one-year-old cleric who was appointed but begged to be excused.[39] Only one was under thirty. The same aging occurred in the Paris

electoral assembly, where the average age rose from forty-three in 1792 to forty-eight in the Year IV.[40]

Nevertheless, this was not a return to the old notables, even if certain individuals had held office under the Old Regime. Only sixteen of the fifty-six men proposed for or appointed to the Civil Committee belonged to notable families established in the Faubourg Saint Marcel before the Revolution. In the space of a few years, an enormous change had taken place. It was in part a result of the turnover in the local elite produced by the abandonment of local loyalties and the preference for citywide marriage alliances, even before 1789. It reflected to some degree a political exodus from the quarter: among those who had left, for example, was André Aclocque. But the shift also reflected the change in the nature of notability brought about by the Revolution. Political allegiance and public service had taken the place of family, while wealth and education were now more important than before.

A glance at the known occupations of the Civil Committee members of 1795 illustrates this (see Table 8.1). The river trades were now poorly represented, and the Gobelins manufactory, the local center of revolutionary agitation, provided only one man. New occupations had made their appearance: teachers and government employees. When the civil committees were abolished, that of the Jardin des Plantes Section pointed out that most of its members had no other income: they had become professional civil servants.[41] This was a sign of things to come.

It is true that the civil committees did not demonstrate much independence. They were, if that of the Finistère Section is typical, obsessed by legality and fearful, following the Terror, of making a mistake.[42] Nevertheless, both they and the members of the Welfare Committee exercised considerable local power. Much of the Civil Committee's time was spent organizing food rationing, a task that earned it the hatred of the local women, who suspected its members of looking after their friends. They also distributed ration tickets for coal and issued residence certificates. In conjunction with the Welfare Committee, they received objections to assessments for the forced loan of December 1795.[43]

These functions, and particularly the power to issue or refuse attestations of good citizenship, which might be required for all sorts of administrative purposes, gave the civil committees a great deal of power over ordinary citizens. The Welfare Committee, which signed certificates on behalf of indigent citizens and for others seeking government jobs, was likewise a source of patronage.[44] The committees almost certainly had a

Table 8.1 Occupations of members of the Civil Committee,
Gobelins/Finistère Section, 1795

Occupation	Number
Manufacturers	
Leather trades	4
Brewers	2
Starch makers	2
Ink maker	1
Dyer	1
Shopkeepers and artisans	
Mercers	2
Spicers	2
Wineshop keeper	1
Retired goldsmith	1
Candle maker	1
Furniture maker	1
Tailor	1
Merchants	
Wood merchants	2
Grain merchant	1
Other	
Building contractors	2
Rentiers	2
Government service (unspecified)	2
Teacher/professor	2
Market gardeners	2
Concierge of Gobelins	1
Clergy	1
Former occupation lost	
Soldier	1
Dancer	1
Procureur au Châtelet	1
Postal employee	1
Total	38

major influence in the sectional assemblies, too. A member of the Civil Committee was president of the Finistère Section General Assembly for a good part of the Year III, and two other *commissaires* acted as secretary at different times. They were well placed to guide the sectional assembly not only in the selection of candidates for the committees themselves, but also in elections for the justice of the peace and the *commissaire de police*.

The notables' control over the sections nevertheless remained shaky. The statement by a deputation from the Faubourg Saint Marcel to the Convention on 17 March 1795, that "we are on the verge of regretting all the sacrifices we have made for the Revolution," did not emanate from the highly deferential committees, who came before the Convention the following day to repudiate it. In Germinal, and again in Prairial, they once more lost control. On 1 Prairial (20 May 1795) illegal sectional assemblies were convened in many parts of Paris, including the Faubourg Saint Marcel, and in the Finistère Section one of their first actions was to try to force the Civil Committee to rearm those who had been dismissed from the National Guard. The following day the Committee was told by a hostile crowd "that it was no longer anything, that the sovereign people had reclaimed their rights."[45]

"Order" was soon restored, of course. The result of these events, in the short term, was actually to increase the powers of the civil committees. They were given the task of disarming former "terrorists" following the Germinal rising, and after Prairial were asked to report on individuals within their section. The sectional assemblies also reassumed the power to arrest and disarm suspects, although it was now the former Jacobins and insurgents who were the targets.[46] It is noticeable, though, that the sections of the Faubourg Saint Marcel were very moderate in these reprisals. Much to the annoyance of the Surveillance Committee of the arrondissement, in July 1795 the Civil Committee of the nearby Panthéon Section refused to sign any more denunciations of former militants. Despite the campaign launched against possible participants in the September massacres of 1792, the Finistère committee reported in late October that no one had been arrested, and the Observatoire Section, which had set up a special commission to seek out the guilty, had received no denunciations. (It is true that the Jardin des Plantes Section arrested thirty-eight alleged *septembriseurs,* but one of the main prisons where the massacres had taken place was in that section.)

The Finistère General Assembly was even prepared to defend some of the accused of Prairial, declaring, for example, that one man, whose participation in the rising was undeniable, "has always shown himself in the section to be a friend of order and of peace."[47] Another was pronounced to have been simply in error and was immediately released. Even Charles Joseph LeBrigand, a member of the Revolutionary Committee at the height of the Terror and president of the illegal sectional assembly on 2 Prairial, was released after less than two months in prison and rearmed shortly after. As soon as the section members realized that disarmament meant dismissal for any public functionary, they immediately retracted the disarming of four former members of the Revolutionary Committee. The members of the Civil Committee showed themselves less forgiving toward the women whom they blamed for the violence against them, but the penalty of two months' imprisonment imposed by the Military Commission on the three eventually convicted does not seem particularly vengeful.[48]

In this area the repression was certainly not the class war that it is sometimes depicted. Did the notables fear eventual reprisals? Was there pressure from the populace of the section to which even the restored notables were vulnerable? Or did the local elite wish to avoid embittering the population further? It is even possible that they did not wish to pursue men who, after all, had left them fairly much alone even during the Jacobin period: although a number were imprisoned, none of the local notables was guillotined and little property was confiscated. Only five men from the section were executed, all for their activities outside the area, and two of them immediately after Thermidor, as Jacobins.[49]

Certainly, the position of the notables was strong by Vendémiaire Year IV, and the insurrection of that month, though generally represented as a royalist or counterrevolutionary insurrection, was in many parts of Paris an attempt by these local notables to defend their own sovereignty. It was not the new constitution that offended them: the requirement for voters to have been resident for one year and to pay tax equivalent to at least three days' labor did not adversely affect any of the local elite, and in practice probably did not disenfranchise a great many militants. It is true that the conditions for becoming a second-tier elector—owning or renting property capable of producing revenue equal to two hundred days' work at a basic wage, later set at 450 francs for Paris—may have excluded some of those who had been politically active since Thermidor.[50] What angered the notables, though, was the requirement that at least two-thirds of the deputies to the new legislative body be members of the existing Convention. "The primary assemblies of Paris are agitating in favor of the sovereignty of the People," wrote Nicolas Ruault, a model moderate republican. "They are almost all opposed to the decree which flings 500 *conventionnels* into the new legislative body. They are not wrong, in my view; this decree violates the national will."[51]

The sections attempted to coordinate their actions, and most defied the order to cease their meetings. The Convention further inflamed the situation by bringing troops into Paris and by rearming many Jacobin supporters. In response, most of the sections themselves took to arms, though it is not known whether the Finistère Section was among them. Only a small number participated in the armed royalist insurrection, while the others probably took up weapons to defend their own quarters against possible attack by brigands and "terrorists."[52]

This attempt to safeguard the sovereignty of the local notables, who like the sansculottes saw themselves as "the People," in the end had precisely the opposite effect, for it gave the Convention an excuse to dissolve the sectional assemblies. No popular societies were permitted, collective petitions were outlawed, and henceforth, under the Constitution of the Year III, the only legal local gatherings were the annual primary assemblies called to elect both the deputies to the legislature and the local administrators. They were to last no more than ten days, and were forbidden to discuss anything other than the election of representatives. If the full number of administrators were not chosen in the time allowed, the Directory would select them. While the sections (now called "divisions") were retained as the primary electoral units, they lost their independence totally. Henceforth, Paris was to have twelve municipalities, one for each of the twelve arrondissements. They were to be responsible for all local administration. The civil committees were to disappear, and the only local bodies retained were the welfare committees, which seem to have lasted until the Year VI.[53]

This change totally destroyed the revolutionary political structure in Paris. The troublesome sections disappeared. There was now no central body, no Commune, through which the citizens of Paris could trouble the government. The twelve municipalities were far larger than the sections, than the quarters of the Old Regime, or the parishes of either old or new regimes, so that local loyalties were diluted and divided. The seven notables elected as administrators of each of the new municipalities, three of whom were replaced one year and four the next, found themselves working with men whom they might never have met before, men whose previous public life had been in another section.

On both a social and a political level, therefore, the new arrangements encouraged the mixing of the Parisian bourgeoisie and the formation of contacts beyond the locality. The administrators of the Twelfth Municipality were drawn from all four of the former sections and represented the full range of bourgeois occupations. The members of the Surveillance Committee of the arrondissement—thirty-three of them in the Years III and IV—were likewise drawn from all parts of the arrondissement and from a wide range of bourgeois professions (see Table 8.2).[54]

Even for these men, the new administrative arrangements greatly limited the opportunities for political activity of any sort after the Year IV (late 1795). Although a larger number of men were eligible to vote than in 1791—in the Finistère Division there were 2,474 potential voters in the Year VII (1798–1799), compared with 774 in 1791 (but 3,783 in the years 1793–1794)—the participation rates were very low. In the Jardin des Plantes Division (4,397 potential voters) in the Year IV, only 103 came on the first day to elect the justice of the peace and 60 for the election of assessor—both on the second attempt, since only a handful

Table 8.2 Occupations of members of the Surveillance Committee of the Twelfth Arrondissement, Years III–IV

Occupation	Number
Manufacturers	
Leather trades	1
Brewers	2
Dyer	1
Furniture makers	2
Shopkeepers and artisans	
Apothecaries	2
Goldsmith	1
Merchants	
Wood merchant	1
Other	
Rentiers	2
Concierge of Gobelins	1
Former clergy	1
Lawyers	4
Librarian	1
Total	19

of citizens had turned up the first time.[55] The electoral process was long and involved, and the assemblies were held during working hours, sometimes over several days and often outside the quarter. In the Year V the elections for the entire Fifth Arrondissement—the area from Saint Nicolas des Champs to La Villette—were held in different parts of the church of Saint Laurent. The same arrangement was used in the Eleventh Arrondissement the following year.[56] The whole electoral system was designed to place electoral power firmly in the hands of a small group of wealthy citizens.

But not just any kind of wealthy citizens. The government ensured that only the right kinds of notables were in positions of authority. In the Year V (1797), after the coup of 18 Fructidor, all the elections were set aside and the administrators of the Paris municipalities appointed by the Directory.[57] In the Year VI (1798), in the First, Tenth, and Eleventh Arrondissements the Department recognized the need to replace "the vicious majority" chosen by the voters. New purges took place in 1799 and again following Napoleon's coup of Brumaire Year VIII (November 1799). Any attempt by the administrators of the municipalities to encourage political discussion resulted in their removal.[58] The most the notables could do was express their displeasure by electing men opposed to the regime, who would not be permitted to take office. Or they could, if themselves chosen by the Directory, refuse the position, as quite a number did.[59] Many, however, were undoubtedly content with the new regime. They were prepared to trade political participation for stability.

The restrictions on the ability even of enfranchised citizens to influence the government were accompanied by the total exclusion, in law, of women. Once again it was the Jacobin regime that began this process, with the closing of women's clubs on 30 October 1793 (9 Brumaire Year II), preceded by more minor but symbolically significant statements such as the exclusion of women from the army in April 1793: military service was a concomitant of citizenship, so removal from the one denoted exclusion from the other. "Anaxagoras" Chaumette's affirmation on 27 Brumaire Year II that "the woman's place [is] in the home and only the man's in politics," and Jean-Baptiste Amar's similar remarks, applauded by the Convention, are frequently quoted.[60]

The Thermidoreans endorsed these sentiments and prohibited women from attending political meetings of any kind, hence excluding them from the sectional assemblies where hitherto some of them had played a significant role. This was accompanied by a law forbidding women from gathering in public places in groups of more than five. It is hard to see how the deputies imagined this could be enforced, given the necessity to line up for bread every day, but it had both symbolic value, as a statement about what they saw as the proper place of women, and practical utility in authorizing the dispersal of potentially troublesome gatherings. Another law tried to get the wives of immigrant Jacobin politicians to return to the provinces.[61]

It is hard to say whether these laws greatly affected bourgeois women in Paris. Not very much in fact, is known about their involvement in the Revolution. But it is difficult to see how the wives of section officials could have enjoyed the luxury of regular political activity, for the weight of running both business and family now fell on them. This may be why, when six ladies were nominated to accompany the men sent to appeal to the National Assembly for the release of those arrested after the sugar riot of 1792, they had to be notified: none of them was present at the meeting. The rarity of couples attending meetings together is confirmed by Dominique Godineau, who indicates rather that it was single or older women who were active. Female relatives of section officials were influential in the general assemblies, and some single or newly married bourgeois women like Pauline Léon regularly attended the clubs and popular societies, as well as participating in the revolutionary *journées*. She and others like her were driven out of political life well before Thermidor.[62]

In the Years III and IV, women played a central role in reopening the churches, just as in the early days of the de-Christianization campaign bourgeois women had kept churches open as long as possible. They were of course not among those to whom the keys of the churches were officially handed over; nor (in the Twelfth Arrondissement, at least) were they among those who came forward to state that they were intending to hold religious services in their premises. Nevertheless, in the former parish of Saint Sulpice a Madame de Soyecourt, who had bought the nearby Carmelite church, made it available to the former parishioners when services were again allowed. In Floréal Year IV, ten priests were officiating regularly, illegally, at the former Filles-Dieu convent, now owned by a Mademoiselle Melon.[63] And it was almost certainly the mass support of women—of all classes—that allowed so many churches to reopen so quickly.

Well-to-do women were often the custodians of church furniture and ornaments: the copes and some seating at Saint Médard; a large collection of hymnbooks and a whole chapel full of furnishings at Saint Laurent (in this case sold back to the church by the two women concerned, presumably in reimbursement of their cost).[64] The running of the churches was confided to men, as it always had been, but local women took an active interest in parish affairs, as is demonstrated by the intervention, mentioned earlier, by fifteen or eighteen determined ladies at Saint Merri in 1801.[65] The government did not look favorably on this sort of activity either.

Bourgeois women, therefore, were just as much the targets of the postrevolutionary measures as the fishwives and stall keepers of Paris. The laws proscribed a group defined not by particular occupational or socioeconomic characteristics, but by gender, and were grounded in arguments about the incapacity of women to act rationally or independently. Furthermore, they were followed by other measures designed to confine *all* women to the sphere of house and family. As Geneviève Fraisse has pointed out, before the Revolution exceptional women, women of science and letters, had been tolerated: the very fact that they were exceptional confirmed the stereotypes. Now, in an age that espoused equality before the law, such women were dangerous examples because what was open to one should be open to all.[66]

But more was at play than simply the internal logic of revolutionary rhetoric. The experience of Revolution had converted a majority of men in power, and many women too, to the view—already in existence before 1789—that women had become too influential. In the 1750s, Rousseau had condemned women's negative influence on public morality. Rétif de la Bretonne developed the same idea in *Les Gynographes* (1777), where he proposed measures "to put Women back in their place." Other writers took the same view. In 1780 the future revolutionary Jacques-Pierre Brissot suggested that one way of reducing crime was for women and children to be taught to respect their fathers and husbands, and men to respect the king.[67]

There was, toward the end of the Old Regime, a vigorous debate over the proper role of women, and particularly over the education of girls. This may have resulted in some measure from a real change in the place of bourgeois women in Paris. The relaxation of patriarchal control by the older generation, thanks in part to the gradual disappearance of local lineages, potentially allowed bourgeois women greater autonomy. Whatever its sources, in 1789 this debate remained unresolved, balanced between those who favored greater economic and public opportunities for women and those who advocated a more restricted role.[68]

The Revolution tipped the balance in favor of the paternalists. After 1795, counterrevolutionaries blamed the apocalypse at least partly on the moral deterioration of French public life during the reign of Louis XVI. The solution, wrote the Vicomte de Bonald (who in 1816 would move the abolition of divorce), was to restore "the natural relations that make up the family." "[The exercise of] power will be gentler, when . . . women have neither control of their persons nor the free disposal of their goods. Peace and virtue will reign in the household . . . when there is no longer, in the home as in public society, either confusion of person or displacement of power." "Families," affirmed the Abbé du Voisin in 1798, "like political societies, essentially presuppose authority and submission."[69]

Moderate republicans, though less pessimistic, were nevertheless shaken by the experience of the Terror and were similarly inclined to attribute its excesses to an overdose of democracy and equality, including the participation of women. A great many more French people, disillusioned after the experience of dearth, war, religious strife, bloodshed, and political turmoil, sought a return to stability and were disposed to accept this argument. As Lynn Hunt has shown, the changing view of women's place was reflected in the official iconography, in which the female figure of Liberty, the representation of the Republic, became more static and conservative. The fierce, bare-breasted figures of 1793 were replaced on the vignette of the Executive Directory of 1798 by a modest, seated figure with no weapons.[70] The ideal woman of the Directory politicians was passive and unthreatening. Even former Jacobins who had not lost their faith in equality, men like Sylvain Maréchal, a member of Babeuf's Conspiracy of the Equals, blamed what they saw as the failure of the Revolution on the excessive interference of women in politics, inspired—in their view—by counterrevolutionary priests.[71] Maréchal's *Projet d'une loi portant défense d'apprendre à lire aux femmes* (1801) linked women's education and politics, and pointed to the dangers that women in public life posed for the family and for private and public morality. The whole arsenal of Enlightenment arguments about women's physical and mental incapacity led Maréchal to the inexorable conclusion—also his first premise—that "the place of women is at home, or in family gatherings."[72]

As Maréchal and others saw clearly, education was central to the exercise of power. Indeed, proposals to reorganize the French education system early in the Revolution had acknowledged this. Talleyrand's proposed law of September 1791 specified that "all lessons given to children in institutions of public education will particularly aim to impart to girls the virtues of domestic life and the talents of utility in the government of a family."[73] After Thermidor the education system was again transformed, and girls were excluded from the future powerhouses of the French administration: the central schools, the Ecole Normale, and the Ecole Polytechnique, all established in late 1794 and early 1795.

In science, too, women were excluded both from the educational and the new professional institutions. Even where legislation did not explicitly mention women—for example, in the practice of medicine—ministers and government servants interpreted it as implicitly banning them.[74] Active citizenship in the Republic of Letters was to be as limited as that in the French Republic. It is no coincidence that this exclusion took place at a time when, more than ever before, science was being drawn into the service and the aureole of the state. It had become one of the gateways to power, and few could enter.[75]

At the same time that they were thus closing off women's access to public life, the Thermidoreans and their successors set about restoring the "natural" order of male dominance in the home. No immediate legislative change ensued, because marital authority had been dismantled as part of the destruction of the monarchy. Because of the close association in the minds of the revolutionaries between the family and the state, the absolute monarch was inseparable from the tyrannical father and husband. "Marital power," declared Camille Desmoulins in August 1793, "is a creation of despotic governments."[76] This association prevented any immediate reversal of the laws giving married women greater freedom, but calls for change became louder.

In July 1795 the Convention asked its Legislation Committee to revise the divorce law, and official attitudes toward divorce gradually became less favorable.[77] An early draft of the Civil Code presented to the Council of Five Hundred in Messidor Year IV (mid-1795) proposed the restoration of the husband's power over his wife's property and the removal of her right to take legal action or enter into contracts. In the event, it was not accepted, but the Directory made divorce by mutual consent harder to obtain. By the time the revised Civil Code was presented in the Year VIII (1800), the climate had changed decisively. "The husband," proclaimed the preamble, "is the head of this government [of the family] . . . He administers all goods, supervises everything, the goods and the morals of his companion."[78]

The reinforcement of authority and hierarchy that took place throughout French society in the second half of the 1790s required the restoration of paternal as well as of marital authority. Although the Revolution had rejected patriarchal imagery in favor of a fraternal concept of the nation, the deputies of the various assemblies firmly retained this ideal of the family.[79] When they realized that in destroying an authority associated with monarchy they had lifted the lid on the Pandora's box of female and juvenile rights, they attempted to close it again by a twin glorification of fatherhood and of seniority. After Thermidor the fraternal images became less conspicuous, those of the strict but benevolent father increasingly common; and paternal authority, impaired by the antimonarchical family legislation of 1792 and of the Year II, was gradually restored.

By September 1794 the Convention had rejected the earlier revolutionary rhetoric of paternal "tyranny" in favor of assertions of the need for parental protection and guidance. It is noticeable that the status of *père de famille* became an essential part of any petition, whether it sought release from prison or a job in the administration. These were not simply evocations of children to be cared for, such as were common both before and during the Revolution. By the Year III, the term acquired a talismanic quality as a guarantee of probity and civic virtue, the qualities of a good citizen. "He is a *père de famille*," added the president of the Finistère Civil Committee in his endorsement of a routine inquiry about whether a committee member could receive both a pension and a salary, "so please reply quickly." Another man selected for the same committee appealed to be excused because of his business and National Guard obligations: "I beg you," he concluded, "to consider my request, it is that of a *père de famille* who will never cease to deserve the esteem of his fellow citizens."[80] Such examples reflect the close association between citizenship and fatherhood that was also embodied in the revolutionary festivals (which invariably excluded the unmarried man) and formally enshrined in the Declaration of the Duties of Man of 5 Fructidor Year III: "No one is a good citizen if he is not a good son, good father, good brother, good friend, good husband."[81]

Growing official stress on seniority followed a similar chronology. As part of the *levée en masse*—the army recruitment of August 1793—old men were to be carried into the public squares to inspire young men to enlist, and in revolutionary festivals old men began to appear on floats and rostrums. A *fête des vieillards* (festival of old age) was introduced in 1796, and the Constitution of 1795 created the Council of Elders, restricted to men over forty who were either married or widowed. The directors themselves were to be over forty. Members of the Council of Five Hundred had to be at least twenty-five, and after 1799 at least thirty. Twenty-five was to be the minimum age for all municipal and departmental administrators, and all generals in the army were to be over thirty. In 1800 the right of partial disinheritance was finally restored, further reinforcing the authority of the propertied parent.[82]

The history of local politics in the years between 1795 and the Napoleonic conquest is, as on the national scene, one of the step-by-step reduction of access to power. "Dependent" sections of the population were the first to be formally excluded, by means of restrictive electoral laws: the poor, servants, women, the young. For those still admitted to the arcadia of citizenship, the suffrage was hedged with restrictions that reduced formal political activity at the local level. Power was taken away from ordinary citizens and vested in central agencies, some political, some bureaucratic. Increasingly, power now flowed from above, rather than from the local level to the center as it had both before the Terror and briefly after Thermidor. Simultaneously, the Directory began the process of restoring hierarchy within the social institutions that the Revolution had attempted to remodel in the image of the fraternal Republic: the parish, with an elected clergy and lay governors, and the family, with a greater equality between husband and wife and early emancipation of children.

These reversals were rich in implications for the Parisian bourgeoisie, now reemerging, like Heracles from his funeral pyre, the same yet transformed. The growth of central agencies based in Paris produced an enormous expansion in the bureaucracy, from some 670 employed in the various ministries in the 1780s to at least 13,000 government officials by 1795.[83] Many of these positions were filled by displaced venal-office holders and by lawyers and Grub Street writers who had made a precarious living in the prerevolutionary capital. Others had come from the provinces, while still more were civic-minded or crisis-stricken merchants and shopkeepers. Bourgeois they had been, and bourgeois they remained, yet their social position and their dependence on the state were quite different.[84]

By the end of the Directory, a new political system and a new organization of power had been put into place.[85] They were to last until 1830. The beneficiaries of this system were those who could adapt to the new conditions and provide the state with services it particularly needed. These people, and the new system, had a profound effect on power relations at the local level.

9

COMMERCE, SCIENCE, ADMINISTRATION

The word notable . . . *designates . . . men exercising public
authority, representatives of the liberal professions, those
most heavily taxed, all the electors . . . [and] finally all those
who by their activity, their fortune or their talents
are to be distinguished from the masses.*

—Journal des conseils de fabrique, *1834*

Commerce

In 1789 Joseph and Claude Salleron were already successful merchants. Sons of a farmer in what was soon to become the Department of the Marne, they were forty-one and thirty-nine respectively,
when the Bastille surrendered. Joseph had come to Paris in 1768, Claude
probably about the same time. Both had qualified as master curriers
there, so had presumably brought with them sufficient capital to pay the
cost of apprenticeship, of reception as a master, and of setting up in
business. In 1774, when Joseph married, he declared his total wealth
(mostly in merchandise) to amount to 4,000 livres, a very modest sum
for a Paris merchant. His wife's dowry was 3,000 livres, plus her share
of her mother's then undetermined estate.[1]

From this modest start, Joseph was to build a remarkable fortune.
Central to his success, and to that of his brother Claude, was close
cooperation between them and their older brother Jean. Within ten years
they had built up substantial businesses, Claude in the rue Galande near
Saint Séverin, Joseph on the other side of the river in the rue de la
Vannerie, and Jean further north in the rue au Maire.

It is clear that corporate regulations did not hinder them greatly. In
principle, the curriers and the tanners were concerned with different
stages of leather production. The tanners produced leather from raw

hides, and the curriers then prepared the leather for manufacture into artifacts of different kinds. By 1789, however, Claude Salleron was acting both as wholesaler and middleman, importing tanned hides in numbers exceeding his own needs and acting as Paris agent for at least one tanner outside the city. A year later he was bringing in raw hides to be processed by a Paris tanner. The arrangement suggests that he was actually in control of much of the production process. Furthermore, the quantities involved were considerable. In one transaction alone, he brought in 5,600 raw calf hides to be tanned: more than the reasonably well-to-do tanner Marin Derenusson had in his entire tannery.[2]

The Salleron brothers were not above infringing the letter as well as the spirit of the corporate regulations. These required that all leather be sold in the central Halle aux Cuirs, and that it be placed on display in lots that any master, large or small, could afford and could bid for. But on at least one occasion, Claude Salleron, officially acting as agent for a tanner, brought some thousands of hides to the market and, according to the authorities, sold only a token lot in open bidding, dividing the rest—at a very advantageous price—between himself and his two brothers. This was quite illegal. When challenged, he maintained that he had not purchased any of the leather himself, and that it was by an inexplicable error that a large quantity had been unloaded at his warehouse. He also stated that, in accordance with the rules, he had placed the whole consignment on open sale. This claim was able to be tested, since leather sold legally in the central market was all stamped by the officials there. But unfortunately, when the authorities arrived to inspect the hides, the whole lot had already been cut up into small pieces ready for further processing.[3]

Despite this incident, which suggests a certain contempt for corporate regulation, Claude Salleron was subsequently elected an official of the combined corporation of tanners and curriers. Joseph, too, was sufficiently prominent to be elected in 1789 to represent the District of Saint Jean en Grève as a member of the Commune: quite an achievement for a leather merchant in a quarter not lacking in wealthy and well-educated men. He was clearly interested in politics, for in 1790 he is listed as a member of the Société des Amis de la Constitution. It is not known precisely what his fortune then was, but Claude's is well documented. In 1782, when he first married, he was worth 50,000 livres—a very substantial sum. The marriage did his affairs no harm, for his bride, a mistress linen maker with her own business, transferred everything to him: 27,500 livres, plus a house in the central rue Saint Denis. In 1789 when she died, their combined assets amounted to nearly 195,000 livres.[4]

When the Paris corporations were dissolved in 1791, the Salleron brothers were well placed to expand their business. They were now permitted to engage openly in the full leather production process, from raw hides to finished leather goods. They were also now able to run an establishment together, and in April 1792 bought a tannery in the Faubourg Saint Marcel, in the rue de l'Oursine. They were to operate it together until at least 1807 and probably until Joseph's death in 1822. It was described by A. J. B. Parent-Duchâtelet in that year as "one of the hugest and most beautiful tanneries in the quarter."[5]

Once again, the Salleron brothers' scant respect for the letter of the law, and in this case for ordinary decency, was to assist their rise. The tannery had belonged to Pierre Planche. When he ran into difficulty with his business in 1791, his largest creditor was Claude Salleron. A few months later, he sold the tannery to the brothers. The sale documents were drawn up privately, so the price and conditions were not made known—even, it would appear, to Planche's family, though they claimed that the sum had been well below market value. The sale was illegal, because half the property had belonged to Planche's deceased wife, and hence to their children. It should not have been disposed of without the consent of their guardian. Once sold, half the proceeds were theirs, and should not have been used to pay off the father's debts. The role of the Salleron brothers in this was certainly not innocent, for both had attended, as "friends" of the family, a meeting called by the justice of the peace in December 1791 to name a guardian for the Planche children.

Nor was that all. The Planche family having obtained a court judgment declaring the sale invalid, Claude and Joseph Salleron came to an arrangement with the children's guardian. The family then challenged this deal, which had been authorized by an assembly of "friends" on the grounds that there were no relatives in Paris. At least six relatives lived in the city, said the family, a fact well known to the Salleron brothers. It took three meetings with the *juge de paix* before they agreed to take the matter to independent arbiters. Unfortunately, the end of the story is not known—but the Salleron brothers kept the tannery.[6]

Now established firmly as major manufacturers, they probably provided leather for the revolutionary armies: Claude's son certainly did. Like many other astute businessmen, the brothers probably bought and sold *biens nationaux*: the declaration of Claude's possessions made after his death includes property in the Seine et Marne and Yonne Departments. He was subsequently to purchase another large tannery in the rue Saint Hippolyte.[7]

During the Revolution, Joseph began his public career in earnest. Early in 1793, soon after moving to the Faubourg Saint Marcel, he became president of the Welfare Committee.[8] Having been briefly in prison, in mid-1794 he resumed his place on the Welfare Committee, and later served on the Civil Committee. In the Year VIII (1800) he became deputy mayor of the Twelfth Arrondissement, a position he held until removed in 1816 for his "bad" (that is, liberal) opinions. In 1801 he served as syndic for the Bièvre administration and drew up the tax lists, and in 1803 he was appointed to the new vestry of Saint Médard. During the Empire, he was also elected to the Tribunal de Commerce, the commercial court of Paris.[9]

By this stage his wealth was considerable. In 1805 he appeared on the list of the sixty most highly taxed men in the department; he was one of only two manufacturers on the list. At about this time he gave one of his sons a marriage portion of 30,000 francs, and in 1809 his third son received 50,000 francs. In the same year, Salleron and his wife purchased a very large house and garden in the rue Neuve Sainte Geneviève, for which they paid 24,000 francs. In 1812 his annual income was 25,000 francs, which probably made him one of the wealthiest manufacturers in the city. When he died he owned real estate in Paris valued at close to 190,000 francs and other effects worth over 40,000 francs (probably an underestimate, since it was for tax purposes): less than one would expect from his prosperity during the Empire, but a substantial fortune none the less.[10]

Claude was even more successful, both politically and financially. He did not venture into public life until the Year VI (1798–1799), when he became assessor for the justice of the peace of the Observatoire Division. In 1810 he was appointed to the vestry of Saint Médard, an honor he was to enjoy until 1822. Also in 1810, he was named to the first *conseil général des manufactures,* together with prominent manufacturers such as François Richard-Lenoir and Guillaume Ternaux, and played an active role in all matters concerning the leather industry. In 1814, like Richard-Lenoir, he was made commander of one of the twelve legions of the newly reorganized Paris National Guard. "When the Patrie is in danger, every citizen is a soldier," he wrote to Napoleon's minister of the interior.[11]

In this case Salleron was fortunate in living in a poor arrondissement,

Rue Neuve Sainte Geneviève, a salubrious street away from the Bièvre River. Joseph Salleron lived at number 23.

for he would certainly not have achieved such a prestigious appointment if he had lived among more prominent citizens. The prefect's original suggestion for this post was the banker Delessert, who perhaps refused. But Salleron clearly did not betray the trust placed in him, for on Napoleon's return from Elba he was named—again alongside Richard-Lenoir—one of the *conseillers généraux* of the Department of the Seine, a very prestigious office. Thus tainted, under the second Restoration he was replaced as legion commander by the Duc de Montmorency—an indication of the status of the post and of the weight the authorities accorded it. But after Montmorency's sudden death in 1818, Salleron was again appointed. This time the mayor had suggested Montmorency's brother, but the minister of the interior replied that the king "wanted a candidate among the citizens resident in the quarter for a reasonably long time."[12]

In the same year, 1818, Salleron was awarded the Légion d'honneur. These accomplishments no doubt assisted him toward the peak of his public career: his election as a liberal in 1822 to the Chamber of Deputies, where he remained for two years. By then he was seventy-three and ready to retire. When he died in February 1833, his Paris estate was valued at 174,000 francs, but he owned a substantial number of properties in the neighboring departments.[13] By any measure, it was a startlingly successful career.

Just as the Salleron brothers typified, in many respects, those who profited from the Revolution and the Empire, their children are representative of the generation that came to maturity under the Empire and to public life during the Restoration. Joseph and Marie Jeanne Salleron had three sons and a daughter. One died young, but in 1811 the elder surviving son, Claude Louis, formed a tanning company with a capital base of 1,000,000 francs, of which he contributed half. In 1821 he provided his daughter with a huge dowry of 85,000 francs, and in 1828 he was one of the most heavily taxed citizens in the entire Twelfth Arrondissement.[14]

But his younger brother Augustin paid even more. He had been launched into marriage in 1809 with 50,000 francs from his parents, and his young wife, the daughter of a wood merchant in the Faubourg Saint Honoré, also brought a dowry of 50,000 francs. Five months later Augustin Salleron signed a contract with Augustin Bricogne, his brother-in-law, to run a tannery into which he put 100,000 francs, presumably the combined dowries. In the 1820s he was involved in what must have been the very lucrative subdivision of the extensive former Cordelières convent in the rue de l'Oursine, and was one of those responsible for opening the rue Pascal. He retained a number of houses on the site.[15] Bricogne, who at a tender age helped to provide furnishings for the reopened church of Saint Médard, had married Marie Françoise Salleron in 1805. In 1807 he was described as one of the principal tanners, and in 1814 as having a "very considerable commerce" and as being "influential in the quarter."[16]

These thriving business careers were matched by recognition in public life. Both Claude Louis and Augustin Salleron were proposed as officers in the National Guard in 1814, and Bricogne was appointed battalion commander. Augustin Salleron and Bricogne were both appointed to the vestry of Saint Médard, and Salleron followed his father in becoming deputy mayor of the arrondissement in 1830. In 1831 he requested a post as prefect.[17]

Claude Salleron's children were younger. In 1814 his daughter married a notary, André Cristy, son of a former employee in the Ministry of War. He claimed his practice and assets to be worth 100,000 francs, while Claude and Marie Perpétue Salleron gave their daughter 106,000 francs in dowry. This huge endowment was witnessed by an impressive group: Jean Joseph Augustin Dessolle, peer of the realm and commander of the National Guard; the Marquis de Dampierre; the Comte de Ségur, also a peer and a member of the prestigious Institut de France, and his wife Elisabeth Daguesseau; Baron Guyot de Chenizot, a former *conseiller d'état*; the army officer Leon Pierre De Vigny and his son Alfred (the future poet); and a host of lesser luminaries. All were present as friends of the Cristy family, but they indicate the illustrious circles into which Claude Salleron was able to marry his children.[18]

Joseph's children were not able to enter quite the same world, but their father's position as deputy mayor and their own marriages placed them firmly in the milieu of wealthy merchants and industrialists and of high-ranking administrators. The alliance with the Bricogne family in 1805 was probably mutually beneficial. Athanase Jean Bricogne was a member of the prestigious mercers' corporation before the Revolution, and a precise contemporary of the Salleron brothers, though unlike them he was Paris-born. In the same year that his son married Marie Françoise Salleron, he became mayor of the Sixth Arrondissement, a useful ally not only for Joseph, deputy mayor since 1800, but also for the younger Salleron generation, particularly Augustin, who also harbored mayoral ambitions. Both Bricogne and Joseph Salleron were liberals, however, and were replaced under the Bourbons.[19]

Another useful marriage, this one during the Restoration, was that of Claude Louis Salleron's only daughter to the son of a former *receveur général des finances* (an important Old Regime office). It was attended by a constellation of *conseillers* from the Cour des Comptes and by a chef and a sous-chef of the Conseil d'Etat.[20] Given the obvious personal ambition of the Salleron brothers, these alliances were certainly part of a deliberate strategy of family advancement.

Nearly all the marriages took place, it should be noted, outside the quarter and even outside the arrondissement. Cristy lived in the rue Neuve des Petits Champs and was born in the parish of La Madeleine, while Claude Louis Salleron's son-in-law Félix Passy probably lived on the Chaussée d'Antin. Claude Louis's own wife hailed from the rue de la Mortellerie and was perhaps a childhood acquaintance, for he had lived in the Grève quarter until he was thirteen. Augustin Salleron's spouse came from the Faubourg Saint Honoré, while Augustin Bricogne had grown up in the rue Saint Denis.

In the previous generation, both of the Salleron brothers had already married outside the quarter in which they were then living, and both subsequently moved to another part of the city altogether. The younger members of the family likewise displayed little attachment to the quarter of their birth: by 1837 Jean François Salleron was the only one still working in the Faubourg Saint Marcel. Claude Louis had retired and moved to the Faubourg Saint Honoré.[21] These were families for whom neither quarter nor parish of origin had any great significance. If this is explicable, in the case of the older Salleron brothers, by the fact that they were immigrants, for their children it is a reflection of the development of a truly citywide bourgeoisie.

But this certainly did not lessen the store they placed in family ties. The business collaboration that had been central to their initial success did not end with the first generation. Claude Louis and his son-in-law, Félix Passy, formed a partnership that had all the trademarks of an apprenticeship, for Passy was not permitted to enter any contracts for the company in the first four years but after that became an equal partner.[22] Augustin Salleron collaborated with his Marcellot brothers-in-law in the subdivision of the Cordelières land, and earlier entered a partnership with his other brother-in-law, Augustin Bricogne. Business cooperation was often accompanied by coresidence. Claude and Joseph

Salleron seem to have lived together briefly when they first moved to the Faubourg Saint Marcel. Augustin Bricogne and Augustin Salleron, during their collaboration, lived in separate wings of the tannery. Félix Passy moved in with his father-in-law Claude Louis Salleron after marrying in 1821.[23]

Close family contact was taken to its extreme in a surprising number of endogamous marriages. Both Claude and Joseph Salleron married distant relatives. The wife of Joseph's eldest son, Charles, had already been married to a Jacques Salleron, and upon Charles's premature death wed Claude Louis Salleron. In the next generation, Adelaide Josephine Salleron married her first cousin.[24] These were very safe marriages that helped concentrate the patrimony in fewer hands. The Salleron family was not alone in this practice, for Adeline Daumard comments on its frequency among the Parisian bourgeoisie and Jean-Pierre Bardet has observed that first-cousin marriages, rare before 1789, became much more common in Rouen after the Revolution.[25] One has the impression of families closing ranks against the uncertainties of the time and returning to many of the strategies of the late-seventeenth- and early-eighteenth-century lineages like the Bouillerot family. But instead of forming alliances with local families whose history and assets were well known, the Salleron family, when not marrying relatives, reached out to other parts of the city, to distant families with very similar social and economic standing but not necessarily the same occupation.

They also differed from the early-eighteenth-century lineages in adopting a conscious strategy of social promotion. A reflection of this is the aspiration to gentility expressed in the exclusion of the women from the business. After the brothers became wealthy, it is very unlikely that any of the women worked either with them or independently. Claude's first wife had been a successful linen maker, but there is no trace in the inventory of her estate in 1789—only seven years after their marriage— that she had continued her business. Joseph's wife almost certainly helped run their business in the 1770s and 1780s, but probably no longer did so after the Revolution. She survived him by three years and upon her death still owned their tannery, but as she was then seventy-seven, and the tannery had for most of the preceding decade been run by Augustin Salleron and Augustin Bricogne, it seems very unlikely that she had played any role in the business for some years.

Further circumstantial evidence comes from the family's residential arrangements. Soon after moving to the Faubourg Saint Marcel and setting up in business with Joseph, Claude and Marie Perpétue Salleron moved into a house in the rue des Postes, within walking distance of the tannery but in a far more salubrious street. The eldest daughter was then an infant, the other two not yet born. No firm evidence shows that Madame Salleron kept away from the tannery, but the new separation of home and work probably reflects the separation of gender roles within the household.[26]

Whatever their parents' views on the subject, Augustin Bricogne and Augustin Salleron had a very clear idea of a wife's role. In the contract establishing their partnership they specified that, should one of them die, the widow could take over, on condition that she pay an agent to help in the running of the company and to look after her interests. Both their wives, it seems, were unfamiliar with business and would need help and protection in such circumstances. The family firm was a male affair.[27]

It was also a male matter in its name. It is no coincidence that businesses established in the early nineteenth century increasingly took the name of the male owners, rather than one taken from the place, the street, or—as invariably happened in the seventeenth or eighteenth centuries—from the shop sign. Men like Joseph and Claude Salleron sought places of honor and influence in public life, and their ambition was reflected in their proud adoption of the business name "Salleron frères." In 1803, when Joseph responded to a neighbor's complaint that he *and his wife* had failed to block up some windows overlooking the adjoining property, he signed the document not with his own name, but as "Salleron frères"! Later, Claude Louis Salleron was to adopt the name "Salleron fils et Compagnie," and in his dealings with partners he always retained control of the firm's affairs. The same desire to keep the firm in the male line underpinned the stipulation in the contract between Augustin Bricogne and Augustin Salleron that should the wife of one of them take over his interest in the company, she could do so only as long as she did not remarry. No outsiders were to be brought in, except on the male partners' own terms.[28]

The Salleron family typify the successful commercial bourgeoisie of the late-eighteenth and early-nineteenth centuries. While retaining close-knit family connections, they married into other families scattered across the city. Their wealth, like that of much of the Parisian bourgeoisie of the period, was recent, their social advancement a product of the Revolution and Empire. The brothers were fortunate that the Revolution came at the precise moment when they were at the peak of their commercial power and able to profit from the opportunities it presented. Under the Old Regime, they might have hoped to purchase minor offices for their sons and to conclude marriages with similar officeholders for their daughters. For themselves, they could not have aspired to more than a wealthy retirement, with positions as churchwardens and a place of honor in the quarter. The Revolution and Empire enabled them to move in circles where they might otherwise never have made the slightest contact.

The Salleron brothers were a little unusual in the height and rapidity of their rise. But a great many similar families in these years achieved far more rapid advancement than they could have hoped for in 1789. The Albinet brothers, in the same quarter, provide another example of family collaboration and steady economic advancement. Originally from the Aveyron, they probably came to the Faubourg Saint Marcel early in the Revolution, at about the same time and almost the same age as the Salleron brothers. They were soon established as major blanket makers. Neither married locally, though some of their children did. Both Etienne and Jean-François Albinet were listed among the principal manufacturers in the quarter, though only Etienne was on the vestry of Saint Médard. His two sons formed a partnership as "Albinet frères"; and whether or not they benefited from government contracts, they certainly profited from the new regime, winning a prize at the industrial exhibition of 1806.[29]

The Aclocque family provides another instance of extraordinary social promotion. André Aclocque was already a successful brewer in 1789. Forced out of the Faubourg Saint Marcel because of his political role during the Revolution, he bought a vinegar distillery near Saint André des Arts. His son took over the business in 1802 and became one of the richest industrialists in the quarter, commander of a legion of the National Guard, member of the Légion d'honneur, and finally a noble under the Restoration.[30]

Yet another example of spectacular advancement, again from the Faubourg Saint Marcel, is Michel Joseph Mattler, a leather manufacturer born in Germany in 1763 who came to Paris and began working in the Faubourg Saint Antoine. In 1793 he married the daughter of a local wagon maker, each of them bringing a small dowry of 3,000 livres. He subsequently inherited 3,000 livres from his parents' estate: a further indication of modest origins. In 1799 the couple were able to pay 12,800 livres toward a house in the Faubourg Saint Marcel, and when she died in 1802 they also owned land at Bagnolet, Charonne, and Montreuil, probably *biens nationaux*. Mattler's second wife, a widow from the Gravilliers Division, brought a dowry of 90,000 francs. In 1807 he was listed as one of the principal manufacturers in the quarter, and in 1812 one finds him diversifying his interests, investing in a dye works. One of his daughters married a local grocer, a second wed a *négociant* in the Marais, the third a hatter in the rue Dauphine. His son worked with him as *commis*. Mattler drops out of sight after 1825, when he resigned from the vestry of Saint Médard and left the quarter, but for an immigrant with few resources he had done extraordinarily well.[31]

There had been such success stories before, of course, but what was unusual about this period was their frequency (accompanied, it is true, by some spectacular collapses). As Adeline Daumard, Louis Bergeron, Serge Chassagne, and others have demonstrated, the times were conducive to exceptional social mobility. Many individuals, like the Salleron and Albinet brothers, like Aclocque and Mattler, were able to capitalize on the economic opportunities opened by the Revolution and Empire, particularly the abolition of the trades corporations, military and government contracts, and the sale of church and émigré land.

Wealth opened the way to social advancement through strategic marriage alliances with both the old and new elites, through office, and through service to the regime. In each case, too, economic and social mobility was accompanied by geographical and occupational mobility. Changes of region, of quarter, and of trade became commonplace among a merchant bourgeoisie with wide connections across the city and, increasingly, across the nation.[32]

Science

On 2 March 1826 the vestry of Saint Médard met to fill a vacancy. The minutes do not reveal how many candidates were proposed, but by the end they had unanimously agreed upon Etienne Geoffroy-Saint-Hilaire, professor of zoology at the Natural History Museum. He joined, on the great bench of honor at the front of the church, the tanners Claude Salleron and Augustin Bricogne, the blanket maker Etienne Albinet, the dye maker Antoine Robert Dheur, and the local schoolteacher Jean-Baptiste Savouré. Two months later this talent was to be supplemented by the skills of André Laugier, professor at the Jardin du Roi and a member of the Royal Academy of Medicine.[33]

Geoffroy-Saint-Hilaire was one of the galaxy of talent that made Paris, at the end of the eighteenth and beginning of the nineteenth century, the scientific capital of the Western world. He was also, in many ways, a typical product of the educational system and extraordinary opportunities provided by those turbulent years. Born in 1772 in Etampes, just south of Paris, Etienne Geoffroy-Saint-Hilaire came from a reasonably affluent but not wealthy family. His father was a minor official in the courts, but apparently with good contacts in Paris.

The family had a tradition of learning, for in the early eighteenth century no fewer than three of its members had become members of the Academy of Sciences; and despite having four brothers and two sisters (another seven died young), Etienne received a sound education at the Collège d'Etampes. Thanks, apparently, to his father's connections, he obtained a scholarship to study in Paris. As he had shown an inclination for academic work, his family decided that he should go into the church and in 1788 obtained him, through an abbot who was a friend of the family, the place of canon in the chapter of Sainte Croix d'Etampes. Nevertheless, having finished at the Collège de Navarre in 1790, young Etienne expressed a desire to continue studying natural history, and soon the proposed career in the church—no doubt looking less promising in revolutionary France—was abandoned.[34]

In March 1793 Louis Daubenton, who became his patron, obtained him a job in the Cabinet d'histoire naturelle in place of the comte de Lacépède, who had left Paris to avoid arrest. A few months later, when the Convention created the Museum of Natural History and twelve chairs within it, Geoffroy-Saint-Hilaire became professor of zoology, even though at that stage it was not his specialty. He thus worked alongside Lamarck and Jussieu, as well as Daubenton. In 1798 he went with Claude Berthollet and Gaspard Monge to Egypt on Bonaparte's campaign, along with his brother Marc-Antoine, who was an engineer in the army. There he met Napoleon, whom he must have impressed, because he was soon after awarded the Légion d'honneur and was offered a prefecture, which he declined. In 1807 he became a member of the Academy of Sciences, and in 1808 was invited to do scientific work in freshly conquered Spain and Portugal. The following year he was appointed to a chair in the newly formed Faculty of Science in Paris.[35]

In 1804, at the age of thirty-two, Etienne married Angélique Jeanne Louise Pauline Brière de Mondétour, eight years his junior. Descended from an old and rich Paris family, she brought a dowry of 80,000 francs (compared with his entire fortune of 15,000 francs, as well as 10,000 francs he subsequently inherited from his parents) and excellent connections. Her father was a former *receveur général,* and was mayor of the wealthy Second Arrondissement (he lived in the rue Saint Honoré), a member of the Légion d'honneur and of the Commission des Finances, an administrator of the Paris *lycées* (upper secondary schools), and *inspecteur aux revues de la Garde de Paris.* He was also at one point elected to the Legislature. His considerable fortune, made up in part of investments in *biens nationaux,* together with his public office, placed him among the sixty most distinguished notables in the department.[36] Angélique was to inherit property worth well over 100,000 francs. Furthermore, one of her brothers was attached to the Conseil d'Etat, a good position in itself but also often a stepping-stone to high administrative posts under the Empire. The notary who drew up many of the family documents was her cousin.[37]

The couple had three children, one of whom seems to have died young. Stéphanie Geoffroy-Saint-Hilaire married in 1831 and was given a dowry of 40,000 francs, plus a trousseau worth 10,000 francs. Her husband was a Bourjot, an old Paris family, though one that had suffered financially from the Revolution.[38] Etienne and Angélique's son Isidore trained in medicine and succeeded his father at the Museum of Natural History and as a member of both the Institut and the Légion d'honneur. In 1830 he was given a marriage portion of 40,000 francs. His wife, Louise Blacque, was the daughter of a *propriétaire* (an investor in real estate) living near the Bourse, a man with mining interests and no doubt other investments. Her dowry was 150,000 francs. She was also related to the Jacquemart family, possibly the same brothers who owned a huge soap works in the Faubourg Saint Antoine and the wallpaper manufacturing plant that had once belonged to Jean-Baptiste Réveillon.[39]

Having found good marriages for their children, Etienne and his wife seem to have enjoyed a prosperous retirement. What she did once the children were grown, apart from overseeing the household, is unclear. She appears to have had musical accomplishments, as befitted a lady of her rank, for she had a collection of instruments. The couple had a cook and a chambermaid, as well as an all-purpose servant. The much greater value of her clothes in the inventory of their goods drawn up immediately after his death—1,300 francs (to which may be added 2,750 francs' worth of jewelry) compared to his worth 430 francs—suggests an investment in female gentility typical of the milieu. His salary brought in nearly 5,000 francs a year, and the income from property he owned outside

Paris amounted to as much again. As a member of the Institut, he earned an additional 1,200, and he had some investments in shares. His wife presumably had some independent income. At the time of his death, the couple's fortune amounted to 168,000 francs after debts were deducted.[40] It was not a huge amount by comparison with commercial fortunes of the time, but it placed the Geoffroy-Saint-Hilaire family firmly among the affluent middle classes of Paris. Their social position, though, is not accurately reflected in such figures. In the milieu of education and science, as in administration and the law, status did not derive primarily from wealth, as is clear both from Etienne's marriage and from those of his children. His was a profession whose standing had risen greatly during the Revolution and Empire, thanks both to the political prominence of many scientists and to the deliberate encouragement of science by the Napoleonic state.

Geoffroy-Saint-Hilaire was not a political person. He took no active part in the Revolution, although one of his cousins was married to a member of the Jacobin Club and of the Convention. The biography written by Geoffroy-Saint-Hilaire's son describes these years as entirely devoted to study (though it claims he rescued twelve priests from the September massacres). Yet science was not politically neutral. As never before, during the Revolution and Empire prominent scientists were public figures, obliged to take a stand. Etienne must have made the right noises, for the Convention named him to his first teaching position in 1793, and he seems to have won the support of Bernardin de Saint-Pierre. Later both he and his military brother supported Napoleon, as the honors showered upon him suggest.

His first active participation in politics came in 1815 when he supported the plebiscite and was elected to the new Chamber by the citizens of his birthplace, Etampes. He does not seem to have suffered for this under the second Restoration. His liberal sentiments are clear from his support for the July Revolution, though once again he does not seem to have participated, except to shelter the highly unpopular archbishop of Paris from the revolutionaries, a very courageous action.[41] Had he wished to, however, at any stage he had the affluence, the contacts, and the respect necessary for far greater political involvement. He could have won election far earlier than he in fact did. He could, like Berthollet or Fourcroy, like Chaptal, Laplace, or Monge, have moved effortlessly into a position of power in the Napoleonic state.

Despite his very different personality, interests, and sources of wealth and prestige, like the Salleron brothers Geoffroy-Saint-Hilaire was very much part of the new Parisian bourgeoisie of the early nineteenth century. Like them he was an outsider, both geographically and socially. Under the Old Regime, sons of provincial *procureurs,* however clever, were a dime a dozen. He might conceivably have become a learned abbé, an amateur scientist like so many of that cloth. Even had he been able to make a career in the university, and perhaps eventually gain entry to the Academy of Sciences like his eighteenth-century forebears, he would not have enjoyed the fame and the favor that the Napoleonic regime lavished on cooperative scientists. Without the Revolution he would not have advanced so rapidly, and it is extremely unlikely that before 1789 he would have been able to marry a Brière de Mondétour. The Museum of Natural History, the Faculty of Sciences, and, above all, the Institut de France were revolutionary and Napoleonic institutions that provided unprecedented prestige and social opportunities for men of science.

Administration

After the July Revolution, the archbishop of Paris and the prefect of the Seine selected new vestrymen for the parish churches of Paris. At Saint Médard the new vestry met for the first time on 23 September 1832, and the man they chose as president was Baron François Mathurin Des Rotours, director of the Gobelins manufactory. Sixty-four years old, he was a native of Normandy who had begun his career in the French army, becoming an artillery officer just before the Revolution at the age of eighteen. He appears to have followed the commander of his regiment, the prince de Condé, into exile and did not return until just before the defeat of Napoleon in 1814.[42]

Des Rotours's fidelity to the Bourbons earned him a minor place in the king's household, in September 1814. He was placed in charge of the Paris theaters, with a salary of 3,000 francs and a clerk to help him. During the Hundred Days he disappeared, but returned to his job in July 1815 with an increment in salary and now four subordinates. In May 1816, out of the blue, he was appointed director of the Gobelins, thanks to the patronage of the comte de Pradel, *secrétaire d'état* responsible for the king's household.[43] He suddenly found his salary doubled. He now had a twenty-room apartment, which admittedly also had to serve as his offices and included reception areas for functions, but which contained a bathroom (a rare luxury in the early nineteenth century). The 1816 budget accorded him 7,700 francs worth of furniture from the royal store.[44]

Des Rotours immediately set about reorganizing the Gobelins along more authoritarian but paternalistic lines. He drew up a new set of regulations that would give him greater authority over the workers, who he felt had profited from the Revolution to increase their pay and reduce the amount of work they did. It might be necessary, he suggested, "to combine my service in the National Guard with my role as administrator, in order to have both civil and military authority over the workers." The next year he was duly promoted to captain in the National Guard. He tried to ban the reading of newspapers in the workshops because the political discussions they provoked took up much valuable working time. At the same time, however, he wanted to introduce a minimum wage and to increase payments to the best workers.[45] A staunch monarchist, he sought information on those whose political opinions were unsatisfactory, and on the anniversary of Marie Antoinette's execution had portraits of the former king and queen placed in the chapel. These he proposed to lend to Saint Médard so that more of the local population would see them: "The sight of this picture would further deepen their horror at the crime committed."[46]

Des Rotours was apparently unmarried and the records reveal nothing of his background or kin. He must have come from a reasonably well connected family in order to join the royal army as an officer. According to Marcel Marion, the title of *chevalier* that he claimed was in principle accorded by the king and was personal, yet in practice was frequently adopted by nonnobles.[47] Despite what must have been an affluent background, Des Rotours appears to have had no property and no income except his salary. In 1820 he paid a derisory 22 francs in tax, insufficient to qualify him for election to an electoral college.[48] But here again, wealth was not a major factor. Public officials enjoyed status by virtue of their positions, and while at the national level a man like Des Rotours could have little influence, as director of the Gobelins he was incontestably a member of the local elite. It was this that made him eligible to preside over the vestry of Saint Médard and to command forty soldiers of the Paris National Guard.[49]

Had he had children, Des Rotours could undoubtedly have found places in the administration for his sons through his own patron, the comte de Pradel, and made marriage alliances for his daughters with families who enjoyed a similar status to his own, though not in the same class as a Salleron or a Geoffroy-Saint-Hilaire. Nevertheless, despite his very different political views, his lack of fortune, his provincial origins and recent arrival in the city, he too was a member of the new Parisian bourgeoisie.

A New Elite

The Salleron family, Geoffroy-Saint-Hilaire, and Des Rotours typify the Parisian bourgeoisie of the early nineteenth century. Commerce and finance, science (and the closely allied areas of medicine and education), and administration were the three areas from which the new elite were recruited. Their position no longer depended on long-standing ties with the quarter, or on family and commercial alliances within it. They were new, both to the quarter and to the status that they enjoyed there.

Three institutions enable one to observe the local elite during this period: the parish vestry, the Welfare Committee, and the National Guard. The first vestry of Saint Médard, appointed in 1803, contained six men. Three of them were manufacturing merchants: a blanket maker, a tanner, and a dye maker, occupations long associated with the quarter. The fourth member was the director of the Gobelins; the fifth was the famous botanist Jussieu; and the sixth was probably a local doctor. Although the members of this first vestry were chosen by the archbishop and the prefect, they did not differ greatly from the men who were to succeed them. Some were in fact reelected, either to a second successive term or some years later. Among the seventeen other men who served on the vestry during the Empire and the eleven additional individuals elected or appointed under the Restoration, the same three main types of occupations dominated (see Table 9.1).

The majority were manufacturers or merchants, all in trade sectors with a long history in the quarter. The others were divided between state employees, ranging from the local *commissaire de police* to two *auditeurs* in the Cour des Comptes, and men engaged in teaching or scientific research. Jussieu was of course in this last group, as were Geoffroy-Saint-Hilaire and the chemist Laugier; all three of them lived and worked at the Jardin des Plantes. These last two groups were entirely missing from the lists of churchwardens before the Revolution.

The thirty-four men who served at Saint Médard between 1803 and 1830 varied in wealth, but by local standards all were well off. At least seven of the merchants and manufacturers earned between 20,000 and

Table 9.1 Occupations of the vestry members of Saint Médard, 1803–1830

Occupation	Number		
	During Empire	During Restoration	1803–1830[a]
Merchants and manufacturers			
Leather trades	7	7	10
Dye makers	1	2	2
Spicers	1	2	2
Brewers	1	1	2
Wood merchants	1	1	2
Mercer	1	0	1
Blanket maker	1	0	1
Négociant (businessman)	1	0	1
Tapestry weaver	1	0	1
All merchants and manufacturers	15	13	22
State employees			
Commissaire de police	1	0	1
Director of Gobelins[b]	1	0	1
Cour des Comptes	2	1	2
Steward of Scipion	1	0	1
Employee at Paris *octroi*	0	1	1
All state employees	5	2	6
Professions, science, and education			
Professors	1	2	3
Doctor	1	0	1
Teacher	1	0	1
Pharmacist	0	1	1
All professions, science, and education	3	3	6
Total	23	18	34

a. Because some individuals served during both the Empire and the Restoration, this number is not always equal to the sum of the figures in the first two columns.

b. Antoine Laurent de Jussieu was a director of the Gobelins but is included here only under his principal occupation (professor).

30,000 francs a year, and at least four more had substantial assets.[50] The state employees and the education/science group had lower incomes, but unlike the merchants had secure positions. They might also possess other property: Geoffroy-Saint-Hilaire left an estate of 184,000 francs (part of which belonged to his wife); Laugier paid tax of 1,700 francs in 1820, a sum that suggests an annual income of nearly 30,000 francs.[51] By comparison, a list of notables in the wealthy Faubourg Saint Honoré in 1809 revealed annual incomes between 12,000 and 200,000 francs, with an average of 35,000 francs. In the central Réunion Division notable incomes ranged from 5,000 to 100,000 francs, with an average of 12,000.[52] The members of the vestry of Saint Médard were not out of place among the Parisian notability as a whole.

If one turns from wealth to look at each man's degree of implantation in the quarter, measured by ownership of property, length of residence, and local economic interests, the picture is much more varied. The merchants nearly all appear to have owned property locally. The state employees and the professors at the Jardin des Plantes did not; job security perhaps reduced the need for such assets. Clearly, too, the manufacturers also had a heavy investment in equipment, and a workforce to consider.[53] Retail merchants, of course, had clients in the quarter.

Of the 34 vestrymen, at least 3 were born in the quarter and 21 almost certainly were not. One came from Germany, another from Poland. Only 2 seem to have come from families present in the quarter for more than two generations. Three had arrived with their parents in the thirty or forty years before the Revolution, and 4 others were there in the 1780s. Twenty arrived after 1789, 7 of them before 1799 and another 7 after 1800. In other words, the overwhelming majority of the vestrymen were immigrants, but had been in the quarter for anywhere from five to twenty years when they were elected or appointed. Again, this is striking testimony to the geographical mobility of the years of the Revolution and Empire.

The same pattern emerges if one looks at their family ties. Seven had another family member in the quarter, more often a brother or an uncle than a full set of kin. Seven married women living in the Faubourg Saint Marcel, while another 8 married outsiders. Some kin ties existed within the vestry. Three members of the Salleron family served, though never at the same time. The schoolteacher Jean-Baptiste Savouré had a son married to the daughter of a fellow vestry member. And Pierre Lallemant's

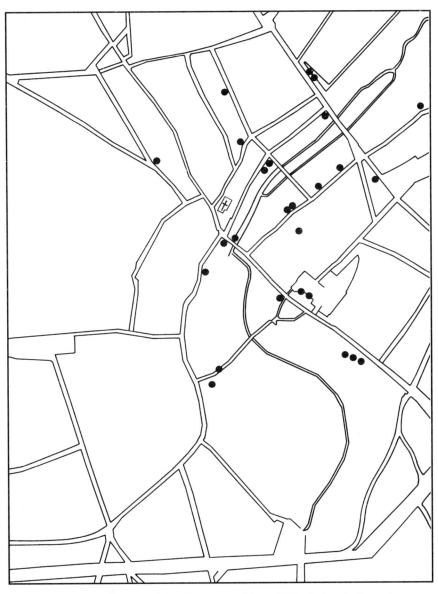

Approximate addresses of churchwardens of Saint Médard elected 1803–1830.

daughter was married to Nicolas Dheur, son of a vestryman and later to become one himself.

The contrast with the eighteenth-century vestry—even that of the 1760s or 1770s—is striking. Except in the case of the Salleron family, the most prominent in the quarter, kin ties were now largely incidental to selection; nor was long association with the area important. Mature years, a solid fortune, a sound business or a middle-ranking position in the administration or, in the case of the scientists, a national reputation, together with a good moral character: these were the components of local notability and the prerequisites for election to the vestry.

This can be tested against the two other forms of local office, one semi-elected—membership in the Welfare Committee of the Finistère Division—and the other appointed—the officer ranks of the local National Guard. The Welfare Committee had 6 members, who were responsible for poor relief in the quarter as well as for the local free primary school. They were appointed by the mayor (though in one case directly by the minister of the interior), but vacancies were filled from a list of names that the continuing members drew up themselves. A surviving register of their deliberations, covering the years 1810 to 1816, names 17 men who were appointed to the committee (of whom 3 refused) and another 16 who were proposed but not appointed.[54] Identification is often difficult, but it is almost certain that 7 of those appointed and 3 who were proposed were also members of the vestry. The occupations of 24 can be identified with reasonable certainty (see Table 9.2).

Missing from this list are scientists, doctors, and teachers, who were well represented in the vestry. This is primarily because the Finistère Division did not include the Jardin des Plantes or the slopes of the Montagne Sainte Geneviève, where such men lived. Otherwise the occupations are similar to those of the vestrymen, although the Gobelins manufactory is much more strongly represented. When one examines the local ties and the background of these men, however, two significant differences emerge. More of them belonged to families who had been in the quarter for two or more generations: at least 8, or possibly 9, of the whole 33 had had forebears (male or female) there in the early eighteenth century, and another 2 were sons of couples who had arrived in midcentury. At least 6 had arrived since 1789, and another 2 just before.

Corresponding to this greater local implantation is the greater role played by some of these men during the Revolution. Whereas only 3 of the vestrymen had held any local office between 1789 and 1794, for the

Table 9.2 Occupations of men proposed for or appointed to the Welfare
Committee, Finistère Division, 1810–1816

Occupation	Number proposed but not appointed	Number appointed	Total
Merchants and manufacturers			
Leather trades	2	4	6
Brewers	1	1	2
Starch makers	1	1	2
Blanket maker	0	1	1
Dye maker	0	1	1
Apothecary	0	1	1
Wood merchant	0	1	1
Grocer	1	0	1
All merchants and manufacturers	5	10	15
State employees			
Director of Gobelins	0	1	1
Employé aux domaines	0	1	1
Inspector at Gobelins	0	1	1
Steward of Scipion	0	1	1
Concierge of Gobelins	1	0	1
Unspecified employee of Gobelins	1	0	1
All state employees	2	4	6
Other			
Clergy (curé of Saint Médard	1	1	2
Propriétaire (investor in real estate)	1	0	1
All other	2	1	3
Unknown	7	2	9
Total	16	17	33

very good reason that most of them had not been in the area, 3 of the members of the Welfare Committee and 2—possibly 3—of the unsuccessful candidates had served on committees during that time. Most notably, Augustin Belle and Jean Etienne Cabouret had both belonged to the Revolutionary Committee in 1793, and Belle had been an elector in 1792. Cabouret had been second in command of the local National Guard in 1792, and had even been president of the popular society, but had fallen out with the principal Jacobins some months before Thermidor. All the men who had held revolutionary office and were later considered for the Welfare Committee had managed to keep a low profile both during the Terror and immediately after Thermidor. Belle had later been one of the administrators of the arrondissement, in the Year VII.[55]

Thus the Welfare Committee, while overlapping significantly with the vestry in membership, had closer and longer-standing ties with the area. This was a help in identifying the needy to whom relief should be given. It was also, in part, because of the smaller size and the geographical location of the division: it was not as large as the parish, and did not include some of the wealthier areas. Although some of the richest men and largest employers did serve on it (Salleron, Albinet), others were far less prominent, drawn from a "second tier" of local notables, whose interests and connections were more restricted. Their presence bears witness to the continuing respect accorded, at a very local level, to prominent citizens of longer standing—in several cases, to men who had played a key political role during the 1790s. There was greater continuity in this neighborhood elite than the list of vestrymen might suggest.

Nevertheless, on balance the composition of the Welfare Committee, like that of the vestry, demonstrates that local family ties to the quarter were now of minor significance. No more than a third of the Welfare Committee could claim any long connection with the Faubourg Saint Marcel, and they were not among the wealthiest. Some of them, unlike their ancestors, now had to leave the quarter to visit their closest kin. Louis Claude Duchemin, for example, descendant of a leather-dressing family long active on the Bièvre, had two children both of whom lived elsewhere (and who were to sell his house after his death in 1819).[56]

The National Guard officers provide another cross-section of the local elite, although the area from which they were drawn was much wider than either the parish or the division. If one takes only the officers of the Fourth Battalion, that drawn from the Faubourg Saint Marcel, and those among the central command of the Twelfth Legion who were from the same area, there are 38 officers for 1814, 37 for 1820. Allowing for a surprisingly small overlap of 9 individuals who remained in place throughout, there are 66 different names for the two years taken together.[57] Some were members of the vestry of Saint Médard or of the Welfare Committee: 8 of the 34 vestrymen and 8 of the 33 Welfare Committee candidates or members also held commands in the National Guard, and 3 men served in all three capacities: Salleron senior, the apothecary Normand, and the dye manufacturer Dheur.

The broad range of the officers' occupations (see Table 9.3) corresponds fairly closely to that of the vestry: a majority of merchants and manufacturers, a number of scientists/teachers, and a group of government employees, though in this case there are also some artisans. The list for 1820 includes the tax each man paid. The merchants and manufacturers paid very substantial sums: three between 300 and 500 francs, five between 500 and 1,000 francs, three more between 1,000 and 2,000, and one over 2,000. Two of the artisans fell slightly outside this range, paying between 200 and 300 francs, but the others paid substantially more. One of the scientists, Laugier, paid 1,700 francs. These men ranged from comfortable to rich. By contrast, five of the officers paid derisory sums: 11 to 22 francs a year. Two of them were former soldiers, presumably promoted because of their military experience. The others were the director of the Gobelins, one of the scientists, and a steward from the Pitié Hospital. One must conclude that they owed their place in the officer corps to the status of their government employment.

The 1820 list also indicates place of birth in 29 cases. Eleven men were born in the provinces, and 5 more came from close to Paris (Montmartre, Versailles, Vaugirard, and Jouy). The remaining 13 were Parisians—45 percent, which corresponds roughly to the proportion of Parisians in the population as a whole. Of them, 4 were almost certainly born in the Faubourg Saint Marcel, while 1 or 2 more may have been. Five of the officers were related by marriage or descent to other residents of the Faubourg Saint Marcel, but none (except the 3 members of the Salleron family) were related to one another.

It cannot be denied that an oligarchy still existed in the Faubourg Saint Marcel. In fact, fewer men had access to positions of authority and honor than at any time in the century before the Revolution. But it was a more open oligarchy than the eighteenth-century ones. A far wider range of occupations was represented; a wider range of ages; and above all, backgrounds were much more diverse. No longer did a small number of

Table 9.3 Occupations of officers in the National Guard of the Faubourg
Saint Marcel, 1814 and 1820

Occupation	Number in 1814[a]	Number in 1820[b]
Merchants and manufacturers		
Leather trades	10	8
Brewers	4	1
Wholesale merchants/ *négociants* (businessmen)	3	1
Spicers	2	3
Blanket maker	1	0
Bookseller	1	0
Dye maker	0	1
All merchants and manufacturers	21	14
Artisans		
Baker	1	2
Furniture maker	0	1
Tapestry weaver (Gobelins)	0	1
Chef	0	1
All artisans	1	5
Professions, science, and education		
Teachers	0	2
Scientists	3	2
Law (notary, *avocat, huissier*)	0	3
Architect	1	0
Doctor	1	0
Musician	0	1
All professions, science, and education	5	8
State employees		
Government service (unspecified)	4	5
Director of Gobelins	0	1
All state employees	4	6
Other		
Propriétaires (investors in real estate)	4	0
Former soldiers	2	2
"Entrepreneur du gouvernement"[c]	1	2
All other	7	4
Total	38	37

a. Includes commander of Twelfth Legion, battalion commanders, officers of Fourth Battalion.

b. Includes commander and general staff officers of Twelfth Legion, officers of Fourth Battalion.

c. Private contractor doing government work.

families dominate the area. Furthermore, it was almost entirely a new oligarchy: most of the notables of the Faubourg Saint Marcel in the first quarter of the nineteenth century were complete newcomers to the quarter. The Revolution and Empire had almost totally renewed the local elite.

This was not confined to the faubourg. The appearance of entirely new groups, who played little part in public life under the Old Regime, is conspicuous both at the local and at the citywide levels. Men of science now enjoyed unprecedented influence, and indeed, scientific achievement now almost obliged participation in public life. Even as reluctant a politician as Geoffroy-Saint-Hilaire found himself, as a well-known scientist, under pressure to take a public stand. Those less timid, or perhaps with more taste for office, welcomed the opportunity and in some cases made of politics a second career. The Revolution had opened the way, providing scientists with an opportunity to create new institutions and to reform the world along rational, statistical lines: the metric system, the eighty-three departments, the revolutionary calendar, and the abortive ten-hour day are obvious examples.

In 1789, men of science immediately took their places in local and city politics: Jean Sylvain Bailly was one; the chemist Claude Berthollet another. When the Republic called, they stepped forward again: Gaspard Monge to run the navy; the chemist Louis-Bernard Guyton de Morveau to lead the first Committee of Public Safety and subsequently to experiment with the military use of hot-air balloons. Berthollet and Chaptal worked to improve the gathering of saltpeter for making gunpowder, and Berthollet again, in association with Alexandre Vandermonde and Monge, applied his work on iron and steel to the manufacture of guns. The chemist Antoine François de Fourcroy served as a member of the Education Committee of the Convention and later on the Thermidorean Committee of Public Safety. The reform of the education system under the Directory was directly due to the efforts of scientist-politicians: the mathematician Monge (and earlier, the Marquis de Condorcet); Fourcroy and Berthollet; the engineer Lazare Carnot, among others.[58]

Under Napoleon, such men continued to play a key role. First the mathematician Pierre Simon Laplace and subsequently the chemist Jean Antoine Chaptal served as minister of the interior. Berthollet and Monge led Geoffroy-Saint-Hilaire and others on the scientific expedition to Egypt. Berthollet also experimented with sugar beets to assist France's survival during the continental blockade. As a *conseiller d'état* under Napoleon, Fourcroy drafted the law establishing the new education system. Pierre Cabanis was a member of the Senate, and Joseph Fourier served as prefect of the Isère Department throughout the Empire. At a humbler level, scientists were appointed to the prestigious but temporary post of president of the electoral assembly: Antoine Laurent de Jussieu and Georges Cuvier both occupied this position in 1812.[59]

It is difficult to see how most of these men could have achieved such prominence under the Old Regime. Berthollet came from a minor noble family and was already a member of the Academy of Sciences before the Revolution, but he would never have had the influence he enjoyed during the Empire as a senator and personal friend of Napoleon. Fourcroy was an apothecary's son who took a medical degree and became the official doctor to the poor in the Faubourg Saint Marcel in the 1780s—not a distinguished start! Admittedly, he had begun a brilliant lecturing career in chemistry before 1789, but he never would have had much political influence had the Revolution not brought him out of the laboratory. Chaptal was the son of small landowners in the Lozère, and although he was ennobled shortly before the Revolution, he was not an obvious candidate for a career as an industrial entrepreneur of the top rank and as a public official.[60] The presence of men like Geoffroy-Saint-Hilaire and Laugier on the vestry of Saint Médard, therefore, and of Cuvier and the lesser known chemist Roard in the officer corps of the National Guard, were local symptoms of the much wider recognition given to scientific achievement.

Likewise, the appearance in such posts of government employees like René Regnard de Barentin, the steward of Scipion, where the bread for the Paris hospitals was baked, or of Rattier, who worked at the library of the Conseil d'Etat, testifies to the greater prestige of government office of all kinds. The dramatic growth of the bureaucracy during the Revolution and Empire provided ideal conditions for advancement.[61] The Restoration was less advantageous, but the weeding out of Bonapartists at the top made career prospects reasonable for those not compromised during the Hundred Days. A man who acceded to the upper echelons of the administration was well remunerated and had the automatic right to participate in the electoral colleges. If he advanced to head a department, he would appear on the lists of notables from whom members of the Senate or the Legislature were chosen: in 1805 administrators of the Department of the Seine and of the Eaux et Forêts (waters and forests) were among the 9 government officials included among the 60 men in the department "most distinguished by their fortune and by their public and private virtues." In 1812 the 36 mayors and deputy mayors of Paris included 2 high-ranking administrators and 2 men who had formerly exercised such functions. Those of 1821 included 4 administrators and 5 former functionaries or magistrates.[62]

The other two occupational groups now conspicuous by their arrival in public office were the lawyers and the manufacturers. While magistrates had before the Revolution been important public figures, they were now joined by notaries and *avocats,* although these were not numerous in the Faubourg Saint Marcel. From other parts of the city, however, they flocked into office: the 36 mayors and deputies of 1812 included 7 legal men, 3 of them notaries. There were also 7 manufacturers: of textiles, leather, paper, fans, and gold and silver artifacts.[63]

A great many Paris manufacturers, like those in the Faubourg Saint Marcel, were men of modest origins who had risen thanks to the Revolution and Empire. Many were recent immigrants from the provinces: there was an influx of merchants from the Atlantic ports, for example.[64] Others were like Bernard L., cited by Adeline Daumard, who made a fortune from shawls. Son of a Lyon cloth merchant, he had 6,000 livres to his name in 1792; yet without any inheritance (though with family collaboration), by 1828 he and his wife were worth more than 4,000,000 francs. Among the 127 Parisian *éligibles* of the Restoration studied by Daumard—those with sufficient property or status to stand for election to the Chamber of Deputies—55 percent were immigrants from the provinces. Of the *négociants* and high-ranking civil servants, 60 percent were born outside Paris. In most cases they had come to the capital with very modest resources. A good number, too, were sons of Paris shopkeepers; but only a small proportion were descended from prominent families that had come unscathed through the 1790s.[65]

A great many fortunes were made from supplying the revolutionary and imperial armies, from speculation in *biens nationaux,* and subsequently from loans to the government. Gabriel Ouvrard, son of a Nantes papermaker, is the most notorious example. He moved to Paris in 1793 and constructed a huge fortune from *biens nationaux* and loans to the government.[66] He is simply the most spectacular example of a phenomenon that allowed a great many provincials, often of modest bourgeois origins, to penetrate the Parisian elite. The Revolution and Empire created the perfect economic and political conditions for such advancement.

Many of the great old Paris bourgeois families, on the other hand—the

Metra, the Quatremère, the Brochant, the Bourjot, and others like them—lost their preeminence, even if their family history still inspired a certain respect. Much of their wealth and power had been derived from offices now abolished, and a large part of their fortune had been invested in government bonds whose worth had been slashed by inflation and by reimbursement at less than face value. Fewer than 20 percent of Daumard's sample of *éligibles* were descended from prerevolutionary notables.[67]

The new, postrevolutionary elite, locally as in Paris as a whole, was an extraordinary mixture. It contained some families who had somehow traversed the 1790s without significant loss of wealth or social standing. Others were of modest origins, enjoying a rank to which they could never have aspired under the Old Regime. Some notables had risen as individuals, while others had floated up as members of professions whose prestige had risen sharply. What nearly all had in common, along with their being members of the early-nineteenth-century bourgeoisie, was geographical mobility. The gradual reduction in the importance of local family connections that was occurring in the second half of the eighteenth century had been dramatically accelerated, as the economic and political turbulence of the 1790s had its equivalent in unprecedented social and geographical movement.

Revolutionary Paris had been a giant cauldron, not only for revolution but for a mixing of the population. New opportunities drew men into new areas, while political expediency led many to leave their former quarters for others more exciting or more peaceful. No longer were key political and honorific positions, like that of *échevin,* reserved for the Paris-born. As Paris sucked back her lost population and attracted new provincial recruits, people without local roots suddenly rose to prominence, buying up church property, establishing businesses to respond to new government and consumer demand, moving in to fill the widening ranks of state employment. Some married into established families in their new quarter, but most sought alliances in other quarters—marriages of power and convenience that joined the bourgeoisie in different parts of the city with the strongest bonds of all: those of family obligation and mutual self-interest. Above all, it was the state, created by the Revolution, that acted as midwife for the new local elite: providing employment and encouragement for industry; showering honors on men of science and of property; closing off the way to political participation and admitting the few to favor and influence.

CHAPTER

10

THE TUTELAGE OF THE STATE

Those chosen to occupy the places of mayor and deputy mayor have always been taken from what was formerly called the "haute bourgeoisie" of Paris—bankers, notaries, lawyers or retired lawyers, all major property owners in Paris who, thanks to their fortune and their former occupations, were able to attract numerous clients to support the government.

—Maître des requêtes *Patry, 1821*

The numbers of people whose occupations and wealth allow them to be classified as bourgeois grew substantially during the period from 1815 to 1830. The careers of the Salleron brothers, of Geoffroy-Saint-Hilaire, and of Des Rotours illustrate the variety of entry points to the new local and citywide elite and the economic prosperity they enjoyed increased during this period, with the overall amount of wealth in Paris doubling while the gap between rich and poor widened.[1] The political caesura of 1814 had little effect on the rising economic or political fortunes of this new bourgeoisie, particularly of those whom Adeline Daumard has termed the *bourgeoisie de quartier*, the local bourgeoisie. They benefited from the remarkable stability that characterized local public office throughout the whole period of the Empire and Restoration.[2]

It was in essence the political and social system created by the Directory that dominated Paris until the revolution of 1830 and beyond. This chapter is concerned with the way the new system operated and how it was maintained. In whose interests did it function, and who was excluded? What was the role of family, and what were the criteria for influence, for public office and political participation? What, in short, were the new "rules" of politics under the Empire and the Restoration?

What characterized the Empire, by contrast with the late Convention and the Directory, was the almost complete control that the state exercised over the local notables. The Consulate and early Empire continued the practice, begun under the Directory, of excluding those groups perceived to be responsible for the "troubles of the Revolution." Women and the working classes were formally excluded from political power. Central control of public office was tightened and power was moved from elected local bodies to government-appointed bureaucracies.

Under the Empire it became virtually impossible for those openly out of sympathy with the regime to engage in any legal political activity, or to occupy any public office. The penalty for opposition was exclusion. The rewards for support were office, honor, and (with luck) lucrative government positions, pensions, or contracts. The Napoleonic regime held the Parisian bourgeoisie in harness, and under its tutelage those prepared to pull the carriage of state were well rewarded. The Restoration continued this policy, though increasingly it was forced to compromise with those whom it had brought to power and on whose support it depended.

Above all, it was through reform of the institutional structure that undesirables were excluded from power. Under both Empire and Restoration only two locally elected bodies remained: the parish vestries and the welfare committees, both of which were clearly considered harmless. Even so, in 1803 and again in 1809 the lay members of the vestries were initially named by the archbishop and by the prefect of the Seine—both of whom were appointed by the emperor. Until 1809 it was officially the archbishop who filled any vacancies, though in practice he simply approved the choice made by the existing members. Subsequently, half the vestry were replaced every three years, and the remaining members were able to elect the new ones, but only from among public functionaries and those paying the highest tax. The vestries were not to contain close relatives. The law expressly stated that the vestrymen were not representatives of the parishioners and had no right to present petitions on their behalf.

Under the 1809 law, which remained in force throughout the Restoration, the vestries could not meet, other than on the statutory dates, without permission either from the archbishop or from the prefect, and any major decisions they made had to be approved by the prefect. Until 1814 even the acceptance of a major donation was the subject of a special decree by the emperor himself! The mayor and deputy mayor of the arrondissement were automatically members, and often did attend.[3] The members of welfare committees were vetted by the mayor, who chose each candidate from a list supplied by the continuing members.[4]

The vestries and welfare committees were clearly not considered capable of crystallizing opposition to the government. The sections, on the other hand, had demonstrated their potential during the Revolution and were therefore totally disarmed. They nevertheless remained as divisions of the basic electoral circumscriptions, now called "cantons," which elected both the candidates for the place of justice of the peace and representatives to the two sorts of electoral colleges. The first of these was the electoral college of the department, whose members were chosen for life, and who in turn elected the *conseil général,* the body that distributed the tax burden to the different parts of the department. The second was the electoral college of each part of Paris, confusingly called the "arrondissement," even though each one was composed of three Paris arrondissements (the electors of the Faubourg Saint Marcel belonged to an electoral "arrondissement" made up of the Tenth, Eleventh, and Twelfth Arrondissements). The electoral college of the "arrondissement" in turn had two tasks. On the one hand, it selected candidates for the *conseil* of the "arrondissement," which was allowed to inform the government of the particular needs of the area and which decided how the tax burden should be shared between the Tenth, Eleventh, and Twelfth Arrondissements. On the other hand, it selected candidates for the Corps législatif (the parliament) and the Tribunat (abolished in 1807).[5]

At every point, the powers of these bodies were strictly circumscribed. The cantonal assemblies could only be convoked by the government, which specified how long they would meet. They could choose their representatives only from the list of the six hundred most highly taxed men of the department, a list that the government was not above rigging. In every case, the electoral colleges were required to name two candidates for each vacant place, leaving the final choice to the government. One of the candidates had to be taken from outside the college that chose him. The colleges were also formally forbidden to make any contact with one another—a way of preventing the kind of coordination that had characterized the Paris sections during the Revolution. Not all of their members, furthermore, were elected, for men granted the Légion d'honneur automatically belonged, and any senior public functionary could also attend and vote. The emperor could add further members at will. Thus there was little chance of their naming candidates hostile to the regime.

Everything, in short, was organized so that the voters could choose only the right sort of men. Electoral assemblies met for short, fixed periods and could not become tiny parliaments. Their presidents were named by the government. The *conseils* of the department and of the "arrondissement" met only once a year, at the behest of the government, and then for a maximum of two weeks. And the potentially dangerous influence of Paris was carefully diluted by plunging it into a department that included a number of more conservative rural cantons. For the same reason, in calculating the tax paid by each individual a heavier weighting was given to land tax. This ensured that rural landowners dominated the list of the six hundred most-taxed men of the department.[6]

Perhaps for all these reasons, participation rates in the primary assemblies were low. In 1803 only 41.6 percent of potential voters turned out in Paris (though 55.2 percent showed up in the Twelfth Arrondissement, which included the Faubourg Saint Marcel), and after 1806, when the suffrage was widened, these figures fell even further. In the 1807 election of a justice of the peace, arguably a matter that more immediately concerned voters than the selection of candidates for the intermittent legislature, 434 voters (53.8 percent) turned out in the Twelfth Arrondissement, out of a total of 807 who were on the roll.[7]

The Restoration made only minor changes to this structure.[8] It further restricted the vote to men at least thirty years of age who paid more than 300 francs a year in tax. Candidates for election had to pay at least 1,000 francs a year and be forty or over.[9] At the same time, though, the notables in the Chamber of Deputies were given limited power. While the government retained a strong influence over the electoral process, in the early years of the Restoration it interfered less. At the local level, however, the new laws did nothing to change the trend, observable since the Directory, toward larger electoral units that threw together men from different areas. This was part of the process of eliminating popular participation in politics, since the need to win electoral support from outside the immediate quarter helped to restrict political influence to a bourgeoisie that over the preceding decades had become increasingly citywide in its social ties, its economic interests, and its political awareness.

Other elected institutions were just as firmly controlled by both imperial and Restoration governments. One of the few important elected bodies was the Paris Chamber of Commerce, established in 1803 and composed of fifteen wealthy merchants. It was chaired by the prefect of the Seine, and all nominations to its ranks had to be approved by the minister of the interior. Also elected were the judges of the Tribunal de Commerce, the commercial court, chosen by a two-tier electoral process. The electors, all prominent merchants, shopkeepers, or manufacturers, were scrutinized by the prefect. Initially at least, the election does not appear to have aroused great enthusiasm: in 1802 only a few merchants turned up at most of the primary assemblies.[10]

The new institutional structure deliberately removed power from elected bodies and transferred it to appointed ones. With the exception of parish and welfare work, local administration was now directly controlled by the government. The body that ran the Paris hospitals, chaired by the prefect of the Seine, was named by the emperor, as were the administrators of the *lycées*. The mayors and deputy mayors of the twelve Paris municipalities were appointed directly by the emperor after very careful selection. During the Restoration the candidates were elected, but still the final choice was made by the government. Among the few remaining local officials were the forty-eight *commissaires de police,* now appointed by the authorities and answerable to the prefect of police.[11]

Similar control was exercised over the other prestigious and potentially powerful institution inherited from the Revolution: the National Guard. It had been suppressed in 1802, but in 1809, when the regime was under pressure and increasingly unpopular, it was revived briefly. In 1814, with the military collapse of the Empire the guard was again mobilized. But there was now no question, of course, of elected officers. The commanders of the twelve "legions" and the captain of each company were chosen by the minister of the interior. Even the ordinary guardsmen were chosen by a council made up of the mayor of the arrondissement, two *commissaires de police* (appointed by the government), the commander of the relevant legion, and the captains. Only citizens who paid a personal tax (the minimum being the equivalent of three days' labor), and the sons of such taxpayers, were to be admitted.[12] Under the Restoration the reorganized National Guard was carefully watched, and any unauthorized mobilization was expressly forbidden.[13] An officer of the National Guard occupied a position of honor and prestige, one that bestowed authority over a large number of fellow citizens but offered little opportunity for overt political activity.

Particularly in the Napoleonic years, but still to a great degree under the Restoration, direct political power was less to be found in elected institutions than in appointed ones, especially in the administration. Not that the administration was any more free from the tutelage of the government than the electoral assemblies. On the contrary, access to its ranks was very firmly controlled. The men chosen for public office and government service were carefully selected according to a number of quite clear criteria. Ability and fidelity to the regime were crucial, but the next most important was influence. "Those chosen to occupy the places of mayor and deputy mayor have always been taken from what was formerly called the 'haute bourgeoisie' of Paris—bankers, notaries, lawyers or retired lawyers, all major property owners in Paris who, thanks to their fortune and their former occupations, were able to attract numerous clients to support the government," wrote the *maître des requêtes* Patry in 1821.[14]

The comments made to the minister about candidates for these posts tell the same story. Unlike the observations made by officials under the Directory, in which the key qualities picked out are "probity," ability, and attachment to the Republic, the imperial and Restoration reports stress stability, reputation, and influence. The goldsmith Louis Cartier, for example, was a desirable candidate for the position of mayor, since he "belongs to the commercial world and is able to exercise influence within the commercial class . . . his reputation is perfect . . . and his fortune considerable."[15]

Even in selecting the members of the parish vestries, the authorities looked for the same qualities: in 1810 the prefect of the Seine requested his subordinates to suggest, for each parish, "two citizens who appear to you to merit the confidence of the government by their morality, their solidity *(consistance),* and the consideration they enjoy."[16] This emphasis on influence explains why a large fortune, although an important factor, was not the sole prerequisite for office. Some of the officers in the National Guard paid derisory amounts in tax yet commanded others with substantial fortunes. The mayors and deputy mayors of Paris in 1812 had annual incomes ranging from a modest 2,000 to a very considerable 60,000 francs.[17] Wealth was often an indication of influence, but it was not enough.

It is the significance of influence that explains why particular occupational categories were favored by the new system. Success in business usually depended on the cultivation of extensive networks of clients. Those with the most significant citywide connections were undoubtedly the bankers who honored the bills of exchange on which every major merchant and manufacturer relied. Stockbrokers, too, knew all the major enterprises in the city, since many manufacturers and wealthy merchants dabbled in state finance and shares.[18] Not far behind these groups were the notaries, who drew up contracts of sale, inventories of deceased estates, marriage contracts, and a variety of other documents, and were well paid for doing so. They also frequently acted as intermediaries in business negotiations and the purchase of real estate. Notaries therefore were in constant contact with the wealthiest and most influential families, and were well informed about the business and domestic affairs of their clients. This enabled them to make judicious investments of their own, which explains why their practices sold for such enormous sums: up to 200,000 francs under the Empire.[19]

There were other reasons why lawyers were a good choice for responsible positions in the administration, of course. They were versed in the law and usually endowed with a devotion to enforcing it to the letter. Scientists, too, thanks to the fame that many of them enjoyed and to their positions in educating the sons of the elite, were men of influence suitable for public office.

Quite apart from occupation and wealth, one measure of influence was a man's links with the quarter: the man chosen as mayor of the Ninth Arrondissement in 1820 "was born in this arrondissement, where he lives . . . has never left it, and his family have been there for more than 200 years . . . He knows perfectly the inhabitants of this quarter of Paris."[20] What was meant by "quarter," however, was not what the eighteenth century understood by the term: it was now the arrondissement, and the emphasis was on the extended influence that a candidate exerted. The same criterion was applied to the departmental "top sixty," which included only men who had been born in the department or who had lived there for at least five years, or else whose family had lived there.[21]

The selection of officers for the National Guard followed a similar pattern: "We can find no one possessing sufficient influence in this arrondissement," reads the entry for the Twelfth Arrondissement in a list of proposed candidates for the place of legion commander in 1814, indicating the primary quality the administration was seeking. The man suggested, therefore, was Benjamin Delessert, "one of the most highly thought of bankers in Paris, and known throughout the city." Among the suggestions for battalion commanders was Briard, a wholesale perfume merchant in the rue Saint Victor, who had "an influence quite widespread in the quarter" and a "good business." A rival candidate was Lafond, a wholesale wine merchant on the Quai de la Tournelle, who possessed "much influence" because of "his fortune and the extent of his commerce." He had the additional advantage of being very tall![22] Local influence was vital for these posts, but the area considered "local" had widened considerably.

Influence also came through family connections. A list of candidates for the position of mayor in 1812 includes comments on their family background: one was "from a very old and highly thought of robe family," while another was the son of a marquis. Yet another was the son-in-law of Louis François Lefevre d'Ormesson, former president of the Paris Parlement. Two were indicated as having sons who were *auditeurs* in the Cour des Comptes, a jumping-off point for high-ranking positions in the administration.[23] A candidate for legion commander in the National Guard was Fraguier, "descended from an old family of magistrates very highly thought of in the arrondissement." Augustin Bricogne, a candidate for battalion commander, not only had a very large tanning business and was influential in the quarter, but was also, the authorities pointed out, the son of the mayor of the Sixth Arrondissement and son-in-law of the deputy mayor of the Twelfth.[24]

These were the sorts of connections that supplicants for posts never failed to stress. The notary Buchère, who applied for a position as mayor in about 1813, pointed to his family's long standing in the city: his father had been *trésorier des pauvres* in the parish of Saint Germain l'Auxerrois for thirty years, and three generations of his family in the male line had been born in Paris. On his mother's side he was descended from a mid-seventeenth-century Paris notary. Buchère's uncle was the recently deceased mayor of the Second Arrondissement, the Chevalier de Mondétour, who had also been a member of the Legislature and of the Commission des Finances. His first cousin was a high-ranking officer in the imperial Cour des Comptes. He requested a place of mayor—in any part of the city.[25] From the point of view of the authorities, the right family background was a guarantee not only of influence but also of fidelity.

This fact, in turn, made it indispensable for an ambitious young man to conclude a good marriage. A single man was less likely to succeed, both because he was likely to have fewer connections and because of widespread official and public condemnation of celibacy as unpatriotic.[26] Only 3 of the 35 mayors and deputies of 1812 whose marital status is given were single, and only 4 of the 68 candidates competing for their posts. Perhaps, too, a reputation as a *père de famille* was among the "private virtues" referred to in the list of the departmental top sixty, since

30 of the 32 married mayors and deputies had children and the 2 who did not were both young, in their mid-thirties. The mayors and their deputies also had large families. If one excludes those under forty whose families may not have been complete, they averaged more than four children each.

Naturally, it was more likely to be older men, who had lived in the city or the arrondissement for some years and had built up a clientele, who possessed the necessary wide influence. The average age of the Paris mayors in 1812 was 52: the youngest was 43 and the oldest 77. The average age of the deputy mayors was 54, but they included youngsters of 29 and 30, as well as old men of 76 and 81. In the same year, the sixty-four other candidates for positions of mayor or deputy were aged between 31 and 76, with an average age of 51.[27] The eighteen vestrymen of Saint Médard whose dates of birth are known also had an average age of 51. The only men appointed in their thirties invariably were lawyers (in the case of the mayors) or sons of wealthy and well-connected families. While not possessing the significance, for its own sake, that age had under the Old Regime, mature years were an informal qualification for public office—an indispensable one for men from a commercial or administrative background for whom government service was a second career. Other offices were closed to most young men because of the income required to become eligible for election to the electoral colleges.[28]

If family connections were the most important ones, they were not the only gateway to prestigious public office. Many dossiers in the files of the Ministry of the Interior are annotated with comments such as "request supported by the president of the Criminal Court of the Department of the Aube," and "recommended by General Baron de Richemont, deputy." Without the right contacts, on the other hand, life was much more difficult. "I have made several requests to Monsieur Pradel, Director of the Maison du Roi . . . but they have all been fruitless, since I have no one to recommend me."[29] Just as under the Old Regime, recommendation was a central element in the political system of the Empire and the Restoration. It too was both a guarantee of fidelity and a way of limiting access to power.

Yet despite the surveillance that the government exercised over its appointees, public figures and administrators had real power over the lives of Parisians and even a certain influence with the government. The position of mayor is a good example. It was undoubtedly the most powerful one in Paris to be filled from the ranks of the citizenry. A list of the registers kept in the Tenth Arrondissement in the first decade of the nineteenth century gives an idea of the matters that fell under the mayors' responsibility. It includes a census of the population, a register for passports issued, and another for citizens eligible to vote and those eligible to become candidates. There was a list of judgments that the criminal court was required to pass on to the municipality, presumably for cross-checking when people applied for passports or to be entered on the voting register. The municipality also kept a register of ministers of religion and another of permits issued to merchants buying food in the area. Yet another book contained the record of certificates of residence issued by the municipal officers; and they also drew up a list of citizens considered suitable to serve on juries. Other documents indicate further matters that the mayor and his staff handled: voters who had changed their address; a list of people injured in an explosion.[30]

The twelve mayors and twenty-four deputies were officially considered to be *fonctionnaires* and were therefore automatically members of the electoral colleges, over which, in fact, they usually presided.[31] Other records reveal that the mayors played a role similar to that of the subprefects in less populous areas of France: they supervised the elections for the Tribunal de Commerce and helped the prefect of the Seine to draw up a list of suitable men. As the prefect himself made clear to one of the mayors, "The relations that you have daily with the principal merchants of your arrondissement and the information that you are able to gather on the order and regularity of their affairs give you the means to know and designate those among them who are the most worthy to carry out the functions of a notable."[32]

For the same reasons, it was to the mayors that the prefect turned when required to gather information on industry and trade in the city. A major inquiry in 1807 produced detailed reports from the mayors on the population and industries of each quarter. They also formed part of the council that decided who should belong to the National Guard, and probably had the preponderant voice: in 1823 it was the mayor who won in a disagreement with the commander of the guard over whether the foreman of a printing shop should serve. It was the mayors, too, who chose replacements for vacancies on the parish welfare committees, from a list provided by the other members, and who selected the primary-school teachers in their arrondissement. The possibilities for patronage were considerable. Even as deputy mayor, Joseph Salleron was able to obtain for his newly graduated son-in-law the position of doctor to the poor of the Faubourg Saint Marcel.[33]

With all this went honor. The mayors had an important place in public ceremonies. Most of those who served the Empire were given the Légion d'honneur, and a number sat in the Senate or the Legislature.[34] This combination of authority and prestige made the posts of mayor and deputy mayor much sought after. The men in office in 1812 included several with enormous incomes: the mayor of the Fifth Arrondissement had an annual revenue of 60,000 francs—five times what a bishop received under the Empire, and twice what a senator was paid. The mayor of the Seventh Arrondissement, director of the Comptoir commercial, enjoyed 50,000 a year. Candidates for the position in that year included Old Regime nobles, magistrates, and administrators, including a Montmorency and a Rochefoucault, men with enormous independent incomes.[35] They did not fear any loss of status in becoming mayor of a Paris arrondissement.

Other positions also opened the way to personal honors and the power of patronage. Members of the Institut de France were consulted about inventions, about appointments to academic and library posts, about whether a government pension should be accorded to a writer. Georges Cuvier, as one of the six inspectors of public education appointed in 1802, was largely responsible for choosing the first professors of the Faculty of Sciences. He placed many of his disciples in teaching jobs or found them work as his assistants. He was even consulted on the appointment of a chemist to oversee the dyes used at the Gobelins.[36]

Office gave access to government, an ability to influence decisions, to secure a post for someone (or for oneself), to obtain a permit or get government support for an enterprise. When in 1807 the priest at Saint Médard, the fiercely anti-Jansenist Louis Bertier, seized the opportunity to dismantle the tomb of François de Pâris on the pretext of putting a path through from his residence to the church, he needed permission from the department to make the necessary alterations. Perhaps anticipating hesitation on the part of the authorities, he approached the director the Gobelins, Charles-Axel Guillaumot, who was also one of the members of the church vestry. Guillaumot, apparently unperturbed by the possibility of violent local reactions, contacted his son-in-law, the architect for the department, who obtained the necessary permit without difficulty.[37]

Guillaumot had other useful contacts, too. In 1804, wishing to reorganize the Gobelins manufactory and needing permission from the minister of the interior, he asked the minister's secretary to intercede for him: "I am persuaded that he will agree with my suggestions, if you think they merit your approval."[38] This system of informal contacts and patronage operated at every level of the administration. The senator Claude Berthollet, wishing to close off the banks of the Bièvre behind a factory he owned, something not permitted by the regulations governing the river, wrote in a commanding tone to "Mon cher Ministre." At the other end of society was Widow Guillaume, a pensioner of the Hospice at Charenton, who in 1815 sought a recommendation from a high-ranking administrator of the "Direction du Commerce."[39]

Even at a very local level, the members of the Welfare Committee in the Faubourg Saint Marcel were in a position to dispense patronage. One of them was responsible for the list of poor families to whom bread and medicine were distributed when available, and another drew up a list of mothers in need of assistance. Collectively they nominated the beneficiary of at least one bed at the hospital for the terminally ill. They awarded prizes to the children of the charity school and purchased clothes and shoes for poor children. In winter they distributed firewood, ran a soup kitchen sponsored by the Société Philanthropique, and on at least one occasion negotiated the return, without payment, of a large number of objects pawned by local people at the Mont-de-Piété, the government pawnbroker. They also had a say in the appointment of a doctor for the poor of the area.[40]

The most humble public office, almost any place in the administration, thus accorded real power over other people, much of it informal. One should not be deceived by the very limited official functions of many offices. Nor should one underestimate the importance of prestige and honor in Paris society under the Empire and the Restoration. The Revolution had not destroyed the significance of titles, of precedence, and of dress as marks of rank. Men cited membership in the Légion d'honneur alongside their occupation, in precisely the same way as a Chevalier de Saint Louis under the Old Regime, and they had their portraits painted with the ribbons and medal prominently displayed.[41] Both elected and appointed office were sources of considerable status. Following the death of Claude Salleron in 1833, nearly ten years after his short service in the Chamber of Deputies, his children gave his occupation not as "tanner," or even as *"négociant,"* but as "ex-deputy."[42]

As commander of the Twelfth Legion of the National Guard, too,

Salleron had met the emperor, had corresponded with the minister of the interior, had actively participated in ceremonial events. As deputy mayor of the arrondissement, Joseph Salleron appeared on the list of the sixty most prominent notables of the whole department, alongside men like Henri François Lefevre d'Ormesson, the former controller general of France, and Jacques Récamier, a famous banker with an equally famous wife.[43]

Mayors and deputy mayors wore smart uniforms, which distinguished them from the run-of-the-mill, black-coated bourgeois: "One felt a nobody if one did not wear a saber or an embroidered uniform," wrote one observer under the Empire.[44] Even as humble a functionary as the *commissaire de police* stood out from the crowd with his tricolor sash and wide hat.[45] An officer in the National Guard was not only distinguished by his uniform: he issued commands to his fellow citizens, perhaps his own neighbors. According to the banker François Cottier, who had a low opinion of stockbrokers, two of them appointed as officers in the National Guard in 1809 "found it pleasant to give orders to bankers and *négociants*."[46] However limited their real authority, such posts could give great personal satisfaction, and in an area like the Faubourg Saint Marcel endowed their holders with a prominence that conferred social power within the quarter.

Even membership in the severely restricted electoral assemblies marked a man out in his own quarter. In any system where the suffrage is limited, its exercise becomes a source of status. In this case, the standing of the independent male householder as citizen distinguished him from the mass of the population and from the dependent members of his household: servants, women, and children. The exclusive electoral colleges, where suffrage was exercised only by those paying high taxes, conferred higher status. Membership in these assemblies gave little real influence over the imperial government (though at certain times during the Restoration it was more significant). Throughout the period, however, it did bestow social power.

This new system involved certain dangers for the government. Although it held the reigns tightly, the regime was nevertheless susceptible to the discontent of those upon whom it bestowed such power and influence. Napoleon could not hold Paris in 1814, when much of the National Guard and most of the notables preferred to capitulate. Likewise, in the last years of the Restoration, Charles X's government was unable to counter the hostile opinion of the Parisian bourgeoisie. Nevertheless, during the Empire and under Louis XVIII the system worked well, both for the rulers themselves and for the bulk of the bourgeois upon whom it conferred public recognition and for whom it brought much-desired stability and order. The imperial government deliberately, through the institutional structure it fashioned, through legislation, through the creation of honorific positions and encouragement of a system of patronage, reinforced hierarchy and authority within French society. In particular, it bolstered the buffers against what many of its supporters now believed to have been primary causes of the excesses of the Revolution: democracy and the excessive power of women.

The wealth requirement effectively excluded the common people from the electoral process. The new status of the *propriétaire,* a man who lived on the proceeds of real estate, helped to exclude the poorer classes. The suppression of workers' associations and the introduction of the *livret,* the booklet that all workers were now supposed to carry, reinforced the authority of employers. A worker had to hand over the *livret* when taken on by a new employer and in theory could not leave without it. The employer was invited to write comments inside. The creation of *conseils de prud'hommes* in 1806, bodies designed to resolve industrial disputes but totally dominated by employers, worked in the same direction.[47]

So did the patronage system. In 1827 François Guilbert, an unemployed blanket maker in the Faubourg Saint Marcel, sought a job as coffin bearer in the now centralized funeral service. He obtained certificates from the parish priest, from the *commissaire de police* of the quarter, and from his former employer's brother, the blanket manufacturer Etienne Albinet: "He is a real *honnête homme,"* wrote Albinet.[48] The role of prominent local employers on the Welfare Committee—the older Albinet had served on it for some years—was a further incentive to workers to do what they were told. Furthermore, as Des Rotours pointed out, the National Guard too could be used to provide "both civil and military authority over the workers."[49]

The new system was also designed to reduce the power of women—again, in part, through legislation. Women were explicitly excluded from electoral assemblies and considered ineligible for public office. Their participation in commerce was made more difficult by restrictions on their ownership of property. Under the Civil Code of 1804, a married woman could not enter into any contract without the authorization of her husband, and a husband could dispose of his wife's property, except for her dowry. Single and widowed women were able to enter into contracts in the same way as men, but powerful economic and family pressures pushed women to marry. In less direct ways, too, the law placed women in a subordinate position. Married women had to live with their husbands. Divorce was made much more difficult to obtain, particularly for women, and was outlawed altogether in 1816.[50]

The exclusion of women from public life was not, however, solely a product of legislation. It was also a result of the ideology of domesticity that had been adopted by most men and women in the wealthier sections of society. It became less common for the wives of wealthy merchants and manufacturers to take any part in the family business.[51] A number of new characteristics of nineteenth-century businesses testify to this trend and served to reinforce it. Increasing separation of home and work, as enterprises grew larger, made it more difficult for women to bring up children, oversee household affairs, and play a role in the firm at the same time. It meant, too, that daughters did not grow up surrounded by the business, picking up aspects of it even if they received no formal training.

Another new development, which was both a mechanism of this exclusion and a way of coping with its practical implications, was the family firm, involving a partnership between male relatives. Whereas in the eighteenth century, even in large enterprises, it was generally the wife who managed the workshop and negotiations with clients when her husband was sick or absent, in the nineteenth her exclusion from the day-to-day running of the business made this impossible. If the husband fell sick, went away on business, or began to spend a great deal of time on politics, there was no one to replace him. An employee could be trusted to do only so much. The solution, therefore, was to go into business with a kinsman, most often a brother, a son or son-in-law, or a nephew. It became increasingly common for a man to take on his son or son-in-law, first as a *commis* and subsequently as an associate. This practice was rare under the Old Regime, when the norm was to set up a son in his own business. But in the early nineteenth century the family firm became a male bourgeois ideal, to the extent that fathers sometimes used their greater legal and social power to force sons into association with them. Hippolyte Ganneron, for example, a prominent businessman under the July Monarchy, was obliged to give up a promising legal career to go into the family enterprise after the premature death of his elder brother.[52]

Other practical reasons encouraged such arrangements, of course.

Stable partnerships, as opposed to short-term agreements, were a response to the need for larger amounts of capital, particularly in industries tendering for state contracts, but were also required by wider markets, and in the precarious economic environment of early-nineteenth-century France it still made sense to rely on kinsmen, whom one knew and trusted. Here the disappearance of the restrictive regulations of the trades corporations, which had often not permitted such arrangements, was a minor facilitating factor, though these regulations had never seriously hindered the most energetic entrepreneurs.

Family firms, in their nineteenth-century form, were not merely a response to new conditions and new gender roles, however. They deliberately excluded women from management and proclaimed this exclusion in their gendered names: "Salleron frères," "Salleron fils et Compagnie." Even where husband and wife continued to work together, as was still the rule in smaller businesses, names now proclaimed masculine ownership. In the seventeenth and eighteenth centuries, the names of shops, displayed on a sign above the door or hanging outside, were rarely gender-specific. In the first half of the nineteenth century, however, the names of shops were increasingly those of the male founder or owner. By 1858 one observer was able to comment that "most of the ordinary signs [are] composed simply of a proper name," and to point to the pride and pretension represented by "those long series of shop fronts that bear only the words BERAUD, DUMONT, DURAND, HENRION, CHARBONNEAU."[53] Prominently displayed across the shop front, the owner's surname stressed individual male achievement and proclaimed to the whole city the proprietor's identity and talents.[54] In very subtle ways, masculinity was being linked with the public domain.

Femininity, on the other hand, was relentlessly tied to family and home. The restoration of stability after the Revolution was widely viewed—by elite men and women alike—as a task in which a central role was to be played by the family, within which female moralizing and civilizing action was deemed crucial. In instilling private virtues in their children, women became a source of public virtue, but this could be achieved only in the home.[55]

An overwhelming emphasis on the domestic and the sexual nature of women, in books on subjects as diverse as education, law, and science, written by authors of all political and intellectual persuasions, helped to locate women firmly within the family sphere. Biological arguments began to be used to justify women's confinement to household and family, notably by the biologists Pierre Cabanis and Julien-Joseph Virey, who claimed that the female reproductive organs had a direct influence on women's moral, intellectual, and social characteristics, making them ill fitted for public life.[56]

In a far more direct and practical way, too, biology may have acted to remove married women from public life: the fertility of bourgeois couples appears to have risen substantially during and just after the Revolution. The thirty-six mayors and deputy mayors of 1812 had on average four or more children each. In Adeline Daumard's much larger sample, 35 percent of *négociants* and nearly 28 percent of *fonctionnaires* and of men in the liberal professions who died in 1820 had three or more children who survived infancy. This contrasts both with the smaller workers' families, and with what is known of the small numbers of children that the Parisian bourgeois had before 1789.[57]

The exclusion of women from public life was not absolute, of course. On the one hand, there are conspicuous examples of women who very successfully ran their own quite substantial businesses, despite the constraints placed upon them by the Civil Code.[58] On the other hand, as a number of writers on nineteenth-century women have shown, when bourgeois women were pushed into the domestic sphere through the front door they often emerged at the back, reentering the public domain through charitable organizations. Both the ideology and the local political role of the Parisian bourgeoisie encouraged this movement. Suspicion of the undeserving poor and the growing distance between worker and employer inclined bourgeois families to channel their limited philanthropy away from direct personal charity and into organizations supervised by like-minded people. The Société Philanthropique, to which Salleron, Geoffroy-Saint-Hilaire, and Bricogne *père* were all subscribers, played a key role both in sponsoring officially approved welfare activities and in identifying worker-run mutual-aid and savings societies that bourgeois subscribers could comfortably support.[59]

Because of the growing gender division in private and public life, bourgeois women took, and were encouraged to take, an active interest in associations concerned with women's health, welfare, and education. They were directly involved in founding schools for poor girls and in the Société de charité maternelle (Society for Maternal Charity), which was concerned with poor pregnant women and those with large families. Recipient of a subsidy from the Société Philanthropique, this body became an official organization under the Empire, but during the Restoration reverted to a more informal status. Its members were largely women—134 of them in 1809, together with 40 men. Many were the wives of administrators and industrialists, and they personally visited and inspected the beneficiaries domiciled in their quarter.[60] This role reinforced that of the men in the local Welfare Committee, creating complementary women's patronage networks within the quarter. While allowing bourgeois women temporary escape from domesticity, therefore, this very public participation of wives in charitable work assisted in building the household's "influence" within the arrondissement, a prerequisite for political office under the Empire and the Restoration.

The creation of a new institutional structure after the Revolution was thus accompanied by a change in the informal and ideological structures of power within Parisian society. More authoritarian than under the Old Regime, but equally paternalistic, the relationship between government and citizens was mirrored in those between employers and employees, between husband and wife, and between parents and children. Few positions accorded any real independence, but many conferred social power, the authority of an official post, and a uniform. At every level the system of informal networks meant that those with the right connections enjoyed enormous unofficial power.

Paradoxically, this gave indirect influence to many women, who by virtue of their husband's position or thanks to the very family connections that made them a desirable match were able to intervene on behalf of petitioners or relatives. How else is one to interpret, for example, the request for a government position addressed in 1807 to "her excellency Madame Minister of the Interior," Madame Cretet, wife of the then minister. One Parisian *commissaire de police,* a later police report suggested, owed his position to the fact that his father gave piano lessons to Madame Decaze, wife of the prime minister.[61] The nineteenth-century belief that women exerted enormous influence from behind the throne may have been promoted by a system that encouraged the exercise of precisely this kind of patronage by men and women alike. The difference was that when women used it they could be accused of meddling in public affairs!

This same system favored families with large numbers of children, provided they were wealthy enough to dower them. Just as in the early eighteenth century it was an advantage to belong to a large family that was well represented in local political office, so in the early nineteenth a couple with numerous well-placed brothers, uncles, or in-laws were extremely likely to obtain positions for their sons and good marriages for their daughters. This was not necessarily a factor in the decision to have more children, but may have removed one of the potential disincentives to doing so.

Unlike the Old Regime or revolutionary system, though, the power structure of the Empire and the Restoration did not offer any advantage to families based in a single quarter. On the contrary, it favored those with wider connections. Power was derived from appointed office rather than from election, as had been the case during the Revolution and in the vestries, trades corporations, and other corporate institutions before 1789. Whereas access to office under both the Old Regime and the new was dependent on "notability"—a subtle mixture of wealth, reputation, family connections, education, and personal qualities—the precise recipe was not the same. After 1800 the possibilities for advancement were far greater, but purely local notability had become a limiting factor, enabling access to the parish vestry but not to the more important municipal and administrative offices. The kind of upward social mobility that was common under the Empire and still possible during the Restoration depended on connections outside the quarter, whereas under the Old Regime and still during the Revolution strong local support was the key for those wishing to enter citywide or even national politics. During the Empire and the Restoration a man with a citywide reputation, widely dispersed acquaintance, and far-reaching family connections was far more likely to be chosen by the voters and, more important, was more likely to be selected by the government. This was one of the factors that made it easier for relative newcomers to succeed: they did not have to have deep local roots. The new political system of the early nineteenth century completed the formation of a citywide, truly Parisian bourgeoisie.

It did not, of course, create one. Important as the Revolution and Empire were in the construction of a new elite in the French capital, the formation of a bourgeoisie that was Parisian in its dimensions and its thinking was a much longer process.

CONCLUSION

*In 1789 a different adversary confronted the court . . . , the Third Estate,
whose power, wealth, stability, and intelligence were growing daily . . . The
Constitution of 1791 . . . was the work of the middle class, at that time
the strongest.*

—François Mignet, 1824

The historians Mignet, Guizot, and Thiers were the foremost
apologists of the French bourgeoisie. They, above all, promoted
the idea of the 1789 Revolution as the triumph of the bourgeoisie over feudalism. Their works, written against the backdrop of the
politically turbulent 1820s and followed by the revolution of 1830,
provided the new Parisian bourgeoisie with the foundation myths and
the self-awareness necessary to their formation as a class. In every other
sense—economic, demographic, ideological—the Parisian bourgeoisie already existed in 1820.

The political background to the awakening of a bourgeois consciousness involved the attempts by the Restoration regime, after the victory
of the ultraconservatives in 1817, to erode the constitutional guarantees
of the Charter of 1814. In particular, the intense student agitation of
1819 and 1820 wakened educated Parisians to the danger, both because
of the publicity it generated and because the young men in the law
schools and the medical faculties were, above all, sons of bourgeois
families. The government appeared to be launching a two-pronged attack: on the political rights of the older middle-class generation and on
the educational institutions that served mainly younger middle-class

males. Rumors flew: of changes to the electoral laws, of a planned indemnity to émigrés.

The repressive measures taken after the assassination of the Duc de Berry in February 1820 aroused further concern in bourgeois circles. But it was the "law of the double vote" of 1820, which provided for the votes of the richest part of the electorate to be counted twice, that provoked open protest in Paris, particularly among a younger population of clerks and students: "no inhabitant of the *faubourg* had joined the rebels," reported the police with satisfaction, not realizing that the alienation of the middle classes was equally serious.[1]

Then the shooting by soldiers of a law student outside the Chamber of Deputies on 3 June provided the focus for riots, which were bloodily suppressed. The dead youth, significantly, was the son of a grain merchant of central Paris, a representative of the prosperous commercial middle classes; but his huge funeral procession assembled a wider social coalition—at its core, the law and medical students drawn from all sectors of the Parisian and provincial bourgeoisie. The experience of repression politicized bourgeois youth and forged an unprecedented solidarity among them.[2]

The faculties created under the Directory and Empire and now threatened by the conservative regime provided a focus for a bourgeois identity: a commonality of experience and a formative political training, particularly under the guidance of men like Victor Cousin and François Guizot—and later, Abel Villemain and Pierre Daunou—all of whose courses attracted huge audiences. The publication between 1823 and 1828 of histories of the Revolution by Thiers, Mignet, Laurent de l'Ardèche, and Thierry, avidly devoured by Paris students, elevated their struggle to a historic mission: the defense of rights for which their fathers had striven and suffered against both aristocracy and populace. The rising bourgeois generation had its foundation myth.[3]

Mobilized by the student struggle, enraged by the "law of the double vote" and by government attempts to remove potential liberal voters from the electoral rolls, the liberal opposition began to organize. The strength of feeling among the well-to-do Paris electorate is demonstrated by the overwhelming victory of opposition candidates in the 1822 elections, which saw a participation rate of 89.3 percent (and even higher figures in the more commercial quarters). It was in these elections that Claude Salleron was elected to the Chamber of Deputies as a liberal. At the same time, there were signs that the predominantly bourgeois National Guard was becoming unwilling to obey orders directed against the liberal opposition.[4]

The conflict provoked at the beginning of the decade was further fueled by the government's later actions: the laws on the church, the indemnity accorded to émigrés, and changes to the Civil Code and to laws on the press all helped to unite the majority of Paris bourgeois against the government. The closure and "reorganization" of the Paris faculties did nothing to appease the anger of students and their families.[5] But the crisis of 1827 was to be even more important in fashioning a distinct bourgeois consciousness in Paris. In April of that year the National Guard was dissolved, following a review by the king at which antigovernment sentiments were expressed by some battalions. Given the importance of the National Guard, not only as an emblem of Parisian autonomy but also as a mark of social prestige for troops and officers alike, this measure represented yet another blow to the Parisian bourgeoisie.

The elections at the end of 1827 resulted in an overwhelming victory for the opposition in Paris. Adeline Daumard has described the mobilization of the local notables, particularly within the electoral colleges, which combined more than one municipal arrondissement. In the first electoral arrondissement, for example, the opposition arranged a caucus in which three hundred voters participated, choosing Jacques Charles Dupont de l'Eure as their candidate. This, and the more systematic organization involved in distributing leaflets, created lasting ties that transcended individual quarters and even municipal arrondissements. These links were renewed in the elections of 1830. Thus the government's actions and the campaign against them finally unified the major part of the Parisian bourgeoisie, giving them a rallying point in the Charter of 1814.[6] The 1820s saw the formation of a politically and ideologically united bourgeoisie.

This process deserves more detailed study than is necessary here, for the developments of the 1820s were only the epilogue to a far-longer-term evolution. It was not these years that formed the Parisian bourgeoisie in a wider sense; nor was it the Revolution of 1789. On the other hand, the Parisian bourgeoisie had not always existed. There had been, it is true, *bourgeois de Paris* since the twelfth century, and many of them were rich, dignified, and powerful.[7] Over the years, some played commanding roles in city and national politics. But their focus, authority, and identity were primarily local. Their power base lay in their quarter, where they served as officers in the bourgeois militia and as *cinquanteniers, dixainiers,* or *quarteniers,* local officials with extensive administrative responsibilities. Through these functions they played a major political role both locally and in the city as a whole. The way to city power in sixteenth-century Paris, Robert Descimon has demonstrated, was through control of individual quarters. He has even suggested that this may account for the geographical distribution of certain trades, which congregated in particular areas so as to consolidate their power.[8] It is a political structure familiar from other Renaissance cities: in Florence, for instance, the *gonfalone* was the basic unit within which even the greatest families resided and schemed, and with which they identified.[9] Renaissance city government was a federal affair, in which the interests of the key lineages and of the quarters in which they lived were in constant competition with those of other families and quarters.

To describe the transformation of the *bourgeois de Paris* of the early modern era into the Parisian bourgeoisie of the nineteenth century, therefore, is in large measure to trace the long-term decline of the quarter as a political, social, and economic unit. The centralizing monarchy was in part responsible, but other powerful social and economic forces were pressing in the same direction. The decline of local lineage as a dominant form of family and political organization, which among the Paris middle classes can be traced to the eighteenth century, is an important part of the story. So is the diminishing importance of the urban parish, in tandem with the shift from religious to secular politics and the remarkable change in religious sensibility in France during the second half of the eighteenth century. A further factor is the gradual adoption by the middle classes, during the eighteenth century, of the twin ideologies of political economy and domesticity—ways of thinking inseparable from the development of capitalism and consumerism during that same period. Accompanying all of this, and traceable to many of the same economic and ideological factors, is the commercial integration of the city. But among these long-term factors, one cannot ignore the enormous demographic, political, and economic impact of the Revolution. Let me look at each of these factors in turn.

The one with the longest history is the centralizing monarchy. The steady erosion of local autonomy occurred earlier in the unruly capital than elsewhere in France.[10] From at least the beginning of the seventeenth century, the crown progressively undermined the influence of the local notables. One of its earliest achievements was to destroy the independence of the Hôtel de Ville—the municipality controlled by the elected representatives of the sixteen quarters of the city, and hence by the bourgeois families who controlled those quarters. Henri IV, seeking to disarm supporters of the Holy League, manipulated the elections of the principal municipal officers, the Prévôt des Marchands and the *échevins,* and by the end of his reign had transformed them into virtual appointees of the crown. He and his successors steadily transferred to royal officials—first the *lieutenant civil,* and subsequently the lieutenant general of police—functions formerly exercised by the municipality.[11]

The effects of these measures can be seen at the local level. In the sixteenth century it was the ward officials—the 16 *quarteniers,* 64 *cinquanteniers,* and 256 *dixainiers*—who organized the militia, drew up the tax lists, and had primary responsibility for law and order, street cleaning and lighting, fire fighting, and public health. They also had an important ceremonial role, wore special costumes, and represented their quarter at the Hôtel de Ville. An edict of 1577 also gave locally elected notables the power to impose fines for breaches of bylaws.[12] In the sixteenth century both the *quarteniers* and the *cinquanteniers* were elected by a restricted group of local bourgeois, but by the mid–seventeenth century the place of *quartenier* had in practice become a venal office. The rebellion by Paris during the Fronde, in the mid–seventeenth century, led Louis XIV to transfer most of their functions to officials of the Châtelet, the royal courts. Henceforth, the office was a purely ceremonial one, though bestowing significant tax exemptions.[13]

Their military role was also removed. In the sixteenth century the officers of the bourgeois militia, initially the same ward officials, had effectively controlled the city and had played a central role in the struggles of the League. Officer rank was a sign of preeminence within the quarter and was reserved for bourgeois of substance. The militias had a very local personality: on at least one occasion, an officer refused to intervene in an incident that took place just outside his quarter.[14] After the Fronde, however, as part of the general disarming of the Paris population, the bourgeois militia was dismantled, although some posts were retained for purchase by those with a taste for forming guards of honor.[15] The militia was replaced initially by officeholders and subsequently by professional soldiers in the pay of the crown. With it disappeared a key role for the local notables and a source of their prestige.[16]

As part of the transfer of power from the local bourgeois to the crown, the seventeenth century also witnessed the creation of a number of new, citywide institutions. One of the most important was the Hôpital

Général. The various hospitals, formerly separate institutions in which the bourgeois had had an administrative role since the sixteenth century, were now under a single, central authority.[17]

The strengthening of the guild structure in the 1670s was yet another move in the same direction. The number of trades corporations more than doubled, while at the same time the separate corporations in the faubourgs were abolished, removing yet another institution of local government and local identity. The tanners' corporation of Saint Marcel was amalgamated with that of Paris in 1675.[18] These measures were largely designed to raise money for the crown, but they further centralized the administration of the city. The self-governing local trades corporations were absorbed into much larger, citywide institutions, to which some of the authority removed from locally elected officials was transferred. The officials of the trades now decided how much of the new capitation tax each master or mistress should pay.

Ironically, there was an element of democratization here, for among the very large number of men and smaller number of women who served as officials of the corporations in the eighteenth century were many of far more modest origins than the wealthy, all-male *quarteniers, cinquan-teniers,* and *dixainiers.* But these men and women could come from any part of the city. Tax assessment was removed from the control of local officials and became a function of men and women elected (in principle) by the whole trade; their authority extended to the whole city and they were answerable to the crown.[19]

In the same year that the *lieutenance générale* was created, 1667, the royal government launched an assault on the seigneurial jurisdictions of the capital. Much of the city was, until then, directly controlled by the great abbeys and priories around which many quarters had originally developed. In much of the Faubourg Saint Marcel, the Abbey of Saint Marcel policed the laws, judged criminal offenses, and made the rules on all kinds of matters, in return for which it enjoyed income from a whole range of feudal dues. It had its own sheriffs, its own mill and wine presses, even its own prison.[20] The archbishop of Paris, the Abbeys of Saint Germain des Prés and of Sainte Geneviève, the priory of Saint Martin des Champs, the Temple and Saint Jean de Latran, to name the major ones—all had similar rights and responsibilities within their extensive jurisdictions: virtually the whole Faubourg Saint Germain came under the Abbey of Saint Germain des Prés; much of north-central Paris under Saint Martin.[21]

Such powers hindered central government control, particularly as some of the abbeys were in the hands of great noble families. In response, the monarchy helped to extend the authority of the archbishop of Paris over other ecclesiastical institutions, giving him control over the secular clergy within each jurisdiction.[22] In 1674, the nineteen seigneurial jurisdictions in Paris were abolished, and although some were subsequently reestablished, their powers and territories were reduced.[23] The legal jurisdiction of the Abbey of Saint Marcel was restricted to the large courtyard off the rue Mouffetard that contained a small farm, the churches of Saint Marcel and Saint Martin, the cemetery, and half a dozen houses, most occupied by the canons themselves. Regular court hearings were still held, staffed by the abbey's own legal officials, who in theory could even pronounce the death penalty for serious offenses committed within the abbey close. But in practice the abbey now became largely irrelevant in the life of the faubourg.[24]

When the seigneurial jurisdictions lost their temporal authority, with it went any real role in local affairs. The Abbey of Saint Marcel still nominated the curés of Saint Martin, Saint Hippolyte, and Saint Jacques du Haut Pas, and its claim to authority over these three churches did lead to bitter disputes that lasted into the 1770s. But the very existence of these disputes is evidence of its declining authority, and by the 1780s its claims on the quarter were so thin that the canons decided to move, eventually settling, in 1787, for amalgamation with Sainte Croix de la Bretonnerie in central Paris. There was no hostility toward the abbey in the Faubourg Saint Marcel on the eve of the Revolution, and the district was prepared to petition the National Assembly on behalf of its fourteen aged clergy, who posed no threat to anyone.[25]

Even before the eighteenth century, therefore, the separate identity of individual quarters was being undermined by the destruction of distinctive local institutions. Their political autonomy was eroded, and the local role of the notables, their authority over their fellow citizens, and the respect that a ward official or an officer in the bourgeois militia enjoyed were all reduced or lost. By the early eighteenth century, only the parishes remained under their control, along with a few special bodies such as the Bièvre administration. The influence of most of these institutions was to dwindle over the following decades.

These changes were linked with those in the local lineages, a form of family organization admirably suited to the political and economic structure of sixteenth- and seventeenth-century Paris but less well adapted to the new conditions of the eighteenth century. The centralization of power, and particularly the removal of local administration from the citizenry to government agencies, eventually rendered them politically obsolete. Their hold on the parishes, together with their possession of real estate, their continued religious and kin ties with the neighborhood, and perhaps, in certain cases (as with the tanners), an occupational focus, were enough to hold some bourgeois lineages together for a time. But the centrifugal forces were growing.

For political and economic reasons alike, outside connections became increasingly important. Influence increasingly lay with such figures as the farmers-general and the administrators of *régies* (autonomous authorities), with manufacturers whose enterprises gave them citywide importance, sometimes with the officials of the guilds, and certainly with those who could use their citywide networks to gain access to government officials. In 1785 and 1786, for example, the government required manufacturers of cotton cloth to obtain the stamp of the Ferme Générale on all the cloth they produced. Fearful of the effect this would have on the Jouy factory, Oberkampf's partner Sarrasin de Maraise enlisted the support of the duc de Choiseul's former private secretary and of the lawyer Cadet de Senneville to write a letter of protest to the controller general, and Madame de Maraise wrote a strong letter to the *intendant du commerce*. Maraise and Oberkampf then visited Controller General Calonne personally and emerged with an assurance that the measure would not apply to them.[26] More formal means of access to government also existed, and they were equally centralized. The Conseil du Commerce gave a voice to many of the principal manufacturers and merchants of the capital.[27] The Academy of Sciences provided a back door into the corridors of power, as in the case of Antoine Deparcieux, one of its members, who in 1762 put forward a project to pipe drinking water to the southern part of the city. Although the plan was never implemented, it was seriously discussed by the King's Council.[28]

In this new, centralized structure, as in the trades corporations, place of residence and the possession of a local power base were no longer of any relevance. Family ties were still important, because patronage at the center was vital. But although officeholders and influential figures tended for convenience to live in the central districts, concentration of families in individual quarters and parishes brought little political advantage.

The decline of local lineages was further hastened by the economic integration of the city. Although the economic history of Paris is little known, it is clear that in the seventeenth and eighteenth centuries the city underwent a process of integration, as did London and other European cities at about the same time. The numbers and the luxury of shops increased, attracting a larger and wider clientele.[29] By the mid–seventeenth century, wealthy merchants were to be found all across the city, no longer concentrated in the right-bank quarters as they had been in the sixteenth.[30] The diversity of products increased as transport improved, and with it, pedestrian and vehicular movement around the city.

Although increasing commercial contact between quarters is hard to document, the improvement of the internal road system and the removal of barriers to movement and trade across the city testify to the change. Both the political and the economic integration of the city in the late seventeenth century are already symbolized by the demolition of a dozen of the old city gates, including the Porte Saint Marcel, which had marked the entrance to the Faubourg Saint Marcel. In the eighteenth century the administration pierced new streets, created the boulevards, paved streets, widened intersections, and straightened street alignments. The chains that had been stretched across the streets at night and at times of crisis were removed, and the police tried to shift artisans who worked in the street, stall keepers, and itinerant street sellers who hindered the traffic.[31]

Another significant symptom of integration was the appearance, around 1680, of the first trade directories, designed to enable customers to find businesses in parts of the city they did not know. In another domain, the abolition of the trades corporations in the faubourgs was a step toward economic unification of the city; and from the mid–eighteenth century, the creation of central registration bureaus for journeymen in quite a number of trades suggests a centralization of the labor market, at least in some industries.[32] The creation in 1726 of the Ferme Générale, which controlled the entry points to the city, was a further move in its unification. The street numbering first seriously attempted in 1779, but not successfully introduced until the Revolution, was a sign both of growing central control and of the need for strangers to be able readily to find their way around the city—further evidence of commercial integration.[33]

This process was hastened by the growth of consumerism and of international trade. Consumer demand grew considerably in the eighteenth century: deceased estates contained goods unimaginable a hundred years before. New forms of advertising, such as trade cards and tokens, also testify to this growing market. The adoption of more elaborate shop signs and of shop displays at the very end of the century indicates a desire to catch the passing customer, not only the locals. All this is evidence of a large, citywide market for luxury goods that was dependent on the growing prosperity of the middle classes, and even of some elements of the working classes.[34] The boulevards, pleasure gardens, and coffeehouses became centers of commercialized leisure, drawing people from all parts of the city. By the early nineteenth century, shopping in the new arcades and on the rue de Rivoli had become a recognized social activity for fashionable women.[35]

Growing consumer demand within Paris, from the provinces, and from abroad fueled industrial and commercial development. While the vast majority of businesses in Paris remained very small, the largest enterprises were now much bigger, certainly in tanning, brewing, and textiles generally. Joint stock companies appeared in many industries, a reflection of the need for larger amounts of outside capital.[36] The growth of banking, the expansion of overseas and international trade, and the burgeoning national market gave Paris a centralized money market, and banks, deluxe shops, and even manufacturers of luxury goods began to cluster in the increasingly fashionable streets around the Bourse. The early nineteenth century witnessed a rapid movement of such businesses into the area.[37]

Increasing numbers of Paris merchants now had, and needed, contacts in Lyon and Rouen, in Amsterdam and London, in Saint Petersburg and Berlin. They also needed to know bankers and financial agents in Paris itself. If they dealt in textiles or wallpaper or fashion clothes, they had to be sensitive to rapidly changing tastes. Even in less fickle industries, they needed to have their ears to the ground. The larger their business and the more clients they had around the city, the more alert they had to be, listening for rumors of an impending bankruptcy or a suspension of payments, even for a serious illness of a major client.

This partly explains the form of bourgeois sociability in the second half of the eighteenth and in the early nineteenth century. Dinner parties and salons were now important ways of making and renewing useful contacts all across the city. Masonic lodges and dining clubs grouped men (and occasionally women) from different quarters who found one another's company congenial but also useful in their business affairs and dealings with government. Bourgeois sociability, for excellent business reasons, no longer recognized the boundaries of parish or quarter.[38]

For the same reasons, marriage alliances outside the quarter became extremely useful. Even if eighteenth-century bourgeois children were more frequently choosing their own partners, they were doing so—young women particularly—within the circles in which their families moved. Parents could encourage or discourage. Marriage ties across quarters in turn created networks that could be activated for borrowing money, finding jobs, or winning protection for an enterprise. In the new political and demographic conditions of the eighteenth century, too, parents were no doubt happier to see their children leave the quarter than they might have been a hundred years earlier. It was, for Parisians, a peaceful period. There was no repetition of the Spanish invasion of 1637, or of the Fronde. Mortality was declining and life expectancy increasing, so that sudden deaths of people in their prime were probably less common than in the seventeenth century.[39] As a result, the need and desire to have close relatives living in the neighborhood was perhaps reduced.

At the same time, economic and political integration facilitated changes of domicile from one quarter to another as young bourgeois and bourgeoises married across the city and sought desirable premises. Relatives living in other quarters could be rejoined rapidly as movement around the city became easier. Carriages had appeared in the Paris streets in the seventeenth century, and by the eighteenth were owned by many thousands of Parisians, including some of the wealthy middle classes. The profusion of vehicles for hire, which also appeared in the seventeenth century and cost only a few sous, made transport easy, cheap, and rapid, if the driver managed to avoid the traffic jams.[40] The accompanying police measures to improve traffic flow, too, were a response to growing commercial and political needs for rapid movement around the city. All of these developments facilitated both commercial and social integration.

The state was a key agent in all these changes, but it was not, of course, a force of nature unconnected with other changes in French society. Its development throughout Western Europe was a response to population growth, to more sophisticated military technology, and to economic development, all of which the local authorities were ill equipped to manage. Powerful interest groups benefited from its development: financiers and merchant capitalists, most obviously, but also the increasing number of its administrators and clients. Many of the very same notables who lost their local political role now profited from supplying goods to the government and the army. The crown stripped the local bourgeois notables of administrative functions and transferred these tasks to the holders of venal offices—offices purchased in many instances by the sons and grandsons of those same bourgeois families.

As in the case of the Bouillerot family, which by the mid–eighteenth century was intermarrying with lawyers as well as with other merchants, a fusion took place between the once distinct merchant and judicial bourgeoisies that Robert Descimon has identified in sixteenth-century Paris. The incentive to purchase offices was not only the prestige they bestowed, but also tax exemptions and income; and since their value rarely declined, they made an ideal investment.[41] Indeed, some of the opposition to the state in the seventeenth century can be traced not only to its dispossession of the local notables but also to its failure to deliver the benefits expected of it by officeholders.[42] The development of the monarchy and of the central state was an important factor in the development of the French bourgeoisie, therefore, not only in its destruction of their former role but in its creation of new opportunities. The bourgeois of Paris as a group had every reason to support and promote the expansion of the state, even when it removed some of their older rights and powers.

Both the decline of local lineage as a form of social organization and the disappearance of the quarter as a political and social unit were accompanied by a very profound shift in ideology among the middle classes. Again, falling mortality was in part responsible for this. The decline of plague, better economic conditions, longer life expectancy, and lower rates of child mortality made death increasingly something that came to the old rather than to those in their prime. This was particularly true for the better-off in society. Eighteenth-century people were less preoccupied with death than their ancestors. Fewer people were requesting burial in their own parish. Later in the century local cemeteries in Paris were closed and burials in churches outlawed, without serious protest. The link with past generations that was characteristic of the older sense of lineage, under challenge at least since the Reformation, was now broken. As death retreated, so the importance of dead ancestors declined, and with it a family sentiment that crossed the generations. In the process, people's identification with distant kin who were linked to them through a common ancestor also declined.

Religious ideology changed in another way, too. Jansenism in its popular form was a quintessentially local worldview particularly attractive to the notables of early eighteenth-century Paris. It saw the parish as the basic unit within the church and within society. The parish church and its cemetery belonged to the laity, not to the clergy. In their long dispute with Coiffrel and with Hardy de Levaré, the churchwardens of Saint Médard were defending their territory, but also their conception of the church. Their struggle, like that of other Jansenist parishes, served to reinforce local bonds, to strengthen them in the face of outside interference.

Yet paradoxically, that same struggle made them aware of broader political issues. They read the *Nouvelles ecclésiastiques* and followed the swings of fortune of the Jansenist "party," as it significantly came to be called. The Jansenist paper provided extensive coverage of events in provincial France, as well as in other Paris parishes—events they knew directly affected them. The latest actions of the Parlement and of the archbishop were closely followed. One has only to read the journal of the bookseller Hardy to see how, admittedly a little later, Jansenism could sharpen and filter an individual's interest in national and city politics: he is constantly on the watch for the latest maneuvers of the "soi-disant ci-devant Jésuites" (the so-called former Jesuits).[43]

The religious disputes of the first half of the eighteenth century not only created a discourse and a "party," as Dale Van Kley has shown, but also stimulated an interest in national affairs that may well have been new for many bourgeois families. Jansenism created a national community of interest, not least with its incorporation of a powerful Gallican element after the publication of *Unigenitus*.[44] It was at once a force that reinforced local ties and that encouraged a more outward-looking worldview.

Through the channels opened by religious disputes, other new ways of thinking were perhaps funneled into the homes of the local bourgeoisie. The *Nouvelles ecclésiastiques* provided an introduction of sorts to the *philosophes*. A lively pamphlet and periodical literature commented on the "affaires du temps." Again, Hardy's journal reveals how a keen interest in religious politics continued to induce one man (admittedly with ample time for such matters) to follow events at court and throughout the city. He did not perceive the dramatic shift from religious to secular politics that is apparent with hindsight. Hardy continued to view politics through religious spectacles right up to at least the 1770s. So did other Parisians.[45] The antiphilosophical best-seller *Année littéraire* explicitly linked attacks on religion with attacks on the government, while itself helping to lay the "theological foundations of secular politics" by attempting to take on the *philosophes* on their own ground.[46] Nobody, in the later eighteenth century, differentiated between religious and secular politics, and there was every reason for an interest in the one to lead directly to an interest in the other.

Access to a literature aimed at a national public was facilitated by the new forms of bourgeois sociability and by the consumer boom, both products of growing prosperity. Reading circles and reading rooms flourished, as did the coffee shops where clients could read and discuss books and papers. Freemasonry, with its deist symbolism, attracted many merchants and professional men.[47] Books became commonplace in middle-class homes. In 1734 Nicolas Bouillerot, a wealthy tanner, left 73 books worth a total of 50 livres, all religious works. In 1792 the tanner Jean Auffray, who was in relation to other local merchants less wealthy than Bouillerot, upon his death in 1792 possessed 500 books and 50 pamphlets valued at 436 livres. They included Latin and French classics, works of history, and an English dictionary. Auffray also owned maps and basic scientific instruments.[48] Each of these items testifies to his membership in the cultured middle class for whom the Enlightenment was "a way of life."[49] He was interested in the world of nature, in the ancients, in public affairs, in the world outside.

Auffray's library reflects, at the end of the Old Regime, a bourgeois culture that was divorced from the locality in two ways. First, it was no longer a religious culture firmly rooted in the parish, but a wider, more secular culture with its sources in scientific curiosity and worldly affairs. Second, it was now quite distinct from the culture of the common people who remained at the heart of the local community. Nicolas Bouillerot, in the 1720s, undoubtedly had a far wider general culture than those who stood at the back of the same church, but he shared with many of them a faith and an attachment to the parish. Jean Auffray's world, some sixty years later, was very different from that of his workers or his servants. The evidence available suggests that the economic gap between the poorer and the better-off halves of Parisian society widened during the eighteenth century, and that this economic difference was accompanied by new forms of recreation and sociability, a new material culture, new social and political values.[50] Auffray was precisely the sort of individual who had distanced himself from the neighborhood community. His life was padded with products from all over France and from other parts of the world: in this sense, too, it was outward-looking. It was moving toward what Nicholas Green has termed a "metropolitan ideology," centered not on the locality but on the shops and the public parades of central Paris. Inherent in this culture was a new perception of public space.[51]

This new notion of space, as Green has shown, was in the early nineteenth century to impose gender roles that the working population could not adopt. Already in the middle of the eighteenth century, merchants and officeholders were adopting the "quality" model of conjugal behavior, part of what historians have called the ideology of domesticity. Complaints made to the Paris police by men and women of the commercial and legal middle classes increasingly stressed the compassion, innocence, and fragility of the female sex—complaints like that of a grocer whose wife had fainted with fright three times when the officials of the *limonadiers* corporation searched their shop.[52] The male displayed sensitivity and consideration. This ideal required the display of conjugal affection—whether or not it was really present—and waxed sentimental over children.

The model is familiar from novels and advice literature of the period, particularly Rousseau's *Nouvelle Héloïse* and Bernardin de Saint-Pierre's *Paul et Virginie*. It was the precursor to the nineteenth-century ideology of separate spheres, for the proper place for the delicate female was naturally in the home, where she could fashion a haven for her menfolk and her children.

This discourse contrasts sharply with that of the working people of Paris, for whom hard work, thrift, and good reputation were the personal qualities stressed by men and women alike. The ideal of domesticity required servants who would do the dirty work and provide a buffer between the lady of the house and the uncouth outer world. It demanded a comfortable conjugal apartment removed from the intrusions of the street, of the neighbors, and of the extended family, precisely the sort of household that was developing among the Paris middle classes in the second half of the eighteenth century. The dream of domesticity was unrealizable and largely irrelevant for men and women who lived in cramped, bare rooms, who worked hard for very long hours, who could not afford the trimmings or the privacy that the ideal required, and who depended for their survival on neighborhood solidarity.

It is true that not all of the middle-class people who aspired to the ideal were in a position to practice it. Contradictions between genteel pretensions and real behavior are legion. But the significance of the ideal lay less in consistency of behavior than in its value as a social indicator.

Conclusion

The spread of the ideal of domesticity accompanied the gradual with-drawal from the neighborhood community of more affluent merchant, legal, artisanal, and shopkeeping groups, and served to distinguish the "middling sort" in late-eighteenth-century Paris from the "common people" (at least in their own eyes). It was among people such as Auffray that these new models of male and female behavior took root.[53]

Auffray's world, therefore, was structured by a system of values that was quite different from that of the early-eighteenth-century Paris bourgeois. He belonged to a sector of society whose humanitarianism had become a proud hallmark. The cahier of Saint Marcel requested the abolition of slavery. What better example of an outward-looking set of mind that no longer saw its own moral responsibility ceasing at the boundary of parish, quarter, or blood ties, but extending to all humanity? What better example of an emerging "public sphere"?[54]

All of these developments were inseparably connected with the rise of the market and with a universalizing belief in the virtues of the free circulation of goods and of people. Such freedom was not by any means in the interests of all Paris merchants, many of whom were protected by guild regulations and by the special rules governing commerce in the capital. Artisans and merchants from other cities could not trade or manufacture in Paris without special permission, whereas most Paris masters could practice their craft anywhere in France. The grain trade was governed by special rules that gave precedence to Paris-bound supplies.[55]

Nevertheless, many *bourgeois de Paris* became converted to a version of free trade. If the Paris cahiers of 1789 are any indication, it meant to them the removal of what they perceived to be government hindrance of trade: duties paid at internal customs barriers, even at the gates of Paris itself; regulations that disrupted their commerce. To the tanners of the Faubourg Saint Marcel, it meant the abolition of the *régie des cuirs,* with its bothersome inspections, its imperious officials, and its impost on leather. For the butchers it meant the removal of the tax on cattle; for the brewers the abolition of duties on beer and of the tax on barley; for the starch makers the duties on the grain they used. These requests were included in the cahiers of both the Saint Marcel and Saint Victor Districts. Freer circulation also most probably meant easier movement within the city of Paris. The same cahiers requested the construction of the projected new bridge over the Seine, between the Faubourg Saint Marcel and the Faubourg Saint Antoine.[56]

An embryonic utilitarianism was another characteristic of this Parisian middle-class ideology. Both André Arnoult Aclocque and Jean Antoine Derubigny, in their individual cahiers in 1789, suggested that monasteries should be made to help the poor, Derubigny arguing that they could provide free education in Latin, geography, religion, arithmetic, agriculture, and Paris customary law. When the District of Saint Marcel petitioned the National Assembly to spare the Chapter of Saint Marcel in 1790, they did so on the grounds of its usefulness to the quarter. It could provide priests to second the efforts of the overworked parish clergy. They did not mention the shrine of Saint Marcel, which several times within living memory had been uncovered to avert famine or disease.[57]

Put together, these elements made up a new ideology that fitted perfectly not only the commercial and consumer interests but also the psychological and family needs of the Paris middle classes in the late eighteenth century. Attachment to domesticity, like the adoption of humanitarianism, utilitarianism, and the beginnings of political liberalism, was intimately linked with the decline of local lineage and of the quarter, and with growing consumerism. A stress on their own virtue and moral superiority—expressed in modesty of dress, in sensibility, and in the place of women within the family—distinguished the middle classes both from the masses and from the "decadent" nobility. As Roddey Reid points out, the new family values were a source of middle-class identity, but at the same time were perfectly compatible with a universalizing political ideology that stressed education, merit (as opposed to birth alone), and domestic virtue.[58] Free circulation was important to both of these: of ideas, for education; of people, for dispersed families; of goods, for commerce and for consumption.

Greater distance from the local community also encouraged faith in universals, rather than in particular saints associated with individual parishes and places. So did daily reliance on the ethical values of distant merchants, on which eighteenth-century commerce was based. This is not to say that such people were not parochial in their own way. The District of Saint Marcel did not have precisely the same interests as every other district, and disputes arose frequently over where the "general will" might lie. Nor did adoption of this new ideology mean complete separation from the local population, or that masters and merchants did not go to wineshops, any more than it prevented bourgeois husbands from beating their wives. But it was significant in public discourse, in creating a distinctive and citywide bourgeois culture.

Conclusion

The long-term nature of this process might seem to suggest that the formation of the Parisian bourgeoisie was little affected by the Revolution. Nothing could be further from the truth. The Revolution spectacularly accelerated the process and at the same time, in certain respects, probably altered the form it took. Of course, the Revolution itself was shaped by the social processes and forces that I have been describing. The format prescribed for the elections to the Estates General—itself a recognition of the growing importance of educated opinion and of the influence of new ideas of representation—opened political participation to men who were often new to the area, at least in the sense that they had no long-standing family ties there. They were sometimes in new industries, often self-made men, and almost all had been excluded from the one remaining local office that conferred honor and a small degree of political influence, the parish vestries.

Very few of the electors or the members of the Faubourg Saint Marcel district and section committees had been churchwardens. This was also true of the Faubourg Saint Antoine. Only three members of the District Committee elected in 1789 had served on the vestry of Sainte Marguerite. Another two former churchwardens were elected in 1790, and one more served on a Civil Committee in 1793. Of the administrators of the two leading confraternities at Sainte Marguerite, only one went on to hold office during the Revolution. Even allowing for the age of many of the former churchwardens, this was not a high rate of continuity, particularly when one remembers that the parish of Sainte Marguerite was divided into three sections. Furthermore, only one member of the five key families whom Richard Andrews identifies as the dominant ones in the Faubourg Saint Antoine during the Revolution had been a churchwarden: the oldest and longest established, Pierre Antoine Damoye, and then only in 1787, at the advanced age (even for a churchwarden) of sixty-six. He was a leader in the relatively new industry of carriage hiring.[59]

Andrews's observation that the revolutionary elite was largely composed of successful newcomers and their sons holds true for both the major faubourgs, as does his conclusion that their "political aggressivity" resulted from this status as parvenus, as new men who owed their positions to hard work, not to inherited wealth or position.[60] They had made their way, some of them with great commercial success, despite the Old Regime, and now that the opportunity presented itself they were determined to exert the leadership that they felt to be rightly theirs. Some were resolved to change the system that had excluded them for so long.

The Parisian Revolution was largely made by such men, in the districts, in the sections, and in the National Guard. They imposed their belief in equality of talent, their faith in public and private virtue, their views on a wide range of issues. Many of them, of course, were not prepared to support all the changes that the Revolution brought: they did not form a united group in this sense. In most cases the men of 1789, of 1790, of 1791, could not stomach the more radical measures. Many found it impossible to accept republicanism, the new religious system, the violations of legality, the taxes on the rich, the attacks on merchants and speculators, or the role played by women and by the common people in the sectional assemblies and popular societies. Their distance from the preoccupations of their poorer neighbors and of their own workers, a hallmark of the new middle classes, forced many of them out of revolutionary politics. Many were later to return, often horrified by what they had witnessed and determined to prevent it ever recurring. The Parisian Revolution did not spring initially from class conflict in any direct sense, but conflicting economic interests and ideological differences between social groups did powerfully shape its course.

The Revolution also created lasting institutions that allowed the bourgeoisie to flourish and handed power to men of property and talent. Debate about its immediate economic effects continues, but in the longer term the elimination of structural barriers to a national market, the unification of weights and measures, and the suppression of trades corporations and legal institutions that had allowed certain categories of workers a voice—these all worked in favor of Paris merchants.[61] The sale of church and émigré land, speculation on assignats, and lucrative army contracts catapulted some modest families to wealth and prominence. Large church properties provided premises for some of the major industrial establishments of the early nineteenth century, particularly in the faubourgs.[62]

The enormous growth of the state bureaucracy provided jobs for the sons of the educated, allowing new families into the previously closed central administration, while the new educational institutions provided openings for teachers and men of science. In politics, a substantial property qualification for the vote, the two-tier electoral system, and the absence of payment not only for deputies but for a whole range of advisory offices ensured that only the affluent could gain access to positions of influence.[63]

The structure of education also favored and integrated a broad bourgeoisie composed of merchants and manufacturers, bureaucrats, lawyers, doctors, intellectuals, and scientists. Particularly important were the new *grandes écoles,* which were to furnish the administrators of the second generation of the nineteenth century, the "generation of 1820."[64] Even female education, largely left in private hands, privileged those who could pay. The patronage system and the role of connections—through kin, work, and later schooling—was in the long term even more effective than institutional structures in limiting access to power to the affluent.

The Revolution was of equal significance in creating the ideology and the social identity of the Parisian bourgeoisie in its nineteenth-century form. In overturning legal privilege for individuals and for corporations, in its emphasis on the benefits of education, its restructuring of the church, in the new systems of administration and of political representation, the Revolution destroyed a way of thinking and created a new set of mental oppositions for the propertied classes. After 1794, the alternative to the rule of law was the rule of the mob; to property, some form of economic equality. The alternative to religion and to the "natural" hierarchy of educated over uneducated, and of husbands over wives, was anarchy.[65]

Key elements of the middle-class ideology of the prerevolutionary years were institutionalized under the Directory and the Consulate, but its ambiguities were now resolved: in particular, the previously implicit contradiction between equality and hierarchy, and its hesitations over the place of women. The experience of Revolution had convinced most middle-class men and women that the fair sex belonged in the home, and that women must be excluded from politics. Thus the prerevolutionary debate over the education of women was resolved, for the moment, in favor of those who had maintained that the sexes required different training, men for the public sphere and women for the private. The Directory and the Empire enshrined this in law.[66]

At the same time, the Revolution had, through its democratic experiment, persuaded most of the same people that equality posed a serious threat to social stability. Again, therefore, postrevolutionary legislation resolved this largely unforeseen ambiguity by instituting an equality limited by gender and by property.[67] The new "political class" was also defined in opposition to the political extremes now termed "Jacobin" and "royalist," both of which now had social connotations: Jacobins were closely associated with sans-culottes and the poor, royalists with aristocrats, however inaccurate the association may have been in a great many cases. The *honnêtes gens,* who included the majority of Parisian bourgeois, were in the middle.

The Revolution helped to shape the Parisian bourgeoisie not only ideologically but also demographically and geographically. Despite increasing movement between quarters during the second half of the eighteenth century, there had been nothing to match the massive displacement of people and the large-scale creation of cross-city ties by the events of the 1790s. The abolition of venal offices obliged many individuals to seek new employment; some went to the faubourgs, where the rents were lower. The changing boundaries of administrative and political units threw together men from different parishes into the district committees, from different districts into the sectional assemblies and offices, and from different sections into the new arrondissements. The National Guard moved men all over the city, and its officers met with those of other units from other quarters, both while on guard duty and in briefings by the battalion commanders.[68]

In addition, the political storms of the 1790s drove some out of their quarter, either to escape, as in the case of André Arnoult Aclocque or Antoine Moinery, or in search of new opportunities, like Jean Junié or Brion, or more notoriously, Léonard Bourdon de la Crosnière, who moved from Saint Marcel to the Gravilliers Section. Antoine Joseph Santerre left the Faubourg Saint Antoine in 1797, probably as a result of pressure from authorities fearful of his influence there.[69]

Others did not change quarter, but were brought into contact with people and issues they would never have encountered had their lives continued as before. The bookseller André Mercier made wide contacts as a member of the Commune of 10 August and was able to begin a new career as director of the printing works where the assignats were produced.[70] Juste Moroy was a more minor figure—he was a jewelry mounter—whom Richard Andrews gives as an example of a man plucked from obscurity as an elector in 1792 and a member of the Civil and later the Revolutionary Committee of the Finistère Section in the Year II. In the Year IV he joined the office staff of the Surveillance Committee of the arrondissement, and had he not also been the local agent of the Babeuf conspiracy might have made a career in administration. As Andrews shows, many of the future Babouvistes met in prison or in revolutionary politics, often in company with future police agents and administrators.[71]

Political clubs, too, created complex cross-city contacts: the Jacobins and the Cordeliers, of course, but also less known ones like the club of the Sainte Chapelle to which nine of the political leaders of the Gobelins Section belonged in 1791, and that brought them together with like-minded and socially similar individuals from all over Paris.[72] Sectional exchanges and common service in municipal assemblies and in the extensive bureaucracy of the Year II linked men whose public life would never otherwise have surpassed the boundaries of their parish, or who would have had no public careers at all. In this sense, too, the Revolution created a new political class, drawing from obscurity men with administrative talent. Not all survived to join the new bourgeoisie, of course, but many gained sufficient influence and experience to remain in place when the adventure was over. Some were to pursue prosperous political or administrative careers under the Empire and occasionally the Restoration, while even those who never occupied another public position had glimpsed the view from the rostrum.

The Parisian bourgeoisie that emerged from the revolutionary crucible was thus a blend of prerevolutionary notables, of leaders from each phase of the Revolution, and of men like the Salleron brothers who had seized with both hands the economic opportunities offered by the abolition of the trades corporations, by lucrative state contracts, and by the sale of church land. The new state bureaucracy, unlike the old, which tended to be largely endogamous, married widely into business circles, forming a new bourgeoisie that was socially, ideologically, and politically more united than the prerevolutionary middle classes.[73]

This process was furthered by the institutions of the Empire and the Restoration. The National Guard was particularly important because it was explicitly bourgeois, and in its officer corps brought together men from different parts of a large arrondissement. As far as the bourgeoisie was concerned, the arrondissement gradually became the most local unit with which they identified: Augustin Cochin could write in the 1860s that "birth, neighborhood, commerce, the exercise on the same day of the same [voting] rights, the proximity created by fulfilling the same duties had little by little made each arrondissement of Paris into a little province, both civic and industrial."[74]

Beyond the arrondissement, educational institutions played a central role in blending a citywide bourgeoisie. The *lycées* and *collèges,* the Paris faculties of law and medicine, and the *grandes écoles* brought together young men and forged ties of solidarity that were tested in the agitation of the years 1820–1822. Lasting personal networks that transcended the boundaries of individual quarters and arrondissements played an important role in the growing bourgeois opposition to the Restoration regime. Schooling begins to be mentioned in the personnel files of the Interior Ministry during the Restoration.[75] The monarchy's attempts to contain bourgeois opposition by dissolving the National Guard, by increasing press censorship and political surveillance, and by using troops against student demonstrations also contributed to the formation of a common political identity among a major portion of the Parisian bourgeoisie.

In demographic terms, a citywide bourgeoisie had already formed by the 1820s. It is striking how many of the churchwardens of the postrevolutionary vestry of Saint Médard resigned because they were leaving the quarter. The prerevolutionary churchwardens almost invariably died there. Those of the Empire and Restoration often moved for business reasons, like the brewer Jean Raoul Chappellet, who founded a new sugar beet factory in Aubervilliers, though he later returned to the Ile de la Cité and died in the Faubourg Saint Antoine.[76] Most were born outside the quarter, and a sizable proportion died elsewhere. Almost all seem to have had a son, daughter, brother, or sister living in another part of Paris.

In all of this they were typical of the early-nineteenth-century Parisian bourgeoisie as a whole. Only 30 percent of Restoration businessmen married women from the same arrondissement, and although the figure for shopkeepers was higher in most areas, even those whom Daumard terms *"notables de quartier"* (local notables) frequently had children living in other parts of the city.[77] The *Parisian* bourgeoisie was a geographical and demographic reality. The events of the years 1826–1830 were to give it an awareness of its own strength and a unity of purpose.

The *bourgeois de Paris* and the Parisian bourgeoisie were not the same people, and for the most part not the same families. Their culture and ideology were different in important respects. The early-nineteenth-century bourgeoisie had a more secular outlook. They were richer, better educated, more powerful both in economic and in political terms. They had significantly different family and business values from their early-eighteenth-century predecessors, and quite a different sense of their place in society. Yet they did retain a belief in the virtues of thrift, of property, and of work. They still drew their income from commerce and manufacturing, from the professions, and from state service. And they continued to dominate local office and to serve the parish. They were linked by a historical process that can be traced back to the seventeenth century and beyond, in which the centralization of city institutions under the Bourbon kings, the ideological and political struggles surrounding Jansenism, the

Conclusion

long-term secularization of politics and society during the seventeenth and particularly the eighteenth century, the economic growth of the early modern period, and the development of capitalism during the eighteenth and early nineteenth centuries all played a major role.

The formation of the Parisian bourgeoisie was not primarily an economic phenomenon, although growing prosperity and changing economic structures were a necessary precondition. It owed much to political struggles and to political institutions and ideas, religious and secular. The story is inseparable, too, from that of the family and of the relationship between kinship and other social relationships. But the formation of the Parisian bourgeoisie was also a geographical process,[78] a product of urbanization and the changing relationship between the people of Paris and their city.

NOTES

A NOTE ON SOURCES

INDEX

Notes

Abbreviations

A capital letter or double capital letter immediately followed by a number indicates a manuscript at the Archives Nationales, Paris (for example, Y15747; LL847).

Uppercase roman numerals followed by a space and a number indicate documents in the Minutier Central des Notaires at the Archives Nationales (for example, LXII 241).

AAP	Archives de l'Assistance Publique, Paris
AN	Archives Nationales, Paris
AP	Archives Privées, Archives Nationales
Arch.P.	Archives de Paris (formerly Archives de la Seine)
Bastille	Bastille collection, Bibliothèque de l'Arsenal, Paris
BHVP	Bibliothèque Historique de la Ville de Paris
BN	Bibliothèque Nationale, Paris
Bod.	Bodleian Library, Oxford
Brongniart	Marcel Brongniart, *La Paroisse Saint Médard au faubourg Saint Marceau* (Paris, Picard, 1951)
JF	Joly de Fleury Collection, Bibliothèque Nationale
lt. gen.	lieutenant general of police
MC	Archives Nationales, Minutier Central des Notaires
Ms. fr.	Manuscrits français, Bibliothèque Nationale
U.P.	University Press

Introduction

1. Albert Babeau, *Les Bourgeois d'autrefois* (Paris, Firmin Didot, 1886). Paul de Crousaz-Crétet, in his series *Paris sous Louis XIV* (Paris, Plon, 1922–1923). Alfred Franklin, *La Vie privée d'autrefois,* 23 vols. (Paris, Plon-Nourrit, 1887–1901).

2. Marcel Reinhard, *Nouvelle histoire de Paris: La Révolution* (Paris, Hachette, 1971), p. 41.

3. William Doyle, *Origins of the French Revolution* (Oxford, Oxford U.P., 1980), pp. 10–11. George C. Comninel, *Rethinking the French Revolution. Marxism and the Revisionist Challenge* (London and New York, Verso, 1987), pp. 8–12.

4. Joseph di Corcia, "*Bourgeois, Bourgeoisie, Bourgeois de Paris* from the Eleventh to the Eighteenth Century," *Journal of Modern History* 50 (1978): 207–233. Michel Vovelle and Daniel Roche, "Bourgeois, Rentiers, and Property Owners: Elements for Defining a Social Category at the End of the Eighteenth Century," in Jeffry Kaplow, ed., *New Perspectives on the French Revolution* (New York, John Wiley, 1965), pp. 25–46. Roland Mousnier, *Social Hierarchies, 1450 to the Present* (London, Croom Helm, 1973; 1st pub. Paris, PUF, 1973), pp. 85–86. See the use of "bourgeois" by Jacques-Louis Ménétra, *Journal de ma vie,* ed. Daniel Roche (Paris, Montalba, 1982); Eng. trans. *Journal of My Life,* trans. Arthur Goldhammer (New York, Columbia U.P., 1986). See also George V. Taylor, "Bourgeoisie," in Samuel F. Scott and Barry Rothaus, eds., *Historical Dictionary of the French Revolution* (Westport, Conn., Greenwood Press, 1985), pp. 117–122, and Elinor G. Barber, *The Bourgeoisie in Eighteenth-Century France* (Princeton, Princeton U.P., 1955), pp. 14–33. For nineteenth-century definitions, see Adeline Daumard, *La Bourgeoisie parisienne, 1815–1848* (Paris, SEVPEN, 1963), pp. 214–216, and Jean-Pierre Chaline, *Les Bourgeois de Rouen: Une Elite urbaine au XIXe siècle* (Paris, Presses de la Fondation nationale des sciences politiques, 1982), pp. 21–48.

5. Louis-Sébastien Mercier, *Tableau de Paris,* 12 vols. (Amsterdam, 1782–1788), 1:53.

6. The *Communist Manifesto* (1848; Harmondsworth, Penguin, 1967), p. 91, states that "the lower middle class, the small manufacturer, the shopkeeper, the artisan, the peasant, all these fight against the bourgeoisie . . ." Georges Lefebvre, in *La Révolution française* (Paris, PUF, 1951), pp. 43–50, used "bourgeois" to include officeholders (even noble ones), members of the liberal professions, wholesale merchants, and entrepreneurs, but not shopkeepers or artisans, and Alfred Cobban seemed happy with this definition, while denying that these groups constituted a class; see Alfred Cobban, *The Social Interpretation of the French Revolution* (Cambridge, Cambridge U.P.,

1964), esp. pp. 54–67. Albert Soboul included artisans and shopkeepers among the "middle classes," but not among the "bourgeoisie" proper; Albert Soboul, *The French Revolution, 1787–1799* (New York, Vintage, 1975), p. 46. Emmanuel Le Roy Ladurie and Bernard Quilliet, on the other hand, distinguish "classe moyenne" from "petite bourgeoisie et peuple qualifié," who include most master artisans; see their article "Déférence sociale et disjonction des valeurs," in Emmanuel Le Roy Ladurie, ed., *Histoire de la France urbaine,* vol. 3, *La Ville classique de la Renaissance aux Révolutions* (Paris, Seuil, 1989), pp. 408–426 (pp. 411, 417).

7. Richard Cobb, *The People's Armies: The* armées révolutionnaires, *Instrument of the Terror in the Departments,* trans. Marianne Elliott (New Haven, Yale U.P., 1987; 1st pub. Paris, Mouton, 1961); *Terreur et subsistances, 1793–1795* (Paris, Clavreuil, 1965). Albert Soboul, *Les Sans-culottes parisiens en l'an II* (Paris, Clavreuil, 1958).

8. Albert Soboul, Introduction to *Mouvement populaire et gouvernement révolutionnaire (1793–1794)* (Paris, Flammarion, 1973); a republication of Soboul, *Les Sans-culottes parisiens* ([1958], pt. 2), p. 15.

9. Cobban, *Social Interpretation,* pp. 54–61.

10. See Robert Descimon, "Milice bourgeoise et identité citadine à Paris au temps de la Ligue," *Annales: ESC* 48 (1993): 885–906 (p. 892 n. 22).

11. François Furet and Adeline Daumard, *Structures et relations sociales à Paris au XVIIIe siècle* (Paris, Armand Colin, 1961).

12. Doyle, *Origins,* pp. 16–24.

13. John F. Bosher, *The Canada Merchants, 1713–1763* (Oxford, Clarendon, 1987); Robert Forster, *Merchants, Landlords, Magistrates: The Depont Family in Eighteenth-Century France* (Baltimore and London, Johns Hopkins U.P., 1980); John G. Clark, *La Rochelle and the Atlantic Economy during the Eighteenth Century* (Baltimore and London, Johns Hopkins U.P., 1981); Paul W. Bamford, *Privilege and Profit: A Business Family in Eighteenth-Century France* (Philadelphia, Pennsylvania State U.P., 1988); Christine Adams, "Defining *état* in Eighteenth-Century France: The Lamothe Family of Bordeaux," *Journal of Family History* 17 (1992): 25–45; Jean-Pierre Hirsch, *Les Deux Rêves du commerce: Entreprise et institution dans la région lilloise (1780–1860)* (Paris, EHESS, 1991). See also the much older works by Bernard Groethuysen, *Origines de l'esprit bourgeois en France* (Paris, Gallimard, 1927); Pierre Goubert, *Familles marchandes sous l'Ancien Régime: Les Danse et les Motte, de Beauvais* (Paris, SEVPEN, 1959), and Barber, *Bourgeoisie.* Also see Geoffrey Crossick, "Petite bourgeoisie et histoire comparée," *Bulletin du Centre Pierre Léon d'histoire économique et sociale,* 1992, no. 1:13–25. The English middle classes have also been the subject of recent work. Most helpful to me have been Leonore Davidoff and Catherine Hall, *Family Fortunes: Men and Women of the English Middle*

Class, 1750–1850 (London, Hutchinson, 1987); Peter Earle, *The Making of the English Middle Class* (London, Methuen, 1989); and Richard J. Morris, *Class, Sect, and Party* (Manchester, Manchester U.P., 1990).

14. Daniel Roche, *The People of Paris* (Leamington Spa, Berg, 1987; 1st pub. Paris, Aubier Montaigne, 1981), and esp. *The Culture of Clothing* (Oxford, Past and Present Publications, 1994; 1st pub. Paris, Fayard, 1989). Annik Pardailhé-Galabrun, *The Birth of Intimacy: Privacy and Domestic Life in Early Modern Paris,* trans. Jocelyn Phelps (Oxford, Polity, 1991; 1st pub. Paris, PUF, 1986). Robert Darnton, esp. *The Business of Enlightenment: A Publishing History of the Encyclopédie, 1775–1800* (Cambridge, Harvard U.P., 1979) and "The Great Cat Massacre of the rue Saint Séverin," in *The Great Cat Massacre and Other Episodes in French Cultural History* (London, Allen Lane, 1984). Ménétra, *Journal of My Life.* Michael Sonenscher, *The Hatters of Eighteenth-Century France* (Berkeley, U. of California Press, 1987); *Work and Wages: Natural Law, Politics, and the Eighteenth-Century French Trades* (Cambridge, Cambridge U.P., 1989); Steven L. Kaplan, *Provisioning Paris: Merchants and Millers in the Grain and Flour Trade during the Eighteenth Century* (Ithaca and London, Cornell U.P., 1984); "Réflexions sur la police du monde de travail, 1700–1815," *Revue historique* 529 (1979): 17–77; "Social Classification and Representation in the Corporate World of Eighteenth-Century Paris: Turgot's Carnival," in Steven L. Kaplan and Cynthia J. Koepp, eds., *Work in France* (Ithaca, Cornell U.P., 1986), 176–228; "The Character and Implications of Strife among the Masters inside the Guilds of Eighteenth-Century Paris," *Journal of Social History* 19 (1986): 631–647; "La Lutte pour le contrôle du marché de travail à Paris au XVIIIe siècle," *Revue d'histoire moderne et contemporaine* 36 (1989): 361–412; "L'Apprentissage au XVIIIe siècle: Le Cas de Paris," ibid. 40 (1993): 436–479. Robert Isherwood, *Farce and Fantasy: Popular Entertainment in Eighteenth-Century Paris* (New York and Oxford, Oxford U.P., 1986). David Garrioch, *Neighbourhood and Community in Paris, 1740–1790* (Cambridge, Cambridge U.P., 1986). Arlette Farge, *Fragile Lives: Violence, Power, and Solidarity in Eighteenth-Century Paris,* trans. Carol Shelton (Cambridge, Harvard U.P., 1993; 1st pub. Paris, Hachette, 1986); "The Honor and Secrecy of Families," in Philippe Ariès and Georges Duby, eds., *A History of Private Life,* vol. 3, *Passions of the Renaissance,* ed. Roger Chartier, trans. Arthur Goldhammer (Cambridge, Harvard U.P., Belknap Press, 1989; 1st pub. Paris, Seuil, 1986). Serge Chassagne, *Oberkampf, un entrepreneur capitaliste au Siècle des Lumières* (Paris, Aubier-Montaigne, 1980); *Une Femme d'affaires au XVIIIe siècle* (Paris, Privat, 1981). See also S. D. Chapman and Serge Chassagne, *European Textile Printers in the Eighteenth Century* (London, Heinemann, 1981).

15. Richard Andrews, "Réflexions sur la conjuration des Egaux," *Annales: ESC*

29 (1974): 73–106; "Social Structures, Political Elites, and Ideology in Revolutionary Paris, 1792–1794: A Critical Evaluation of Albert Soboul's *Les Sans-culottes parisiens en l'an II,*" *Journal of Social History* 19 (1985–1986): 71–112; "Paris of the Great Revolution," in Gene Brucker, ed., *People and Communities in the Western World,* 2 vols. (Homewood, Ill., Dorsey, 1979). Haim Burstin, *Le Faubourg Saint-Marcel à l'époque révolutionnaire* (Paris, Société des Etudes Robespierristes, 1983). Raymonde Monnier, *Le Faubourg Saint-Antoine* (Paris, Société des Etudes Robespierristes, 1981); *Un Bourgeois sans-culotte: Le Général Santerre* (Paris, Publications de la Sorbonne, 1990). Louis Bergeron, *Banquiers, négociants, et manufacturiers parisiens du Directoire à l'Empire,* 2 vols. (Lille, Atelier de reproduction des thèses de l'Université de Lille III, 1975; republished in 1 vol., Paris, EHESS, 1978).

16. E. P. Thompson, *The Making of the English Working Class* (London, Victor Gollanz, 1963).

17. Mercier, *Tableau de Paris,* 4:194–195.

18. Robert Descimon, *Qui était les Seize?* (Paris, Fédération Paris et Ile-de-France, 1983) and, esp. "Paris on the Eve of Saint Bartholomew: Taxation, Privilege, and Social Geography," in Philip Benedict, ed., *Cities and Social Change in Early Modern France* (London, Routledge, 1989), pp. 69–104; also, with Elie Barnavi, *La Sainte Ligue, le juge, et la potence* (Paris, Hachette, 1985).

19. On Jansenism and its political implications, Dominique Julia, "Le Déclin institutionel et politique du catholicisme français," in Jacques Le Goff and René Rémond, eds., *Histoire de la France religieuse* (Paris, Seuil, 1991), pp. 9–40; David A. Bell, *Lawyers and Citizens: The Making of a Political Elite in Old Regime France* (New York, Oxford U.P., 1994), pp. 68–73; John McManners, "Jansenism and Politics in the Eighteenth Century," in Derek Baker, ed., *Church, Society, and Politics* (Oxford, 1975), pp. 253–273.

20. Mercier, *Tableau de Paris,* 1:269.

21. Jean-Jacques Rousseau, *Les Confessions,* ed. Bernard Gagnebin (Paris, Livre de Poche, 1972), vol. 1, bk. 4 (1730–1731), p. 243. Nikolai Karamzin, *Letters of a Russian Traveler, 1789–1790* (New York, Columbia U.P., 1957), p. 179. See also Simon Davies, "L'Idée de Paris dans le roman du dix-huitième siècle," in *La Ville au XVIIIe siècle* (Aix-en-Provence, Edisud, n.d. [1975], pp. 11–17.

22. On this quarter at the end of the eighteenth century, Burstin, *Faubourg Saint-Marcel.* For its earlier history, C. Eyraud et al., *Du Bourg Saint Marcel aux Gobelins* (Paris, Editions municipales/Société historique et archéologique du treizième arrondissement, 1971); Louis Joly, "Saint-Marcel-lez-Paris, collégiale et seigneurie," doctoral thesis, Faculté de Droit, Paris, 1949). On the Gobelins, A.-L. Lacordaire, *Notice historique sur les manufactures impériales de tapisseries des Gobelins et de tapis de la Savonnerie . . .* (Paris,

Gobelins, 1853); Haim Burstin, "Travail, entreprise, et politique à la Manufacture des Gobelins pendant la période révolutionnaire," in Gérard Gayot and Jean-Pierre Hirsch, eds., *La Révolution française et le développement du capitalisme,* special issue of *Revue du Nord* (Lille, 1989), pp. 369–379. See also Charles Manneville, *Une Vieille Église de Paris: Saint Médard* (Paris, Champion, 1906); Marcel Brongniart, *La Paroisse Saint Médard au faubourg Saint Marceau* (Paris, Picard, 1951); Jean Gaston, *Une Paroisse parisienne avant la Révolution: Saint Hippolyte* (Paris, Librairie des Saints Pères, 1908).

23. David Garrioch, "Parish Politics, Jansenism, and the Paris Middle Classes in the Eighteenth Century," *French History* 8 (1994): 403–419.

24. Garrioch, "Parish Politics." Marie-José Michel, "Clergé et pastorale jansénistes à Paris (1669–1730)," *Revue d'histoire moderne et contemporaine* 26 (1979): 177–197.

1. The Work of Satan

1 December 1730

This description is modeled on the 1745 ceremony at Saint Eloi de Roissy, whose curé was also a canon of Sainte Geneviève; XLIX 631, 8 Aug. 1745. The same ceremony was used at Saint Gervais in 1761; Louis Brochard, *Saint Gervais: Histoire de la paroisse* (Paris, Didot, n.d. [1950]), pp. 164–165. On the church and liturgy, Charles Manneville, *Une Vieille Eglise de Paris: Saint Médard* (Paris, Champion, 1906), pp. 28–32, 61. Marcel Brongniart, *La Paroisse Saint Médard au faubourg Saint Marceau* (Paris, Picard, 1951; hereafter cited as Brongniart), p. 47, says the Roman liturgy was adopted because it was printed and therefore cheaper than the manuscript Paris liturgy.

26 December 1730

Bastille 10171, letter of 28 Dec. 1730. B. Robert Kreiser, *Miracles, Convulsions, and Ecclesiastical Politics in Early Eighteenth-Century Paris* (Princeton, Princeton U.P., 1978), p. 163. Brongniart, p. 73. On Saint Etienne, Edmond Jean François Barbier, *Journal historique et anecdotique du règne de Louis XV,* 4 vols. (Paris, J. Renouard, 1847–1851), 1:328 (8 Oct. 1730).

21 January 1731

Bastille 10196, Archbishop Vintimille to [Hérault?], 17 Jan. 1731; police report on Desroches, n.d.; list of churchwardens of Saint Médard, 1730, on which Coiffrel has written next to Desroches's name, "Celui-ci anime tous les autres [This one stirs up all the others]." On Pâris, the *Unigenitus* controversy, and events at Saint Médard, Kreiser, *Miracles,* pp. 10–54, 81–98, 161–163. See also Brongniart, p. 74.

30 December 1731

Nouvelles ecclésiastiques, 31 Feb., 21 June, 14 July, 15 Dec., 29 Dec. 1731. Archbishop Vintimille to Cardinal Fleury, 18 Apr. 1731, quoted in Kreiser, *Miracles,* p. 164. "Arrêt du Grand Conseil," 11 June 1731, quoted ibid. On exile of priests, Kreiser, *Miracles,* pp. 203–204. On convulsions, ibid., pp. 173–176; Barbier, *Journal historique* 1:352 (July 1731); Catherine Maire, *Les Convulsionnaires de Saint Médard* (Paris, Gallimard/Julliard, 1985), chap. 4; Jeffry Kaplow, *The Names of Kings* (New York, Basic Books, 1972), pp. 121–126. See Bastille 10196, *mémoire,* n.d. [early 1732], for comment on miracles; police report, 29 Oct. 1731, on hawkers; police reports of 22 Nov., 24 Nov., 27 Nov., 14 Dec. 1731 on cemetery. Also Brongniart, p. 74.

17 May 1732

Bastille 10196, Coiffrel to Hérault, 17 May 1732. Kreiser, *Miracles,* pp. 214–217, 296–297. Bastille 10196, police reports, 3 Feb., 4 Feb., 16 Apr., 22 Apr. 1732, and LeJeune (*vicaire* of Saint Médard), to Cardinal Fleury. For prayers seeking Pâris' intercession, Bastille 10199, Mathieu Marais, *Journal et mémoires de Mathieu Marais sur la Régence et le règne de Louis XV,* 4 vols. (Paris, Didot, 1863–1868), 4:361 (4 May 1732). On wider political struggle, Kreiser, *Miracles,* chap. 5. On Coiffrel's court cases, Marais, *Journal,* 4:344, 358 (22 Feb., 24 Apr. 1732); Barbier, *Journal historique,* 1:399 (Feb. 1732); *Remontrances des anciens marguilliers de Saint Médard* (1733), Bod 3 Delta 515 19 (hereafter cited as *Remontrances*). Churchwarden signatures (in photograph), MC XVII 674, extract from register of deliberations, 14 Dec. 1732.

15 April 1733

Bastille 10197, fol. 238, "Déclaration du curé du 15 avril 1733."

3 April 1735

Brongniart, pp. 78–79. Bastille 10196, Coiffrel to [Cardinal Fleury], n.d. [before Oct. 1732]; police report, 12 Dec. 1732. *Remontrances.* Bastille 10197, Coiffrel to [lieutenant general of police], 5 Apr. 1733; Etienne Bouillerot to lt. gen., 1 Apr. 1733. On Dupin, Bastille 10197, Coiffrel to lt. gen., 10 May and 22 May 1733. XVII 678, "Délibération des anciens marguilliers de Saint Médard," 2 Aug. 1733. *Remontrances.* On Coiffrel's plans, Bastille 10196, Coiffrel to Cardinal Fleury, 2 Oct. [1732], Bastille 10200, Coiffrel to lt. gen., 23 Aug. [1733]; On divisions in parish, Bastille 10197, fols. 354, 372, 384, police reports of 2 Feb.,

25 Apr., 15 May 1734. For deaths of churchwardens, JF 1569, fol. 84, *mémoire* for churchwardens of Saint Médard, n.d. [c. 1755]. For Coiffrel's debts, Bastille 10198, 1 Apr. 1736; Bastille 10201, *mémoire* on Saint Médard, n.d. [c. 1740]. On Jansenism in the parish, Bastille 10197, fol. 296; fol. 302, Coiffrel to lt. gen., 16 May, 15 July 1734; Bastille 10198, *mémoire*, n.d. [1735]. On schoolmaster, BN Ms. fr. 11356, fol. 342. On Tavignot affair, Brongniart, pp. 80–81; Kreiser, *Miracles*, pp. 296 n. 79, 322 n. 6; JF 126, fols. 296–483; Bastille 10916.

18 March 1736
Bastille 10198, Coiffrel to lt. gen., 18 Mar. and 1 Apr. 1736, 3 Apr. 1735. Bastille 10197, fol. 332, Coiffrel to [lt. gen.], 21 Dec. 1734.

5 September 1740
Bastille 10199, abbé of Sainte Geneviève to [lt. gen.], 2 Sept., 3 Sept., 5 Sept. 1740.

23 December 1740
This is a free translation of most of the letter in Bastille 10199.

4 May 1741
Bastille 10200, Delecluze, *vicaire* at Saint Médard, to Archbishop Vintimille, 4 May 1741. Bastille 10199, petitions to lt. gen., 15 Nov., 23 Dec. 1740. Bastille 10200, petitions, n.d.

13 July 1741
Bastille 10200, Gerbault to lt. gen., 13 July 1741; Gaillande to [lt. gen.], 6 May 1741; Grandval to lt. gen., 6 June 1741; unsigned *mémoire*, n.d. [1741]; Gerbault to 1st secretary of Cardinal Fleury, 24 Aug. 1741.

24 March 1742
Bastille 10200, *mémoire*, 12 Oct. 1741; police reports, 7 Dec., 27 Dec. 1741, 13 Feb., 15 Feb., 19 Feb. 1742; petition to lt. gen., n.d. [Jan. 1742]. Brongniart, p. 82. On Hardy de Levaré's arrival, Bastille 10200, police reports, 12 Mar., 13 Mar., 24 Mar. 1742, and on Huguet, Bastille 10200, Gaillande to [lt. gen.], 6 May 1741; Dubut to [lt. gen.], 15 May 1741; Cheret (curé of Saint Roch), to [lt. gen.], 11 June 1741.

31 July 1742
Bastille 10200, police reports, 24 May, 23 July, 25 July, 31 July 1742; exposé by

Hardy de Levaré, n.d. [May 1742]; same to [lt. gen.], 7 May, 28 May, 19 July, 27 July 1742; Hardy de Levaré, "Mémoire concernant le commissaire des pauvres de Saint Médard," n.d. [early June 1742].

1 May 1749

Bastille 10201, police reports, 1 May 1749, 4 Oct. 1743; Hardy de Levaré to [lt. gen.], 28 May 1743. On Jansenism, Bastille 10200, same to [lt. gen.], 27 Oct. 1742. For battles with vestry, Bastille 10201, same to [lt. gen.], 25 Apr., 17 June, 23 June 1744, 19 Sept. 1747. On pastoral work, Bastille 10201, unsigned "Mémoire concernant l'état de la paroisse Saint Médard," 1743; Hardy de Levaré to lt. gen., 8 Nov. 1743, 27 Aug. 1744. On cantor, Bastille 10201, same to lt. gen., 23 May 1744. For provocations of vestry, Bastille 10201, lt. gen. to Dupont (magistrate in Châtelet court), 15 Jan. 1749; Hardy de Levaré to lt. gen., 31 Dec. 1748.

29 December 1751

Bastille 10202, archbishop of Paris to Berryer, 21 Dec. 1751; Dupont to [archbishop], 29 Dec. 1751; summary of events at Saint Médard, n.d. [mid-1751]; unsigned "Mémoire pour la fabrique de Saint Médard," n.d. [early 1751]. Bastille 10201, "Extrait des délibérations des marguilliers de Saint Médard," 7 Mar. 1750; "Arrêt du Conseil," 17 Mar. 1750.

17 December 1752

Brongniart, pp. 85–87. René L. de Voyer de Paulmy d'Argenson, *Journal et mémoires du Marquis d'Argenson*, ed. E. J. B. Rathery, 9 vols. (Paris, Veuve Renouard, 1859–1867; reprint New York, Johnson Reprint, 1968), 7:184 (6 Apr. 1752). Dale Van Kley, *The Damiens Affair and the Unraveling of the Ancien Régime, 1750–1770* (Princeton, Princeton U.P., 1984), pp. 107–112. See also Jacques Parguez, *La Bulle Unigenitus et le jansénisme politique: Avant-coureur de la Révolution française* (Paris, Librairie Maurice Glomeau, 1986).

7 February 1755

26 AP 58, Pointard papers, "Etat de la chambre de conseil de la fabrique" [de Saint Médard], n.d. [1790]. JF 1569, fol. 67, "Extrait des délibérations de la paroisse Saint Médard," 7 Feb. 1755; fol. 71, "Délibération du 5 mars 1754"; fol. 69, "Requête des marguilliers de Saint Médard," 8 Feb. 1755; fols. 80–81v, unsigned *mémoire* for churchwardens, n.d. [1755]; fol. 73, "Délibération du 17 janvier 1755." On Declaration of Silence (2 Sept. 1754), Van Kley, *Damiens Affair*, pp. 131–133.

4 October 1759

JF 1569, fols. 185–188, on 4 Oct. 1759; fol. 110, churchwardens of Saint Médard to *procureur général*, n.d. [1758]; fol. 112, Bertin (lt. gen.) to *procureur général*, 22 Sept. 1758; fol. 82, invitation to service for curés, 1 Mar. 1758. Bastille 10202, police reports, 4 Oct. 1756. Brongniart, pp. 88–89. For background, Van Kley, *Damiens Affair*, pp. 137–143, 159–160. The Gothic facade was replaced in 1773; Brongniart, p. 93.

2. The Elect

1. Bastille 10202, unsigned letter, n.d. [1731 or 1732].
2. Bastille 10196, Le Jeune (*vicaire* of Saint Médard), to Cardinal Fleury, 2 Apr. 1732.
3. Bastille 10200, unsigned petition to lt. gen., n.d. [1741].
4. JF 126, fol. 296.
5. Bastille 10196, list of churchwardens, 1730.
6. BN Ms. fr., nouvelles acquisitions 4264, fols. 31v, 35.
7. Bastille 10198, *mémoire* concerning Jean Camet, n.d. [1735]; letter to lt. gen., 28 Feb. 1745. Camet was "connu de tous les Bouillerot." For Nicolas Bouillerot's library, XVII 683, 25 May 1734.
8. Bastille 10196, unsigned police report, n.d. [1731].
9. Bastille 10197, fol. 302, Coiffrel to lt. gen., 16 May 1734.
10. Bastille 10196, Duval (priest at Saint Médard) to [archbishop], 11 Aug. 1731. Bastille 10197, fol. 370, police report, 2 Mar. 1734.
11. Bastille 10201, Hardy de Levaré to lt. gen., 28 Dec. 1743.
12. H5 3792, L685, and esp. L686. Marie-José Michel, "Clergé et pastorale jansénistes à Paris (1669–1730)," *Revue d'histoire moderne et contemporaine* 26 (1979): 177–197 (pp. 180–185).
13. L685, no. 52. L686, dossier 4. Brongniart, p. 105. Jean Gaston, *Une Paroisse parisienne avant la Révolution: Saint Hippolyte* (Paris, Librairie des Saints Pères, 1908), p. 91. LL847, fol. 138, 28 Dec. 1738.
14. Bastille 10196, Le Jeune to lt. gen., 2 Apr. 1732. Unsigned note to "Monsieur Le Clerc, officier du guet," n.d. Guillotte (police employee) to lt. gen., 29 Oct. 1731. Bastille 10196, police reports, 24 Nov., 27 Nov., 14 Dec. 1731. Bastille 10199, police reports, 4 Oct. 1738, 1 May 1739. The churchwardens allowed the famous convulsionary Marquis de Légal to sit in their pew at mass; Bastille 10196, police reports, 27 Jan., 2 Feb. 1732.
15. Bastille 10200, "Mémoire concernant le commissaire des pauvres de Saint Médard," received by police office 5 June 1742. Bastille 10202, police reports, 4 Oct. 1756, 4 May 1757. Bastille 10196, police report, 7 Sept. 1732.
16. Bastille 10196, Pillerault, *exempt de robe courte*, to [lt. gen.], n.d. [1730].

17. Bastille 10196, Coiffrel to [Cardinal Fleury], n.d. [late 1732]. Bastille 10196, letter to lt. gen., 17 Jan. 1731 [signature indecipherable]. Michel, "Clergé," p. 179. Bastille 10197, fol. 296, n.d. [c. 1733]. Bastille 10201, unsigned *mémoire* in Hardy de Levaré's hand, of 1743.

18. Bastille 10200, police report, 31 July 1742. JF 345, fol. 139, unsigned *mémoire* in Hardy de Levaré's hand, n.d.

19. Bastille 10197, 3 May 1733. See also Bastille 10196, police reports, 15 Apr., 5 Oct. 1732; Bastille 10197, fol. 143 (3 Sept. 1733), fol. 389 (20 May 1734). Bastille 10200 and 10201, Hardy de Levaré's letters.

20. Bastille 10196, Coiffrel to [Cardinal Fleury], n.d. [late 1732]. Bastille 10197, unsigned *mémoire* [1733?]. Bastille 10196, police reports on Saint Médard, 1730s and 1740s. Bastille 10200, list of frequent visitors, 1741. On Paris curés, Bastille 10171, 22 Apr. 1732.

21. Bastille 10199, reports, 1738. Bastille 10202, police reports, May 1751. Bastille 10200, police report, 23 July 1742.

22. Bastille 10171, unsigned *mémoire*, 28 Dec. 1730. Bastille 10197, Mennessier to [lt. gen.], 30 Oct. 1734.

23. Bastille 10171, Dulac (Doyen of Saint Marcel), to [archbishop], 19 Mar. 1733. Laurence Winnie, "Aegis of the Bourgeoisie: The Cochin of Paris, 1750–1922)," (Ph.D. diss., U. of Michigan, 1988), pp. 67–68. Bastille 10200, Hardy de Levaré to [lt. gen.], n.d. [1742].

24. Bastille 10201, unsigned *mémoire* describing events at Saint Médard since 1732, n.d. [c. 1740].

25. Dale Van Kley, *The Damiens Affair and the Unraveling of the Ancien Régime, 1750–1770* (Princeton, Princeton U.P., 1984).

26. At Saint Germain l'Auxerrois in 1757, 58,000 livres; at Saint Gervais, 61,000 livres in 1747 and 32,500 livres in 1762; at Saint Hippolyte, a poor parish, around 5,000 livres annually; S 7493, statements of income for church gift to King (therefore very conservative).

27. Archives of Saint Médard, accounts, 1779. H5 3795, 1786 accounts. Assets calculated from interest on investments, 1730, at 3 percent per annum; L686. On dowries, Adeline Daumard and François Furet, *Structures et relations sociales à Paris au XVIIIe siècle* (Paris, Colin, 1961), pp. 18–19.

28. S3445, 1781 accounts. 26 AP 58, revenue, n.d. [1790]. Bastille 10197, *mémoire* for churchwardens, n.d. [c. 1733]. S3443, Saint Martin du Cloître, 1790.

29. Bastille 10201, unsigned "Mémoire concernant l'état de la paroisse Saint Médard," 1743. S 7493, dossier Saint Jacques du Haut Pas.

30. According to most parish statutes, other parish notables were to be invited to participate in elections, but this seems to have been a dead letter. See statutes in BN Ms. fr. 21609, 21610. Registers of elections for Sainte Marguerite (LL836) and Saint Martin du Cloître (LL847). See also JF 1588, fol.

48, and Louis Brochard, *Saint Gervais: Histoire de la paroisse* (Paris, Didot, n.d. [1950]), pp. 181–183. At Saint Cristophe en la Cité in 1746, however, other notables did attend; L634, fol. 37v.

31. S 7493, Saint Hippolyte. See also S 3371, Saint Hippolyte, 16 Mar. 1789, no. 48; XI 344, 24 Mar. 1696 (Saint Etienne du Mont).

32. Brongniart, p. 65. XI 344, 24 Mar. 1696 (Saint Etienne du Mont). L634 (Saint Cristophe en la Cité). Louis Brochard, *Histoire de la paroisse et de l'église Saint-Laurent* (Paris, Champion, 1923), p. 68 n. 1.

33. Bastille 10202, Hardy de Levaré to lt. gen., n.d. [28 Dec. 1743]. The final page of this letter is in Bastille 10201.

34. L634, Saint Cristophe en la Cité, fol. 1.

35. On introduction of churchwardens' pews, Orest Ranum, *Paris in the Age of Absolutism* (Bloomington and London, Indiana U.P., 1979; 1st pub. New York, John Wiley and Sons, 1968), p. 181. 26 AP 58, "Etat de la chambre de conseil de la fabrique," Saint Médard, 1790. LL847, Saint Martin du Cloître, fols. 45v (26 Mar. 1702), 212v, (21 Feb. 1757). Michel, "Clergé," p. 189. Maurice Vimont, *Histoire de l'église et de la paroisse Saint-Leu Saint-Gilles* (Paris, Florange and Margraff, 1932), p. 103.

36. Y11452, *scellé après décès,* 9 Jan. 1730.

37. LL847, fol. 136, 28 Sept. 1738 (Saint Martin du Cloître). L634, Saint Cristophe en la Cité, fol. 7v, 19 May 1737. LL707, fol. 112, Saint Etienne du Mont, 1 Apr. 1725.

38. LL847, fol. 108v. Bastille 11040, fol. 9, Pommard to Rossignol (police officer), 31 Aug. 1729.

39. Brongniart, p. 107. LL836, fol. 18, 3 Feb. 1763. L685, nos. 52–56. David Garrioch, *Neighbourhood and Community in Paris, 1740–1790* (Cambridge, Cambridge U.P., 1986), pp. 164–165. JF 1569, fol. 126 [1758].

40. [D. Jousse], *Traité du gouvernement spirituel et temporel des paroisses* (Paris, Debure, 1769), p. 402. JF 1588, fol. 3, 7 Sept. 1745 (Sainte Marguerite). JF 1587, fol. 5 (Saint Jean en Grève). Brochard, *Saint Gervais,* p. 296.

41. Winnie, "Aegis of the Bourgeoisie," pp. 83–86. Bastille 10171, Saint Séverin, 1734–1736. Bastille 10200, police report, 3 Mar. 1742.

42. JF 345, fol. 79, 28 Oct. 1757.

43. Daniel Roche, "A Pauper Capital: Some Reflections on the Parisian Poor in the Seventeenth and Eighteenth Centuries," *French History* 1 (1987): 182–209 (p. 196). Bastille 10199, Dame Tirman to archbishop, 23 Dec. 1740. Bastille 10201, unsigned "Mémoire concernant l'état de la paroisse de Saint Médard,' 1743.

44. LL847, fol. 199v, 23 Apr. 1752.

45. JF 1586, fol. 159, *arrêt* of 3 July 1755. See JF 1586, fol. 243 (Saint Jean en Grève); LL847, fols. 150v, 186, 198 (Saint Martin du Cloître); BN 4° Fm 23877 (Saint Etienne du Mont, 1766); 4° Fm 35552 (Saint Eustache, 1708).

46. BN Ms. fr. 21620, fols. 275–282. L635, p. 12, *arrêt du Parlement*, n.d. [July 1751]. Vimont, *Saint-Leu*, p. 107. LL847, fol. 45, 26 Mar. 1702. Y14667, complaint of 20 Jan. 1747 (Sainte Croix en la Cité); BN 4° Fm 23895, *Extrait d'un mémoire de MM. les marguilliers de Saint Hilaire du Mont*, n.d. [1781].

47. The BN collection of factums contains many *mémoires* concerning such disputes. See also David Garrioch, "Parish Politics, Jansenism, and the Paris Middle Classes in the Eighteenth Century," *French History* 8 (1994): 403–419.

48. Bastille 10171, curé of Saint Jacques de la Boucherie to [lt. gen.], 25 Dec. 1734.

49. BN 4° Fm 23890, *Mémoire pour Remy Chapeau, curé de . . . Saint Germain l'Auxerrois*, 1761.

50. Bastille 10196, Coiffrel to lt. gen., 23 Aug. [1733].

51. BN Ms. fr. 21610, fol. 127. See also Ms. fr. 21609, fol. 29 (Saint-Leu); [Jousse], *Traité du gouvernement* pp. 385–402 (Saint Louis en l'Ile).

52. BN Ms. fr. 21609, fols. 29–32 (Saint-Leu Saint Gilles); Ms. fr. 21610, fol. 127 (Saint Jean en Grève); JF 1586, fol. 46v (Notre Dame de Bonne Nouvelle, 1735). [Jousse], *Traité du gouvernement*, p. 387 (Saint Louis en l'Ile).

53. Y13925, division of Bouillerot estate, 31 Aug. 1740. Another wealthy churchwarden, the tanner Nicolas Bouillerot, left an estate worth 90,196 livres; XVII 687, 21 Oct. 1734.

54. Annik Pardailhé-Galabrun, La *Naissance de l'intime* (Paris, PUF, 1986), pp. 155, 464. Daumard and Furet, *Structures et relations,* pp. 18–19. Daumard and Furet give the total of male and female dowries added together. I have conservatively estimated the dowry of the other partner at two-thirds that of the Bouillerot daughters and used the combined total for comparison with the 1749 sample.

55. Y13916, 31 Aug. 1735.

56. Y13916, division of estate and *compte de tutelle,* 31 Aug. 1735. Daumard and Furet, *Structures et relations,* p. 19 table.

57. XXVIII 409, 4 June 1768. Pardailhé-Galabrun, *Naissance,* p. 465.

58. The wife of silk merchant Jean Pichard left 32,504 livres; XVII 671, 25 Apr. Henry Devaux owned an office purchased for 38,000 livres, devalued to 20,050 livres by 1732; 26 Mar. 1732; Y11457B, 13 Dec. 1740. Candle maker Charles Labbé left 56,000 livres Y13925, 31 Aug. 1740. Pierre Bouillerot left an estate of 101,790 livres; Y12581, division of estate, 14 May 1738. Jean Genneau, who married in 1692, had a dowry of 14,000 livres; LXIX 474, 10 Feb. 1692.

59. Steven L. Kaplan, "The Character and Implications of Strife among the Masters inside the Guilds of Eighteenth-Century Paris," *Journal of Social History* 19 (1985–1986): 631–647; "La Lutte pour le contrôle du marché

de travail à Paris au XVIIIe siècle," *Revue d'histoire moderne et contemporaine* 36 (1989): 361–412; Michael Sonenscher, *Work and Wages: Natural Law, Politics, and the Eighteenth-Century French Trades* (Cambridge, Cambridge U.P., 1989), p. 4; Garrioch, *Neighbourhood*, pp. 105–108.

60. Alfred Franklin, *Dictionnaire historique des arts, métiers, et professions exercés dans Paris depuis le treizième siècle* (Paris, H. Welter, 1906), p. 774; Jacques Savary des Bruslons, *Dictionnaire du commerce*, 5 vols. (Copenhagen, 1759–1765), "Cordonniers." According to a complaint of 1764, a smaller number of masters' representatives were summoned, giving the *anciens* an absolute majority; Y11952, 11 July 1764 (shoemakers).

61. Z1E 307, tax list for Bièvre, 1749–1750.

62. S. Dupain, *La Bièvre: Nouvelles recherches historiques* (Paris, Champion, 1886), pp. 52, 56. BN Ms. fr. 21689, fols. 138–139.

63. Dupain, *La Bièvre*, pp. 65–70, 105. BN Ms. fr. 21689, fol. 199, *arrêt de la Table de Marbre du 26 octobre 1678*. Z1E 307, reports of the river guard, 1733.

64. Z1E 307, Arrêt du Conseil d'Etat, 26 Feb. 1732. Z1E 308, ordonnance du Grand Maître des Eaux et Forêts, 30 May 1751. Z1E 308, état de curage, 7 Sept. 1784. Z1E 307, ordonnance du Grand Maître des Eaux et Forêts, 24 Sept. 1743. Z1E 308, accounts for 1749–1750.

65. Z1E 308, ordonnance du Conseil d'Etat, 18 May 1756.

66. Z1E 308, deliberation of *intéressés à la Bièvre*, 3 Oct. 1745. Z1E 307, accounts for 1749–1750. Z1E 308, ordonnance du Grand Maître des Eaux et Forêts, 8 Mar. 1757.

67. Z1E 308, elections of 28 June 1750, 30 June 1754, 29 June 1755; "Requête au Grand Maître des Eaux et Forêts," 30 July 1736.

68. Z1E 308, elections. Emile Dacier and Albert Vuaflart, *Jean de Jullienne et les graveurs de Watteau au XVIIIe siècle*, 3 vols. (Paris, Société pour l'étude de la gravure française, 1929).

69. XVII 720, 16 Jan. 1740.

70. Z1E 307. I exclude the assembly of 1755, when the Eaux et Forêts threatened to fine those who did not come and twenty-seven attended.

71. Ibid.

3. The Ruling Families

1. BN Ms. fr. 18803, tax roll for street cleaning, 1637, fol. 86. André E. Guillerme, *The Age of Water: The Urban Environment in the North of France, AD 300–1800* (College Station, Texas A&M University Press, 1988; 1st pub. Paris, Editions du Champ Vallon, 1983), p. 155. XVII 426, inventory of François Bouillerot, 15 June 1691. S*1664, Sainte Geneviève, ensais-

inements pour les faubourgs, 25 Apr. 1704; S*1753, *terrier* of Sainte Geneviève, fol. 338.

2. Roland Mousnier, *Les Institutions de la France sous la monarchie absolue,* 2 vols. (Paris, PUF, 1974, 1980), vol. 1, chap. 2. Jack Goody, *The Development of the Family and Marriage in Europe* (Cambridge, Cambridge U.P., 1983), esp. App. 1. Goody prefers the term *lignage*. See also F. W. Kent, *Household and Lineage in Renaissance Florence* (Princeton, Princeton U.P., 1978). Christiane Klapisch-Zuber, *La Maison et le nom: Stratégies et rituels dans l'Italie de la Renaissance* (Paris, EHESS, 1990). Robert Descimon, "Paris on the Eve of Saint Bartholomew: Taxation, Privilege, and Social Geography," in Philip Benedict, ed., *Cities and Social Change in Early Modern France* (London, Routledge, 1989), pp. 69–104 (pp. 93–97). René Pillorget, *La Tige et le rameau: Familles anglaise et française, 16e–18e siècle* (Paris, Calmann-Lévy, 1979), pp. 60–61.

3. The following reconstruction is based primarily on inventories, *scellés,* and marriage contracts in the notarial archives, on the *censive* records of Sainte Geneviève, and on the *insinuations* kept in the AN Y series and in Arch. P.

4. S*1752, fol. 189. XVII 667, transfer of *rente,* 10 Aug. 1731. XXVIII 409, *licitation,* 4 June 1768; S*1668, fol. 53.

5. S5683, fol. 51; S*5695 (4), fol. 25. XVII 662, *délaissement,* 24 Apr. 1730.

6. S*1753, fol. 319. S*1666, fol. 411.

7. David Garrioch, *Neighbourhood and Community in Paris, 1740–1790* (Cambridge, Cambridge U.P., 1986), pp. 92–93. Yves Durand, *Les Fermiers généraux au XVIIIe siècle* (Paris, PUF, 1971), pp. 75–76, 326–383. See also Sharon Kettering, "Patronage and Kinship in Early Modern France," *French Historical Studies* 16, no. 2 (fall 1989), 408–435.

8. Bastille 10171, letter from Boivriaux [?], 28 Dec. 1730. Bastille 10197, fol. 144, report of 3 Sept. 1733. Bastille 10201, undated petition from Antoine LeBis to lt. gen., n.d. [c. 1741]. See also Coiffrel's list of "all those individuals capable of troubling us"; Bastille 10197, fol. 302, Coiffrel to [Cardinal Fleury], 16 May 1734. At least thirteen of the twenty-two named belonged to the Bouillerot kin network.

9. Arch.P. DC6 212, fol. 51, Mar. 1714.

10. Y13925, 31 Aug. 1740.

11. Arch.P. 5 AZ 3911, n.d. [1740s]. For another example, XVII 739, 21 Oct. 1742.

12. Arch.P. DC6 232, fol. 254v, 27 Nov. 1747. Y 14667, *scellé,* 11 Aug. 1747.

13. MC, index of *affiches.* See also Arch.P. DC6 238, fol. 74, 13 Aug. 1755; DC6 243, fol. 174v, 7 Jan. 1762. André Burguière observes that throughout France godparents were carefully chosen from both sides of the family, most often grandparents, then aunts and uncles; "Prénoms et parenté," in Jacques

Dupâquier et al. eds., *Le Prénom: Mode et histoire* (Paris, EHESS, 1984), pp. 29–35 (p. 30).

14. S*1664, fol. 97v. XVIII 95, 14 Feb. 1681.

15. John G. Clark, *La Rochelle and the Atlantic Economy during the Eighteenth Century* (Baltimore and London, Johns Hopkins U.P., 1981), p. 135; John F. Bosher, "Success and Failure in Trade to New France, 1660–1760," *French Historical Studies* 15, no. 3 (spring 1988):444–461 (p. 455).

16. Haim Burstin, *Le Faubourg Saint-Marcel à l'époque révolutionnaire* (Paris, Société des Etudes Robespierristes, 1983), p. 204. BN Ms. fr. 11356, fols. 427–428, Assemblée de police, 1 Sept. 1740. F12 2457, Auffray, "Considérations sur le commerce de la tannerie," unpublished MS, n.d.

17. Arch.P. D4 B6 4, dossier 212, bankruptcy Jacques Bouillerot de Longchamp, 13 Nov. 1742. Arch.P. D4 B6 13, dossier 609, bankruptcy François Huguet, 10 Dec. 1753. See also Burstin, *Faubourg Saint-Marcel,* pp. 206–207.

18. Déclaration du Roi, 12 Nov. 1692, *French Royal and Administrative Acts, 1256–1794* (Woodbridge, Conn.: Research Publications, 1978). Arch.P. D4 B6 21, bankruptcy Jean Dorigny, 23 Nov. 1759. Y10852, *scellé* Marie Nicole Lepy, 29 June 1742.

19. XVII 683, inventory of Nicolas Bouillerot, 25 May 1734. S*1664, fol. 108, 10 May 1698.

20. XVII 662, 27 May 1730; XVII 663, 6 July 1730; XVII 665, two *constitutions* of 19 Feb. 1731.

21. XI 425, *partage* (division of deceased estate), 31 July 1714. S*1664, fols. 107v–108v. Agnès Devaux, wife of Jacques Médard Bouillerot, did the same. Y75, fol. 108, will of Agnès Devaux, 8 Aug. 1780.

22. XVII 663, 19 July 1730; XVII 665, 17 Jan. 1731.

23. For other examples, Y10852, 29 June 1742, opposition 28; Arch.P. D4 B6 4, dossier 212; Arch.P. D4 B6 13, dossier 609; Arch.P. D4 B6 21, Françoise Dorigny to Jean Dorigny (she was not a sister, niece, or aunt, so can have been no closer than first cousin).

24. XVII 469, 21 Feb. 1700, marriage contract Arnoult–Saint Martin; Y13916, *partage* Arnoult, 31 Aug. 1735. *Extrait des registres du Conseil d'Etat,* 24 Mar. 1714. XVII 670, 20 Jan. 1732, marriage contract Deheuqueville-Gaudouin. See also S*1668, fol. 661, 9 June 1788. Y72, 21 Aug. 1772, will of Marie Osmont; XVII 739, 21 Oct. 1742, marriage contract of Jean Chevalier.

25. Bosher, "Success and Failure," p. 455. Clark, *La Rochelle,* pp. 59–62, 79–82. Robert Wheaton, "Affinity and Descent in Seventeenth-Century Bordeaux," in Robert Wheaton and Tamara K. Hareven, eds., *Family and Sexuality in French History* (Philadelphia, U. of Pennsylvania Press, 1980), 111–134. Peter Dobkin Hall, "Family Structure and Economic Organization: Massa-

chusetts Merchants, 1700–1850," in Tamara K. Hareven, ed., *Family and Kin in Urban Communities, 1700–1930* (New York, New Viewpoints, 1977), pp. 38–61.

26. Arlette Farge and Michel Foucault, *Le Désordre des familles* (Paris, Gallimard/Julliard, 1982).

27. Bastille 11040, fols. 18–25, dossier Hubert Bouillerot.

28. Bastille 10878, fols. 179–189, dossier N. Dorigny.

29. Jean Ganiage, "Le Choix des prénoms au XVIIe siècle: L'Exemple du Beauvaisis," in Dupâquier et al., *Le Prénom,* pp. 369–372. (Despite its title, covers the eighteenth century.)

30. Unsigned *mémoire* for churchwardens of Saint Médard, n.d. [c. 1734], Bastille 10197, fol. 282.

31. JF 1588, will of Jean Michelin, 2 May 1785.

32. Pierre Chaunu, *La Mort à Paris* (Paris, Fayard, 1978), pp. 436, 442.

33. S*1664, fols. 107v, 92. S*1641, rue Censier nos. 16, 14, 26; rue Triperet no. 4. See David Garrioch, "House Names, Shop Signs, and Social Organization in Western European Cities, 1500—1900," *Urban History* 21 (1994): 18–46.

34. Marcel Marion, *Dictionnaire des institutions de la France aux XVIIe et XVIIIe siècles* (Paris, Picard, 1923), "Retrait." Mousnier, *Institutions* 1:62. S*1666, fol. 366, 13 Feb. 1741. S*1954 (2), fol. 233v. For other examples, S*5693, fols. 5, 9; S*1953 (1), fol. 503.

35. JF 345, fol. 139, unsigned *mémoire* from Hardy de Levaré to [Joly de Fleury], n.d. [1758].

36. Arch.P. DC6 224, 8 Feb. 1736. On entailments, Robert Forster, *Merchants, Landlords, Magistrates: The Depont Family in Eighteenth-Century France* (Baltimore and London, Johns Hopkins U.P., 1980), pp. 55–59.

37. Arch.P. DC6 248, 7 Oct. 1767.

38. Y29, 15 Apr. 1682.

39. Y67, 4 Sept. 1755.

40. XVIII 881, 12 Mar. 1789, will of Suzanne LeRoy.

41. XVIII 515, 6 Jan. 1728. Jacques Lelièvre, *La Pratique des contrats de mariage chez les notaires au Châtelet de Paris, de 1769 à 1804* (Paris, Editions Cujas, 1959), p. 72. Similar strategies were used by the Depont family; Forster, *Merchants,* pp. 52–53.

42. Hall, "Family Structure," pp. 42–43.

43. For examples, XVII 674, 12 Dec. 1732, inventory of Jeanne Bouillerot. Y11492, *scellé* Dorigny, 22 May 1772. Arch.P. D4 B6 21, bankruptcy Dorigny, 23 Nov. 1759. Y15740, *scellé* François Bouillerot, 2 June 1691. XVIII 95, 14 Feb. 1681, marriage Doyrieu-Michelin. MC index, XVIII 745, Lepy.

44. XVII 683, 25 May 1734, inventory of Nicolas Bouillerot. For other examples, S*1752, fol. 215. S*1664, fol. 136, 8 Nov. 1700. XI 344, 10 Apr. 1696. LXXVI 451, 4 Aug. 1774. S1953 (1), fol. 344.

45. S*1665, fol. 235v, 19 Apr. 1720.

46. MC, index of artisans in seventeenth- and eighteenth-century Paris. Arch.P. 5AZ 3911, Tronchet family. S*5695 (4), p. 30.

47. Forster, *Merchants*, pp. 16–17, 25–26. See also Christine Adams, "Defining *état* in Eighteenth-Century France: The Lamothe Family of Bordeaux," *Journal of Family History* 17 (1992): 25–45.

48. Margaret Darrow suggests that the Montauban elite used wide marriage alliances for this reason; *Revolution in the House* (Princeton, Princeton U.P., 1989), p. 133.

49. MC, placard 3.436. Y13935, *partage* Bouillerot, 31 Aug. 1740. On the *commissaires*, Alan Williams, *The Police of Paris* (Baton Rouge, Louisiana State U.P., 1979), pp. 119–124; Steven L. Kaplan, "Note sur les commissaires de police de Paris au XVIIIe siècle," *Revue d'histoire moderne et contemporaine* 28 (1981): 669–686.

50. S3445, copy of title to *rente*, 7 Jan. 1745.

51. Y13925, 31 Aug. 1740. Bastille 10198, Coiffrel to [lt. gen.], 18 Mar. 1736. Bastille 10202, *Mémoire pour le Sieur Coiffrel, au sujet du jugement de M. Barangue, Conseiller au Châtelet, du 12 février 1738*. Bastille 10201, Hardy de Levaré to lt. gen., 25 Jan. 1743.

52. François Bouillerot, born 1713, married Marie Madeleine Huguenet in the church of Sainte Opportune, but they returned to live near Saint Médard. Arch.P., reconstitution de l'ancien état civil.

53. XVII 420, 17 Mar. 1690. Arch.P. DC6 212, fol. 51. XVIII 478, 15 July 1716.

54. Bastille 10200, Gaillande to [lt. gen.], 6 May 1741; Dubut to [lt. gen.], 14 May 1741. Bastille 10201, *Mémoire pour les marguilliers de Saint Médard, au sujet de leur sacristie*, n.d. [Oct. 1743]. For an example in the neighboring parish of Saint Martin, XVII 678, 5 Aug. 1733.

55. *Nouvelles ecclésiastiques*, 31 Feb. 1731.

56. Bastille 10200, Cheret, curé of Saint Roch, to [lt. gen.], 11 June 1741. Gaillande to [lt. gen.], 6 May 1741.

57. JF 1569, fols. 133–133v.

58. XVIII 702, 1 Mar. 1769.

59. Orest Ranum, *Paris in the Age of Absolutism* (Bloomington and London, Indiana U. Press, 1979; 1st pub. New York, John Wiley and Sons, 1968), pp. 171–173, 180–183.

60. S*1953 (1), fols. 197, 209, 299, 338, 491. S1954 (2), fol. 237v. Another cluster comprised the Benard, Gosselin, Lacroix, Mouette, and Mouton families. The list of Saint Hippolyte churchwardens was reconstructed primarily from S3371 and L655. For Saint Martin, LL847, register of elections.

61. Jean Gaston, *Une Paroisse parisienne avant la Révolution: Saint Hippolyte* (Paris, Librarie des Saints Pères, 1908), esp. appendix. Burstin, *Faubourg Saint-Marcel,* pp. 219–225; A.-L. Lacordaire, *Notice historique sur les manufactures impériales de tapisseries des Gobelins et de tapis de la Savonnerie . . .* (Paris, Gobelins, 1853); Jules Guiffrey, "Etat-civil des tapissiers des Gobelins au dix-septième et au dix-huitième siècles, recueillis par M. A.-L. Lacordaire, ancien Directeur de la Manufacture des Gobelins," *Nouvelles archives de l'art français,* 3d series, 13 (1897): 1–60. Charles Du Peloux, *Répertoire biographique et bibliographique des artistes du XVIIIe siècle français,* 2 vols. (Paris, Champion, 1930, 1931), 1:2–3, 309; Mireille Rambaud, *Documents du Minutier central concernant l'histoire de l'art (1700–1750),* 2 vols. (Paris, SEVPEN, n.d.), 1:115–119.

62. The Clabaux, Gromau, Genneau, and Benard families formed one. Another was the Chevalier, Osmont, Barre, and Poupart clans.

63. Louis Brochard, *Saint Gervais: Histoire de la paroisse* (Paris, Didot, n.d. [1950]), appendix 8 and pp. 189–190; *Histoire de la paroisse et de l'église Saint-Laurent* (Paris, Champion, 1923), pp. 337–343.

64. Steven L. Kaplan, *Provisioning Paris: Merchants and Millers in the Grain and Flour Trade during the Eighteenth Century* (Ithaca and London, Cornell U.P., 1984), pp. 131–135. Garrioch, *Neighbourhood,* p. 100. Emile Coornaert, *Les Corporations en France avant 1789* (Paris, Gallimard, 1941), p. 198. Nicole Mounier, "Le Quartier des Porcherons (1720–1789)" (thesis of Ecole nationale des Chartes, Paris, 1978), pp. 295–307. Laurence Winnie, "Aegis of the Bourgeoisie: the Cochin of Paris, 1750–1922" (Ph.D. diss., U. of Michigan, 1988), pp. 17, 126, 153.

65. François de Salverte, *Les Ebénistes du XVIIIe siècle* (Paris, De Nobele, 1962), pp. 6–7, 142–143. Annik Pardailhé-Galabrun, *La Naissance de l'intime* (Paris, PUF, 1986), p. 185. *Les Ebénistes du XVIIIe siècle français* (Paris, Hachette, 1963), pp. 16, 87, 95, 109, 135, 183. Daniel Roche, *The Culture of Clothing* (Oxford, Past and Present Publications, 1994; 1st pub. Paris, Fayard, 1989), pp. 349–350. JF 1570, fol. 24, and Y12424, 15 Nov. 1753. Christine Legrand, "La Maison et le foyer parisien: Maîtres boulangers, marchands bouchers, et fruitiers-orangers à travers les inventaires après décès au milieu du XVIIIe siècle," maîtrise, Paris I, 1981, p. 26, cited in Pardailhé-Galabrun, *La Naissance,* p. 184. Garrioch, *Neighbourhood,* p. 70.

66. Adeline Daumard and François Furet, *Structures et relations sociales à Paris au XVIIIe siècle* (Paris, Colin, 1961), pp. 74–75.

4. Power and Local Politics

1. Keith Baker, "Politics and Public Opinion under the Old Regime: Some Reflections," in Jack Censer and Jeremy Popkin, eds., *Press and Politics in*

Pre-Revolutionary France (Berkeley, U. of California Press, 1987), pp. 204–246. See also: Baker's introduction to *The Political Culture of the Old Regime,* vol. 1 of *The French Revolution and the Creation of Modern Political Culture* (Oxford, Pergamon, 1987), pp. xi–xxiii; Mona Ozouf, "L'Opinion publique," ibid., 419–434; and Keith Baker, "Defining the Public Sphere in Eighteenth-Century France: Variations on a Theme by Habermas," in Craig Calhoun, ed., *Habermas and the Public Sphere* (Cambridge and London, MIT Press, 1992), pp. 181–211.

2. Baker, *Political Culture of the Old Regime,* p. xii.
3. Nora Temple, "Municipal Elections and Municipal Oligarchies in Eighteenth-Century France," in John F. Bosher, ed., *French Government and Society, 1500–1850* (London, Athlone Press 1973), pp. 70–91. Lynn A. Hunt, *Revolution and Urban Politics in Provincial France* (Stanford, Stanford U.P., 1978). Gail Bossenga, "City and State: An Urban Perspective on the Origins of the French Revolution," in Baker, *Political Culture of the Old Regime,* pp. 115–140.
4. Steven L. Kaplan, "Social Classification and Representation in the Corporate World of Eighteenth-Century Paris: Turgot's Carnival," in Steven L. Kaplan and Cynthia J. Koepp, eds., *Work in France* (Ithaca, Cornell U.P., 1986), pp. 176–228; "Les Corporations, les 'faux ouvriers,' et le faubourg Saint Antoine au XVIIIe siècle," *Annales ESC* 43 (1988): 353–378; "La Lutte pour le contrôle du marché de travail à Paris au XVIIIe siècle," *Revue d'histoire moderne et contemporaine* 36 (1989): 361–412; "The Character and Implications of Strife among the Masters inside the Guilds of Eighteenth-Century Paris," *Journal of Social History* 19 (1985–1986): 631–647. Michael Sonenscher, *Work and Wages: Natural Law, Politics, and the Eighteenth-Century French Trades* (Cambridge, Cambridge U.P., 1989), esp. chaps. 2, 3, 4. See also Jacques Revel, "Les Corps et communautés," in Baker, *Political Culture of the Old Regime,* pp. 225–242 (pp. 234–235, 239–240). On journeymen, Sonenscher, "French Journeymen, the Courts, and the French Trades, 1781–1791," *Past and Present* 114 (Feb. 1987): 77–109, and David Garrioch and Michael Sonenscher, "*Compagnonnages,* Confraternities, and Associations of Journeymen in Eighteenth-Century Paris," *European History Quarterly* 16 (1986): 25–45.
5. Hunt, *Revolution and Urban Politics,* pp. 6–7. Bossenga, "City and State," pp. 115–117.
6. See esp. B. Robert Kreiser, *Miracles, Convulsions, and Ecclesiastical Politics in Early Eighteenth-Century Paris* (Princeton, Princeton U.P., 1978); Dale Van Kley, *The Damiens Affair and the Unraveling of the Ancien Régime, 1750–1770* (Princeton, Princeton U.P., 1984). On Calas, David D. Bien, *The Calas Affair: Persecution, Toleration, and Heresy in Eighteenth-Century Toulouse* (Princeton, Princeton U.P., 1960).

7. Hunt, *Revolution and Urban Politics,* p. 7.
8. Bastille 10196, police report, 14 Feb. 1732. Bastille 10201, unsigned *mémoire* on events at Saint Médard since 1730, n.d. [c. 1740]. Bastille 10196, Coiffrel to lt. gen., 23 Aug. [1733].
9. Bod. 3 Delta 515 (19), *Remontrances des anciens marguilliers de Saint Médard* (1733). There is a large collection of similar *mémoires* in the BN Factum collection.
10. *Nouvelles ecclésiastiques,* 14 July 1731. JF 1569, fol. 82.
11. Bastille 10200, Coiffrel to Cardinal Fleury, 2 Oct. [1732].
12. Marquis d'Argenson, *Journal et mémoires du Marquis d'Argenson,* ed. E. J. B. Rathery, 9 vols. (Paris, Veuve Renouard, 1859–1867; reprint New York, Johnson Reprint, 1968) 7:184 (6 Apr. 1752).
13. See David Garrioch, *Neighbourhood and Community in Paris, 1740–1799* (Cambridge, Cambridge U.P., 1986), chap. 1.
14. Bastille 10202, unsigned letter, n.d. [1731 or 1732].
15. Ibid. Bastille 10196, unsigned letter, n.d.
16. Bastille 10198, Coiffrel to lt. gen., 3 Apr. 1735. Bastille 10200, LeBis to lt. gen., Nov. 1741.
17. Bastille 10196, police reports, 16 Apr. 1732. Bastille 10197, police report, 25 Apr. 1734.
18. Bastille 10197, fol. 143, police report, 3 Sept. 1733.
19. Mathieu Marais, *Journal et mémoires de Mathieu Marais sur la Régence et le règne de Louis XV,* 4 vols. (Paris, Didot, 1863–1868), 4:344 (22 Feb. 1732). See also Edmond Jean François Barbier, *Journal historique et anecdotique du règne de Louis XV,* 4 vols. (Paris, J. Renouard, 1847–1851), 1:399 (Feb. 1732).
20. Marais, *Journal et mémoires* 4:358, 361 (24 Apr., 4 May 1732).
21. Bastille 10196, complaint, 18 Aug. 1732.
22. Bastille 10197, fol. 309.
23. Bastille 10202, chronology of events, 1750–1751.
24. JF 1569, fol. 67, 7 Feb. 1755. JF 345, fol. 133, extract from deliberations of vestry, 24 Feb. 1758. JF 345, fol. 139v. JF 1569, fol. 115, Joly de Fleury to his brother, 27 Sept. 1758.
25. Bastille 10196, Coiffrel to [lt. gen.], 23 Aug. [1733]. Bastille 10200, Coiffrel to Cardinal Fleury, 2 Oct. [1732].
26. Bastille 10198, Coiffrel to [lt. gen.], 18 Dec. 1734. Bastille 10200, "Mémoire concernant le commissaire des pauvres de Saint Médard," received by police office 5 June 1742.
27. Bastille 10201, Hardy de Levaré to lt. gen., 8 Nov. 1743.
28. Bastille 10171, Hardy de Levaré to [lt. gen.], 21 Mar. 1743. Bastille 10201, Hardy de Levaré to [lt. gen.], 27 Jan., 29 May 1744.
29. JF 1569, fol. 133v, deliberation of 17 Dec. 1758.

30. Bastille 10196, police report, 3 Feb. 1731. Barbier, *Journal historique,* 1:412 (12 May 1732).
31. Bastille 10196, police report, 16 Apr. 1732; Coiffrel to Hérault, 17 May 1732.
32. Bastille 10197, fol. 252, Coiffrel to [lt. gen.], 22 May 1733.
33. S*1641, rue neuve Sainte Geneviève no. 13. S*1668, fol. 33, 14 Oct. 1771.
34. Bastille 10197, fol. 256, Coiffrel to [lt. gen.], 10 May 1733.
35. S*1637, p. 484. Delestre also held the office of *cinquantenier,* worth 600 livres: XVII 661, 19 Jan. 1730.
36. JF 1569, fol. 8ov, 1755.
37. On Hure family, S*1668, fol. 53, 12 July 1772. On Petiton, Bastille 10197, fol. 372, police report, 25 Apr. 1734; Bastille 10200, *Mémoire* cited in n. 26.
38. On Merillon, Bastille 10200, police report, 23 July 1742; XVII 667, 2 July 1731; XVII 662, 24 Apr. 1730. On Bonjean, Bastille 10197, fol. 372, police report, 25 Apr. 1734, and Bastille 10200, police report, 23 July 1742.
39. Bastille 10201, Hardy de Levaré to [lt. gen., 19 Sept. 1747.
40. Bastille 10202, Hardy de Levaré to lt. gen., 28 Dec. 1743. XVII 678, 30 July 1733.
41. XVII 671, 22 Apr. 1732.
42. See Jean Gaston, *Les Images des confréries parisiennes avant la Révolution* (Paris, A. Marty, 1910); Garrioch and Sonenscher, "*Compagnonnages.*"
43. Brongniart, p. 108. XVII 671, 22 Apr. 1732. Bastille 10197, fol. 163, police report, 20 Sept. 1733. On Paris confraternities in general, see JF 1590, survey of 1761. See also JF 1586–1588, parish affairs, Paris. On Saint Médard, JF 345, fol. 133. On Saint Martin du Cloître, LL847, fols. 54v–56 (8 Sept. 1707).
44. Y11454, *scellé* of Michel Velut de la Crosnière, 14 Nov. 1734.
45. JF 1586, fol. 159, "*Arrêt pour la fabrique de Saint Hippolyte,*" 3 July 1755.
46. Louis Brochard, *Histoire de la paroisse et de l'église Saint-Laurent* (Paris, Champion, 1923), pp. 63, 68, 204. See also LL847, fols. 100–101, 14 June 1722 (Saint Martin du Cloître); JF 1586, fol. 243 (Saint Jean en Grève).
47. JF 1586, fol. 159, *Arrêt pour la fabrique de Saint Hippolyte,* 3 July 1755; fol. 243 (Saint Jean en Grève). See also LL847, fols. 54, 100 (Saint Martin du Cloître).
48. XVII 671, both statements dated 22 Apr. 1732.
49. Bastille 10197, fol. 105, police report, 4 June 1733.
50. *Nouvelles ecclésiastiques,* 3 Nov. 1731.
51. JF 1569, fols. 230–239.
52. Bastille 10198, Coiffrel to [lt. gen.], 4 July [1736].
53. There is disagreement about the exact number of parishes, because some chapels fulfilled parish functions within a very limited jurisdiction—for ex-

ample, the Sainte Chapelle for the area of the Palais de Justice, and those of the hospitals; Pierre Chaunu, *La Mort à Paris* (Paris, Fayard, 1978), pp. 211–212.

54. The survey in 1760 lists 76 confraternities in parish churches and 71 in monastery, chapter, or convent churches, but only half the churches responded; JF 1590, fols. 24–35, 65–66.

55. See lists of administrators in JF 1590, fol. 152 (Saint Sacrement at Saint Etienne du Mont); LL837, Saint Sacrement at Sainte Marguerite; A. Zephirin, "La Confrérie du Très Saint Sacrement à Saint Médard," *La Montagne Sainte Geneviève et ses abords,* no. 238 (Jan. 1982): 59–60; LXXXVIII 622, 12 Nov. 1751 (Saint Laurent at Sainte Marie du Temple; CV 1236, 29 June 1751 (Sainte Vierge at Saint Paul). I owe these last two references to Michael Sonenscher.

56. Sonenscher, *Work and Wages,* p. 63.

57. Garrioch and Sonenscher, *"Compagnonnages."* Sonenscher, *Work and Wages,* p. 83, adds several more, and I have subsequently found two more at Saint Marcel: LL580, fols 108, 240.

58. Alfred Franklin, *Dictionnaire historique des arts, métiers, et professions exercés dans Paris depuis le treizième siècle,* (Paris, H. Welter, 1906), "Edit de 1691," "Sages-femmes," "Grainiers." Sonenscher, *Work and Wages,* p. 66.

59. JF 1590, fol. 29. L661, no. 5.

60. Laurence Winnie, "Aegis of the Bourgeoisie: The Cochin of Paris, 1750–1922" (Ph.D. diss. U. of Michigan, 1988), p. 99.

61. Bastille 10200, unsigned petition, n.d. [late Dec. 1740]. For other complaints, Bastille 10200, 1741.

62. See engraving by Abraham Bosse, reproduced in Georges Duby, ed., *Histoire de la France urbaine,* vol. 3 of *La Ville classique,* ed. Emmanuel Le Roy Ladurie, 4 vols. (Paris, Seuil, 1981), p. 240.

63. One churchwarden of Saint Médard later did go bankrupt, and disappeared owing some 500 livres; JF 1588, fol. 15, requête au Parlement, 28 May 1784.

64. Cissie Fairchilds, *Domestic Enemies: Servants and Their Masters in Old Regime France* (Baltimore and London, Johns Hopkins U.P., 1984), p. 138. Jeremy Boulton points out that wealthy households, being larger, bestowed greater social power on their heads; *Neighbourhood and Society: A London Suburb in the Seventeenth Century* (Cambridge, Cambridge U.P., 1987), p. 138.

65. Bastille 12369, fol. 12, Bourgoin to lt. gen., 8 May 1769.

66. On varieties of notability in sixteenth-century Paris, Robert Descimon, *Qui était les Seize?* in *Paris et Ile-de-France: Mémoires publiés par la Fédération des sociétés historiques et archéologiques de Paris et de l'Ile-de-France* 34 (1983): 59–60.

67. This point is made, in regard to the Directory, by Colin Lucas, "The Rules

of the Game in Local Politics under the Directory," *French Historical Studies* 16:2 (fall 1989): 344–371. On the corporations, Sonenscher, *Work and Wages*. More generally, Anthony Giddens, *Profiles and Critiques in Social Theory* (London, Macmillan, 1982), pp. 197–199.

68. Marie-José Michel, "Clergé et pastorale janséniste à Paris (1669–1730)," *Revue d'histoire moderne et contemporaine* 26(1979):177–197 (pp. 188–189).

69. See Chapter 12 on these offices and their fate.

5. The Decline of Lineage

1. JF 1569, fol. 133, deliberation of 17 Dec. 1758.

2. S3445, agreement of 16 Nov. 1760 and accounts, 1781. XVIII 845, extract of burial in *notoriété*, 19 Jan 1785. Y11492, 22 May 1772. Arch.P. D4 B6 21, 23 Nov. 1759.

3. S*1753, *terrier de* Sainte Geneviève, 1668–1719, fols. 333, 335. XVII 676, will of Bouillerot de Vinente, 6 Apr. 1733.

4. XVII 420, *renonciation*, 16 Mar. 1690. S*1753, fol. 308. XVIII 427, marriage contract, 1 Apr. 1704.

5. XVIII 427, 1 Apr. 1704. Y13935, *partage* Bouillerot, 31 Aug. 1740. S*1753, fol. 300. S*1665, fol. 30. Y12577, *scellé* Pierre Bouillerot, 25 June 1735. Marcel Marion, *Dictionnaire des institutions de la France aux XVIIe et XVIIIe siècles* (Paris, Picard, 1923), p. 130.

6. Y13925, 31 Aug. 1740. Y12577, 25 June 1735. Y45, fol. 67. XI 425, 13 July 1714. XVII 683, 25 May 1734. Y11452, 13 Dec. 1730. The *juges consuls* were chosen from the Six Corps, the wine merchants, or the booksellers and printers; Marion, *Dictionnaire*, p. 139.

7. Y13925, 31 Aug. 1740.

8. Ibid.

9. Ibid.

10. XVIII 702, 18 Mar. 1769. Louis Brochard, *Saint Gervais: Histoire de la paroisse* (Paris, Didot, n.d. [1950]), p. 166.

11. XVII 683, 22 June 1734.

12. Y14667, 11 Aug. 1747. XVII 674, 12 Dec. 1732.

13. XVII 674, 12 Dec. 1732. XVII 683, 25 May 1734. XVII 687, 21 Oct. 1734.

14. S*1641, rue Censier nos. 24, 25. XXIX 488, 3 June 1751.

15. MC index of Paris artisans. Arch.P., reconstitution of the Old Regime état civil. Y12167, 31 Jan. 1766. XLII 417, 25 Sept. 1747. Arch.P. DC6 23, fol. 156. Y10787, 16 Feb. 1773. Arch.P. D4 B6 103, bankruptcy, 31 Dec. 1788.

16. Compare Robert Forster, *Merchants, Landlords, Magistrates: The Depont Family in Eighteenth Century France* (Baltimore and London, Johns Hopkins U.P., 1980), p. 125.

17. S*5695 (4), fol. 115. LL847, Saint Martin du Cloître, election of sacristan, 14 Aug. 1729, fol. 7v from back of register; and fol. 163. Y15765, *procès-verbal* for leather dressers, 16 Mar. 1722. S*1953 (1), fols. 268, 270. S1954 (2), fol. 282v. Adeline Daumard, *La Bourgeoisie parisienne, 1815–1848* (Paris, SEVPEN, 1963), p. 319.

18. S*5695 (4), fol. 115. S5683, fol. 78. Daumard, *Bourgeoisie parisienne,* p. 319. Another example is the Hannen family: XVII 720, marriage of Françoise Hannen, 7 Feb. 1740; Y14857, *scellé* Pierre Hannen, 4 Apr. 1739.

19. Laurence Winnie, "Aegis of the Bourgeoisie: The Cochin of Paris, 1750–1922" (Ph.D. diss., U. of Michigan, 1988), pp. 9, 17, 68, 126, 163, 169–177.

20. XVIII 884, inventory Derenusson, 5 June 1789.

21. Christiane Klapisch-Zuber, "Constitution et variations temporelles des stocks de prénoms," in Jacques Dupâquier et al., eds., *Le Prénom: Mode et histoire* (Paris, EHESS, 1984), pp. 37–47 (p. 41).

22. See Christiane Klapisch-Zuber, "Le Nom refait," *L'Homme* 20, no. 4 (Oct.–Dec. 1980): 77–104, a special issue on "Formes de nomination en Europe," cited in Dominique Schnapper, "Essai de lecture sociologique," in Dupâquier et al., *Le Prénom,* pp. 13–21 (p. 18).

23. André Burguière, "Un Nom pour soi," *L'Homme* 20, no. 4 (Oct.–Dec. 1980): 25–42, cited in Schnapper, "Essai," p. 19.

24. Pierre Chaunu, *La Mort à Paris* (Paris, Fayard, 1978), pp. 436, 442.

25. Information on family size comes primarily from the *censive* records of Sainte Geneviève and Saint Marcel. Thanks to the equal-inheritance provisions of Paris customary law, when a property changed hands through inheritance all the heirs were listed, even those who had renounced their claim. Because the children of direct heirs were entitled to their parents' inheritance, deceased heirs had to be mentioned. Even those who died childless had to be listed, for their share was divided equally among the others. The only family members who escape being included are children who died in infancy and stepchildren. Comparison with notarial records indicates that the abbey records are very accurate.

26. Jean-Pierre Bardet, *Rouen aux XVIIe et XVIIIe siècles,* 2 vols. (Paris, Société d'Edition d'enseignement supérieur, 1983), 1:271, 279–281, 287; "Acceptation et refus de la vie à Paris au XVIIIe siècle," in Jean-Pierre Bardet and Madeleine Foisil, eds., *La Vie, la mort, la foi, le temps* (Paris, PUF, 1993), pp. 67–83. Bardet's data show a drop in Paris birthrates between 1690 and 1789, most markedly among nobles, professionals, and merchants. See also Alfred Perrenoud, "Variables sociales en démographie urbaine: L'Exemple de Genève au XVIIIe siècle," in *Démographie urbaine, XVe–XXe siècle* (Lyon, Université de Lyon II, Centre d'histoire économique et sociale de la région lyonnaise, n.d. [1977]), pp. 143–172. M. Delassise, "Essai d'étude démographique des familles consulaires lyonnaises du XVIIIe siècle," cited

by Maurice Garden, "La Démographie des villes françaises du XVIIIe siècle: Quelques approches," ibid., pp. 43–85 (pp. 65–66). Benoît Garnot, "La 'Fécondité naturelle' et les chartrains au XVIIIe siècle," *Annales de démographie historique,* 1988, pp. 91–98. John G. Clark, *La Rochelle and the Atlantic Economy during the Eighteenth Century* (Baltimore and London, Johns Hopkins U.P., 1981), pp. 55–56, 71. For an overview, Massimo Livi-Bacci, "Social Group Forerunners of Fertility Control in Europe," in Ansley J. Coale and Susan Cotts Watkins, eds., *The Decline of Fertility in Europe* (Princeton, Princeton U.P., 1986), pp. 182–200, esp. p. 197.

27. René Pillorget, *La Tige et le rameau: Familles anglaise et française, 16e–18e siècle* (Paris, Calmann-Lévy, 1979), p. 123.

28. J. G. C. Blacker, "Social Ambitions of the Bourgeoisie in Eighteenth Century France and their Relation to Family Limitation," *Population Studies* 11 (1957–1958): 46–63. The Depont family, studied by Robert Forster, frowned on people marrying outside their station; *Merchants,* p. 16. Christine Adams reaches the same conclusion in: "Defining *état* in Eighteenth-Century France: The Lamothe Family of Bordeaux," *Journal of Family History* 17 (1992): 25–45.

29. This is the implication in Bardet, *Rouen,* p. 304.

30. Margaret Darrow, *Revolution in the House* (Princeton, Princeton U.P., 1989), p. 99 n. 44. Mme de Sévigné, *Lettres,* quoted in Etienne van de Walle, "Motivations and Technology in the Decline of French Fertility," in Robert Wheaton and Tamara K. Hareven, eds., *Family and Sexuality in French History* (Philadelphia, U. of Pennsylvania Press, 1980), pp. 135–178 (p. 141). This is also the implication of Alfred Perrenoud's suggestions in "Espacement et arrêt dans le contrôle des naissances," *Annales de démographie historique,* 1988, pp. 59–78.

31. Angus McLaren, *Reproductive Rituals* (London, Methuen, 1984); *A History of Contraception* (Oxford, Blackwell, 1990). Jean-Louis Flandrin, *Familles: Parenté, Maison, Sexualité dans l'ancienne société,* rev. ed. (Paris, Seuil, 1984; 1st pub. 1976), pp. 190–191, 208–212.

32. Flandrin, *Familles,* pp. 212–217. Darrow, *Revolution,* p. 99 n. 44. McLaren, *Contraception,* p. 168. See also Wally Seccombe, "Men's 'Marital Rights' and Women's 'Wifely Duties': Changing Conjugal Relations in the Fertility Decline," in John R. Gillis, Louise A. Tilly, and David Levine, eds., *The European Experience of Declining Fertility, 1850–1970* (Cambridge, Mass., and Oxford, Blackwell, 1992), pp. 66–84.

33. Norbert Elias, *The Civilizing Process,* 2 vols. (Oxford, Blackwell, 1982). Compare Flandrin, *Familles,* p. 216. See also Seccombe, "Men's 'Marital Rights.'"

34. Jean Gaston, *Une Paroisse parisienne avant la Révolution: Saint Hippolyte*

(Paris, Librairie des Saints Pères, 1908), pp. 97–102. Winnie, "Aegis of the Bourgeoisie," pp. 62–63.

35. John McManners, "Jansenism and Politics in the Eighteenth Century," in Derek Baker, ed., *Church, Society, and Politics* (Oxford, Blackwell, 1975), pp. 253–273. On effects of Protestant theology, see Ulrich Pfister, "Mobilité sociale et transition de la fécondité: Le Cas de Zurich (Suisse) au XVIIIe siècle," *Annales de démographie historique*, 1988, pp. 111–125 (p. 114).

36. See McManners, "Jansenism," pp. 264–265; F. Ellen Weaver, "Erudition, Spirituality, and Women: The Jansenist Contribution," in Sherrin Marshall, ed., *Women in Reformation and Counter-Reformation Europe* (Bloomington and Indianapolis, Indiana U.P., 1989), pp. 188–206. See also Monique Cottret, "Le Républicanisme janséniste: Mythe de l'Eglise primitive et primitivisme des Lumières," *Revue d'histoire moderne et contemporaine* 31 (1984): 99–115.

37. David Garrioch, *Neighbourhood and Community in Paris, 1740–1790* (Cambridge, Cambridge U.P., 1986).

38. Annik Pardailhé-Galabrun, *The Birth of Intimacy: Privacy and Domestic Life in Early Modern Paris,* trans. Jocelyn Phelps (Oxford, Polity, 1991; 1st pub. Paris, PUF, 1986). Philippe Ariès, *L'Enfant et la vie familiale sous l'Ancien Régime* (Paris, Plon, 1960), p. 451.

39. Perrenoud links economic expansion with new family norms; "Espacement," p. 75.

40. Roland Mousnier, *Les Institutions de la France sous la monarchie absolue,* 2 vols. (Paris, PUF, 1974, 1980), 1:82.

41. Garrioch, *Neighbourhood*.

42. Edmond Jean François Barbier, *Journal historique et anecdotique du règne de Louis XV,* 4 vols. (Paris, J. Renouard, 1847–1851), 2:440–441 (Feb. 1745). On Barbier, ibid., pp. xv–xxi. See also Roddey Reid, *Families in Jeopardy. Regulating the Social Body in France, 1750–1910* (Stanford, Stanford U.P., 1993), esp. introduction, chap. 1.

6. The New Families and the New Politics

1. Haim Burstin, *Le Faubourg Saint-Marcel à l'époque révolutionnaire* (Paris, Société des Etudes Robespierristes, 1983), pp. 194–195.

2. S. D. Chapman and Serge Chassagne, *European Textile Printers in the Eighteenth Century* (London, Heinemann, 1981), p. 145. XVIII 912, *quittance,* 15 Dec. 1793. Arch.P. D11 U5 34, dossier 2217, bankruptcy Jean-Baptiste Vérité, 10 Mar. 1806. Alfred Franklin, *Dictionnaire historique des arts, métiers, et professions exercés dans Paris depuis le treizième siècle* (Paris, H. Welter 1906), "Bleu de Prusse."

3. Françoise Teynac, Pierre Nolot, and Jean-Denis Vivien, *Wallpaper: A History* (London, Thames and Hudson, 1982; 1st pub. Paris, Berger-Levrault, 1981), pp. 40, 66, 74, 87, 98, 101. See also Jean Antoine Claude Chaptal, *De l'industrie française* (Paris, Renouard, 1819), p. 45.

4. F7* 2517, fols. 213v, 214v, 23 Pluviôse Year II. F7 4794, cartes de sûreté, 7e compagnie. S3444, Saint Médard, saisie des papiers, 21 Floréal Year II. Z1E 307, tax roll, Nov. 1738.

5. F7*2517, fol. 213v, 216v, 27 Pluviôse Year II. F30 157, exchange of assignats, Observatoire Section. F30 157, exchange of assignats, Gobelins Section. F7 4794, cartes de sûreté, 7e and 11e compagnies. V 820, inventory of Jeanne Lorillard, 7 Apr. 1790.

6. F7 4794, 11e compagnie. S*1642, rue d'Orléans no. 32. H5 3792, roofing expenses, Saint Médard. F30 159.

7. F7 4794, 7e compagnie. F7* 2517, fols. 213v, 215. S*1641, rue Censier no. 9.

8. XVII 683, 23 May 1734. Z1E 307, tax lists, 1735–1736, 24 Oct. 1738. Z1E 307, tax list, 1757, nos 24, 25. S*1641, no. 10 rue Censier.

9. F7 4670, dossier Derubigny, letter of 1 Floréal. Z1E 307, tax lists, 1757, 1764. S*1641, nos. 3, 4 rue Censier.

10. D12 U1 39, 15 Feb. 1792. Burstin, *Faubourg Saint-Marcel*, p. 210.

11. H. Depors, *Recherches sur l'état de l'industrie des cuirs en France pendant le XVIIIe siècle et le début du XIXe siècle* (Paris, Imprimerie nationale, 1932), p. 69 n. 4.

12. F12 2457, Auffray, "Considérations sur le commerce de la tannerie," unpublished MS, n.d.; [Jean Antoine Derubigny de Berteval], *Réflexions sur le Mémoire du Régisseur des Cuirs*, n.p., n.d. [1775]. On 1759 edict, Burstin, *Faubourg Saint-Marcel*, pp. 209–210.

13. Depors, *Recherches*, pp. 20, 69–72, 111.

14. Z1E 307, tax roll, 1738.

15. Arch.P. VD* 6699, owners of property on Bièvre [c. Year VI/1798]. Z1E 308, tax roll, 1784. S*1668, fol. 45. Burstin, *Faubourg Saint-Marcel*, pp. 207, 210. F20 255, report of mayor of Twelfth Arrondissement to Ministry of the Interior, 14 May 1807. F30 159, exchange of assignats, Derubigny. 1792.

16. Alexandre Jean-Baptiste Parent-Duchâtelet, "Recherches et considérations sur la rivière de la Bièvre, ou des Gobelins . . ." (1822), in *Hygiène publique; ou, mémoires sur les questions les plus importantes de l'hygiène appliquée aux professions et aux travaux d'utilité publique* (Paris, 1836), quoted in Joel Audefroy, *La Formation du Val de Bièvre: Essai d'interprétation architecturale de l'histoire* (Paris, Corda, 1977), pp. 64–65.

17. Louis Bergeron, *Banquiers, négociants, et manufacturiers parisiens du Directoire à l'Empire*, 2 vols. (Lille, Atelier de reproduction des thèses de

l'Université de Lille III, 1975; republished in 1 vol., Paris, EHESS, 1978), 1:278.

18. Burstin, *Faubourg Saint-Marcel,* pp. 172–174.

19. Ibid., pp. 174–175. Geneviève Aclocque, *Un Défenseur du roi, André-Arnoult Aclocque, commandant général de la garde nationale parisienne, 1748–1802* (Paris, A. and J. Picard, 1947), pp. 25, 32. LL581, fol. 162, 25 Sept. 1780. H1956, "Ordonnance du Prévôt des Marchands," 25 Sept. 1785.

20. S*1642, rue neuve Saint Médard no. 3; rue Mouffetard nos. 26, 31, 33; rue des Postes nos. 21, 22. S*1668, fol. 639. S5683, fol. 99. Y61, fol. 340, will of Charles Delongchamp, 28 Apr. 1781.

21. Raymonde Monnier, *Un Bourgeois Sans-culotte: Le Général Santerre* (Paris, Publications de la Sorbonne, 1990), p. 14.

22. Michael Sonenscher, *Work and Wages: Natural Law, Politics, and the Eighteenth-Century French Trades,* (Cambridge, Cambridge U.P., 1989), pp. 145, 26, 63; *The Hatters of Eighteenth-Century France* (Berkeley, U. of California Press, 1987), pp. 44–51. Statutes of the seamstresses' corporation *(couturières),* 1675, in Franklin, *Dictionnaire,* p. 774. Jacques Savary des Bruslons, *Dictionnaire du commerce,* 5 vols. (Copenhagen, 1759–1765), "Cordonniers." See also Steven L. Kaplan, "Social Classification and Representation in the Corporate World of Eighteenth-Century Paris: Turgot's Carnival," in Steven L. Kaplan and Cynthia J. Koepp, eds., *Work in France* (Ithaca, Cornell U.P., 1986), pp. 176–228, (p. 194 n. 57).

23. Y11952, 11 July 1764. Y14560, 13 Sept. 1775. For further examples, see Steven L. Kaplan, "The Character and Implications of Strife among the Masters inside the Guilds of Eighteenth-Century Paris," *Journal of Social History* 19 (1985–1986): 631–647.

24. Emile Coornaert, *Les Corporations en France avant 1789* (Paris, Gallimard, 1941), p. 198. Compre. Y15363, 29 July 1753. Y12596, 3 July. Y11239, 30 Oct. Y15350, 7 Oct., witness 5. Y12596, 3 July 1752. On exemptions for sons of masters, Coornaert, *Corporations,* pp. 197–198, and Franklin, *Dictionnaire* (entries for various trades). See also David T. Pottinger, *The French Book Trade in the Ancien Regime, 1500–1791* (Cambridge, Harvard U.P., 1958), pp. 136–138.

25. Sonenscher, *Work and Wages,* pp. 100–104, 107–108. Haim Burstin, "Conditionnement économique et conditionnement mental dans le monde du travail parisien à la fin de l'ancien régime," *History of European Ideas* 3 (1982): 23–29. See also Burstin, *Faubourg Saint-Marcel,* pp. 95–100. But the prestigious corporations probably remained more closed; Pottinger, *French Book Trade,* p. 138.

26. Edict of 23 Aug. 1776, in Franklin, *Dictionnaire,* pp. 786–792. Kaplan, "Character and Implications of Strife," p. 634.

27. In larger corporations electioneering was already common before 1776; Kaplan, "Character and Implications of Strife," p. 637.

28. Burstin, *Faubourg Saint-Marcel,* p. 100.

29. The goldsmiths complained that 150 of the former 400 masters, some of them the "wisest and most experienced," would be excluded from the corporation altogether: Kaplan, "Social Classification," pp. 212–213.

30. France Weber, "La Famille Santerre et la brasserie parisienne au XVIIIe siècle," *Le Brasseur français,* no. 704 (20 May 1905), no. 705 (27 May 1905). S*1641, no. 22 rue Censier. On Schveinfelt, S*1642, no. 5 rue du Noir, no. 37 rue d'Orléans.

31. Kaplan, "Social Classification," p. 211.

32. Neither Ménétra's skepticism nor his recent arrival in the area were barriers to his being invited to become administrator of a parish confraternity toward the end of the Old Regime; Jacques-Louis Ménétra, *Journal de ma vie,* ed. Daniel Roche (Paris, Montalba, 1982), p. 180.

33. Sonenscher, *Work and Wages,* p. 216. On "manufactures royales," Jean-Pierre Hirsch, *Les Deux Rêves du commerce: Entreprise et institution dans la région lilloise (1780–1860)* (Paris, EHESS, 1991), p. 115.

34. De la Lande, "L'Art de l'Hongroyeur," in J.-E. Bertrand, *Descriptions des arts et métiers faites ou approuvées par Messieurs de l'Académie royale des sciences de Paris,* new ed., 19 vols. (Neuchâtel, Société typographique, 1771–1783), 3:380, cited in Burstin, *Faubourg Saint-Marcel,* p. 213 n. 150. He is credited with this invention in the *Bibliothèque physico-économique instructive et amusante,* vol. 1 (1787), p. 398. Thanks to Michael Sonenscher for this reference.

35. F12 1464, "Mémoire du Sieur De Rubigny de Berteval, tanneur au faux-bourg Saint Marcel, à Monsieur le Controlleur Général," 1786, quoted in Burstin, *Faubourg Saint-Marcel,* p. 213.

36. Ibid.

37. Auffray, "Considérations"; [Derubigny], *Réflexions;* Derubigny, *Extrait du mémoire présenté au Roi et à l'Assemblée des Notables* (1788), and letters in F12 1464 and F12 2286. For Derubigny's *cahier particulier,* Charles-Louis Chassin, *Les Elections et les cahiers de Paris en 1789,* 4 vols. (Paris, Jouaust and Sigaux 1888–1889), 3:172–173. Derubigny referred to his *Observations* in seeking release from prison during the Revolution, F7 4670. On Derubigny, Burstin, *Faubourg Saint-Marcel,* pp. 210–214.

38. A whole series of works on different industries was commissioned by the Académie. See also J.-E. Bertrand, *Descriptions des arts et métiers.* Liliane Perez, "Invention, politique, et société en France dans la deuxième moitié du dix-huitième siècle," *Revue d'histoire moderne et contemporaine* 37 (1990): 36–63.

39. Sonenscher, *Work and Wages,* p. 24 n. 47, 25, 200. Serge Chassagne,

Oberkampf, un entrepreneur capitaliste au Siècle des Lumières (Paris, Aubier-Montaigne, 1980), pp. 10–17. See also Margaret Darrow, *Revolution in the House* (Princeton, Princeton U.P., 1989), pp. 34–35; Cissie Fairchilds, "Three Views on the Guilds," *French Historical Studies* 15, no. 4 (fall 1988): 688–692 (p. 690); "The Production and Marketing of Populuxe Goods in Eighteenth-Century Paris," in John Brewer and Roy Porter, eds., *Consumption and the World of Goods* (London and New York, Routledge, 1993), pp. 228–248; Gail Bossenga, "Protecting Merchants: Guilds and Commercial Capitalism in Eighteenth-Century France," *French Historical Studies* 15, no. 4 (fall 1988): 693–703; Perez, "Invention, politique, et société," p. 37.

40. The fairground theater proprietors, particularly Jean-Baptiste Nicolet and Nicholas Audinot, were similarly encouraged by the Paris police and by the hospitals, in defiance of the monopoly granted to the official theaters; Michèle Root-Bernstein, *Boulevard Theatre and Revolution in Eighteenth-Century Paris* (Ann Arbor, Mich., UMI Research Press, 1984), pp. 236, 238, and Robert Isherwood, *Farce and Fantasy: Popular Entertainment in Eighteenth-Century Paris* (New York, Oxford U.P., 1986), pp. 167–191.

41. F12 2457, *Lettres patentes portant privilège pour la manufacture de cuirs,* 5 June 1765. JF 369, fol. 53. NII Seine 148.

42. Teynac, Nolot, and Vivien, *Wallpaper,* pp. 87, 90. For Réveillon's claim and Didot's rebuttal, F12 2281, dossier I 9. Christian-Marc Bosseno, "Réveillon, ou le philosophe incompris," in *Le Monde de la Révolution française* 4 (Apr. 1989), p. 11. On the Didot brothers, Gustave Brunet, *Firmin Didot et sa famille* (Paris, Bachelin-Deflorenne, 1870), pp. 7–8.

43. Weber, "Famille Santerre," *Le Brasseur français,* no. 706 (3 June 1905), p. 4; no. 710 (1 July 1905), p. 4; no. 704 (20 May 1905), p. 4. Monnier, *Un Bourgeois Sans-culotte,* pp. 10, 19–21.

44. Suzanne Tucoo-Chala, *Charles-Joseph Panckoucke et la librairie française, 1736–1796* (Pau and Paris, Marrimpouey jeune/Touzot, 1977), pp. 49, 79, 93, 176, 416.

45. Chassagne, *Oberkampf.*

46. Serge Chassagne, *Le Coton et ses patrons: France, 1760–1840* (Paris, EHESS, 1991), pp. 94–95. Among them was Jacques Baron, who migrated to Paris as a young man in 1750 and became a mercer. He then created a very successful printed-cotton factory at Corbeil; Chassagne, *Oberkampf,* p. 71, and *Le Coton,* p. 105. Baron was accepted extraordinarily rapidly into the vestry of Sainte Marguerite; LL836, fol. 2, 15 Apr. 1759. Another successful self-made man was Antoine Pierre Damoye, founder of a cab company in the Faubourg Saint Antoine, whose father had come to Paris in 1733; Richard Andrews, "Réflexions sur la conjuration des Egaux," *Annales: ESC* 29 (1974): 73–106 (p. 83). Yet another example was the wood merchant Joseph Gandolphe, who came to Paris in the 1730s, married into

a carpenter family, and built up a huge fortune; Evelyne Bouvet-Bensimon, "L'Ascension sociale d'un marchand de bois au XVIIIe siècle," *Revue d'histoire moderne et contemporaine* 34 (1987): 282–304. In Lille, too, a flood of newcomers entered the ranks of *négociants* after 1750; Hirsch, *Deux Rêves*, pp. 41–50.

47. Serge Chassagne, *Une Femme d'affaires au XVIIIe siècle* (Paris, Privat, 1981), pp. 8–31.

48. Régine de Plinval de Guillebon, "La Manufacture de porcelaine de Dihl et Guérhard, rue de Bondy et rue du Temple," *Bulletin de la Société de l'histoire de Paris et de l'Ile de France* 109 (1982): 177–212 (pp. 177, 180).

49. Emile Liez and Pierre de Nouvion, *Ministre des modes sous Louis XVI: Madame Bertin* (Paris, H. Leclerc, 1912), pp. 7–30. See also William Reddy, *The Rise of Market Culture: The Textile Trade and French Society, 1750–1900* (Cambridge, Cambridge U.P., 1984), p. 22; Hirsch, *Deux Rêves*, pp. 140–141; John McManners, *Death and the Enlightenment* (Oxford, Oxford U.P., 1981), p. 461.

50. Chassagne, *Femme d'affaires*, pp. 24–33. On 1776 edicts, Kaplan, "Social Classification," p. 211.

51. F7 4670. Chassin, *Les Elections*, 3:172–173.

52. *Pétition particulière d'un habitant du district de Saint Marcel,* in Chassin, *Les Elections*, 2:480–482.

53. F12 2457.

54. On barometers, Annik Pardailhé-Galabrun, *La Naissance de l'intime* (Paris, PUF, 1986), p. 158.

55. Lenoir was given the job of going through all of these: Bibliothèque municipale d'Orléans, MS 1423, dossier 3, fol. 357. Many are in AN F12 series.

56. On economic milling, Steven L. Kaplan, *Provisioning Paris: Merchants and Millers in the Grain and Flour Trade during the Eighteenth Century* (Ithaca and London, Cornell U.P., 1984), chap. 11. On Solignac and other kneading machines, Alexandra Michell, "Innovations and Innovators in the Baking Trades in Eighteenth-Century Paris (1700–1789)" (B.A. [Hons] thesis, Monash U., 1989), pp. 41–43, and Pierre Legrand d'Aussy, *Histoire de la vie privée des François,* 3 vols. (Paris, 1782), 1:67. Chapman and Chassagne, *European Textile Printers,* p. 144. For other examples, Alexandre Tuétey, *Répertoire général des sources manuscrites de l'histoire de Paris pendant la Révolution française,* 10 vols. (Paris, Imprimerie nouvelle, 1890–1912), vol. 7, no. 1709.

57. Christopher Todd, "French Advertising in the Eighteenth Century," *Studies on Voltaire and the Eighteenth Century* 266 (1989): 513–547. Robert Darnton, *Mesmerism and the End of the Enlightenment in France* (Cambridge, Harvard U.P., 1968), chap. 1. On Réveillon's advertising, Teynac, Nolot, and Vivien, *Wallpaper,* pp. 87, 89–90. For the best studies of eighteenth-cen-

tury advertising, Neil McKendrick, John Brewer, and J. H. Plumb, *The Birth of a Consumer Society: The Commercialization of Eighteenth-Century England* (London, Europa Publications, 1982).

58. Emile Dacier and Albert Vuaflart, *Jean de Jullienne et les graveurs de Watteau au XVIIIe siècle*, 3 vols. (Paris, 1929), 1:201–203.

59. JF 1588, fol. 15, requête du procureur général, 28 May 1784. Louis Brochard, *Histoire de la paroisse et de l'église Saint-Laurent* (Paris, Champion, 1923), pp. 68–70. Pardailhé-Galabrun, *Naissance,* p. 36. L634, dossier Saint Cristophe en la Cité, register of deliberations, 1746.

60. JF 1590. LL836, fol. 8, 15 June 1760.

61. BN 4° Fm 23906, deliberation of 10 Aug. 1758.

62. LL847, fols. 198, 186. Brochard, *Saint-Laurent,* pp. 196–197.

63. Nicole Mounier, "Le Quartier des Porcherons, 1720–1789: Description d'un processus d'urbanisation d'un faubourg de Paris" (thesis of the Ecole des Chartes, 1978), p. 59.

64. Owen Chadwick, *The Popes and European Revolution* (Oxford, Clarendon, 1981), pp. 29–31.

65. S7493, Saint Jacques de la Boucherie. See also LL847, fols. 47, 54 (Saint Martin du Cloître).

66. L635, *Arrêt de règlement pour les confréries du Saint Sacrement établies à Paris, dans les églises paroissiales de Saint Etienne du Mont, Saint Sulpice et Saint Roch,* 1786.

67. Marcel Brongniart, *La Paroisse Saint Médard au faubourg Saint Marceau* (Paris, Picard, 1951), pp. 108–110. XVII 671, *procuration,* 22 Apr. 1732. Archives of Saint Médard, accounts for 1779. Brochard, *Saint-Laurent,* pp. 184–205; *Saint Gervais: Histoire de la paroisse* (Paris, Didot, n.d. [1950]), pp. 251–267. On decline of confraternities, John Bossy, "The Counter-Reformation and the People of Catholic Europe," *Past and Present* 47 (May 1970): 51–70 (p. 60); McManners, *Death,* p. 233. Robert Schneider, *Public Life in Toulouse, 1463–1789* (Ithaca, Cornell U.P., 1989), pp. 303–307.

68. McManners, *Death,* pp. 308–319.

69. Pierre Chaunu, *La Mort à Paris* (Paris, Fayard, 1978), pp. 435–436, 442–445. Ralph Gibson, *A Social History of French Catholicism, 1789–1914* (London, Routledge, 1989), pp. 3–8. Charles Manneville, *Une Vieille Eglise de Paris: Saint Médard* (Paris, Champion, 1906), p. 91 n. 2.

70. LL 836, fols. 101–102, 4 June 1780.

71. R. B. Rose, "How to Make a Revolution: The Paris Districts in 1789," *Bulletin of the John Rylands University Library* 59 (1977): 426–457 (p. 445).

72. Arch.P. 4AZ 1294, *Observations pour les propriétaires et intéressés à . . . la Bièvre . . . contre le prétendu projet de l'Yvette* (1789). S. Dupain, *La Bièvre:*

Nouvelles recherches historiques (Paris, Champion, 1886), pp. 34–37. *Arrêt du Conseil d'Etat,* 1 Dec. 1789, summarized in Tuétey, *Répertoire,* vol. 3, no. 2651.

73. Arch.P. 4AZ 1294, tax roll, 1774–1775; convocation for 23 June 1768. Derenusson was one of the wealthiest tanners, but never became church-warden (he may have been too young); Burstin, *Faubourg Saint-Marcel,* pp. 206–207. Nor did Etienne Cayrol, "entrepreneur de la manufacture des draps et de teinture"; Arch.P. D4 B6 68, dossier 4473, 3 Aug. 1778.

74. Sonenscher, *Work and Wages,* p. 290.

75. Quoted in Coornaert, *Corporations,* p. 159.

76. XVIII 703, 6 June 1769. Teynac, Nolot, and Vivien, *Wallpaper,* pp. 87–88, 90. On postal service, Marcel Rouff, "Une Grève de gagne-deniers en 1786 à Paris," *Revue historique* 105 (1910): 332–347 (pp. 338–339). On *privilèges,* Sonenscher, *Work and Wages,* pp. 216–217.

77. Charles-Joseph Panckoucke, "Sur les chambres syndicales," *Mercure de France,* 23 Jan. 1790, quoted in Tucoo-Chala, *Panckoucke,* p. 429. See also the *Cahier du Tiers-Etat du District de Saint Victor,* BHVP, 10070, no. 16.

7. The Revolution in Local Politics

1. See esp. Keith Baker, ed., *The Political Culture of the Old Regime* (Oxford, Pergamon, 1987) and Colin Lucas, ed., *The Political Culture of the Revolution* (Oxford, Pergamon, 1988), vols. 1 and 2 of *The French Revolution and the Creation of Modern Political Culture;* Lynn Hunt, *Politics, Culture, and Class in the French Revolution* (Berkeley, U. of California Press, 1984), esp. chap. 5.

2. JF 345, fol. 139v.

3. JF 345, fol. 133. Extract from deliberations of vestry, 24 Feb. 1758.

4. Michael Sonenscher, "French Journeymen, the Courts, and the French Trades, 1781–1791," *Past and Present* 114 (Feb. 1987): 77–109.

5. Pierre Le Maistre, *Coutume de Paris,* new ed. (Paris, 1741), pp. 262–263. Paul Viollet, *Précis de l'histoire du droit français* (Paris, Larose and Forcel, 1886), pp. 670–671. For an example from a religious community, see XVII 662, 6 May 1730.

6. See also Gail Bossenga, "City and State: An Urban Perspective on the Origins of the French Revolution," in Baker, *Political Culture of the Old Regime,* pp. 115–140 (p. 133).

7. Malcolm Crook, "Les Français devant le vote: Participation et pratique électorale à l'époque de la Révolution," in *Les Pratiques politiques en province à l'époque de la Révolution française* (Montpellier, Université de Montpellier, 1988), pp. 27–37.

8. Compare Hunt, *Politics,* p. 217: the "nearly-in" take over from the established elites.

9. On schoolteachers, Raymonde Monnier, "La Lecture en milieu populaire dans le Département de Paris," *Dix-huitième siècle* 21 (1989): 217–231 (pp. 229–230); Hunt, *Politics,* p. 216.

10. Richard Andrews, "Réflexions sur la conjuration des Egaux," *Annales: ESC* 29 (1974): 73–106. See also Hunt, *Politics,* chap. 6.

11. Alexandre Tuétey, *Répertoire général des sources manuscrites de l'histoire de Paris pendant la Révolution française,* 10 vols. (Paris, Imprimerie nouvelle, 1890–1912), vol. 2, no. 1681, 12 Nov. 1790.

12. Marcel Brongniart, *La Paroisse Saint Médard au faubourg Saint Marceau* (Paris, Picard, 1951), p. 114. F7* 2517, fol. 227v.

13. André Arnoult Aclocque, "Pétition particulière d'un habitant du district de Saint Marcel pour réunir au cahier du tiers état de la Ville de Paris," reproduced in Charles-Louis Chassin, *Les Elections et les cahiers de Paris en 1789,* 4 vols. (Paris, Jouaust and Sigaux 1888–1889), 2:480–482.

14. Ba 64A, dossier 2, fols. 1–5, Jean Antoine Derubigny de Berteval, "Cahier du Sieur de Rubigny de Berteval, tanneur et habitant du District de Saint Marcel"; dossier 4, no. 30, "Cahier du District de Saint Marcel."

15. BN Lb40 1621, *District de Saint Marcel: Assemblée général de la Commune dudit District, pour le mardi 1er septembre 1789,* n.p., n.d. [1789].

16. Edict of August 1776, Alfred Franklin, *Dictionnaire historique des arts, métiers, et professions exercés dans Paris depuis le treizième siècle* (Paris, H. Welter, 1906), pp. 86–92.

17. Jacques Michel, *Du Paris de Louis XV à la marine de Louis XVI: L'Oeuvre de Monsieur de Sartine* (Paris, Editions de l'Erudit, 1983), pp. 99–100.

18. Municipal law of 21 May/27 June 1790, reproduced in Ernest Mellié, *Les Sections de Paris pendant la Révolution française* (Paris, Société de l'histoire de la Révolution française, 1898), pp. 9–22.

19. Jean-Paul Poisson, "Les Déplacements professionnels d'un notaire parisien à la fin de la Restauration," *Revue d'histoire moderne et contemporaine* 29 (1982): 125–140. *Procureurs* seem to have had clients concentrated in certain areas of the city.

20. R. B. Rose, "Claude Fauchet, 1789, and the Theology of Revolution" (unpublished paper presented to the Fourth George Rudé Seminar, Melbourne, 27 Aug. 1984).

21. Maurice Genty, *L'Apprentissage de la citoyenneté: Paris, 1789–1795* (Paris, Messidor/Editions sociales, 1987), p. 21.

22. Ages known for 23 of the 36 members of the 1789 committee, 15 of 25 members of 1790 committee, 37 of 41 electors and committee members of the years 1792–1793, 25 of 29 members of Revolutionary Committee of Year II, for 9 of 16 members of Civil Committee of Year II.

23. Raymonde Monnier, *Le Faubourg Saint-Antoine* (Paris, Société des Etudes Robespierristes, 1981), pp. 121, 134.

24. Norman Hampson, *Social History of the French Revolution* (London, Routledge, 1963), p. 132. Alison Patrick, *The Men of the First French Republic* (Baltimore and London, Johns Hopkins U.P., 1972), pp. 247–252. On other parts of France, Hunt, *Politics,* pp. 151, 173, 217.

25. Monnier, *Faubourg Saint-Antoine,* p. 134. Emile Ducoudray, "Bourgeois parisiens en révolution, 1790–1792," in Michel Vovelle, ed., *Paris et la Révolution* (Paris, Publications de la Sorbonne, 1989), pp. 71–88, (pp. 72, 80).

26. David G. Troyansky, *Old Age in the Old Regime* (Ithaca, Cornell U.P., 1989), pp. 28, 66–71, 199–207. Jean-Pierre Gutton, *Naissance du vieillard* (Paris, Aubier, 1988), pp. 133–166.

27. Jacques Lelièvre, *Pratique des contrats de mariage chez les notaires au Châtelet de Paris,* (Paris, Cujas, 1959), p. 100. Bernard Schnapper, "Liberté, égalité, autorité: La Famille devant les assemblées révolutionnaires (1790–1800)," in Marie-Françoise Lévy, ed., *L'Enfant, la famille, et la Révolution française* ([Paris], Olivier Orban, 1990), pp. 325–340 (p. 333), and Jean Carbonnier, "Le Statut de l'enfant en droit civil pendant la Révolution," ibid., pp. 297–305 (p. 298). See also Lynn Hunt, *The Family Romance of the French Revolution* (Berkeley, U. of California Press, 1992), pp. 40–43.

28. William Doyle, "The Price of Offices in Prerevolutionary France," *Historical Journal* 27 (1984): 831–860. Margaret Darrow, *Revolution in the House* (Princeton, Princeton U.P., 1989), pp. 124–125.

29. Pierre Goubert and Daniel Roche, *Les Français et l'Ancien Régime,* 2 vols. (Paris, Armand Colin, 1984), pp. 298–299.

30. Lelièvre, *Pratique des contrats de mariage,* pp. 181–185.

31. Jacques Godechot, "Fragments des mémoires de Charles-Alexis Alexandre sur les journées révolutionnaires de 1791 et 1792," *Annales historiques de la Révolution française* 24 (1952): 113–251. Albert Soboul and Raymonde Monnier, *Répertoire du personnel sectionnaire parisien en l'an II* (Paris, Publications de la Sorbonne, 1985), p. 527; *Almanach national,* Year II.

32. Arch.P. D12 U1 36, 4 Thermidor Year II. F7* 2519, fol. 34v. *Almanach national,* 1793. Etienne Charavay, *Assemblée électorale de Paris, 18 novembre 1790–15 juin 1791* (Paris, Quantin, 1890), p. 80. DIII 256 (4), dossier 4, nos. 5, 44.

33. BN Lb40 1621, *District de Saint Marcel: Assemblée générale de la Commune dudit District, pour le mardi 1er septembre 1789,* n.p., n.d. [1789] *Almanach national,* 1793. F7* 2517, fols. 15v, 54v, 263v. Soboul and Monnier, *Répertoire,* p. 525. Arch.P. D12 U1 39, avis de parents, 10 Feb. 1791. For another example of revolutionary brothers-in-law, see Sophie Faguay, "Bourgeois du faubourg Saint-Antoine, 1791–1792," in Vovelle, *Paris et la Révolution,* pp. 89–95 (p. 93).

34. Andrews, "Réflexions." Raymonde Monnier, *Un Bourgeois Sans-culotte: Le Général Santerre* (Paris, Publications de la Sorbonne, 1990), p. 32. France Weber, "La Famille Santerre et la brasserie parisienne au XVIIIe siècle," *Le Brasseur français* no. 706 (3 June 1905), p. 4.

35. Soboul and Monnier, *Répertoire*, pp. 526–527. Richard Cobb, "Note sur Guillaume Bouland, de la section du Finistère," *Annales historiques de la Révolution française* 22 (1950): 152–155.

36. Dale Lothrop Clifford, "The National Guard and the Parisian Community, 1789–1790," *French Historical Studies* 16 (1990): 849–878 (p. 856).

37. Tuétey, *Répertoire*, vol. 8, no. 2960, deliberation of Revolutionary Committee, 13 June 1793.

38. Godechot, "Fragments des mémoires." Etienne Charavay, *Assemblée électorale de Paris, 2 septembre 1792–17 frimaire an II* (Paris, Quantin, 1905), p. 87. F7 4774 (70), nos. 475–476. Two recent exceptions to the general neglect of the National Guard are Clifford, "National Guard," and Raymonde Monnier, "La Garde citoyenne, élément de la démocratie parisienne," in Vovelle, *Paris et la Révolution*, pp. 147–159.

39. Charavay, *Assemblée électorale, 2 septembre 1792*, p. 87. Godechot, "Fragments des mémoires," p. 122. Geneviève Aclocque, *Un Défenseur du roi, André-Arnoult Aclocque commandant général de la garde nationale parisienne, 1748–1802* (Paris, A. and J. Picard, 1947), p. 109. Haim Burstin, *La Politica alla prova* (Milan, Franco Angeli, 1989), pp. 131–132. Fritz Braesch, "Les Lazowski," *La Révolution française* 80 (1927): 263–266.

40. F7 4794.

41. F7 4751, dossier Jouzeau.

42. Haim Burstin, *Le Faubourg Saint-Marcel à l'époque révolutionnaire* (Paris, Société des Etudes Robespierristes, 1983), pp. 224–231; "Travail, entreprise, et politique à la manufacture des Gobelins pendant la période révolutionnaire," in Gérard Gayot and Jean-Pierre Hirsch, eds., *La Révolution française et le développement du capitalisme,* special issue of *Revue du Nord* (Lille, 1989), pp. 369–379.

43. F1bII Seine 25, Twelfth Arrondissement, Year VII.

44. F7 4774 (97), dossier Rognon. Revolutionary Committee signatures (in photograph), AN F7* 2523, 12 Vendémiaire Year III.

45. F7 4635, dossier Castille, quoted in Richard Andrews, "Paris of the Great Revolution," in Gene Brucker, ed., *People and Communities in the Western World* (Homewood, Ill., Dorsey, 1979), p. 74.

46. NII Seine 148. Charavay, *Assemblée électorale, 2 septembre 1792*, p. 86 n. 1. H1956 (1), list of *dixainiers*, 1785. F7* 2517, fols. 23, 261. F7* 1519, fol. 36. F7 4774 (42), dossier Mercier.

47. For the idea of a revolutionary political class, see Hunt, *Politics,* esp. chap. 5.

48. Quoted in Albert Soboul, *Les Sans-culottes parisiens en l'an II* (Paris, Clavreuil, 1958), p. 669.
49. Ibid. pp. 442–444. Monnier, *Faubourg Saint-Antoine*, pp. 128–133. Andrews, "Réflexions," p. 83; "Social Structures, Political Elites, and Ideology in Revolutionary Paris, 1792–1794: A Critical Evaluation of Albert Soboul's *Les Sans-culottes parisiens en l'an II*," *Journal of Social History* 19 (1985–1986): 71–112 (pp. 85–92). Morris Slavin, *Revolution in Miniature: Section Droits de l'Homme* (Princeton, Princeton U.P., 1984), pp. 217–230. R. B. Rose, *The Making of the Sans-culottes* (Manchester, Manchester U.P., 1983), p. 181. The revolutionary committees had a more modest membership; Slavin, *Revolution,* pp. 247–264; Soboul, *Sans-culottes,* pp. 444–449.
50. F7* 2519, fols. 1–2, 30 Prairial and 3 Messidor Year II. Soboul, *Sans-culottes,* p. 118.
51. Burstin, *Politica alla prova,* chaps. 2, 3.
52. Georges Garrigues, *Les Districts parisiens pendant la Révolution française* (Paris, Spes, 1931), p. 9.
53. DIV bis 13, extract from the deliberations of the Saint Marcel District, 16 Dec. 1789. BHVP 196655, *District de Saint Marcel: Extrait des registres de ses délibérations, du 21 mars 1790* [Paris, 1790].
54. Charavay, *Assemblée électorale, 18 novembre 1790,* pp. viii–x. Etienne Charavay, *Assemblée électorale de Paris, 26 août 1791–12 août 1792* (Paris, Quantin, 1894), p. vii. Genty, *Apprentissage,* p. 266. Soboul, *Sans-culottes,* p. 1094, cites a list of 1791 giving only 774 active citizens for the Gobelins Section. DIII 256 (4), dossier 8, no. 1, petition of Dec. 1791. DIII 256 (4), dossier 8, no. 4.
55. Soboul, *Sans-culottes,* pp. 1095–1097.
56. Ibid., pp. 587–588, 1094, 1098–1103.
57. DIV 51, no. 1488, listed in Tuétey, *Répertoire,* vol. 2, no. 1438. Rose, *Making,* pp. 128–129, 158. Genty, *Apprentissage,* pp. 132–133.
58. Genty, *Apprentissage,* pp. 203, 206–209, 217–220. F7* 2517, fol. 27, 6 June 1793. Rose, *Making,* p. 160.
59. Rose, *Making,* pp. 154, 178. Dominique Godineau, *Citoyennes tricoteuses: Les Femmes du peuple à Paris pendant la Révolution française* (Paris, Alinea, 1988), p. 213. DIII 256 (4), dossier 8, no. 4. Soboul, *Sans-culottes,* p. 77. Mellié, *Sections,* p. 108.
60. DIII 264, no. 15, late July 1792. F7*2517, fol. 228, 22 Ventôse Year II. F7 4774 (42), dossier Mercier. W547, no. 52, interrogation of Marie Jacqueline Elisabeth Beschepoix. Richard Cobb, *Les Armées révolutionnaires,* 2 vols. (Paris, Mouton, 1961), 2:892.
61. Cobb, "Guillaume Bouland"; Soboul and Monnier, *Répertoire,* pp. 526–527; F7* 2517, fols. 163v, 228, 258, 281v.
62. Burstin, *Politica alla prova,* pp. 80–81.

63. On Gency, Paul Sainte-Claire Deville, *La Commune de l'an II: Vie et mort d'une assemblée révolutionnaire* (Paris, Plon, 1946), p. 162. For Carrel, W547, no. 52, 7 Messidor Year III.

64. Slavin, *Revolution*, pp. 217–219.

65. Genty, *Apprentissage*, pp. 182–195, 203–205. Soboul, *Sans-culottes*, pp. 600, 606–608. Slavin, *Revolution*, pp. 214–215.

66. Marcel Reinhard, *Nouvelle histoire de Paris: La Révolution* (Paris, Hachette, 1971), p. 293. Soboul, *Sans-culottes*, p. 611. Genty, *Apprentissage*, pp. 229–235. Slavin, *Revolution*, pp. 216, 246.

67. Quoted in Soboul, *Sans-culottes*, p. 954. On growing central control, Cobb, *Armées révolutionnaires*, p. 493; Soboul, *Sans-culottes*, pp. 602, 611–612, 851–916; Genty, *Apprentissage*, pp. 230–240; Reinhard, *Nouvelle histoire*, pp. 288–289.

68. On Droulot, F7* 2517, fols. 106v, 188. On Véron, F7* 2517, fol. 46, and Soboul and Monnier, *Répertoire*, p. 525. On Langlois, ibid. For other examples, Soboul, *Sans-culottes*, pp. 446–447. See also Andrews, "Social Structures," p. 99.

69. Olwen Hufton, "Women in Revolution, 1789–1796," *Past and Present* 53 (Nov. 1971): 90–108; *Women and the Limits of Citizenship in the French Revolution* (Toronto, U. of Toronto Press, 1992), chap. 3.

8. Interregnum

1. Richard Andrews, "Réflexions sur la conjuration des Egaux," *Annales: ESC* 29 (1974): 73–106 (esp. pp. 82–83); "Paris of the Great Revolution," in Gene Brucker, ed., *People and Communities in the Western World* (Homewood, Ill., Dorsey, 1979), pp. 56–112 (pp. 72–74).

2. Joseph Grente, *Le Culte catholique à Paris de la Terreur au Concordat* (Paris, Lethielleux, 1903), p. 442. Arch.P. 4 AZ 698, 28 Thermidor III.

3. Brongniart, pp. 119–121. Louis Brochard, *Histoire de la paroisse et de l'église Saint-Laurent* (Paris, Champion, 1923), p. 273. *Annales de la Religion* 1 (1795):162–164.

4. Maurice Vimont, *Histoire de l'église et de la paroisse Saint-Leu Saint-Gilles à Paris* (Paris, Florange and Margraff, 1932), p. 39. Brongniart, p. 125.

5. F3 II Seine 23, dossier 1, "Monuments religieux," petition of 20 Pluviôse Year IV. Abbé Baloche, *Eglise Saint-Merri de Paris: Histoire de la paroisse et de la collégiale*, 2 vols. (Paris, Oudin, n.d. [1911]), 1:104. L. Soutif, "Une Société du culte catholique à Paris pendant la première séparation: La Paroisse Saint-Eustache de 1795 à 1802," *Revue des questions historiques* 84 (1908): 145–177 (pp. 148–149).

6. Grente, *Culte catholique*, p. 10.

7. Charles Manneville, *Une Vieille Eglise de Paris: Saint Médard* (Paris, Cham-

pion, 1906), p. 124 n. 4. The level of popular support may also be measured by baptisms: 2,640 at Saint Médard between October 1795 and May 1802; Brongniart, p. 126.

8. P. Pisani, "Une Paroisse parisienne pendant la Révolution: Saint Gervais (1789–1804)," *Le Correspondant,* 10 Feb. 1908, pp. 444–473 (pp. 455, 457). F19 4145, inventory of Saint Marcel, Year X. On Bertier, Brongniart, p. 125. At Saint Leu and at Saint Laurent, too, many ornaments were donated; Vimont, *Saint-Leu,* p. 39; Brochard, *Saint-Laurent,* pp. 276–277.

9. F19 4145, fabriques, Paris. Dossier Saint Médard.

10. Arch.P. 2 AZ 230. Manneville, *Vieille Eglise,* p. 104. Albert Soboul and Raymonde Monnier, *Répertoire du personnel sectionnaire parisien en l'an II* (Paris, Publications de la Sorbonne, 1985), p. 525. DIII 256 (4), dossier 4, no. 31.

11. F20 255, report of mayor of Twelfth Arrondissement to minister of the interior, 1807. F7 4794, 7e compagnie.

12. F20 255, Twelfth Arrondissement, 1807. Sigismond Lacroix, *Actes de la Commune de Paris pendant la Révolution,* 16 vols. (Paris, L. Cerf, 1894–1914), 1st ser., index.

13. Arch.P. 2 AZ 230, document 3, benediction of the flag of the National Guard of Saint Marcel, 1789. S*1642, fol. 34. F7* 2517, fol. 222, 10 Ventôse II.

14. F19 4145, dossier Saint Médard.

15. Brochard, *Saint-Laurent,* pp. 274–275. Jean Boussoulade, *L'Eglise de Paris du 9 thermidor au Concordat* (Paris, Procure générale du clergé, 1950), pp. 66, 71. Baloche, *Saint-Merri,* 2:41–42, 104–109, 199. LL836, register of elections, Sainte Marguerite. Soutif, "Saint-Eustache," pp. 160–164. Pisani, "Paroisse parisienne," p. 467.

16. F3 II Seine 23, dossier 1, "Monuments religieux," petition of Nivôse Year IV. Soutif, "Saint-Eustache," p. 159 n. 1, 171).

17. Brongniart, pp. 121, 125–126. Baloche, *Saint-Merri,* 2:99, 106–110. T 782, papers of Gaston Marie Cécile Margarita. Marcel Reinhard, *Nouvelle histoire de Paris: La Révolution* (Paris, Hachette, 1971), p. 393. Soutif, "Saint-Eustache." Albert Mathiez, *La Révolution et l'église* (Paris, Armand Colin, 1910), p. 189. On Saint Etienne du Mont, see Boussoulade, *Eglise de Paris,* p. 71. Pisani, "Paroisse parisienne," p. 456.

18. Boussoulade, *Eglise de Paris,* pp. 71, 84, 161. Baloche, *Saint-Merri* 2:154–165.

19. Baloche, *Saint-Merri,* 2:181. For complaint from Saint Laurent, F19 4145, [prefect of the Seine] to minister of the interior, 15 Nivôse Year XIII.

20. Reinhard, *Nouvelle histoire,* pp. 396–398. Albert Mathiez, *La Théophilanthropie et le culte décadaire, 1796–1801* (Paris, Alcan, 1903), p. 413n.

21. Brochard, *Saint-Laurent,* pp. 288–295. Boussoulade, *Eglise de Paris,* p. 138.

22. *Nouvelles ecclésiastiques,* 24 Apr. 1800.

23. Baloche, *Saint-Merri*, 2:166–175.

24. Ibid., 2:234.

25. On Bertier, Brongniart, pp. 125–126. *Nouvelles ecclésiastiques,* 13 Sept. 1802, 29 Mar. 1803. F19 4145, archbishop to minister for religious affairs, 6 May 1808. Ordinance of Monseigneur de Belloy, Aug. 1803, in Boussoulade, *Eglise de Paris,* p. 210.

26. Baloche, *Saint-Merri*, 2:642–646.

27. F19 4145, curé of Saint Leu to Conseiller d'Etat for religious affairs, 22 Frimaire Year XII.

28. Arch.P. VD* 6690. S. Dupain, *La Bièvre: Nouvelles recherches historiques* (Paris, Champion, 1886), pp. 114, 125. On Vérité, F7* 2523, fol. 86; F30 159. On Salleron, see chap. 9. On Huguet nephew, Etienne Charavay, *Assemblée électorale de Paris, 2 septembre 1792–17 frimaire an II* (Paris, Quantin, 1905), p. 86.

29. Arch.P. VD* 6536. VD* 6548, 12 Thermidor Year V. On Rivaud, F7* 2517, fols. 117v, 227v; DIII 256 (4), dossier 4, no. 6; F7 4774 (93); Soboul and Monnier, *Répertoire,* p. 524.

30. Arch.P. VD* 6557–6602, 6617, 6623, 6632, 6634, 6688, 6692.

31. Arch.P. VD* 6685, 14 Thermidor Year VII; VD* 6719, 6720, 17 and 19 Frimaire Year VIII (8 and 10 Dec. 1799).

32. F12 2286, minister of the interior to Derubigny, 30 Thermidor Year XIII (18 Aug. 1805).

33. Albert Soboul, *Les Sans-culottes parisiens en l'an II* (Paris, Clavreuil, 1958), pp. 851–916, 930, 951–965; Richard Cobb, *Les Armées révolutionnaires,* 2 vols. (Paris, Mouton, 1961), 2:493. Maurice Genty, *L'Apprentissage de la citoyenneté: Paris, 1789–1795* (Paris, Messidor/Editions sociales, 1987), pp. 230–238.

34. Decrees of 4 Fructidor Year II (21 Aug. 1794); 28 Vendémiaire Year III (19 Oct. 1794); 22 Frimaire Year III (12 Dec. 1794); 7 Fructidor Year II (24 Aug. 1794). Genty, *Apprentissage,* pp. 241–243. Jean Tulard, *Paris et son administration (1800–1830)* (Paris, Ville de Paris, Commission des travaux historiques, 1976), p. 57.

35. DIII 256 (4), dossier 4, no. 48, 16 Thermidor Year III (3 Aug. 1795). See also ibid., no. 12, 17 Messidor Year III (5 July 1795).

36. DIII 256 (4), dossier 4, nos. 12, 13, 19, 26, 32.

37. See Genty, *Apprentissage,* p. 242, and Raymonde Monnier, *Le Faubourg Saint Antoine* (Paris, Société des Etudes Robespierristes, 1981), pp. 132–133.

38. Evelyne Bouvet-Bensimon, "L'Ascension sociale d'un marchand de bois au XVIIIe siècle, d'après un compte de tutelle," *Revue d'histoire moderne et contemporaine* 34 (1987): 282–304 (p. 294).

39. DIII 256 (4), dossier 4, no. 12.

40. Emile Ducoudray, "Bourgeois parisiens en révolution, 1790–1792," in Michel Vovelle, ed., *Paris et la Révolution* (Paris, Publications de la Sorbonne, 1989), pp. 71–88, (p. 72).

41. F1bI 124–130, Civil Committee of Jardin des Plantes Section to minister of the interior, 29 Pluviôse Year IV.

42. They pestered the Legislation Committee on the most trivial matters. For an example, DIII 256 (4), dossier 4, no. 3.

43. Genty, *Apprentissage,* p. 242. F7* 2523, fol. 6. W547, no. 52. F1b I 124–130.

44. DIII 256 (4), dossier 4, no. 44. F7* 2523, fol. 16. F1dII D10, dossier Deperthes, Fructidor Year VI. See also F1bI 124–130, Jardin-des-Plantes Section, 29 Pluviôse Year IV.

45. *Moniteur,* 30 Ventôse Year III (20 Mar. 1795). Denis Woronoff, *La République bourgeoise* (Paris, Seuil, 1972), pp. 25–29. Kåre D. Tonnesson, *La Défaite des sans-culottes* (Oslo, Universitetsforlaget, 1978), pp. 291–297. F7* 2523, fol. 45. Genty, 247–250.

46. F7*2523, fol. 23. F7* 2523, fol. 52. DIII 256 (4), dossier 4, no. 3, Civil Committee to Legislation Committee, 6 Prairial Year III (25 May 1795). Genty, *Apprentissage,* p. 249. F7* 2523, fols. 40, 53.

47. F7*2523, fols. 87, 148, 166. George Rudé, *The Crowd in the French Revolution* (Oxford, Oxford U.P., 1959), p. 166. W547, no. 62, extract from deliberations of Finistère Section, 10 Messidor Year III (28 June 1795). Tonnesson says the Finistère General Assembly was unusual in its clemency; *Défaite* p. 335.

48. F7* 2523, fols. 56–57. F7* 2517, fol. 279v. Soboul and Monnier, *Répertoire,* p. 524. F7 4775 (21), dossier Soyer. W547, no. 52. The General assembly also defended Denis Vian: F7 4775 (45), dossier Vian.

49. Antoine Gency and André Mercier were members of the rebel Commune. Louis D'Hervilly was involved in a prison conspiracy at Saint Lazare; Etienne Charavay, *Assemblée électorale de Paris, 26 août 1792,* (Paris, Quantin, 1894), p. 68. A man named Roussel, who played little role in the faubourg, was accused of leading a counterrevolutionary revolt at the Palais-Royal; Alexandre Tuétey, *Répertoire general des sources manuscrites de l'histoire de Paris pendant la Révolution française,* 10 vols., (Paris, Imprimerie nouvelle, 1890–1912), vol. 7, no. 1047). Manguelschot was arrested as a royalist and was executed on 9 Thermidor. F7 4774 (32), dossier 4; F7 4774 (97); F7*2517, fol. 228v; Charavay, *Assemblée électorale 26 août 1791,* p. 69.

50. Isser Woloch, *Jacobin Legacy: The Democratic Movement under the Directory* (Princeton, Princeton U.P., 1970), p. 241.

51. Jean-René Suratteau, *Les Elections de l'an VI et le "coup d'état du 22*

floréal" (Paris, Société les Belles Lettres, 1971), pp. 19–25. Nicolas Ruault, *Gazette d'un Parisien sous la Révolution: Lettres à son frère, 1783–1796* (Paris, Perrin, 1976), p. 386 (see also pp. 388–389). Also see Genty, pp. 250–252, and Rudé, *Crowd,* pp. 165–170.

52. Rudé, *Crowd,* pp. 170–174. F7 4774 (9), dossier Urbain Leclerc.

53. Genty, p. 254. F1dII D10, dossier Deperthes; F1dII G11, dossier Pierre Guibert.

54. For administrators, F1bII Seine 8, 25. For Surveillance Committee, F7* 2523.

55. Soboul, *Sans-culottes,* p. 1094. Arch.P. D12 U1 108, Division Jardin des Plantes, 10, 15, and 16 Brumaire Year IV.

56. Woloch, *Jacobin Legacy,* p. 242. T782, dossier Margarita, Fifth Municipality to Margarita, 25 Ventôse Year V. F1bII Seine 25, commissaire du Directoire exécutif, Department of the Seine, to minister of the interior, 23 Messidor Year VI.

57. F1bII Seine 25, List of the members of municipal administrations, Messidor Year VI. More generally, Woloch, *Jacobin Legacy,* pp. 230–232.

58. F1bII Seine 25, commissaire du directoire exécutif, Department of the Seine, to minister of the interior, 23 Messidor Year VI. More generally, see Sigismond Lacroix, *Le Département de Paris et de la Seine pendant la Révolution* (Paris, Société de l'histoire de la Révolution française, 1904), pp. 353–354.

59. F1bII Seine 25, orders of du Directoire exécutif, 28 Messidor Year VII, 29 Fructidor Year VII, 28 Vendémiaire Year VIII, Frimaire Year VIII. F1bII Seine 8, commissaire du directoire exécutif, Department of the Seine, to minister of the interior, 16 Vendémiaire Year VI.

60. Darline Gay Levy, Harriet B. Applewhite, and Mary Durham Johnson, eds., *Women in Revolutionary Paris, 1789–1795* (Urbana, U. of Illinois Press, 1979), pp. 215–216, 161–166, 169–170.

61. F7* 2523, fol. 55, 8 Prairial Year III. Olwen Hufton, *Women and the Limits of Citizenship in the French Revolution* (Toronto, U. of Toronto Press, 1992), p. 49.

62. DIII 256 (4), dossier 8, no. 7, deliberations of Gobelins Section, 25 Apr. 1792. Dominique Godineau, *Citoyennes tricoteuses: Les Femmes du peuple à Paris pendant la Révolution française* (Paris, Alinea, 1988), pp. 190–192, 213. On Pauline Léon, F7 4774 (9), dossier Leclerc.

63. Pisani, "Paroisse parisienne," p. 464. Boussoulade, *Eglise de Paris,* p. 56.

64. Olwen Hufton, "The Reconstruction of a Church, 1796–1801," in Gwynne Lewis and Colin Lucas, eds., *Beyond the Terror* (Cambridge, Cambridge U.P., 1981), pp. 21–53. F19 4145, Saint Médard. Brochard, *Saint-Laurent,* pp. 276–277, 282.

65. Baloche, *Saint-Merri,* 2:164.

66. Geneviève Fraisse, "Rupture révolutionnaire et l'histoire des femmes," in Danielle Haase-Dubosc and Eliane Viennot, eds., *Femmes et pouvoirs sous l'ancien régime* (Paris, Rivages, 1991), pp. 291–305 (p. 295).

67. Fraisse, "Rupture," p. 293. Jeanne Peiffer, "L'Engouement des femmes pour les sciences au XVIII siècle," in Haase-Dubosc and Viennot, *Femmes et pouvoirs,* pp. 196–222 (pp. 200, 214). Jacques Pierre Brissot de Warville, *Théorie des loix criminelles* [1780], 2 vols. (Paris, 1836), 1:40–100, quoted in Antoinette Wills, *Crime and Punishment in Revolutionary Paris* (Westport, Conn., Greenwood, 1981), p. 18. For another example, "De l'influence de la Révolution sur les femmes," *Les Révolutions de Paris,* no. 83, pp. 226–235.

68. Candice E. Proctor, *Women, Equality, and the French Revolution* (Westport, Conn., Greenwood, 1990), pp. 20–39. Joan B. Landes, *Women and the Public Sphere in the Age of the French Revolution* (Ithaca and London, Cornell U.P., 1988), pt. 1. Jane Rendall, *The Origins of Modern Feminism: Women in Britain, France, and the United States, 1780–1860* (Basingstoke, Macmillan, 1985), pp. 7–32. Madelyn Gutwirth, *The Twilight of the Goddesses: Women and Representation in the French Revolutionary Era* (New Brunswick, N.J., Rutgers U.P., 1992), chaps. 3, 4.

69. Barbara Corrado Pope, "Angels in the Devil's Workshop: Leisured and Charitable Women in Nineteenth-Century England and France," in Renate Bridenthal and Claudia Koonz, eds., *Becoming Visible: Women in European History* (Boston, Houghton Mifflin, 1977), 296–324 (p. 302). Vicomte de Bonald, *Du Divorce considéré au XIXe siècle relativement à l'état domestique et à l'état public de la société* (Paris, 1801), quoted in Geneviève Fraisse, *Muse de la Raison: La Démocratie exclusive et la différence des sexes* (Paris, Alinea, 1989), p. 107. Abbé du Voisin, *Défense de l'ordre social contre les principes de la Révolution française* (1798), quoted in Margaret Darrow, "French Noblewomen and the New Domesticity, 1750–1850," *Feminist Studies* 5 (1979): 41–65 (p. 55).

70. Lynn Hunt, *Politics, Culture, and Class in the French Revolution* (Berkeley, U. of California Press, 1984), pp. 93, 113, and esp. 118, where the vignette is reproduced.

71. Fraisse, "Rupture," p. 293. See also the example of Portal in Hufton, *Women and the Limits of Citizenship,* p. 137.

72. Fraisse, *Muse,* pp. 13–36 (quote on p. 36). See also Marcel Reinhard, *La France du Directoire,* cours de Sorbonne, n.d., p. 71; Susan Grogan, *French Socialism and Sexual Difference* (Basingstoke, Macmillan, 1992), p. 8.

73. Peiffer, "Engouement des femmes," p. 214.

74. Ibid. Martyn Lyons, *France under the Directory* (Cambridge, Cambridge U.P., 1975), pp. 91, 95. Colin Jones, *The Longman Companion to the*

French Revolution (London, Longman, 1988), pp. 271–274. Jacques Léonard, "Women, Religion and Medicine," in Robert Forster and Orest Ranum, eds., *Medicine and Society in France* (Baltimore and London, Johns Hopkins U.P., 1980), 24–47 (pp. 24–25). Nicole and Jean Dhombres, *Naissance d'un pouvoir: Sciences et savants en France (1793–1824)* (Paris, Payot, 1989), pp. 218–222. Proctor, *Women*, pp. 171–172.

75. N. and J. Dhombres, *Naissance d'un pouvoir*, pp. 553–604.

76. Bernard Schnapper, "Liberté, égalité, autorité": La Famille devant les assemblées révolutionnaires (1790–1800),' in Marie-Françoise Lévy, ed., *L'Enfant, la famille, et la Révolution française* ([Paris], Olivier Orban, 1990), p. 328. See also Lynn Hunt, *The Family Romance of the French Revolution* (Berkeley, U. of California Press, 1992), chaps. 2, 6.

77. Themistocles Rodis, "Marriage, Divorce, and the Status of Women during the Terror," in Morris Slavin and Agnes M. Smith, eds., *Bourgeois, Sans-culottes, and Other Frenchmen* (Waterloo, Ont., Wilfrid Laurier U.P., 1981), pp. 41–57 (p. 49). Marcel Garaud, *La Révolution française et la famille* (Paris, PUF, 1978), p. 83.

78. Schnapper, "Liberty," p. 330. Garaud, *Révolution*, p. 86.

79. Hunt, *Politics*, pp. 29–32, 34–35.

80. DIII 256 (4), dossier 4, nos. 4, 57. See also F7 4775 (45), dossier Denis Vian, letter of 29 Thermidor Year III.

81. Mona Ozouf, *La Fête révolutionnaire, 1789–1799* (Paris, Gallimard, 1976), p. 315. John Hall Stewart, *A Documentary Survey of the French Revolution* (New York, Macmillan, 1951), p. 574. See also Jean Bart, "La Famille bourgeoise, héritière de la Révolution?" in Lévy *L'Enfant*, pp. 357–372 (pp. 362–363).

82. David G. Troyansky, *Old Age in the Old Regime* (Ithaca, Cornell U.P., 1989), pp. 206, 209–213. Alison Patrick, *The Men of the First French Republic* (Baltimore and London, Johns Hopkins U.P., 1972), pp. 247–248. Constitution of the Year III, in Stewart, *Documentary Survey*, pp. 572–612, articles 74, 83, 134, 148, 175. Schnapper, "Liberté," p. 339. See also Lyons, *France,* pp. 18–19.

83. Clive H. Church, *Revolution and Red Tape: The French Ministerial Bureaucracy, 1770–1850* (Oxford, Clarendon, 1981), pp. 30, 94.

84. Over a third of justices of the peace and *commissaires de police* from 1792 to early 1795 went into positions to which they were appointed by government; Richard Andrews, "Social Structures, Political Elites, and Ideology in Revolutionary Paris, 1792–1794: A Critical Evaluation of Albert Soboul's *Les Sans-culottes parisiens en l'an II,*" *Journal of Social History* 19 (1985–1986): 71–112 (p. 99).

85. Andrews, "Réflexions," pp. 110–111.

9. Commerce, Science, Administration

1. F7 4794, cartes de sûreté, 4e compagnie. XXXIII 602, marriage contract Salleron-Salleron, 14 May 1774.
2. Y11207B, 14 Nov. 1789. Y11207A, 17 Feb. 1789. Arch.P. D12 U1 36, *scellé* Planche, 25 Nov. 1791. XVIII 884, inventory Derenusson, 5 June 1789.
3. Y11207A, 17 Feb. 1789.
4. Etienne Charavay, *Assemblée électorale de Paris, 18 novembre 1790–15 juin 1791* (Paris, Quantin, 1890), p. 31. VI 863, inventory Jouanin, 5 Nov. 1789.
5. Arch.P. D12 U1 48, no. 375, 25 Nivôse Year XIII, Hossart and Planche against Salleron brothers. F20 255, Twelfth Arrondissement. Parent-Duchâtelet, "Recherches" (cited in chap. 6 n. 16), p. 64.
6. Arch.P. D12 U1 36, *scellé* Planche, 25 Nov. 1791. D12 U1 39, *avis de parents* Planche, 24 Dec. 1791. D12 U1 48, no. 375, *citation* Salleron, 25 Nivôse Year XIII.
7. Parent-Duchâtelet, "Recherches." Louis Bergeron, *Banquiers, négociants, et manufacturiers parisiens du Directoire à l'Empire,* 2 vols. (Lille, Atelier de reproduction des thèses de l'Université de Lille III, 1975; republished in 1 vol., Paris, EHESS, 1978), 1:159 n. 95. Arch.P. DQ7 3955, fol. 14.
8. Jean Boussoulade, "Soeurs de charité et comités de bienfaisance des faubourgs Saint Marcel et Saint Antoine (septembre 1793–mai 1794)," *Annales historiques de la Révolution française,* no. 200 (April–June 1970): 350–374 (pp. 352, 354). Olwen Hufton, *Women and the Limits of Citizenship in the French Revolution* (U. of Toronto Press, 1992), pp. 84–85.
9. W547, no. 52, deposition of 7 Messidor Year III (26 June 1795). *Almanach impérial,* 1810. F1bII Seine 9, "Renouvellement de 1816," note to minister of the interior, 20 Mar. 1816. S. Dupain, *La Bièvre: Nouvelles recherches historiques* (Paris, Champion, 1886), p. 138. Archives of Saint Médard, "Registre des délibérations," fol. 1v (20 Nov. 1803). F1bII Seine 9, no. 37, mayors and deputy mayors, 1812.
10. XXVII 772, inventory Dangin, 29 Apr. 1843. XVII 1120, 7 Sept. 1809. F1bII Seine 1812. Arch.P. DQ8 1002, no. 45. Capital value of real estate is calculated by multiplying estimated annual revenue by twenty. See Adeline Daumard, "Une Source d'histoire sociale: L'Enregistrement des mutations par décès. Le XIIe arrondissement de Paris en 1820 et 1847," *Revue d'histoire économique et sociale* 35 (1957): pp. 52–78. On economic crisis, Georges and Hubert Bourgin, *Le Régime de l'industrie en France de 1814 à 1830,* 2 vols. (Paris, Picard, 1912–1941), 2:272–297.
11. *Almanach national,* 1810–1822. Archives of Saint Médard, "Registre des délibérations de la fabrique, 1803–1848." Bertrand Gille, *Le Conseil général des manufactures* (Paris, SEVPEN, 1961), p. xxvi. F9 658, Claude Salleron to minister of the interior, 12 Jan. 1814.

12. F9 658, candidates for legion commander. F9 671, mayor and deputy mayors of Twelfth Arrondissement to Maréchal de Reggio, n.d. [late 1818]. Minister of the interior to Maréchal de Reggio, 1 Feb. 1819. F9 670, Paris National Guard, Twelfth Legion, 1820.

13. F1bII Seine 9, appointments to Conseil général du département, 11 Apr. 1815. *Notes biographiques sur les membres des assemblées municipales parisiennes et des Conseils généraux de la Seine de 1800 à nos jours* (Paris, Commission des travaux historiques de la Ville de Paris, n.d.), p. 49. F9 670, Paris National Guard, Twelfth Legion, 1820. Arch.P. VD6 629, no. 2, "Liste des électeurs du septième collège de l'arrondissement électoral, 1828." Arch.P. DQ7 3955, fol. 14.

14. XXVII 772, inventory Dangin, 29 Apr. 1843. Arch.P. D31 U3 5, no. 44, *acte de société* Montessuy-Salleron, 23 Feb. 1811. LXXI 220, marriage contract Passy-Salleron, 16 Apr. 1821. Adeline Daumard, *La Bourgeoisie parisienne, 1815–1848* (Paris, SEVPEN, 1963), p. 150. Arch.P. VD6 629, no. 2, "Liste des électeurs," 1828.

15. Arch.P. VD 629, no. 2, "Liste des électeurs," 1828. CVIII 907, marriage contract Salleron-Marcellot, 10 Jan. 1809; *acte de société* Salleron-Bricogne, 16 June 1809. Dupain, *La Bièvre*, p. 174. Arch.P. 6 AZ 1292, "Discours de M. le Préfet de la Seine, 4 Nov. 1828." Arch.P. D12 U1 103, *citation* Marcellot, 21 Feb. 1826. See also Arch.P. VN4 56, sale of house, 26 and 28 Nov. 1860. AN, *Catalogue général des cartes, plans, et dessins d'architecture: Répertoire des plans cadastraux de Paris, côtes F31 3 à 72* (Paris, SEVPEN, 1969), rue de l'Oursine, rue Pascal.

16. I 715, *donations mutuelles* Bricogne-Salleron, 12 Sept. 1809. F20 255, Twelfth Arrondissement. F9 658, candidates for battalion commanders, 1814. Arch.P. VD6 629, no. 2, "Liste des électeurs," 1828.

17. F9 658, decree of 11 Jan. 1814; candidates for captain and lieutenant, 1814. Archives of Saint Médard, "Registre des délibérations," fols. 61, 62, 70v, 81, 93v. *Almanach royal*, 1830. F1dII S2, dossier Salleron.

18. XIX 944, marriage contract Cristy-Salleron, 28 July 1814.

19. Arch.P., reconstitution of old *état civil*. F1bII Seine 9, prefect to minister of the interior, 9 Dec. 1815; notes on mayors, n.d. [1815]; Renouvellement de 1816, note to minister, 20 Mar. 1816.

20. LXXI 220, marriage contract Passy-Salleron, 16 Apr. 1821.

21. Claude's wife came from the other side of the river and Joseph's from near Vitry, right outside the city. XIX 944, birth extract of André Cristy, 22 July 1814. Arch.P., Chambre de Commerce, Série I, 2.23, *Liste des notables-commerçants de la Ville de Paris, pour l'élection des juges au Tribunal de Commerce*, 1837. Arch.P. DQ7 3980, no. 557.

22. Arch.P. D31 U3 19, no. 522, *acte de société* Salleron-Passy, 27 Dec. 1821.

23. CVIII 907, *acte de société* Salleron-Bricogne, 16 June 1809.

24. Arch.P. DQ7 3980, no. 557. XLVII 591, marriage contract Gérardin-Salleron, 6 Aug. 1814.

25. Daumard, *Bourgeoisie parisienne,* p. 401. Jean-Pierre Bardet, *Rouen aux XVIIe et XVIIIe siècles,* 2 vols. (Paris, Société d'Edition d'enseignement supérieur, 1983), 1:258.

26. VI 863, inventory Jouanin, 5 Nov. 1789. Arch.P. DQ8, 1002, nos. 45, 58. VI 886, constitution, 15 Ventôse Year II. XVII 1120, sale of house, 7 Sept. 1809.

27. CVIII 907, *acte de société,* 16 June 1809. Serge Chassagne makes the same observation regarding cotton manufacturers; *Le Coton et ses patrons: France, 1760–1840* (Paris, EHESS, 1991), p. 583.

28. Arch.P. D12 U1 46, no. 238, *citation,* 25 Frimaire Year XII. D31 U3 5, no. 44, *acte de société* Montessuy-Salleron, 23 Feb. 1811, and D31 U3 19, no. 522, *acte de société* Salleron-Passy. See also David Garrioch, "House Names, Shop Signs, and Social Organization in Western European Cities, 1500–1900," *Urban History* 21 (1994): 18–46, and Daumard, *Bourgeoisie parisienne,* pp. 459–474.

29. Arch.P. D12 U1 49, no. 452. F7* 2519, fol. 1v. BN Vp 29832, *Liste des notables commerçants de la Ville de Paris, pour l'élection des juges du Tribunal de Commerce* (1810). Arch.P. D31 U3 25, no. 543. Jean Tulard, *Paris et son administration (1800–1830)* (Paris, Ville de Paris, Commission des travaux historiques, 1976), p. 236 n. 29.

30. Geneviève Aclocque, *Un Défenseur du roi, André-Arnoult Aclocque, commandant général de la garde nationale parisienne, 1748–1802* (Paris, A. and J. Picard, 1947), pp. 165–179. Paul Robiquet, *Le Personnel municipal de Paris pendant la Révolution,* 2 vols. (Paris, Jouaust, 1890), 1:87.

31. XXVIII 613, 1 and 20 Nivôse Year XII. XXVIII 671, 7 July 1812. Archives Saint Médard, register of deliberations, 1825, fol. 93v.

32. Daumard, *Bourgeoisie parisienne,* esp. pp. 291–300, 386, 395. Bergeron, *Banquiers.* Serge Chassagne, *Oberkampf, un entrepreneur capitaliste au Siècle des Lumières* (Paris, Aubier-Montaigne, 1980), and *Le Coton.* See also careers of Jean Hermann Nast and of Christophe Dihl; Régine de Plinval de Guillebon, *La Porcelaine à Paris sous le Consulat et l'Empire* (Paris, Arts et métiers graphiques, 1985), pp. 69–72, 130–137.

33. Archives of Saint Médard, register of deliberations, 1825 fols. 93v, 96, 96v.

34. Isidore Geoffroy-Saint-Hilaire, *Vie, travaux, et doctrine scientifique d'Etienne Geoffrey Saint-Hilaire, par son fils* (Paris, Bertrand, 1847), pp. 1–6.

35. Ibid. pp. 7–10, 20–25, 30, 39, 71–83, 170, 190. Théophile Cahn, *La Vie et l'oeuvre d'Etienne Geoffroy Saint-Hilaire* (Paris, PUF, 1962), p. 59.

36. CXXI 847, inventory Geoffroy-Saint-Hilaire, 9 Sept. 1844. Cahn, *Geoffroy Saint-Hilaire* p. 55. F1bII Seine 9, no. 120, Buchère to minister of the

interior, n.d. [c. 1813]. AFIV 1427, *Liste des 60 plus imposés du Département de la Seine,* n.p., Year XIII.

37. CXXI 847, 9 Sept. 1844. See F1bII Seine 9, no. 28, Maury to [minister of the interior], 11 Feb. 1812.

38. CXXI 847, inventory Geoffroy-Saint-Hilaire, 9 Sept. 1844.

39. XLI 895, marriage contract Blacque–Geoffroy-Saint-Hilaire, 18 Jan. 1830. XLI 895, *mainlevée* Blacque, 18 Jan. 1830. Raymonde Monnier, *Le Faubourg Saint Antoine* (Paris, Société des Etudes Robespierristes, 1981), p. 223.

40. CXXI 847, inventory, 9 Sept. 1844. Adeline Daumard, *Les Bourgeois et la bourgeoisie en France depuis 1815* (Paris, Aubier, 1987), p. 99.

41. Geoffroy-Saint-Hilaire, pp. 6–23, 199–200, 389. Maurice Genty, *L'Apprentissage de la citoyenneté Paris, 1789–1795* (Paris, Messidor/Editions sociales, 1987), p. 127. Frédéric Bluche, "Un Aspect de la vie politique à Paris: Le Plébiscite des cent-jours," *Bulletin de la Société de l'histoire de Paris et de l'Ile de France* 98 (1971): 207–219 (p. 212). Toby Appel, *The Cuvier-Geoffroy Debate,* (Oxford, Oxford U.P., 1987) p. 166.

42. Archives of Saint Médard, "Registre des délibérations," fol. 109v. F9 670, officers of National Guard, 1820, Twelfth Legion. O3 1515, report to king on Des Rotours, 1816.

43. O3 896, Maison du Roi, payment of employees, 1814–1816. O3 1515, letter of appointment, 4 May 1816; Des Rotours to Comte de Pradel, 4 May 1816; report on Des Rotours, 5 May 1816.

44. O3 1515, reports to *directeur général,* 6 May, 10 Oct. 1816; *intendant* of Garde Meuble to Pradel, 20 July 1816.

45. O3 1515, Des Rotours to Pradel, 21 May, 22 Aug., 29 Aug. 1816. F9 671, nomination of officers, 1817, Twelfth Legion.

46. O3 1515, Des Rotours to Pradel, 21 May, 14 Oct. 1816.

47. Marcel Marion, *Dictionnaire des institutions de la France aux XVIIe et XVIIIe siècles* (Paris, Picard, 1923), "Chevalier."

48. F9 670, list of officers, 1820, Twelfth Legion.

49. F9 681, dossier on incident of 1826, report of D'Agier.

50. Tax paid known for nine of twenty-two merchants and manufacturers; Arch.P. VD6 629, no. 2, electoral list for seventh college. I have used Adeline Daumard's multiplier of 17 to calculate approximate annual income. Daumard, "La Hiérarchie des biens et des positions," in Fernand Braudel and Ernest Labrousse, eds., *Histoire économique et sociale de la France,* vol. 3, *L'Avènement de l'ère industrielle (1789–années 1880)* (Paris, PUF, 1976), cited in Thomas D. and Martha W. Beck, *French Notables: Reflections of Industrialization and Regionalism* (New York, Peter Lang, 1987), p. 77. On others, Arch.P. D11 U3 49, 1074, 14 Mar. 1814.

51. Director of the Gobelins earned 6,000 francs a year, professors about the

same. O3 1515, report on salary of director of Gobelins, to director of Maison du Roi, 6 May 1816. On Geoffroy-Saint-Hilaire, Daumard, *Bourgeois et la bourgeoisie*, p. 99. On Laugier, F9 670, National Guard, Twelfth Legion, Fourth Company.

52. Jean Tulard, "Problèmes sociaux de la France impériale," *Revue d'histoire moderne et contemporaine* 17 (1970): 639–663 (p. 650).

53. The blanket maker Etienne Albinet employed 400 workers in 1807, though only about 80 locally. F20 255, Twelfth Arrondissement. G. and H. Bourgin, *Régime de l'industrie* 2:291–292.

54. AAP, nouvelle série 96, première liasse, register 2, "Registre des séances du Bureau de Bienfaisance de la Division du Finistère," 4 Jan. 1810–20 June 1816.

55. On Cabouret, F7* 2517, fols. 27v, 107, 233v; DIII 264, no. 2, testimony of Deliens, 25 June 1792; *Almanach national*, Year IV. On Belle, F7* 1517, fols. 2, 21v, 216v, and *Almanach national* 1792, 1793, Year VII; F1bII Seine 25.

56. Archives of Saint Médard, register of deliberations, fol. 85v. On Duchemin, Arch.P. état civil reconstitué; DQ18 85, rue Censier no. 33; DQ7 3955, no. 127.

57. F9 658, Twelfth Legion. F9 670, Twelfth Legion.

58. Jean Dhombres, "Savants en politique, politique des savants: Les Expériences de la Révolution française," in Gisèle Van de Vyver and Jacques Reisse, eds., *Les Savants et la politique à la fin du XVIIIe siècle* (Brussels, Editions of U. of Brussels, 1991), pp. 23–41. Owen Connelly, ed., *Historical Dictionary of Napoleonic France, 1799–1815* (Westport, Conn., Greenwood Press, 1985), "Berthollet," "Fourcroy." See also Antoine Léon, "Promesses et ambiguités de l'oeuvre d'enseignement technique en France, de 1800 à 1815," *Revue d'histoire moderne et contemporaine* 17 (1970): 846–859. William A. Smeaton, *Fourcroy, Chemist and Revolutionary* (London, Heffer, 1962), pp. 1, 39–45. Marcel Reinhard, *Nouvelle histoire de Paris: La Révolution* (Paris, Hachette, 1971), pp. 382–387. Erwin H. Ackerknecht, *Medicine at the Paris Hospital, 1794–1848* (Baltimore, Johns Hopkins U.P., 1967), pp. 37–38.

59. Martyn Lyons, *France under the Directory* (Cambridge U.P., 1975), p. 121. Jean Bernard Robert, "L'Itinéraire d'un savant: Joseph Fourier," in Van de Vyver and Reisse, *Les Savants*, pp. 57–68. F1bII Seine 9, no. 4, presidents of cantonal assemblies, 1812. See also career of Bernardin de Saint-Pierre, who rose through a combination of administrative and educational activity. Roddey Reid, *Families in Jeopardy: Regulating the Social Body in France, 1750–1910* (Stanford U.P., 1993), p. 103.

60. Bergeron, *Banquiers*, 1:94–95; Connelly, *Historical Dictionary*, "Chaptal."

61. Boguslaw Lesnodorski, "The State of the Jacobin Dictatorship: Theory and

Reality," in Jaroslaw Pelenski, ed., *The American and European Revolutions, 1776–1848: Sociopolitical and Ideological Aspects* (Iowa City, U. of Iowa Press, 1980), pp. 148–181 (p. 164). Robert Forster, "The French Revolution and the 'New' Elite," ibid., pp. 182–207 (p. 190). Clive H. Church, *Revolution and Red Tape: The French Ministerial Bureaucracy, 1770–1850* (Oxford, Clarendon, 1981), pp. 72, 94, 267–270.

62. Jean-Paul Bertaud, *La France de Napoléon* (Paris, Messidor/Editions sociales, 1987), pp. 140–141. Jean Tulard, "Problèmes sociaux de la France napoléonienne," *Annales historiques de la Révolution française,* no. 199 (1970): 135–160 (p. 149). AF IV 1427. F1bII Seine 9, no. 37, mayors and deputies, 1812. Daumard, *Bourgeoisie parisienne,* p. 537.

63. Nicole Célestin, "Le Notariat parisien sous l'Empire," *Revue d'histoire moderne et contemporaine* 17 (1970): 694–708 (p. 704 n. 4).

64. Paul Butel, "Revolution and the Urban Economy: Maritime Cities and Continental Cities," in Alan Forest and Peter Jones, eds., *Reshaping France: Town, Country, and Region during the French Revolution* (Manchester, Manchester U.P., 1991), pp. 37–51 (pp. 47–48).

65. For other examples, Daumard, *Bourgeoisie parisienne,* pp. 292–297; Tulard, *Paris,* p. 417. Raymonde Monnier concludes that there was little social mobility but uses "mobility" to mean movement from one category into another (merchant to noble, for instance), and in fact gives many examples of individuals who prospered greatly. Furthermore, she mostly compares the position of notables under the Empire with their position during the Revolution, rather than the Old Regime. Thus she mentions the appearance of schoolmasters, but does not see it as significant. Nor does she consider movement between quarters significant. *Faubourg Saint Antoine,* pp. 107, 177–217, 279–286.

66. On Ouvrard, Bergeron, *Banquiers,* 2:408–415, 438; Albert Soboul, *Dictionnaire historique de la Révolution française* (Paris, PUF, 1989), pp. 802–803. For other examples, Bergeron, *Banquiers,* chap. 2. On fortunes from supplying army, ibid., vol. 2 pp. 395–427. On benefits from *biens nationaux,* Daumard, *Bourgeoisie parisienne,* pp. 300–302.

67. Ibid., *Bourgeoisie parisienne,* pp. 291, 297.

10. The Tutelage of the State

1. Adeline Daumard, *La Bourgeoisie parisienne, 1815–1848* (Paris, SEVPEN, 1963), pp. 18, 65–67.

2. Pamela Pilbeam, *The Middle Classes in Europe, 1789–1914* (Chicago, Lyceum Books, 1990), p. 122.

3. F19 4145, prefect of Seine to minister for religious affairs, 3 Oct. 1810. Ordinance of archbishop of Paris, 21 July 1803; imperial decrees of 26 July

1803 and 30 Dec. 1809. Félix Ponteil, *Les Institutions de la France de 1814 à 1870* (Paris, PUF, 1966), pp. 110–112. Archives of Saint Médard, register of deliberations, 1803–1848, fols. 1, 12, 15, 23, 35v-36, 43, 46. F3II Seine 23, decree of 23 May 1806; requests for authorization to accept bequests for several parishes, 1814. Extract from deliberations of vestry, Saint Germain l'Auxerrois, 24 May 1813.

4. AAP, nouvelle série, no. 96, première liasse, register 2, 29 Mar. 1810. Jacques Godechot, *Les Institutions de la France sous la Révolution et l'Empire* (Paris, PUF, 1951), pp. 606–607. Ponteil, *Institutions*, pp. 98–101.

5. P. H. J. Allard, *Annuaire administratif et statistique du département de la Seine pour l'an XIII/1805* (Paris, 1805), pp. 23–25, 33, 179–185, 196–197. Godechot, *Institutions*, p. 497. See also Jean Tulard, *Nouvelle histoire de Paris: Le Consulat et l'Empire* (Paris, Hachette, [1970]), pp. 171–174.

6. Tulard, *Nouvelle histoire*, pp. 171–174; "Problèmes sociaux de la France napoléonienne," *Annales historiques de la Révolution française*, no. 199 (1970): 135–160 (pp. 146–147).

7. Jean Yves Coppolani, *Les Elections en France à l'époque napoléonienne* (Paris, Albatros, 1980), pp. 69–74, 223–225. F1bII Seine 8, candidates for justice of the peace, 1807.

8. Daumard, *Bourgeoisie parisienne*, p. 532. Ponteil, *Institutions* p. 30; Jean Tulard, *Paris et son administration (1800–1830)*, (Paris, Ville de Paris, Commission des travaux historiques, 1976), p. 372.

9. Ponteil, *Institutions*, p. 20. F1cIII Seine 7, elections, 1818–1819. Daumard, *Bourgeoisie parisienne*, pp. 32–33.

10. Allard, *Annuaire*, pp. 78, 261. Arch.P. VD4 472, poster announcing elections, Year VIII. Arch.P. VD4 412, prefect of Seine to mayor of Sixth Arrondissement, 16 Mar. 1808. F3II Seine 50, *assemblées de commerce*, 1802–1807.

11. Allard, *Annuaire*, pp. 38, 66. See reports on candidates for mayor, F1bII Seine 9 and F1bII Seine 25; on *commissaires de police*, F7 9866 and F7 9867.

12. Tulard, *Paris*, p. 153; and *Nouvelle histoire de Paris*, p. 364. F9 658, garde nationale, 1814, "Organisation de la Garde nationale," approved 27 Dec. 1813.

13. See the fuss in 1826 when the colonel of the Twelfth Legion disobeyed this rule: F9 681, Garde nationale, Douzième Légion, 1826.

14. F1bII Seine 26, quoted in Daumard, *Bourgeoisie parisienne*, pp. 147–148.

15. F1bII Seine 25, "Etat nominatif des membres des administrations municipales," Year VII. Report on Cartier quoted in Daumard, *Bourgeoisie parisienne*, p. 150. On importance of influence, ibid., p. 536.

16. Arch.P. DV2, Fabriques, prefect of Seine to sub-prefect of Saint Denis, 25 Aug. 1810.

17. F1bII Seine 9, no. 37, mayors and deputy mayors, 1812.

18. Louis Bergeron, *Banquiers, négociants, et manufacturiers parisiens du Directoire à l'Empire,* 2 vols. (Lille, Atelier de reproduction des thèses de l'Université de Lille III, 1975; republished in 1 vol., Paris, EHESS, 1978), 1:218–320.

19. Nicole Célestin, "Le Notariat parisien sous l'Empire," *Revue d'histoire moderne et contemporaine* 17 (1970): 694–708 (p. 697).

20. Daumard, *Bourgeoisie parisienne,* p. 148.

21. AFIV 1427, minutes of Commission des Finances, 23 Ventôse Year XIII.

22. F9 658, candidates for legion and battalion commanders, Twelfth Arrondissement, 1814.

23. F1bII Seine 9, candidates, 1812.

24. F9 658, candidates for legion and battalion commander, Sixth and Twelfth Arrondissements, 1814.

25. F1bII Seine 9, Buchère to minister of the interior, n.d. [c. 1813]. Many requests for positions, from the Convention to the July Monarchy, are in series F1dII. The importance of local influence of family is stressed in Pilbeam, *Middle Classes in Europe,* p. 122.

26. Jacques Gélis, "L'Enfant et l'évolution de la conception de la vie sous la Révolution," in Marie-Françoise Lévy, ed., *L'Enfant, la famille, et la Révolution,* ([Paris], Olivier Orban, 1990), pp. 69–77 (p. 70). Mona Ozouf, *La Fête révolutionnaire, 1789–1799* (Paris, Gallimard, 1976), p. 315. See also condemnation of the "selfish" celibate by Antoine Caillot, *Mémoires pour servir à l'histoire des moeurs et usages des Français* (Geneva, Slatkine Reprints, 1976; 1st pub., 2 vols., Paris, Dauvin, 1827), 2:69–71.

27. F1bII Seine 9, candidates, 1812.

28. Daumard, *Bourgeoisie parisienne,* p. 293.

29. F1dII G11, dossier Guillemart (1807). F1dII V3, dossier Vaure (1822). F1dII D12, dossier Deslauriers.

30. Allard, *Annuaire,* p. 33. F3II Seine 51. See Tulard, *Nouvelle histoire,* p. 171.

31. F1bII Seine 8, "Liste des fonctionnaires du département de la Seine," n.d. [1808]. F1cIII Seine 6, proceedings of fourth electoral college of the Seine, 1816. F1cIII Seine 7, elections of 1818–1819, candidates for presidents and vice-presidents of electoral college, 1818.

32. Arch.P. VD4 412, prefect of Seine to mayor of Sixth Arrondissement, 16 Mar. 1808. See also F3II Seine 50, prefect of Seine to mayor of Tenth Arrondissement, 13 June 1807.

33. F20 255. F9 681, Garde nationale, Douzième Légion, dossier Raffelin. AAP, nouvelle série 96, première liasse, "Registres du Bureau de bienfaisance de la Division du Finistère, 4 janvier 1810–20 juin 1816," 29 Mar. 1810, 9 Apr. 1812, 13 May 1813. Allard, *Annuaire,* p. 65. Daumard, *Bourgeoisie parisienne,* pp. 540–541. Tulard, *Paris,* pp. 100–103.

34. Tulard, *Paris,* p. 100.
35. Jean-Paul Bertaud, *La France de Napoléon* (Paris, Messidor/Editions socialies, 1987), p. 141. F1bII Seine 9, mayors and deputy mayors, 1812; candidates for mayor and deputy mayor, 1812. See also Daumard, *Bourgeoisie parisienne,* pp. 536–537.
36. F1dII S2, dossier Saint Simon. Toby Appel, *The Cuvier-Geoffroy Debate* (Oxford, Oxford U.P., 1987), pp. 53, 59–65. O3 1515, Cuvier to Comte de Pradel, 22 Aug. 1816. For other examples, Daumard, *Bourgeoisie parisienne,* p. 342.
37. "Exposé de ce qui s'est passé au Cimetière de Saint Médard le 7 janvier 1807," in Paul Valet, "Le diacre Pâris et les convulsionnaires de Saint Médard," *Bulletin de la Montagne Sainte Geneviève et ses abords* 2 (1897–1898): 343–420 (pp. 391–394). For another highly colored account, BN Ms. fr., nouvelle acquisition 4264, fols. 99–106.
38. F1dII G11, dossier Guillaumot, letter of 19 Vendémiaire Year XI.
39. F13 979, letter of 18 Floréal Year XII. F1dII G11, dossier Guillaume, 12 Jan. 1815.
40. AAP, nouvelle série 96, première liasse, register 2, "Registres des séances du bureau de bienfaisance de la Division du Finistère," 25 Jan., 10 May, 7 June, 2 Aug., 20 Sept., 25 Oct., 13 Dec. 1810; 10 Jan., 30 May, 8 June, 30 Nov. 1811.
41. See portrait of Louis-Guillaume Ternaux in Tulard, *Nouvelle histoire,* p. 69.
42. DQ7 3955, fol. 14.
43. AFIV 1427, list of notables, Department of the Seine, Year XIII.
44. Quoted in Jean Tulard, "Problèmes sociaux de la France napoléonienne," *Annales historiques de la Révolution française,* no. 199 (1970): 135–160 (p. 149). Original source not indicated.
45. See illustration in Tulard, *Nouvelle histoire de Paris,* p. 170.
46. François Cottier to Dominique André, 24 Aug. 1809, quoted in Jean-Jacques Hémardinquer, "Une correspondance de banquiers parisiens (1808–1815): Aspects socio-politiques," *Revue d'histoire moderne et contemporaine* 17 (1970): 514–539 (p. 522).
47. Tulard, *Nouvelle histoire,* pp. 93–94; see photograph of *livret* on p. 91, where employer's comment is clearly legible. Bertaud, *La France de Napoléon,* p. 49.
48. F1dII G11, dossier Guilbert.
49. O3 1515, Des Rotours to Comte de Pradel, 21 May 1816.
50. Daumard, *Bourgeoisie parisienne,* pp. 357–360. Godechot, *Institutions,* pp. 597–599. Marcel Garaud, *La Révolution française et la famille* (Paris, PUF, 1978), pp. 172–174. Barbara Corrado Pope, "Revolution and Retreat: Upper-Class French Women after 1789," in Carol R. Berkin and Clara M.

Lovett, eds., *Women, War, and Revolution* (New York, Holmes and Meier, 1980), pp. 215–232 (p. 220).

51. Daumard, *Bourgeoisie parisienne*, pp. 368–369. Daumard nevertheless gives examples of widows who took over quite large businesses; ibid., pp. 372–373. On ideology of domesticity, Geneviève Fraisse, *Muse de la Raison: La Démocratie exclusive et la différence des sexes* (Paris, Alinea, 1989); Margaret Darrow, "French Noblewomen and the New Domesticity, 1750–1850," *Feminist Studies* 5 (1979): 41–65; Susan Grogan, *French Socialism and Sexual Difference* (Basingstoke, Macmillan, 1992), esp. pp. 1–19. Barbara Corrado Pope, "Angels in the Devil's Workshop: Leisured and Charitable Women in Nineteenth-Century England and France," in Renate Bridenthal and Claudia Koonz, eds., *Becoming Visible: Women in European History* (Boston, Houghton Mifflin, 1977), pp. 296–324 (pp. 302–303).

52. Daumard, *Bourgeoisie parisienne*, p. 177. For other examples, pp. 459–466; Bergeron, *Banquiers*, 1:60; Serge Chassagne, *Oberkampf, un entrepreneur capitaliste au Siècle des Lumières* (Paris, Aubier-Montaigne, 1980), p. 281.

53. Victor Fournel, *Ce qu'on voit dans les rues de Paris* (Paris, Delahaye, 1858), p. 289.

54. David Garrioch, "House Names, Shop Signs, and Social Organization in Western European Cities, 1500–1900," *Urban History* 21 (1994): 18–46.

55. Darrow, "Noblewomen." Pope, "Revolution and Retreat," pp. 228–229. Grogan, *French Socialism*, pp. 4–5.

56. Fraisse, *Muse de la Raison*, pp. 72–95. Yvonne Knibiehler, "Les Médecins et la 'nature féminine' au temps du Code Civil," *Annales: ESC* 31 (1976): 824–845 (pp. 828–835). For valuable observations on linking of women's sexuality with domesticity and use of the middle-class family as a model for class relationships in England, Sonya O. Rose, *Limited Livelihoods: Gender and Class in Nineteenth-Century England* (Berkeley, U. of California Press, 1992), esp. pp. 39–45, 186–187.

57. Daumard, *Bourgeoisie parisienne*, p. 337. Figures for the part of Paris that included the Faubourg Saint Marcel were slightly lower; Adeline Daumard, "Une Source d'histoire sociale: L'Enregistrement des mutations par décès. Le XIIe arrondissement de Paris en 1820 et 1847," *Revue d'histoire économique et sociale* 35 (1957): 52–78.

58. XXVIII 613, marriage contract, 20 Nivôse Year XII.

59. Daumard, *Bourgeoisie parisienne*, pp. 527–528. Pope, "Angels," *Rapports et comptes rendus de la Société philanthropique de Paris, pendant l'année 1807* (Paris, Baron, 1808), report of M. du Pont de Nemours, 31 Jan. 1808; and list of subscribers, pp. 82, 88, 89. A similar body was the Société pour l'enseignement secondaire, founded 1815 and supported by liberal bourgeois such as Guizot, Delessert, and Périer.

60. Stuart Woolf, "The Société de charité maternelle, 1788–1815," in Jonathan Barry and Colin Jones, eds., *Medicine and Charity before the Welfare State* (London, Routledge, 1991), pp. 98–112 (pp. 102–104).

61. F1dII G11, dossier Guillemart, 3 Dec. 1807. F7 9866, dossier Correspondance 1807–1823, Twelfth Arrondissement, Marrigues.

Conclusion

1. Alan B. Spitzer, *The French Generation of 1820* (Princeton, Princeton U. Press, 1987), p. 57.

2. Adeline Daumard, *La Bourgeoisie parisienne, 1815–1848* (Paris, SEVPEN, 1963), pp. 564–565. Spitzer, *Generation of 1820*, pp. 55–70. Jean-Claude Caron, *Générations romantiques: Les Etudiants de Paris et le quartier latin (1814–1851)* (Paris, Armand Colin, 1991), pp. 239–247.

3. On *lycées*, Spitzer, *Generation of 1820*, pp. 19–20. Caron, *Générations romantiques*, pp. 272, 284; François Furet and Denis Richet, *La Révolution française* (Paris, Fayard, 1965), pp. 468–9. On Restoration historians: Douglas Johnson, *Guizot: Aspects of French History* (London, Routledge and Kegan Paul, 1963), pp. 75, 320–376; Peter McPhee, *A Social History of France, 1780–1880* (London and New York, Routledge, 1992), p. 114; Eric Hobsbawm, *Echoes of the Marseillaise* (London, Verso, 1990), p. 24. The idea of a middle class defining itself through particular events is developed for England by Catherine Hall in "Gender and Working-Class Culture," in Harvey J. Kaye and Keith McClelland, *E. P. Thompson: Critical Perspectives* (Oxford, Polity, 1990), esp. p. 94.

4. Daumard, *Bourgeoisie parisienne*, pp. 565–569. See also Caron, *Générations romantiques*, p. 269.

5. Spitzer, *Generation of 1820*, pp. 25, 239–248. Caron, *Générations romantiques*, pp. 266–267.

6. Daumard, *Bourgeoisie parisienne*, pp. 571–575, 623–633; "Progrès et prise de conscience des classes moyennes," in Fernand Braudel and Ernest Labrousse, eds., *Histoire économique et sociale de la France*, 4 vols. (Paris, PUF, 1976–1982), 3:897–929 (p. 926). Sherman Kent, *The Election of 1827 in France* (Cambridge, Harvard U.P., 1975), pp. 5–32, 80–129. On caucus, p. 125. David H. Pinkney, *The French Revolution of 1830* (Princeton, Princeton U.P., 1972), pp. 32, 55–57. Jean Louis Bory, *La Révolution de Juillet* (Paris, Gallimard, 1972), pp. 178, 185.

7. Joseph di Corcia, "*Bourgeois, bourgeoisie, bourgeois de Paris* from the Eleventh to the Eighteenth Century," *Journal of Modern History* 50 (1978): 207–233.

8. Robert Descimon, "Paris on the Eve of Saint Bartholomew: Taxation, Privilege, and Social Geography," in Philip Benedict, ed., *Cities and Social*

Change in Early Modern France (London, Routledge, 1989), pp. 69–104, (pp. 91, 101).

9. F. W. Kent, *Household and Lineage in Renaissance Florence* (Princeton, Princeton U.P., 1978).

10. Yves-Marie Bercé, *Fête et révolte* (Paris, Hachette, 1976), esp. pp. 118–125. Nora Temple, "Municipal Elections and Municipal Oligarchies in Eighteenth-Century France," in John F. Bosher, ed., *French Government and Society, 1500–1850* (London, Athlone Press 1973), pp. 70–91. Lynn A. Hunt, *Revolution and Urban Politics in Provincial France* (Stanford, Stanford U.P., 1978), chap. 2.

11. Orest Ranum, *Paris in the Age of Absolutism* (Bloomington and London, Indiana U.P., 1979; 1st pub. 1968), pp. 51–67. Leon Bernard, *The Emerging City: Paris in the Age of Louis XIV* (Durham, N.C., Duke U.P., 1970), pp. 40–46. Marc Chassaigne, *La Lieutenance générale de police de Paris* (Paris, A. Rousseau, 1906); Alan Williams, *The Police of Paris,* (Baton Rouge, Louisiana State U.P., 1979), chap. 2. Robert Descimon slightly modifies this picture, arguing that the Hôtel de Ville actually cut itself off from the bourgeois notables; "L'Echevinage parisien sous Henri IV (1594–1609); Autonomie urbaine, conflits politiques et exclusives sociales," in Neithard Bulst and J.-P. Genet, eds., *La Ville, la bourgeoisie, et la genèse de l'état moderne* (Paris, Editions du CNRS, 1988), pp. 113–150.

12. Robert Descimon, "Contrôle de l'espace parisien" (papers presented to Denis Richet's seminar at the Ecole des Hautes Etudes en Sciences Sociales, Paris), Nov.–Dec. 1978). Chassaigne, *Lieutenance générale,* p. 26. Jean-Pierre Babelon, *Nouvelle histoire de Paris: Paris au XVIe siècle* (Paris, Hachette, 1986), pp. 217, 274–277.

13. Georges Picot, "Recherches sur les quartiniers, cinquanteniers, et dixainiers de la ville de Paris," *Mémoires de la société de l'histoire de Paris et de l'Ile de France* 1 (1875): 132–166. Bernard, *Emerging City,* pp. 31–32, 53–55. Descimon, "Paris on the Eve of Saint Bartholomew," p. 75.

14. Descimon, "Contrôle," 29 Nov. 1978.

15. Jean Chagniot, *Paris et l'armée au XVIIIe siècle* (Paris, Economica, 1985), pp. 77, 84, and *Nouvelle histoire de Paris: La Révolution* (Paris, Hachette, 1988), pp. 94–95.

16. Chagniot, *Paris,* pp. 85–162.

17. Ranum, *Paris,* pp. 240–241. Marcel Marion, *Dictionnaire des institutions de la France aux XVIIe et XVIIIe siècles* (Paris, Picard, 1923), "Hôpital." Bernard, *Emerging City,* p. 229.

18. Ranum, *Paris,* pp. 179–180. Bernard, *Emerging City,* pp. 110–111. Marion, *Dictionnaire,* "Corporation." Alfred Franklin, *Dictionnaire historique des arts, métiers, et professions exercés dans Paris depuis le treizième siècle* (Paris, H. Welter 1906), pp. 208, 290–291. XVII 420, 29 Mar. 1690.

19. Marion, *Dictionnaire,* "Capitation." Franklin, *Dictionnaire,* "Jurés."
20. S1914, Déclaration du temporel, 1673.
21. Chassaigne, *Lieutenance générale,* p. 45.
22. Maarten Ultee, *The Abbey of Saint Germain des Prés in the Seventeenth Century* (New Haven, Yale U.P., 1981), pp. 176–180.
23. Bernard, *Emerging City,* pp. 46–47.
24. Z2 3699, register of court proceedings, Bailliage Saint Marcel, 10 Apr. 1781–5 Jan. 1790.
25. LL581, deliberations of Chapter of Saint Marcel, 1760–1790, fols. 171, 211v. On projected move, J. Meuret, *Le Chapitre de Notre-Dame de Paris en 1790* (Paris, Picard, n.d. [1903]), pp. 38–39. For district's defense of chapter, LL581, fol. 228v, D XIX 53, fol. 114, 28 Apr. 1790.
26. Serge Chassaigne, ed., *Une Femme d'affaires au XVIIIe siècle* (Paris, Privat, 1981), pp. 22–23.
27. Louis Bonnassieux, *Conseil de Commerce et Bureau du Commerce* (Paris, Imprimerie nationale, 1900).
28. S. Dupain, *La Bièvre: Nouvelles recherches historiques* (Paris, Champion, 1886), p. 34.
29. Fernand Braudel, *The Wheels of Commerce,* trans. Siân Reynolds (New York, Harper and Row, 1982; 1st pub. Paris, Armand Colin, 1979), pp. 67–75.
30. Robert Descimon, "Contrôle," 29 Nov. 1978.
31. Ranum, *Paris,* pp. 63–65. David Garrioch, *Neighbourhood and Community in Paris* (Cambridge, Cambridge U.P., 1986), pp. 213–215. Alan Williams, *Police,* pp. 125–129.
32. Christopher Todd, "French Advertising in the Eighteenth Century," *Studies on Voltaire and the Eighteenth Century* 266 (1989): 513–547 (pp. 523–524). Michael Sonenscher, *Work and Wages: Natural Law, Politics, and the Eighteenth-Century French Trades* (Cambridge, Cambridge U.P., 1989), pp. 284–287. Steven L. Kaplan, "La Lutte pour le contrôle du marché du travail à Paris au XVIIIe siècle," *Revue d'histoire moderne et contemporaine* 36 (1989): 361–412.
33. Jeanne Pronteau, *Les Numérotages des maisons de Paris du XVe siècle à nos jours* (Paris, Ville de Paris, Commission des travaux historiques, 1966). Todd, "Advertising."
34. Annik Pardailhé-Galabrun, *The Birth of Intimacy: Privacy and Domestic Life in Early Modern Paris,* trans. Jocelyn Phelps (Oxford, Polity, 1991; 1st pub. Paris, PUF, 1986). Todd, "Advertising," pp. 523–524. Colin Jones, "Bourgeois Revolution Revivified: 1789 and Social Change," in Colin Lucas, ed., *Rewriting the French Revolution* (Oxford, Clarendon, 1991), pp. 69–118 (p. 92). David Garrioch, "House Names, Shop Signs, and Social Organization in Western European Cities, 1500–1900," *Urban History* 21

(1994): 18–46. Daniel Roche, *The People of Paris* (Leamington Spa, Berg, 1987), chap. 5; *The Culture of Clothing* (Oxford, Past and Present Publications, 1994). Cissie Fairchilds, "The Production and Marketing of Populuxe Goods in Eighteenth-Century Paris," in John Brewer and Roy Porter, eds., *Consumption and the World of Goods* (London and New York, Routledge, 1993), pp. 228–248.

35. Nicholas Green, *The Spectacle of Nature: Landscape and Bourgeois Culture in Nineteenth-century France* (Manchester, Manchester U.P., 1990), pp. 23–24. Jones, "Bourgeois Revolution," pp. 88–91.

36. S. D. Chapman and Serge Chassagne, *European Textile Printers in the Eighteenth Century* (London, Heinemann, 1981). Jean-Paul Poisson, "Constitutions et dissolutions des sociétés commerciales à Paris au XVIIIe siècle, d'après les registres du greffe de la juridiction consulaire," *Bulletin de la Société de l'histoire de Paris et de l'Ile de France* 101–102 (1974–1975): 103–107.

37. Green, *Spectacle of Nature*, pp. 22–25.

38. Garrioch, *Neighbourhood*, pp. 170–171, 173–180. For another example, Chassagne, *Une Femme d'affaires*, pp. 24–25.

39. John McManners, *Death and the Enlightenment* (Oxford, Oxford U.P., 1981), pp. 93–104. Kathryn Norberg, *Rich and Poor in Grenoble, 1600–1814* (Berkeley, U. of California Press, 1985), pp. 301, 303, suggests a decline in fear among Grenoblois, and links this with the reduction in charitable bequests.

40. Bernard, *Emerging City*, pp. 56–64.

41. William Doyle, "The Price of Offices in Prerevolutionary France," *Historical Journal* 27 (1984): 831–860. Descimon, "Paris," p. 101.

42. For instance, the debates over the *paulette;* Roland Mousnier, "Some Reasons for the Fronde: The Revolutionary Days in Paris in 1648," in P. J. Coventry, ed., *France in Crisis, 1620–1675* (London, Macmillan, 1977), 169–200 (pp. 185–186). Robin Briggs, *Early Modern France, 1560–1715* (Oxford, Oxford U.P., 1977), pp. 101–104, 124, 132–133.

43. BN Ms fr. 6680–6687.

44. Dale Van Kley, *The Damiens Affair and the Unraveling of the Ancien Régime, 1750–1770* (Princeton, Princeton U.P., 1984); "The Jansenist Constitutional Legacy in the French Prerevolution," in Keith Baker, ed., *The Political Culture of the Old Regime* (Oxford, Pergamon, 1987), pp. 169–201.

45. Van Kley, *Damiens Affair*, chap. 4.

46. Amos Hofman, "The Origins of the Theory of the *Philosophe* Conspiracy," *French History* 2 (1988): 153–172. Jeffrey Merrick, *The Desacralization of the French Monarchy in the Eighteenth Century* (Baton Rouge, Louisiana State U.P., 1990). The phrase "theological foundations of secular politics"

is taken from Bernard Plongeron, who explores this theme in *Théologie et politique au siècle des Lumières (1770–1820)* (Geneva, Droz, 1973).

47. Garrioch, *Neighbourhood,* pp. 175–180.

48. Annik Pardailhé-Galabrun, *La Naissance de l'intime* (Paris, PUF, 1986), pp. 404, 416. XVII 683, inventory Bouillerot, 25 May 1734. XXVIII 558, inventory Auffray, 11 Oct. 1792. Arch.P. D12 U1 36, *scellé* Auffray, 29 Sept. 1792.

49. Norman Hampson, *The Enlightenment* (Harmondsworth, Penguin, 1968), chap. 4.

50. Roche, *People of Paris,* pp. 75–76. Garrioch, *Neighbourhood,* chap. 5.

51. Green, *Spectacle of Nature,* pp. 12–41. Roche, *People of Paris,* chaps. 5, 6; *Culture of Clothing.*

52. Y11239, 21 Apr. 1752. Garrioch, *Neighbourhood,* pp. 72–77. See also Carol Duncan, "Happy Mothers and Other New Ideas in Eighteenth-Century French Art," in Norma Broude and Mary D. Garrard, eds., *Feminism and Art History: Questioning the Litany* (New York, Harper and Row, 1982), pp. 201–219 (esp. pp. 213–217).

53. Garrioch, *Neighbourhood,* pp. 72–77, 87.

54. Ba 64 A, dossier 4, no. 30. Thomas L. Haskell, "Capitalism and the Origins of the Humanitarian Sensibility," *American Historical Review* 90 (1985): 339–361, 547–566.

55. Steven L. Kaplan, *Bread, Politics, and Political Economy,* 2 vols. (The Hague, Martinus Nijhoff, 1976), 1:52–96.

56. Ba 64A, dossier 4, no. 23, cahier of Third Estate, District of Saint Victor; no. 30, Cahier of Third Estate, District of Saint Marcel. See also dossier 2, fols. 1–5, "Cahier du Sr de Rubigny de Berteval, tanneur et habitant du District de Saint Marcel," and [André Arnoult Aclocque], "Pétition particulière d'un habitant du district de Saint Marcel," in Charles-Louis Chassin, *Les Elections et les cahiers de Paris en 1789,* 4 vols. (Paris, Jouaust and Sigaux, 1888–1889), 3:172–173, 2:480–482.

57. Ba 64A, dossier 2, fols. 1–5, "Cahier du Sr de Rubigny de Berteval"; [Aclocque], "Pétition particulière." D XIX 53, fol. 114, 28 Apr. 1790. Steven L. Kaplan, "Religion, Subsistence, and Social Control: The Uses of Saint Genevieve," *Eighteenth Century Studies* 13 (1979–1980): 142–168 (p. 163).

58. Hans-Jürgen Lüsebrink, "L'Innocence persecutée et ses avocats: Rhétorique et impact public du discours 'sensible' dans la France du XVIIIe siècle," *Revue d'histoire moderne et contemporaine* 40 (1993): 86–101. Reid, *Families in Jeopardy* (Stanford, Stanford U.P., 1993), chap. 3, esp. pp. 116–118.

59. LL836, vestry of Sainte Marguerite, 1759–1788. LL837, elections, confraternity of the Saint Sacrement, 1738–1791. LL838, elections, confraternity of Sainte Marguerite, 1729–1790. Richard Andrews, "Réflexions sur la conjuration des Egaux," *Annales: ESC* 29 (1974): 73–106 (pp. 82–83);

"Social Structures, Political Elites, and Ideology in Revolutionary Paris, 1792–1794: A Critical Evaluation of Albert Soboul's *Les Sans-culottes parisiens en l'an II*," *Journal of Social History* 19 (1985–1986): 71–112 (p. 98).

60. Andrews, "Réflexions," p. 88. Colin Lucas, "Nobles, Bourgeois, and the Origins of the French Revolution," *Past and Present* 60 (Aug. 1973): 84–126.

61. Louis Bergeron, "The Revolution: Catastrophe or New Dawn for the French Economy," in Colin Lucas, ed., *Rewriting the French Revolution* (Oxford, Clarendon, 1991), pp. 119–131.

62. Serge Chassagne, *Le Coton et ses patrons: France, 1760–1840* (Paris, EHESS, 1991), pp. 108–109, 142, 286, 300.

63. Clive H. Church, *Revolution and Red Tape: The French Ministerial Bureaucracy, 1770–1850* (Oxford, Clarendon, 1981), p. 49.

64. Adeline Daumard, "Les Elèves de l'école polytechnique de 1815 à 1848," *Revue d'histoire moderne et contemporaine* 5 (1958): 226–234 (p. 227); Spitzer, *Generation of 1820*, pp. 19–20, 35–53, 263.

65. Not that the early nineteenth-century bourgeoisie were personally very religious. But they recognized that religion encouraged "the spirit of subordination of the inferior classes" (as the Société de persévérance in Montpellier put it in 1820); quoted in Roger Price, *A Social History of Nineteenth-Century France* (London, Hutchinson, 1989), p. 294.

66. See Chapter 8, and Geneviève Fraisse, *Muse de la Raison: La Démocratie exclusive et la différence des sexes,* (Paris, Alinea, 1989).

67. Fraisse, *Muse de la Raison*. Geneviève Fraisse, "Rupture révolutionnaire et l'histoire des femmes," in Danielle Haase-Dubosc and Eliane Viennot, eds., *Femmes et pouvoirs sous l'ancien régime* (Paris, Rivages, 1991), pp. 291–305.

68. Jacques Godechot, "Fragments des mémoires de Charles-Alexis Alexandre sur les journées révolutionnaires de 1791 et 1792," *Annales historiques de la Révolution française* 24 (1952): 113–251. See also Andrews, "Social Structures," p. 99.

69. Raymonde Monnier, *Un Bourgeois Sans-culotte: Le Général Santerre* (Paris, Publications de la Sorbonne, 1990), p. 73.

70. F7 4774 (42), dossier Mercier. Among his contacts, perhaps through the printery, was Nicolas Ruault; *Gazette d'un Parisien sous la Révolution* (Paris, Perrin, 1976), p. 319.

71. Andrews, "Réflexions," pp. 77–79. On Moroy, Albert Soboul and Raymonde Monnier, *Répertoire du personnel sectionnaire parisien en l'an II* (Paris, Publications de la Sorbonne, 1985), p. 526; Richard Cobb, *Les Armées révolutionnaires,* 2 vols. (Paris, Mouton, 1961), 2:880; F1bI 124–130, employees dismissed [Year IV]; DIII 256 (4), dossier 4, no. 34.

72. Etienne Charavay, *Assemblée électorale de Paris, 18 novembre 1790–15 juin 1791* (Paris, Quantin, 1890), pp. 539–542.

73. Church, *Revolution and Red Tape,* p. 36. Jean de La Monneraye, "Le Mariage dans la bourgeoisie parisienne (1789–1804)," in *Assemblée générale de la Commission centrale et des comités départementaux de la Commission de Recherche et de publication des documents relatifs à l'histoire de la vie économique de la Révolution, 1939,* vol. 1 (Besançon, 1942), pp. 195–208 (p. 202).

74. Augustin Cochin, *Paris, sa population, son industrie* (1864), quoted in Daumard, *Bourgeoisie parisienne,* p. 210.

75. Spitzer, *Generation of 1820,* pp. 19–20, 25–26, 35–64, 258. F7 9866, dossier Chapuis.

76. Archives of Saint Médard, register of deliberations, fol. 44. XVII 1133, *acte de société* Chappellet, 19 June 1813. Louis Bergeron, *Banquiers, négociants, et manufacturiers parisiens du Directoire à l'Empire,* 2 vols. (Lille, Atelier de reproduction des thèses de l'Université de Lille III, 1975; republished in 1 vol., Paris, EHESS, 1978), 2:825. Arch.P. D32 U3 51, *acte de société,* 17 Feb. 1829; reconstitution of état civil.

77. Daumard, *Bourgeoisie parisienne,* pp. 293–297, 382, 384, 386.

78. On the role of place in class formation, Mike Savage, "Urban History and Social Class: Two Paradigms," *Urban History* 20 (1993): 61–77 (esp. pp. 70–75).

A Note on Sources

A complete bibliography of the primary and secondary sources used for a book of this scope would take up many pages. Full references to manuscript and printed material are given in the endnotes, and where a work is rare I have given the location and call number. The Jansenist newspaper *Nouvelles ecclésiastiques* is held in almost complete runs in the Bibliothèque Nationale, Paris, and in the Bibliothèque Municipale of Grenoble.

It is not possible to acknowledge, in all notes, all of the sources used to compile lists of churchwardens at Saint Médard, Saint Hippolyte, and Saint Martin, nor all the material for the reconstitution of families. The loss of so many sources for Paris makes research on families and on parish life difficult. There are no tax records. The prerevolutionary parish registers are gone, and even after 1800 the records are fragmentary. An attempt has been made to reconstitute something of the pre-1870 *état civil* (registers of baptisms, marriages, and funerals) at the Archives de Paris, but it remains very incomplete.

At Saint Médard parish registers survive for the period after 1796, but the staff were unable to find them when I returned to consult these records, and the conditions in which the parish archives are stored jeopardize their survival. Fortunately, the notarial archives make it possible to fill some of the gaps. Marriage contracts, wills, inventories, and occasionally commercial contracts offer much information about middle- and upper-class Parisians. Tracing individuals and particular families, however, is not easy. There were over 120 notaries working in Paris whose records survive, and although most kept chronological inventories, no complete indexes exist. Catalogs at the Archives Nationales cover a few of the notaries for part of the period, and a complete computer listing is available for 1749, but beyond this it is largely a matter of chance. The notaries had many clients in the area where they lived, but families and institutions often went to a particular notary, who might live anywhere in the city.

For the early nineteenth century, among the most valuable records for family reconstitution are the *déclarations des mutations après décès*, the declarations families were required to make when someone died that state the value of the estate and the identity of the heirs. But the difficulties of using them to trace families are considerable. Separate records were kept in each arrondissement and were chronological. A second series of volumes, one or more for each letter of the alphabet, served as an index, and these contain a summary of the declaration. Within these volumes, however, the order is again chronological, each one covering perhaps a twenty-year period. This means that the researcher must know where the person died and the approximate year. Furthermore, many of the volumes are missing, either permanently or misplaced in the recent move of the Archives de Paris to the Porte des Lilas.

Strangely enough, the early nineteenth century is the most difficult period for research on the Paris middle classes. Few electoral lists exist. That for 1819, held by the Bibliothèque historique de la Ville de Paris, is missing. I had hoped to find information on the vestries in the archives of the Ministère des Cultes, the F19 series, but they are in considerable disorder. The municipal records for this period do not exist for the (pre-1860) Twelfth Arrondissement, and the cadastre is fragmentary. A detailed description of other sources for this period may be found in Jean Tulard, *Paris et son administration (1800–1830)* (Paris, Ville de Paris, Commission des travaux historiques, 1976).

For the prerevolutionary period, the most useful sources for family reconstitution, apart from the notarial archives, are the neglected archives of the abbeys and seigneurial jurisdictions. These institutions collected dues annually on each property in their jurisdiction, and did so again when property changed hands. They therefore maintained careful records of ownership and, particularly, of changes in ownership. Their records comprise two series. The *ensaisinements,* a running register of sales of property, normally include a copy of the contract of sale, but they exclude changes of ownership through inheritance. The *terriers,* or *censiers,* are compilations drawn up every twenty or thirty years that list all the current owners. They give less information on sales, but trace all changes of ownership since the previous version was drawn up. In general, the *terriers* list all the heirs—both males and females, thanks to the inheritance system of Paris customary law—who received equal shares in a property. They also list any deceased heirs, whether or not there were descendants. It thus is possible to trace both the male and the female lines. In most cases, too, the name of the owner's spouse is given: always if the owner was female, for it was part of her legal identity even though she retained her maiden name; and often a wife's name, because the marriage community rules governing most Paris alliances meant that she was co-owner of property bought with the couple's joint funds, even though the husband was free to dispose of it and she was not.

INDEX

Index